D1480003

Decorate Something Great!

Dear Friend,

In this 2008 Yearbook you can create a castle cake the way it was meant to be–larger than life. Castles have long been a favorite shape for party cakes, but you've never seen castles like the ones in this book.

In our *Castle Parties!* special section, we showcase 7 spectacular castle scenes for all types of celebrations. Start with our cover design--the ideal cake to thrill any birthday girl. It's the ultimate princess palace, with 11 sparkling peaked towers, sprays of fondant flowers and windows laced with lattice. Complete the scene with fondant-covered mini cakes of the princess and her court and a candy shell coach to whisk them away. What a perfect way to make the day magical.

The key is our Romantic Castle Cake Set, with beautifully-detailed turrets and accents that transform a stacked tier cake into a towering centerpiece. From King Arthur's fondant fortress to a candy-topped toyland tower, you'll be amazed by the number of exciting looks possible with the Castle Cake Set. Let the great *Castle Parties!* ideas in this Yearbook inspire you to enter your own design in our Castle Decorating Contest. Visit www.wilton.com for all the details.

Castles are just the beginning of the exciting theme ideas you'll find in the 2008 Yearbook. Look for cute bugs and fun flowers for summer birthdays. Celebrate holidays in new ways, with witches' brooms to greet trick-or-treaters or a snow-topped mountain of cupcakes for Christmas. The star performers your kids want at the party are here as well, including Go, Diego, Go!, The Backyardigans, Tinkerbell and Ariel.

This 2008 edition also has our biggest wedding collection ever. As always, the Yearbook features the most contemporary colors and shapes for your reception cake. Be sure to see the beautiful ruffled floral design made with our Paisley Tier Pan Set—it's an elegant curved shape which will set your celebration apart.

Your year of decorating excitement starts here. I hope this 2008 Yearbook will add to your enjoyment of celebrations to come.

Vince Naccarato

Vince Naccarato
Chairman and CEO
Wilton Industries, Inc.

Cake Decorating!
2008 WILTON YEARBOOK

Make Them Stars! . . . . . . *p. 22*

The cakes kids want to be seen with. New friends The Backyardigans, Diego and Tinkerbell join Pooh, Scooby-Doo, SpongeBob SquarePants and Elmo for a party that will be your claim to fame.

Birthday Cheer! . . . . *p. 4*

Desserts worth shouting about! Planes and cranes for boys, poodles and purses for girls and stand-up clown cakes or cupcakes any kid will love. From 1st birthday bears to bug and blossom designs, you'll find the perfect birthday theme here.

p. 7

Your Holidays are Hot! . . . *p. 36*

Something pleasing in each season! Witch broom cakes, candies and appetizer to sweep Halloween guests off their feet. Peek inside a house on the Night Before Christmas and find a very surprised Santa. Spot all the dotted eggs for Easter, including a cookie pop flower pot and a fondant basket cake.

The Big Event! . . . . *p. 60*

Save the date! Toy boxes and teddy bears greet the mom-to-be. Honor the confirmation boy with a traditional cross cake in a beautiful mosaic of fondant. Make a grad glad with tiers linked by a garland of roses and topped by a fondant diploma.

Your Day to Shine! . . . . *p. 70*

Every detail is perfect, each cake with a signature touch that will be remembered. Delicate ruffled cake top flowers and side strips touched with a pink blush. Bold fondant loops and clusters of grapes peeking between scrolled tiers. Amazing curved cakes in white etched with dramatic black flowers.

p. 54

p. 93

CREATIVE DIRECTOR
Daniel Masini

ART DIRECTOR/CAKE DESIGNER
Steve Rocco

DECORATING ROOM SUPERVISOR
Cheryl Brown

SENIOR CAKE DECORATORS
Mary Gavenda
Susan Matusiak

CAKE DECORATORS
Jenny Jurewicz
Diane Knowlton
Mark Malak
Tracey Wurzinger
Debbie Friedman
Judy Wysocki

EDITOR/WRITER
Jeff Shankman

WRITER/COPY EDITOR
Jane Mikis

WRITERS
Mary Enochs
Marita Seiler

PRODUCTION MANAGER
Challis Yeager

ASSOCIATE PRODUCTION MANAGER
Mary Stahulak

GRAPHIC DESIGN/PRODUCTION
Deborah Casciato
RNB Graphics
Courtney Kieras

PHOTOGRAPHY
Peter Rossi—PDR Productions
Dale DeBolt—DeBolt Photography
Black Box Studios

PHOTO STYLIST
Carey Thornton

CREATIVE SERVICES ASSISTANT
Sharon Gaeta

PRODUCT DEVELOPMENT/PUBLICATIONS
Tina Celeste

IN U.S.A.
Wilton Industries, Inc.
2240 West 75th Street, Woodridge, IL 60517
www.wilton.com

Retail Customer Orders:
Phone: 800-794-5866 • Fax: 888-824-9520
Online: www.wilton.com

Class Locations:
Phone: 800-942-8881
Online: www.wilton.com/classes/classlocator.cfm

IN CANADA
Wilton Industries Canada Company
98 Carrier Drive, Etobicoke, Ontario M9W5R1 Canada
Retail Customer Orders: Phone: 416-679-0798

Class Locations:
Phone: 416-679-0790, ext. 200
E-mail: classprograms@wilton.ca

¡SE HABLA ESPAÑOL!
Para mas informacion, marque 800-436-5778
In Mexico: www.wiltonmexico.com.mx

Birthday Cheer!

It's "a rule"—everyone has to treat you nicely on your birthday. There's no better way to treat a birthday buddy than with the decorated desserts you'll find here! We have something for every personality: A cake construction crane for boys or a pampered poodle cake for girls. A summer flower party with blossoms of fondant, ice cream, mousse and cheese, plus a bug bash with sandwiches, cereal treats and a great fondant and candy cake. Or, stand up and cheer our Wonder Mold clown here—displayed on our Silly-Feet! Cake Stand and surrounded by stand-up cupcakes in a rousing birthday shout-out!

Instructions for projects shown on these two pages are on page 6.

What a Cut-Up!

Pans: 10 x 2 in. Round, p. 153; Classic Wonder Mold, p. 155
Tips: 1M (2110), 5, 18, p. 142-143
Colors:* Kelly Green, Lemon Yellow, Orange, Rose, Violet, Royal Blue, Red-Red, Christmas Red, Black, Copper (skin tone), p. 136
Fondant/Gum Paste: White Ready-To-Use Rolled Fondant (24 oz.), p. 130; Gum-Tex™, Rolling Pin, Roll & Cut Mat, p. 133
Recipes: Buttercream, Royal Icings, p. 114
Also: 2008 Pattern Book (Head, Hands, Hat), p. 128; Silly-Feet! Cake Stand, p. 145; Fanci-Foil Wrap, Cake Boards, p. 233; Meringue Powder, p. 137; White Candy Melts®†, p. 166; 11¾ in. Lollipop Sticks, p. 169; Plastic Dowel Rods, p. 232; red, blue, yellow curling ribbon (12 in. of each color) and balloons, cornstarch, knife, scissors, waxed paper

In advance: Make fondant head and hat. Tint 3 oz. fondant copper (skin tone) and 2 oz. yellow; combine copper with ½ teaspoon Gum-Tex and yellow with ¼ teaspoon. Roll out ⅛ in. thick; cut head and hat using patterns and knife. Let dry 48 hours on cornstarch-dusted surface. When dry, decorate using royal icing on waxed paper covered board. With tip 5, outline and pipe in mouth; add bead tongue (smooth with finger dipped in cornstarch). Pipe tip 5 dot eyes, nose and cheeks (flatten and smooth with finger); add dot pupils (flatten and smooth). Pipe tip 18 C-motion hair. Attach hat, pipe tip 18 pull-out pompom and fringe; let dry 48 hours. **Also:** Make right hand (left hand holding balloons will be made when cake is assembled). Roll out white fondant ½ in. thick; cut hand using pattern and knife. Shape fingers. Insert lollipop stick in hand; let dry 48 hours on cornstarch-dusted surface. Attach two lollipop sticks to back of head with melted candy for support; let dry.

Bake and cool 1-layer round cake and Classic Wonder Mold cake (use firm-textured batter such as pound cake). Prepare for Stacked Construction (p. 112) on double-thick, foil-wrapped board. Trim 10 in. cake to match angle of Wonder Mold Cake. Cut dowel rods 6 in. long for arms; insert in cake sides leaving 3 in. exposed. Ice cake and arms smooth in buttercream. Tint 4 oz. fondant yellow, roll out ⅛ in. thick and cut into 1 x 3 in. strips. Attach to bottom of cake, 1 in. apart. Pipe tip 1M zigzags around waist, neck and sleeves. Pipe tip 1M swirl buttons. Use wide opening of tip 18 to imprint dots on costume; pipe in dots with tip 5 (smooth with finger dipped in cornstarch).

Make left hand. Cut 2 lollipop sticks to 7 in. long and 1 to 8 in. long. Slightly bend sticks 2 in. from one end and attach 2 in. inside of dowel rod arm with melted candy, placing longer stick in middle; let set. Roll out white fondant ½ in. thick. Reverse pattern and cut hand with knife. Shape fingers; wrap around to form fist. Tie balloons to lollipop sticks; tie on curling ribbon. Insert head into cake. Position on stand at party. Serves 26.

*Combine Violet with Rose for violet shown. Combine Red-Red with Christmas Red for red shown.

†Brand confectionery coating.

Friends in Good Standing

Pans: Cookie Sheet, Cooling Grid, p. 154
Tips: 2, 2A, 3, 7, 21, p. 142-143
Colors:* Lemon Yellow, Golden Yellow, Royal Blue, Violet, Rose, Orange, Black, Brown, Copper (skin tone), p. 136
Fondant/Gum Paste: White Ready-To-Use Rolled Fondant (24 oz.), p. 130; Rolling Pin, Roll & Cut Mat, p. 133
Candy: White Candy Melts®† (14 oz. for 50 treats), Primary, Garden Candy Color Sets, p. 166; Party Time Lollipop Mold, p. 168; 4 in. Lollipop Sticks, p. 169
Recipe: Buttercream Icing (stiff consistency), p. 114
Also: 2008 Pattern Book (Hands), p. 128; Silly-Feet! Silicone Baking Cups, p. 147; cornstarch, knife

In advance: Tint melted white candy yellow, blue, pink, green using candy colors. Mold hats in candy mold without sticks. Refrigerate until firm; unmold. **Also:** Make hands. Tint fondant skin tone and roll out ⁵⁄₁₆ in. thick. Use pattern and knife to cut 2 hands per treat; reverse pattern for 2nd hand. Let dry on cornstarch-dusted surface.

Bake and cool cupcakes in silicone cups supported by cookie sheet. Cover top with tip 2A icing mound; smooth with spatula and finger dipped in cornstarch. Cut lollipop sticks to 3 in.; insert stick 1¾ in. into bag fitted with tip 21; squeeze as you pull out stick to pipe arms. Clean off icing from ½ in. at end of stick; attach hands. Insert other end of stick into cupcake. Pipe hairdos with tip 2 and tip 3 lines, curls and pull-outs or tip 7 pull-out spikes. Attach hats with icing; trim with tip 2 pull-out fringe and pompom. Pipe tip 3 dot eyes (smooth with finger dipped in cornstarch). Pipe tip 7 dot nose; flatten slightly. Use tip 2 to pipe in mouth, outline closed eyes and add dot pupils (flatten slightly). Each serves 1.

*Combine Lemon Yellow with Golden Yellow for yellow shown. Combine Violet with Rose for violet shown.

Feast Your Eyes!

Candy: Party Time Lollipop Mold, p. 168; Candy Melts®† (14 oz. makes 15 treats), Primary, Garden Candy Color Sets, p. 166; Decorator Brush Set, p. 167
Also: Parchment Triangles, p. 140; Cake Boards, p. 233; waxed paper, paper

Tint portions of candy violet, orange, blue, pink, red and yellow using candy colors. Make gift and cupcake candies using painting method (p. 125). Refrigerate until firm; unmold. For base pattern, draw 1¾ in. circles on paper; tape to cake board then cover with waxed paper. Pipe candy circles using melted candy in cut parchment bag. Refrigerate until firm; remove from paper. Attach molded candies to bases with melted candy; hold upright until candy sets. Chill. Each serves 1.

▶ Birthday with the Works!

Pan: 11 x 15 in. Sheet, p. 153
Tips: 18, 21, p. 143
Color: Lemon Yellow, p. 136
Recipe: Buttercream Icing, p. 114
Also: Sparkle Gel (Blue, Green, Red, Yellow), p. 137; Star Plastic Nesting Cutter Set, p. 163; 13 x 19 in. Cake Boards, Fanci-Foil Wrap, p. 233

Ice 1-layer cake sides smooth in yellow; ice top white. Pipe tip 18 shell top border and tip 21 rosette bottom border. Using Sparkle Gel tubes, print message. Use smallest star cutter from set to imprint random stars; outline and fill in with gel. Pipe gel dots and outline motion lines. Serves 30.

◀ They're All Big Fans!

Pan: Cookie Sheet, p. 154

Tips: 2, 21, p. 142-143

Colors:* Sky Blue, Violet, Rose, Lemon Yellow, Black, p. 136

Fondant/Gum Paste: Natural Colors Fondant Multi Pack, p. 130; Gum-Tex™, Rolling Pin, Roll & Cut Mat, p. 133; Brush Set, p. 131

Recipe: Buttercream (stiff consistency), Royal Icings, p. 114

Also: 2008 Pattern Book (Hand), p. 128; Silly-Feet! Silicone Baking Cups, p. 147; Fine Tip Primary Colors FoodWriter™ Edible Color Markers, p. 130; 101 Cookie Cutters Set, p. 162; 6 in. Lollipop Sticks, p. 169; Meringue Powder, p. 137; construction paper, glue, scissors, waxed paper, cornstarch, knife

In advance: Make fondant head and hands (p. 122).

Bake and cool cupcakes in silicone cups supported by cookie sheet. Use spatula to build up and mound icing; smooth. Insert heads. Ice arms by pushing 3 in. lollipop stick through tip 21 into bag of icing; squeeze as you pull out stick. Clean end and insert into cupcake. Slide out lollipop sticks which were positioned in hands before drying. Cut 1 x 1¼ in. triangle pennants from construction paper; print guest's name with FoodWriter. Attach to lollipop stick with glue. Attach hands to arms using royal icing; let set. Slide pennant stick back into hand. Each serves 1.

*Combine Violet with Rose for violet shown.

▲ Have a Banner Birthday

Pan: Pennant, p. 155

Tip: 10, p. 142

Colors:* Violet, Rose, p. 136

Recipe: Buttercream Icing, p. 114

Also: Happy Birthday with Balloons Icing Decorations, p. 189; Flowerful Medley Sprinkles Assortment, p. 138; Cake Boards, Fanci-Foil Wrap, p. 233; Wooden, Plastic Dowel Rods, p. 232; large gumball, red curling ribbon, cellophane tape, knife

Ice cake sides smooth in light violet; ice top white. Using tip 10, pipe outline top border in dark violet and ball bottom border in light violet. Use knife to cut small hole in gumball; insert wooden dowel rod. Wrap ribbon around 6 in. of plastic dowel rod; secure with tape. Insert plastic dowel rod into cake from bottom; insert wooden dowel rod into cake from top, sliding it inside plastic dowel rod. Position icing decorations; sprinkle with confetti from assortment. Serves 12.

*Combine Violet with Rose for violet shown.

▶ Wish We Were in Your Shoes!

Pans: Decorator Preferred® 8 x 3 in. Round, p. 152; Cooling Grid, p. 154

Tips: 4, 21, p. 142-143

Colors:* Violet, Rose, p. 136

Candy: White Candy Melts®†, Primary, Garden Candy Color Sets, p. 166

Recipe: Buttercream Icing, p. 114

Also: Cake Boards, Fanci-Foil Wrap, p. 233; Silly-Feet! Cake Stand, p. 145; Smiley Flames Chunky Candles (2 pks.), p. 185; Flowerful Medley Sprinkles Assortment, p. 138; Round Comfort Grip™ Cutter, p. 164; Round Cut-Outs™, p. 132; Wooden Dowel Rods, p. 232; Disposable Decorating Bags, p. 140

Bake and cool 1-layer cake 2 in. high and 2-layer cake 5 in. high (bake two 2½ in. high cakes). Ice 2-layer cake smooth and prepare for Stacked Construction (p. 112) on double-thick, foil-wrapped board. Cut mini cakes from 1-layer cake using round Comfort Grip cutter for bottom tier and large and medium Cut-Outs for top 2 tiers. Cover mini cakes with melted candy (p. 126); let set. Stack mini cakes, securing with dots of melted candy, position bottom tier on same-size foil-covered board. Pipe tip 4 bead bottom borders on top and middle tiers using buttercream icing. Using melted candy, pipe swag garland on all mini cakes. Set aside.

On 2-layer cake, pipe tip 21 top shell and bottom rosette border. Pipe tip 4 message. Attach confetti sprinkles from assortment. **At party:** position 2-layer cake on stand; position mini cakes on cake top, secure with dot of icing. Pipe tip 4 bead bottom border on bottom tier of mini cake. Pipe tip 21 rosette candleholders; insert candles. Serves 23.

*Combine Violet with Rose for violet shown.

▶ Starting Out On Top!

Pans: Number 1, p. 155; 10 x 3, 14 x 3 in. Decorator Preferred® Rounds, Heating Core, p. 152

Tips: 2, 5, p. 142

Colors:* Rose, Lemon Yellow, Leaf Green, Sky Blue, Violet, p. 136

Fondant/Gum Paste: White Ready-To-Use Rolled Fondant (24 oz.), p. 130; Gum-Tex™, Rolling Pin, Roll & Cut Mat, p. 133; Fondant Ribbon Cutter/Embosser Set, Brush Set, p. 131; Round Cut-Outs™, p. 132

Candy: White Candy Melts®† (2 pks.), p. 166; Alphabet Candy Mold, p. 168; 6 in. Lollipop Sticks, p. 169

Recipes: Buttercream Icing, p. 114; Thinned Fondant Adhesive, p. 115

Also: Baby Face Topper, p. 237; 101 Cookie Cutters Set, p. 162; Plastic Dowel Rods, p. 232; 16 in. Round Silver Cake Base, Cake Boards, p. 233; cornstarch, waxed paper, knife

In advance: Make fondant "Happy Birthday." Mix ¾ teaspoon Gum-Tex into 8 oz. fondant; tint blue. Roll out ⅛ in. thick. Cut out letters using alphabet cutters from 101 Cutters Set. Let set at least 1 hour. Turn over and set flat on waxed paper-covered board. Roll out remaining blue fondant ¼ in. thick. Cut 13 circles using smallest Cut-Out; attach a circle to the back of each letter using damp brush. Cut lollipop sticks to 3 in. long. Dip end in water and push into circle at right angle to letter. Shape circle fondant around stick for support. Let dry. **Also:** Make candy plaque (p. 126). Use Number 1 pan, filling just the recessed number area with melted candy. Refrigerate until firm; unmold; return to room temperature. Roll out remaining blue fondant ⅛ in. thick. Use smallest Cut-Out to cut circles; attach around edge of plaque with melted candy. Tint 6 oz. fondant violet. Press into Alphabet Candy Mold dusted with cornstarch to make name letters. Unmold; use knife to trim and smooth edges. Reserve leftover fondant. Attach name letters to candy plaque with melted candy. Store out of direct sunlight to prevent fading. **And:** Make baby's hat. Tint 6 oz. fondant yellow; roll out a small amount ³⁄₁₆ in. thick; reserve remainder. Cut a 1½ x 2 in. high triangle with knife. Trim curve at base to fit on baby's head; reserve leftover fondant. Let dry on cornstarch-dusted surface.

Bake and cool 1-layer 14 in. cake and 2-layer 10 in. cake. Ice smooth and prepare for Stacked Construction (p. 112) on cake base. Tint 6 oz. portions of fondant green and rose; use remaining violet. Roll out colors ⅛ in. thick. Use medium Cut-Out to cut 6 circles in each color. Attach to sides of 10 in. cake; use extra icing if needed. Use Cutter/Embosser Set to make 9-10 strips in yellow, green and violet for side of 14 in. cake. Cut yellow using 2 wavy cutting wheels with ⅓ in. spacer. Cut green using 2 zigzag cutting wheels with ¼ in. spacer. Cut violet using 2 straight cutting wheels with 2 beaded embossing wheels. Attach to cake sides, about 1 in. apart; use extra icing if needed. Pipe tip 5 ball bottom border on both cakes. Attach hat to baby topper with fondant adhesive. Use icing to pipe tip 2 pull-out dot fringe and pompom. Use melted candy to attach 2 plastic dowel rods to back of candy plaque, leaving 6 in. exposed at bottom; let set. Insert letters on sides of 10 in. cake, set about 1 in. away from cake side. **At Party:** Insert candy plaque and position baby topper. Serves 48.

*Combine Violet with Rose for violet shown. Combine Leaf Green with Lemon Yellow for green shown.

†Brand confectionery coating.

▶ This Baby Holds the Road!

Pans: Baby Buggy, p. 156; Cookie Sheet, Cooling Grid, p. 154

Tips: 2, 3, 4, 5, 7, 10, 16, 18, 129, p. 142-143

Colors: Rose, Brown, Black, p. 136

Recipes: Buttercream, Royal Icings, Roll-Out Cookies, p. 114

Also: 2008 Pattern Book (Horse, Crown), p. 128; 101 Cookie Cutters Set, p. 162; Meringue Powder, p. 137; Jumbo Hearts Sprinkle Decorations, p. 138; Cake Board, Fanci-Foil Wrap, p. 233; waxed paper, paring knife, toothpick, cornstarch

In advance: Make flowers. Using royal icing, pipe 50 tip 129 dark rose drop flowers with tip 3 white dot centers. Let dry. **Also:** Bake and decorate cookies. Prepare and roll out dough; trace horse pattern with toothpick and cut with knife. Using cutters from set, cut out 1 medium circle for baby's head and 3 small hearts. Bake and cool all cookies. Using royal icing, ice heart cookies smooth and attach jumbo heart sprinkle at center; let set. Cover crown pattern with waxed paper; position circle cookie just below pattern. Using dark rose royal icing, pipe in tip 5 center heart and tip 4 side hearts; overpipe, building up hearts to same thickness of head cookie. Pipe tip 3 light rose heart in center of larger heart (smooth with finger dipped in cornstarch). Attach heart sprinkle; let dry. Pipe tip 2 dot and outline facial features and hair. Decorate horse using royal icing. Outline cookie with tip 3. Ice saddle smooth with spatula (smooth with finger dipped in cornstarch). Using tip 4, outline saddle and add zigzag stirrup, hooves and bridle. Pipe tip 3 dot eye and nose; outline mouth and pipe in inside ear. Cover body with tip 16 stars; add tip 18 pull-out star mane and tail. Attach heart cookie and heart sprinkles with icing.

Ice wheels, blanket on side and background areas of cake smooth in buttercream. Outline carriage with tip 3 and cover with tip 16 stars. Pipe tip 7 spokes on wheels; attach drop flowers at center and rim. Pipe tip 3 drop strings ½ in. deep and 1¾ in. apart; attach flowers at points. Pipe tip 3 dots on carriage hood; attach heart cookies with icing. Pipe tip 10 handle on carriage. Attach head. Cake serves 12; cookies each serve 1.

▼ Driver in Training Pants

Pans: 3-D Cruiser, p. 160; Cookie Sheet, Cooling Grid, p. 154

Tips: 2, 2A, 3, 4, 5, 12, 16, p. 142

Colors: Sky Blue, Lemon Yellow, Copper (skin tone), Black, Orange, p. 136

Candy: Light Cocoa Candy Melts®†, Garden Candy Color Set, p. 166; 8 in. Lollipop Sticks, p. 169

Recipes: Buttercream Icing, Roll-Out Cookies, p. 114

Also: 2008 Pattern Book (Windshield), p. 128; Rocking Horses, p. 235; Baby Blocks Favor Containers (2 pks.), p. 234; 101 Cookie Cutters Set, p. 162; Round Cut-Outs™, p. 132; Cake Boards, Fanci-Foil Wrap, p. 233; 9 x 4 x ½ in. craft block, sugar ice cream cone, jelly ring candy, ruler, knife, cornstarch, waxed paper, double-stick tape

In advance: Make cookie head. Prepare dough; roll out and cut cookie using largest round cutter from set. Bake and cool. Ice smooth in copper. Using tip 2, pipe dot nose, outline ears and eyes. Outline and pipe in tip 3 mouth (pat smooth with finger dipped in cornstarch). **Also:** Make 4 candy tires. Melt cocoa candy and tint black. Place largest round Cut-Out on waxed paper-covered board. Fill ¼ in. deep; refrigerate until firm and unmold. **And:** Prepare foil-wrapped pieces. Use pattern to cut windshield from cake board; wrap. Use melted candy to attach lollipop sticks to back of each end, leaving 3 in. extended to insert into cake. Cut cake board to cake shape; wrap. Wrap craft block.

Bake and cool cake using firm-textured batter such as pound cake. Place on wrapped board; position on wrapped craft block. Trim off top of car. Using melted candy, attach tires to cake sides. Using buttercream, ice passenger area smooth. Use tip 4 to outline car details; cover with tip 16 stars, overpiping wheel wells for dimension. Add tip 12 headlights and hubcaps (pat smooth with finger dipped in cornstarch). Pipe tip 2A outline bumpers and running boards (pat smooth). Cut lollipop stick to 7 in. Using melted candy, attach stick to back of cookie head, leaving 2 in. extended above head; insert in cake top. Position jelly ring steering wheel. Using buttercream, pipe tip 12 outline arms, tip 5 pull-out fingers and tip 3 outline shirt. Insert windshield; cover with tip 16 stars. Cut sugar cone to 3 in. for hat; ice smooth. Slip hat over extended stick on top of head and attach with melted candy. Use tip 3 and buttercream to pipe outline number, pull-out pompom and brim. Position baby blocks and rocking horse behind head. Cake serves 12; cookie serves 1.

◄ Teddy in a Tutu!

Pan: Teddy Bear, p. 156

Tips: 3, 8, 16, 127D, 131, 225, 349, p. 142-143

Colors: Rose, Brown, Kelly Green, Red-Red, Black, p. 136

Fondant/Gum Paste: White Ready-To-Use Rolled Fondant (4 oz.), p. 130; Gum-Tex™, Rolling Pin, Roll & Cut Mat, p. 133

Recipe: Buttercream Icing, p. 114

Also: 2008 Pattern Book (Crown), p. 128; Meringue Powder, p. 137; Cake Boards, Fanci-Foil Wrap, p. 233; 6 in. Lollipop Sticks, p. 169; waxed paper, cornstarch, knife

In advance: Make fondant crown. Mix ½ teaspoon Gum-Tex with 4 oz. fondant. Roll out ⅛ in. thick. Use pattern to cut crown; let dry on cornstarch-dusted surface. **Also:** Make 6 tip 131 and 18 tip 225 drop flowers with royal icing. Make extras to allow for breakage and let dry. Add tip 3 dot centers. **And:** Cut lollipop stick in half. Attach 3 in. pieces to back of dried crown using royal icing; leave 2 in. exposed to insert into cake.

Use tip 3 to outline and pipe-in eyes, pupils, nose, inside of ears and paw pads (smooth with finger dipped in cornstarch). Outline mouth. Cover cake with tip 16 stars. For tutu, pipe tip 127D double ruffles; add tip 8 outline waistband. Insert crown in cake. Attach flowers to crown and tutu; pipe tip 349 leaves. Pipe tip 3 number. Serves 12.

► Rookie of the Year!

Pans: Pennant, p. 155; Teddy Bear, p. 156; Cookie Sheet, Cooling Grid, p. 154

Tips: 3, 6, 9, 14, 16, p. 142-143

Colors:* Brown, Red-Red, Royal Blue, Lemon Yellow, Golden Yellow, Orange, Black, p. 136

Recipes: Buttercream, Royal Icings, Roll-Out Cookies, p. 114

Also: 101 Cookie Cutters Set, p. 162; 8 in. Cookie Treat Sticks, p. 165; Flowerful Medley Sprinkles Assortment, p. 138; Cake Boards, Fanci-Foil Wrap, p. 233; Meringue Powder, p. 137; cornstarch

In advance: Make sports ball cookies. Prepare and roll out dough; cut 1 football and 2 medium round cookies using cutters from set. Bake and cool. Outline cookies with tip 3 and royal icing; pipe in with tip 3 and thinned royal icing. Let dry. Pipe tip 3 stitching lines on baseball. Outline and pipe in black panels and lines on soccer ball; cover black panels with tip 14 stars. Pipe tip 14 outline stitching and zigzag stripes on football. Let dry.

Bake and cool bear and pennant cakes. Ice pennant smooth. Outline with tip 9; add tip 6 message. Add confetti sprinkles. On bear, ice smooth paw pads, inside ears and muzzle. Pipe tip 3 dot eyes, pupils and nose (pat smooth with finger dipped in cornstarch). Pipe tip 3 outline mouth. Cover bear and shirt with tip 16 stars. Pipe tip 16 zigzag collar and shirt trim; add tip 3 number. Position cookie stick between pennant and bear cakes. Position cookies. Cakes serve 24; each cookie serves 1.

*Combine Lemon Yellow with Golden Yellow for yellow shown.

◄ This is a First!

Pans: Teddy Bear, p. 156; Cookie Sheet, Cooling Grid, p. 154

Tips: 3, 5, 16, 233, p. 142-143

Colors:* Lemon Yellow, Royal Blue, Leaf Green, Violet, Rose, Black, p. 136

Recipes: Buttercream, Royal Icings, Roll-Out Cookies, p. 114

Also: 2008 Pattern Book (Hat), p. 128; 101 Cookie Cutters Set, p. 162; Flowerful Medley Sprinkles Assortment, p. 138; 6 in. Lollipop Sticks, p. 169; Cake Boards, Fanci-Foil Wrap, p. 233; Parchment Triangles, p. 140; Meringue Powder, p. 137; curling ribbon, waxed paper, cornstarch, knife, toothpicks

In advance: Make cookies. Prepare and roll out dough. Use pattern to cut hat; use largest round cutter from set to cut 3 balloons. Bake and cool cookies. Cover with thinned royal icing (p. 126); let dry. Set hat on waxed paper. Use royal icing to pipe tip 5 number and tip 16 pull-out star pompom. Let dry. When dry, attach lollipop stick to back of hat, leaving 3 in. exposed to insert into cake.

Bake and cool cake; position on foil-covered cake board. Mark oval on tummy. Use tip 3 and buttercream to pipe in inside ears, paw pads and tummy (smooth with finger dipped in cornstarch). Print tip 3 name. Add confetti sprinkles. Use spatula to build up icing and ice muzzle smooth. Pipe in tip 3 nose and mouth; overpipe for dimension (smooth with finger). Pipe tip 5 eyes. Cover body with tip 233 pull-out fur. Insert hat. Use royal icing to pipe tip 16 pull-out star brim and to attach ribbons to balloon backs. Attach ribbons to paw with dots of icing. Serves 12.

*Combine Violet with Rose for violet shown.

▶ Grab Them Bear-Handed!

Pans: Round Cookie Treat Pan, p. 165; Non-Stick 12-Cup Mini Muffin, p. 151

Candy: White, Light Cocoa Candy Melts®†, Primary, Garden Candy Colors Set, p. 166

Also: Parchment Triangles, p. 140; 6 in. Cookie Treat Sticks, p. 165; ¼ in. wide ribbon (12-14 in. for each treat), waxed paper

Mold candy bear heads on sticks in Cookie Treat Pan. Refrigerate until firm; unmold. Fill cavities of Mini Muffin pan ¼ in. deep to mold 2 ears for each treat. Refrigerate until firm; unmold. Attach ears to back of head with candy. Tint portions of white candy yellow and black. Using melted candy in cut parchment bags, pipe muzzle, eyes and inside ears; let set. Pipe dot pupils, nose and outline mouth; let set. Tie ribbon around stick. Each serves 1.

†Brand confectionery coating.

▶ Kitty-cat Princess

Pans: Animal Crackers, p. 157; Sports Ball Set, p. 159; Cookie Sheet, Cooling Grid, p. 154

Tips: 3, 4, 7, 12, 16, p. 142-143

Colors:* Rose, Black, Violet, p. 136

Recipe: Buttercream Icing, Roll-Out Cookies, p. 114

Also: 2008 Pattern Book (Crown, Tail, Paw and Legs), p. 128; White Candy Melts®†, p. 166; Cake Board, Fanci-Foil Wrap, p. 233; 4 in. Lollipop Sticks, p. 169; knife, cornstarch, toothpicks

In advance: Make cookies. Prepare and roll out dough. Use patterns to cut out crown, tail and bottom paw. Bake and cool cookies. Ice crown smooth and attach lollipop stick to back with melted candy. Let set.

Bake and cool Animal Crackers cake and ½ Sports Ball cake. Trim ears of animal cake to shape pointed cat ears; trim ½ in. off bottom (neck). Trim about ¾ in. off top (neck) and 1¾ in. off bottom of ball cake. Position cakes next to each other on foil-covered cake board; join with icing. Position paw and tail cookies on board, securing with icing. Use tip 7 to outline and pipe in inner ears plus eyes, nose and mouth (smooth with finger dipped in cornstarch). Use patterns to mark legs; build up with tip 12 and round with spatula. Pipe tip 4 outline claws. Cover cake with tip 16 stars. Pipe tip 4 outline whiskers and tip 3 outline eyelashes. Insert crown in cake. Pipe tip 3 name. Pipe tip 4 balls at crown points. Pipe tip 3 pull-out fringe at base of crown. Serves 16.

*Combine Violet with Rose for violet shown.

◀ See Spot Celebrate!

Pans: Animal Crackers, p. 157; Sports Ball Set, p. 159; Cookie Sheet, Cooling Grid, p. 154

Tips: 3, 4, 7, 12, 16, p. 142-143

Colors:* Brown, Red-Red, Black, Rose, Royal Blue, p. 136

Recipes: Buttercream Icing, Roll Out Cookies, p. 114

Also: 2008 Pattern Book (Hat, Paw, Tail, Legs), p. 128; Cake Board, Fanci-Foil Wrap, p. 233; 4 in. Lollipop Sticks, p. 169; White Candy Melts ®†, p. 166; toothpicks, paring knife, cornstarch

In advance: Make cookies. Prepare and roll out dough. Use patterns and knife to cut out hat, bottom paw and tail; bake and cool cookies. Ice hat smooth and attach lollipop stick to back with melted candy. Let set.

Bake and cool Animal Crackers cake and ½ Sports Ball cake. Trim bottom of ears off Animal Crackers cake. Trim 1¾ in. off top edge of Sports Ball cake (neck) and 1½ in. off bottom. Position cakes next to each other on foil-wrapped cake board; join with icing. Position paw and tail on board, securing with icing. Use toothpick to trace front and back leg patterns on cake and build up area with tip 12. Pipe whites of eyes with tip 7 (smooth with finger dipped in cornstarch). Pipe tip 7 dot pupils and nose; smooth; pipe tip 4 mouth and bead tongue; smooth. Pipe tip 16 star spots and tip 4 outline claws. Cover remainder of cake with tip 16 stars; Build up muzzle area. Pipe tip 3 dot whiskers on muzzle. Insert hat in cake; pipe tip 3 message, pull-out fringe and pom-poms. Serves 16.

*Combine Brown with Red-Red for brown shown.

†Brand confectionery coating.

▶ A Quackin' Snack

Pans: 3-D Rubber Ducky, p. 157; Oval Set (13½ x 9⅞ in. used), p. 153

Tips: 5, 7, 18, 21, p. 142-143

Colors:* Black, Golden Yellow, Lemon Yellow, Orange, Violet, Rose, Royal Blue, p. 136

Recipe: Buttercream Icing, p. 114

Also: 11¾ in. Lollipop Sticks, p. 169; Cake Boards, Fanci-Foil Wrap, p. 233; Flowerful Medley Sprinkles Assortment, p. 138; Dowel Rods, p. 232; balloons, curling ribbon, party horn, waffle ice cream cone, cornstarch, scissors

Bake and cool 1-layer oval and duck cake using firm-textured batter such as pound cake. Ice oval cake smooth on foil-wrapped cake board and prepare for Stacked Construction (p. 112). Print tip 5 message; add confetti sprinkles from assortment. Pipe tip 21 shell bottom border.

On duck, ice beak smooth. Pipe tip 7 dot eyes (pat smooth with finger dipped in cornstarch). Add tip 5 dot pupils. Cover cake with tip 18 stars. For wings, overpipe tip 18 pull-out stars. For wing holding balloons, pull stars toward front of duck. For party hat, trim cone to 4 in. high; ice smooth. Attach cone to head with buttercream; add tip 5 pull-out fringe pompom and brim. Pipe tip 5 number.

At party: Position duck on oval cake. Cut one lollipop stick to 4 in.; insert in beak to support party horn, leaving 2 in. extended. Trim horn approximately 2 in. and insert end over lollipop stick. Tie curling ribbon to balloons, then to lollipop sticks; trim sticks as needed and insert in cake. Serves 27.

*Combine Lemon Yellow with Golden Yellow for yellow shown. Combine Violet with Rose for violet shown.

◀ He's Right On Time!

Pans: Lady Bug, p. 157; Cookie Sheet, Cooling Grid, p. 154

Tips: 3, 16, p. 142-143

Colors:* Kelly Green, Leaf Green, Lemon Yellow, Violet, Rose, Black, p. 136

Recipes: Buttercream Icing, Roll-Out Cookies, p. 114

Also: 2008 Pattern Book (Eyes, Hat, Feet, Tail, Spots, Mouth), p. 128; Cake Boards, Fanci-Foil Wrap, p. 233; toothpicks, cornstarch, knife

In advance: Make cookies. Prepare and roll out dough; use patterns to cut hat, tail and 4 feet. Bake and cool.

Bake and cool Lady Bug cake. Trim off eye, antennae and about ¾ in. of bottom to make a straight edge. Use patterns to mark eyes, mouth and spots with toothpick. Use tip 3 to outline and pipe in eyes (smooth with finger dipped in cornstarch). Use tip 3 to pipe dot nostrils and outline and pipe in pupils and mouth (smooth with finger). Sandwich 2 cookies for each foot using icing. Position feet and tail. Cover cake and cookies with tip 16 stars. Ice hat cookie smooth and position on cake. Pipe tip 16 pull-out fringe border and pompom; print tip 3 name. Serves 12.

*Combine Leaf Green with Lemon Yellow for green on face, feet and tail; use 2 shades of Kelly Green for shell. Combine Violet with Rose for violet shown.

▶ It Carries the Day!

Pan: Purse, p. 156
Tips: 2A, 5, p. 142
Colors*: Rose, Leaf Green, Lemon Yellow, Violet, p. 136
Fondant/Gum Paste: White Ready-To-Use Rolled Fondant (24 oz.),
    p. 130; Cutter/Embosser, Brush Set, p. 131; Alphabet/Number
    Cut-Outs™, p. 132
Recipe: Buttercream Icing, p. 114
Also: Cake Board, Fanci-Foil Wrap, p. 233; ruler

Ice cake sides and background areas smooth in white buttercream.
Ice body of purse smooth in violet. Tint 9 oz. fondant rose and 2 oz.
green. Roll out fondant ⅛ in. thick, cut into ½ in. wide strips. Keep
covered. Score line down center of rose strips using wavy-edge
wheel of Cutter/Embosser. Using straight-edge wheel, score 2 lines
on green strips. Position pairs of green and rose strips on cake
top, ½ in. apart. Using buttercream icing, pipe tip 5 dots in violet
areas. Roll out rose fondant ⅛ in. thick. Using pan as a pattern, cut
out purse flap. Position on cake and smooth. For snap, roll a 1 in.
diameter green ball, flatten and attach with damp brush. Roll out
remaining green fondant ⅛ in. thick. Cut letters using Cut-Outs;
position on cake top. Pipe tip 2A balls for handle. Pipe tip 5 bead
bottom border. Serves 12.

*Combine Leaf Green and Lemon Yellow for green shown. Combine Violet with
  Rose for violet shown.

◀ Fun In Full Flower

Pan: Dancing Daisy Flower, p. 158
Tips: 6, 12, 127, p. 142-143
Colors: Rose, Lemon Yellow, Leaf Green, p. 136
Fondant/Gum Paste: White Ready-To-Use Rolled Fondant, p. 130;
    Rolling Pin, Roll & Cut Mat, p. 133
Recipe: Buttercream Icing, p. 114
Also: 2008 Pattern Book (Leaf), p. 128; Fine Tip Primary Colors
    FoodWriter Edible Color Markers, p. 130; Cake Board, Fanci-
    Foil Wrap, p. 233; Yellow Cake Sparkles, p. 139, knife

In advance: Make stem and leaf. Tint a 3 in. ball of fondant green.
Roll out ⅛ in. thick; cut leaf using pattern and knife. Shape
remaining green fondant into a ½ in. wide rope; position against
cake pan. Let dry overnight.

Ice cake sides smooth; lightly ice cake top. Cover petal areas
with tip 127 ruffles. Outline and pipe in center with tip 12; smooth
with spatula. Sprinkle center with Cake Sparkles. Pipe tip 6 bead
bottom border. Write name on leaf with FoodWriter marker.
Position stem and leaf. Serves 12.

▶ Lip-Smackin' Treats

Pan: Mini Loaf, p. 154
Candy: Girl Power Mold Set, p. 168; Yellow, White Candy Melts®†, Garden Candy Colors Set, p. 166; Decorator Brush Set, p. 167
Also: Parchment Triangles, p. 140

In advance: Mold candies. Mold lipsticks in Girl Power mold using painting method (p. 125). Mold name plaques (p. 126) in Mini Loaf Pan, filling cavities about ¼ in. deep. Refrigerate until firm; unmold.

Using melted candy in cut parchment bags, pipe wavy line border and dot accents; print name. Attach lipstick with melted candy. Each serves 1.

†Brand confectionery coating.

◀ Primped-Up Pup

Pans: Mini Ball, Sports Ball Set, p. 159
Tips: 18, 32, p. 143
Color: Rose, p. 136
Fondant/Gum Paste: White Ready-To-Use Rolled Fondant (24 oz.), p. 130; Gum-Tex™, Rolling Pin, Roll & Cut Mat, p. 133
Recipe: Buttercream Icing, p. 114
Also: 2008 Pattern Book (Poodle Head, Bow, Ear), p. 128; Wooden Dowel Rods, p. 232; Cake Boards, Fanci-Foil Wrap, p. 233; large marshmallows, knife, cornstarch

In advance: Make ear. Add 1 teaspoon Gum-Tex to 2 oz. fondant. Roll out ⅛ in. thick. Use pattern to cut ear. Let dry for several days on cornstarch-dusted surface.

Bake and cool 1 Mini Ball and ½ Sports Ball cake; position on foil-covered board, about 2 in. apart, for head and body. Tint fondant: 6 oz. light rose, 6 oz. dark rose. Roll out ⅛ in. thick. Use pattern to cut light rose face; position on board. Use patterns to cut dark pink bow and nose; also cut a 1 x 1½ in. strip for collar and position on board between cakes. Cut dowel rods to make two 3½ in. legs and 2 in. tail. Reroll light rose fondant ¼ in. thick. Wrap dowel rods with fondant; smooth seams. Cut slit in marshmallows and insert dowel rods; position on board. Shape ½ x 1¾ in. light rose logs for feet and position on board. Roll small pointed fondant logs for eyelashes and toenails; attach with damp brush. Attach nose. Use buttercream to pipe tip 18 rosettes over leg and tail marshmallows and tip 32 rosettes on head and body cakes. Position ear; prop up with 2 stacked marshmallows. Cover ear with tip 32 rosettes. Position bow. Use wide end of decorating tip to cut circle for knot; attach with damp brush. Serves 7.

▶ Fly Guy

Pans: 3-D Cruiser, p. 160, Mini Ball, p. 159; Cookie Sheet, Cooling Grid, p. 154

Tips: 3, 5, 6, 8, 10, 16, p. 142-143

Colors:* Lemon Yellow, Leaf Green, Violet, Rose, Copper (skin tone), Brown, Black, Orange, Royal Blue, Red-Red, p. 136

Recipes: Buttercream Icing, Roll-Out Cookies, p. 114

Also: 2008 Pattern Book (Wings, Windshield, Tail Fin and Cloud), p. 128; Comfort Grip™ Flower Cutter, p. 164; White Ready-To-Use Rolled Fondant, p. 130; Brush Set, p. 131; Cake Board, Fanci-Foil Wrap, p. 233; Flower Nail No. 7, p. 140; 4 in. Lollipop Sticks, p. 169; Wooden Dowel Rods, p. 232; White Candy Melts®†, p. 166; drinking straw (bendable), knife, white cardstock paper, colored markers

In advance: Make cookies. Prepare and roll out dough. Using knife, cut 2 main wings, 1 each tail wings, tail fin, windshield and a 3 in. circle for back of propeller. Using flower cutter, cut propeller; use knife to cut petal divisions to ¾ in. Bake and cool all cookies.

Bake and cool Cruiser and 2 Mini Ball cakes using firm-textured batter such as pound cake. Trim off roof and bumper areas from Cruiser. Position Cruiser cake on foil-wrapped board; insert 2 dowel rods through sides, about 4 in. from front and 1 in. from top, to support main wings. Attach four lollipop sticks to tail wings cookie and 1 stick at each end of windshield cookie with melted candy, leaving 1½ in. of sticks extended; let set. Attach tail fin to tail wings with melted candy; let set. Insert windshield and tail wings into cake. Ice mini ball cakes together for head and attach to cake top with icing. Pipe tip 3 outline mouth and eyes; pipe tip 5 outline ears. Cover face with tip 16 stars; overpipe nose. Add tip 16 pull-out hair. Cover Cruiser cake, main wings, tail wings and tail fin with tip 16 stars. Pipe tip 6 stripes, dots and numbers. Ice 3 in. circle cookie smooth; attach to back of propeller cookie. Cover propeller with tip 16 stars; add tip 10 dot hub. Make steering wheel using head of flower nail; pipe tip 6 outline spokes and tip 8 wheel. Cut straw to

2½ in.; insert stem of flower nail and insert into cake; place stem of flower nail so that 1 in. extends at top. For arms and hands, tint 4 oz. fondant orange and 1 oz. copper. Shape 4 x ⅝ in. logs for arms. Bend and position arms on cake. Shape ⅝ in. ball hands; flatten slightly and score fingers with knife. Attach hands to arms with damp brush; position on cake. From construction paper, cut cloud shape. Draw dots, squiggles and write message with markers. Attach to cake with icing. Serves 13.

*Combine Leaf Green with Lemon Yellow for green shown. Combine Violet with Rose for violet shown. Combine Brown and Red-Red for brown shown.

†Brand confectionery coating.

▼ Party Pitch

Pans: Soccer Ball, Mini Ball, p. 159

Tip: 2, p. 142

Colors: Red-Red, Royal Blue, Black, Brown, p. 136

Fondant/Gum Paste: White Ready-To-Use Rolled Fondant (24 oz.), p. 130; Brush Set, p. 131; Gum-Tex™, Rolling Pin, Roll & Cut Mat, p. 133

Recipe: Buttercream Icing, p. 114

Also: 2008 Pattern Book (Mouth, Tongue, Eyes, Hand, Mitt, Hat Brim), p. 128; Plastic Dowel Rods, p. 232; Parchment Triangles, p. 140; Cake Boards, Fanci-Foil Wrap, p. 233; knife, cornstarch, waxed paper

In advance: Prepare fondant pieces. Add 2 teaspoons Gum-Tex to 17½ oz. fondant. Tint as follows: 4½ oz. light brown, 3½ oz. dark brown, 4 oz. black, 2 oz. blue; reserve remaining 3½ oz. white. For Hat Brim: Roll out blue ⅛ in. thick. Use pattern to cut brim. For Bat: Shape a light brown circle ¼ x 1 in. for bottom. Use remaining light brown to shape 7½ in. long bat with 4 in. diameter top, 2½ in. diameter bottom. For Mitt: Using pattern, shape dark brown fondant, about ¾ in. thick at wrist. Press with thumb to form ball pocket. Push onto 4 in. dowel rod; use knife to shape fingers and thumb. For Hand: Using pattern, shape white fondant, about ¾ in. thick at wrist, tapering to ⅜ in. at fingers. Insert 4 in. dowel rod at wrist. Use knife to cut slits for fingers; shape and wrap around another dowel rod, lightly greased to avoid sticking. For Shoes: Shape black fondant into 2 tapered ovals, about ¾ x 3 in. long. Push onto end of 4½ in. dowel rods. Let all pieces dry 2-3 days on cornstarch-dusted surface.

Bake and cool 1 Mini Ball and ½ Soccer Ball cake. Position soccer ball on foil-covered board; ice smooth. Tint fondant as follows: 2½ oz. blue, 2 oz. red, 1½ oz. black; reserve ½ oz. white. Roll out all ⅛ in. thick. Use patterns to cut whites of eyes, pupils, mouth and tongue; position on cake. Cut ¼ in. red strips for sock stripes; attach to dowel rod with damp brush, trimming to fit. Cut ¼ x 11 in. long red strips for baseball seams; cut ¼ x 1 in. strips for stitches, pinching to V-shape. Attach using damp brush. Position arms and legs by pushing dowel rods into cake. Attach bottom circle to bat with icing and slide bat into hand. Shape ¼ in. fondant cones for spikes; use icing to attach to bottom of shoes in 2 rows, 4 spikes each. Prepare Mini Ball for rolled fondant (p. 115). Roll out blue fondant ⅛ in. thick; cover cake, trimming bottom edges. Divide into 8ths. Cut ⅛ in. wide strips; using damp brush, attach over marks for seams. Roll small ball and flatten for top button; attach with damp brush. Attach hat cake to fondant brim with icing. Position hat on ball. Serves 13.

HAPPY BIRTHDAY SAM

▲ Junior Jet Set

Pan: Mini Loaf, p. 154
Candy: White Candy Melts®† (1 pk. makes 3 plaques), Primary, Garden Candy Color Sets, p. 166; Transportation Mold, p. 168; Decorator Brush Set, p. 167
Also: Parchment Triangles, p. 140

Tint a portion of melted white candy light blue. Make candy plaques (p. 126), filling each pan cavity ¼ in. thick; refrigerate until firm and unmold. For planes, tint portions of melted white candy red, green and dark blue; reserve a portion of white. Mold planes using painting method (p. 125); refrigerate until firm and unmold. Attach airplane to plaque with melted candy; let set. Use melted candy in cut parchment bag to pipe clouds and print message. Each serves 1.

▼ Custom Built

Pans: Choo-Choo Train Set, p. 160; 6 x 2 in. Round, p. 153; Cooling Grid, p. 154

Tips: 1, 2, 3, 6, 8, 12, 17, p. 142-143

Colors:* Royal Blue, Lemon Yellow, Golden Yellow, Black, Copper (skin tone), Red-Red, Brown, p. 136

Fondant/Gum Paste: White Ready-To-Use Rolled Fondant (4 oz.), p. 130; Gum-Tex™, Rolling Pin, Roll & Cut Mat, p. 133; Brush Set, p. 131

Candy: Dark Cocoa Candy Melts®†, Garden Candy Colors Set, p. 166

Recipe: Buttercream Icing, p. 114

Also: 2008 Pattern Book (claw), p. 128; Smiley Flames Chunky Candles (2 pks.), p. 185; Jumbo Stars Sprinkle Decorations, p. 138; Chocolate Ready-To-Use Decorator Icing, p. 137; Plastic Dowel Rods, p. 232; Cake Boards, Cake Circles, Fanci-Foil Wrap, p. 233; Disposable Decorating Bags, p. 140; plain donuts, waxed paper, wooden skewer, 3 x 7½ x 1 in. craft block, double-stick tape, 6 in. black cord, cornstarch, ruler, knife, toothpicks

In advance: Prepare crane claw and arm. Tint 4 oz. fondant black. Add ¼ teaspoon Gum-Tex to 1½ in. ball of fondant; roll out ⅜ in. thick. Use pattern to cut out claw; use wooden skewer to make a hole from top through bottom. Thread cord through hole, tie a knot at the bottom end and pull knot up to hole. Position candle in claw and shape to loosely hold head. Let dry on cornstarch-dusted surface at least 24 hours. Roll out remaining black fondant ⅛ in. thick. Cut a 3 x 7 in. rectangle; wrap around dowel rod, leaving 5½ in. uncovered to insert into cake, and secure with damp brush. Carefully lift candle out of dried claw. Use tape to attach

cord to wooden skewer, leaving claw and 2½ in. of cord swinging free. Slide skewer into dowel rod and insert fondant in end to secure. Let dry. **Also:** Prepare tires. Tint candy black. Set donuts on Cooling Grid; cover with melted candy in cut disposable decorating bag. Let set. **And:** Prepare baseboards. Cover 8 in. cake circle, 5¼ x 8 in. cake board and craft block with Fanci-Foil. Use tape to secure craft block to center of rectangle to support crane cake.

Bake and cool 1-layer round and 3-D train cake (use firm-textured batter, such as pound cake). Create crane shape by cutting smokestack and cap off train; trim back end level. Slice about ¾ in. off front. Cut a square, approximately 3½ in., from cake slice; attach to cab top to increase height. Position crane on cut-to-fit foil-covered cake board; use tape to secure that cake board to prepared craft block base. Ice cake side smooth, building up areas as needed to make flat surfaces. Ice cab window areas smooth; cover rest of crane with tip 17 stars. For boy, pipe tip 12 ball head (smooth with finger dipped in cornstarch), tip 8 arm/body; add tip 1 outline eyes and mouth, tip 2 swirl hair, dot nose and pull-out hands. Pipe tip 6 outline details on sides. For grill, pipe tip 8 vertical supports and tip 6 horizontal lines. Pipe large dot headlights using tip 12 and small lights using tip 8. Attach tires to sides with icing; pipe tip 6 V-shaped outline treads. Insert crane arm into cake at a 45° angle; slide candle into claw, secure with melted candy if needed. Position round cake on covered cake board; ice smooth. Use tip 17 to pipe shell top and rosette bottom border. Pipe tip 3 name; position sprinkle stars. Pipe tip 17 rosette candleholders; insert candles. Serves 18.

*Combine Lemon Yellow with Golden Yellow for yellow shown.

◀ Roll Weevils

Pan: Mini Ball, p. 159

Tips: 1, 4, p. 142

Also: Disposable Decorating Bags, p. 140; 16 oz. hot roll mix, black olives, green olives with pimentos, carrots, uncooked spaghetti, cherry tomato, cream cheese, chicken, egg or ham salad, knife, vegetable shortening

Prepare hot roll mix following package directions. Lightly grease mini ball pan with vegetable shortening and place hot roll mix in each cavity. Bake 15 minutes at 375°F; cool. Slice roll ½ in. from bottom. Cut a small circle of bread from top piece; fill with your choice of salad and replace bottom piece. Cut ¾ x ½ in. long carrot feet; cut thin slices of green olive for spots. Stir cream cheese until softened; attach feet and spots with tip 4 dots of cream cheese. Cut 1 in. long carrot tail; trim ends to a point. Cut hole in roll; insert tail and secure with cream cheese. For head, insert portion of 2 in. length of uncooked spaghetti into cherry tomato; insert remainder into roll. Pipe tip 4 dot eyes and outline mouth with cream cheese. Cut black olive pupils using wide end of tip 1; position on eyes. Refrigerate until ready to serve. Each serves 1.

▼ A Slice of Summertime

Pan: 8 x 2 in. Round, p. 153

Tip: 789, p. 142

Colors:* Leaf Green, Kelly Green, Red-Red, p. 136

Fondant/Gum Paste: White Ready-To-Use Rolled Fondant (24 oz.), p. 130; Rolling Pin, Roll & Cut Mat, p. 133; Cutter/Embosser, p. 131

Recipe: Buttercream Icing, p. 114

Also: Fine Tip Neon Colors and Bold Tip Primary Colors FoodWriter™ Edible Color Markers, p. 130; 16 in. Featherweight® Decorating Bag, p. 140; Cake Board, Fanci-Foil Wrap, p. 233; Cake Leveler, p. 134; mini chocolate chips

Prepare favorite white cake mix; tint with ¼ teaspoon of Red-Red color. Blend in ½ cup mini chocolate chips. Bake and cool 1-layer cake. Refrigerate cake until mini chocolate chips are hardened; trim off top of cake with Cake Leveler. Ice cake sides with tip 789 and Featherweight Bag. For rind, tint 8 oz. fondant green, roll out ⅛ in. thick. Using Cutter/Embosser, cut a 1 in. wide strip and attach to cake sides; trim to fit. Draw lines on rind with FoodWriter markers. Serves 6.

*Combine Leaf Green with Kelly Green for green shown.

▶ Crispy Bee

Pans: Mini Ball, p. 159; Cooling Grid, p. 154

Colors: Lemon Yellow, Black, Royal Blue, p. 136

Fondant/Gum Paste: White Ready-To-Use Rolled Fondant (24 oz.), Neon Colors Fondant Multi Pack, p. 130; Cutter/Embosser, p. 131; Gum-Tex™, Rolling Pin, Roll & Cut Mat, p. 133; Heart Cut-Outs™, p. 132

Candy: White Candy Melts®†, Primary, Garden Candy Color Sets, p. 166

Recipe: Favorite crisped rice cereal treats (1 recipe)

Also: Flower Former Set, p. 140; sugar ice cream cones, black shoestring licorice, waxed paper, cornstarch, vegetable pan spray

In advance: Make fondant wings. Tint 2 in. ball of fondant light blue and add ¼ teaspoon of Gum-Tex. Roll out fondant ⅛ in. thick; cut 2 wings using medium heart Cut-Out. Let dry inside medium flower former dusted with cornstarch.

Prepare crisped rice cereal treats (1 recipe makes 10 treats); tint melted butter/marshmallow mixture yellow, add crisped rice cereal and mix. Press into lightly sprayed mini ball pan and inside sugar cones; remove mini ball shapes and place on waxed paper sprayed lightly with vegetable pan spray. Tint melted white candy green using green and yellow candy colors. Stand sugar cone on cooling grid; cover with melted candy (p. 126) and let set on waxed paper-covered board. Attach mini ball treat to cone with melted candy, shaping treat mixture around top of cone; let set. Roll out neon orange fondant ⅛ in. thick; cut an 18 x ½ in. wide strip using wavy-edge wheel of Cutter/Embosser. Wrap strip around cone and attach with melted candy. For eyes, roll ¾ in. balls of white fondant and ¼ in. flattened balls of black fondant; attach with melted candy. For nose, shape a 1 x ½ in. wide purple cone; attach. Cut licorice antennae and mouth; attach. For antenna ends, roll ¼ in. pink balls; push onto licorice. Attach wings with melted candy; let set. Each serves 1.

†Brand confectionery coating.

▶ They're Guests, Not Pests!

Pans: 8, 12 x 2 in. Round, p. 153; Sports Ball Set, Mini Ball, p. 159; Cookie Sheet, p. 154

Tip: 5, p. 142

Colors:* Sky Blue, Leaf Green, Lemon Yellow, Golden Yellow, Violet, Rose, Orange, Black, p. 136

Fondant/Gum Paste: White Ready-To-Use Rolled Fondant, p. 130 (37 oz.), p. 130; Gum-Tex™, Rolling Pin, Roll & Cut Mat, p. 133; Ribbon Cutter/Embosser Set, Brush Set, p. 131

Candy: White, Yellow, Orange Candy Melts®† (1 pk. each), Primary, Garden Candy Color Sets, p. 166

Recipe: Buttercream Icing, p. 114

Also: Heart Plastic Nesting Cutter Set, p. 163; Flower Nail No. 7, p. 140; Wooden Dowel Rods, p. 232; 4 in. Lollipop Sticks, p. 169; 14 in. Silver Cake Base, 8 in. Cake Circle, p. 233; 6 in. Separator Plate, p. 231; toothpicks, knife, cornstarch, waxed paper, ruler, pastry brush, craft knife

In advance: Make fondant pieces (p. 121). When pieces are dry, complete small bugs. For spider, roll 2¼ and 1¼ in. balls for body; position on toothpick. Roll 3 x ¼ in. logs for legs; shape with a 45° angle. Roll small balls for feet. Insert spider legs in body. Insert wings and attach stinger and spider feet with damp brush. For inchworm, roll balls for body in graduating sizes, ½, ¾, 1, 1¼, 1 and ¾ in. diameter. Roll and flatten small balls of fondant for eyes and pupils; roll thin logs for mouths. Attach features on small bugs using damp brush. Use a toothpick to poke holes in head and ball antennae tips. Assemble and position antennae; secure with melted candy.

Mold large candy bee. Melt yellow and orange candy; add candy color for brighter shades shown. Using mini ball pan for head and sports ball pan for body, mold candy shells (p. 125), 2 of each size, by brushing melted candy up insides of pans with a pastry brush. Let set. Add additional layers for a thicker shell; chill completely and unmold. Rub edges over warm cookie sheet and attach halves to form ball; smooth seams. Roll out black fondant ⅛ in. thick. Using ribbon cutter with zigzag wheel and 1 in. spacer, cut stripes. Wrap around body and secure with melted candy. Roll a 2 in. cone for stinger; attach with melted candy. Roll fondant balls for eyes and pupils, log for mouth. Using melted candy, attach features and nose; attach head to body. Bend lollipop sticks for antennae; use tip of craft knife to make small, tight-fitting holes in head and insert sticks. Paint with melted candy; when dry, push on ball tips. Cut ¾ in. off bottom of heart wings; attach lollipop stick to back with melted candy. Using warm tip of flower nail, make small, tight-fitting holes in body and insert sticks; secure with melted candy. Bee will be attached to legs at party.

Ice smooth 1-layer 12 in. and 2-layer 8 in. cakes and prepare for Stacked Construction (p. 112) on base. Pipe tip 5 bead bottom border on 8 in. cake. For grass, roll out green fondant ⅛ in. thick. Cut 1 in. strips; use knife to make ¾ in. slits, ⅛ in. apart. Attach 2 layers of grass around base of cake; separate and shape blades of grass. Cut 4 dowel rods to 7 in. long. Roll out black fondant ⅛ in. thick; cut 3 x 1 in. rectangle and wrap around one end of rod, securing with damp brush. Use separator plate to mark feet on cake top. Push dowel rod legs into cake at marks. Take a 1½ in. ball of fondant and wrap around leg for each foot. Using melted candy, attach small bugs. **At party:** Attach large bee to legs with melted candy. Serves 40.

▶ Daisy Dipper

Pan: Dancing Daisy Flower, p. 158; Cookie Sheet, Cooling Grid, p. 154
Recipes: Your 2 favorite dips
Also: Leaf Cut-Outs™, p. 132; hot roll mix (two 1 lb. boxes),
3½ in. diameter custard cup, knife, sandwich bread, cherry
tomatoes, carrot and celery sticks, lemon leaves, serving platter

In advance: Mix and bake bread in flower pan according to package
directions; you will need 1½ recipes to fill pan. Press dough into
greased pan; let rise. Bake and cool. Prepare dips; refrigerate until
serving time.

Use largest leaf Cut-Out to cut sandwich bread leaves (about 20).
Place on cookie sheet and toast in 400° oven for 7-8 minutes.
Arrange bread leaves and lemon leaves on platter; position daisy
bread. Use knife to cut and pull bread out of center and petals. Fill
petals with dip; place custard cup in center and fill with vegetables.

◀ Cheese Daisies

Fondant: Flower, Round Cut-Outs™, p. 132
Also: 11¾ in. Lollipop Sticks, p. 169; 4 in. clay flower pot, craft block, deli-style yellow
Cheddar and white American cheese (½ in. thick), cream cheese, parsley, knife

Use medium and largest flower Cut-Outs to cut 12 assorted Cheddar and American
cheese blossoms. Use smallest round Cut-Out to cut centers in opposite color cheese;
attach with cream cheese. Insert Lollipop Sticks. Cut craft block to fit snugly in bottom
of pot. Arrange flowers in pot just before serving; trim sticks to vary heights. Use cream
cheese to attach some parsley to sticks; arrange remaining parsley around bottom.
Each serves 1.

▶ Sunflower Mousse

Pan: Sunflower, p. 155
Colors: * Lemon Yellow, Golden Yellow, p. 136
Recipe: Cream Cheese Mousse, p. 114
Also: Cake Boards, Fanci-Foil Wrap, p. 233; large chocolate chips,
vegetable oil pan spray

Lightly spray pan with vegetable oil pan spray. Prepare mousse
recipe; tint yellow. Pour into prepared pan. Refrigerate at least 6 hours
or overnight to set. Unmold onto serving plate. To unmold, dip bottom of
pan in cool water for no more than 10 seconds. Position chocolate chips
at center. Refrigerate until serving time. Serves 16.

*Combine Golden Yellow with Lemon Yellow for yellow shown.

◄ Polar Pansies

Pans: Silicone Mini Flower Mold, p. 149; Cookie Sheet, Cooling Grid, p. 154
Candy: White Candy Melts®†, Primary Candy Colors Set, p. 166
Also: Yellow Colored Sugar, p. 139; 8 in. Cookie Treat Sticks, p. 165; Cake Boards, p. 233; Disposable Decorating Bags, p. 140; ice cream, vegetable pan spray, jelly spearmint leaves, knife, waxed paper

Spray mold cavities with vegetable pan spray. Fill with softened ice cream, pressing firmly. Freeze for at least 6 hours. Unmold onto waxed paper-covered board; refreeze for about 30 minutes. Tint candy yellow. Remove flowers from freezer and insert sticks. Spatula ice backs with melted candy; refreeze for about 30 minutes. Place Cooling Grid over pan lined with waxed paper. Place flowers, iced side down, on grid. Quickly coat with melted candy in cut disposable bag; tap grid to smooth coating. Sprinkle with colored sugar; refreeze for about 1 hour. Cut small slit in spearmint leaves; press onto stick. Attach Candy Melts wafer to center using melted candy. Freeze until serving time. Each serves 1.

► Fluffy Flower

Pans: Silicone Mini Flower Mold, p. 149; Cookie Sheet, Cooling Grid, p. 154
Tip: 32, p. 143
Candy: White Candy Melts®†, Garden Candy Colors Set, p. 166; Decorator Brush Set, p. 167
Recipe: Strawberry Mousse, p. 114 .
Also: Flower Formers Set, Disposable Decorating Bags, p. 140; fine tip artist brush, lemon leaves, candy-coated chocolates

In advance: Prepare candy shells (p. 125) in flower mold. Let set.
Also: Make candy leaves. Tint melted white candy green. Brush melted candy onto back of lemon leaf; let dry in medium flower former. Later, peel off leaf and paint vein lines on candy using fine tip brush and green candy color.

Prepare mousse and fill candy shells using tip 32 rosettes. Position candy-coated chocolate in center. Position leaf. Each serves 1.

†Brand confectionery coating.

◄ Sprays of Color

Pans: Petal Set (12 x 2 in. used), 6 x 2 in. Round, p. 153
Tips: 2A, 3, 12, p. 142
Colors:* Royal Blue, Lemon Yellow, Kelly Green, Violet, Rose, p. 136
Fondant/Gum Paste: White Ready-To-Use Rolled Fondant, p. 130; Gum Tex™, Rolling Pin, Roll & Cut Mat, p. 133; Cutter/Embosser, Brush Set, p. 131; Flower, Leaf Cut-Outs™, p. 132
Recipe: Buttercream Icing, p. 114
Also: 2008 Pattern Book (Flower Pot), p. 128; White Candy Melts®†, p. 166; Cake Boards, Fanci-Foil Wrap, Dowel Rods, Flower Spikes, p. 232; Parchment Triangles, p. 140; 22-gauge florist wire, wire cutters, ruler, cornstarch, waxed paper

In advance: Make fondant flowers and leaves. Mix 8 oz. fondant with 2 teaspoon Gum-Tex. Tint yellow, rose, violet and green; roll out ⅛ in. thick. Using Cut-Outs, cut 14 large and 21 medium flowers in assorted colors; cut 35 leaves using smallest cutter from leaf set. Roll out white fondant ⅛ in. thick. Cut large flower centers using wide end of tip 2A, small centers using narrow end; roll into balls. Attach centers using damp brush. Let all dry on cornstarch-dusted surface. Cut 20 wires each in 5 and 8 in. lengths; attach flowers and leaves using melted candy in cut parchment bag.

Ice smooth 1-layer round and 2-layer petal cakes; prepare for Stacked Construction (p. 112). Pipe tip 3 ball bottom border around 6 in. cake. Tint 2 oz. portions of fondant blue, yellow, violet and rose. Roll out fondant ⅛ in. thick. Use pattern to cut flower pots; attach to cake sides, curving to fit petals. Cut 4½ x ½ in. strips for flower pot front rims; trim to fit and attach to edge of cake. Cut 4½ x ⅜ in. strips for flower pot back rims; trim to fit and position on cake top. Decorate rose and blue pots with ¼ in. fondant strips; cut to fit and attach. Decorate yellow and violet pots with small fondant balls. Roll out fondant ¼ in. thick and cut circles with narrow end of tip 12; roll into balls and attach. Pipe tip 3 ball border between pots. Insert flower spikes in pots and cake top; position flowers. Trim wires to fit; use a bit of fondant inside spike as needed for support. Serves 44.

*Combine Violet with Rose for violet shown.

Make Them Stars!

Ask any kid—there's a big difference between seeing their favorite characters on the screen and having them make a birthday house call. Imagine how much it would mean to have a decorated Diego waiting at the table with a handful of balloon cakes and cookie place markers that spell everyone's name in candy! Or think of the thrills when kids see Pablo from The Backyardigans smiling back against a galaxy of colorful fondant stars. In our superstar lineup, you'll also find classic characters with fresh new looks, including Tink, Ariel, Superman and Spider-Man. Plus big hits like Cars, with Lightning McQueen cruising through a cityscape of neon fondant. Give them a birthday that's ready for prime time!

Instructions for projects shown on these two pages are on page 24.

2008 WILTON YEARBOOK | 23

The *Diego* Dash

Pans: *Go, Diego, Go!*, p. 170; Mini Ball, p. 159

Tips: 3, 16, 366, p. 142-143

Colors: *Go, Diego, Go!* Icing Color Set (skin tone, brown, blue, black), p. 170; Royal Blue, Red-Red, Lemon Yellow, Terra Cotta, Leaf Green, Orange, p. 136

Recipe: Buttercream Icing, p. 114

Also: Cake Boards, Fanci-Foil Wrap, p. 233; Flowerful Medley Sprinkles Assortment, p. 138; red, yellow and blue curling ribbon (18 in. each), toothpicks, cornstarch

Bake and cool 3 Mini Ball balloon cakes. Position on cut-to-fit cake boards and cover with tip 16 stars. Pipe tip 16 rosette knot and insert ribbon. Bake and cool *Diego* cake. Position on foil-covered cake board cut 1 in. wider than cake on all sides. Ice cake sides and background areas smooth. Using tip 3, pipe details. Outline and pipe in mouth, tongue, eyes and irises (smooth with finger dipped in cornstarch). Add dot pupils and highlights. Outline and pipe in watch, vest patch, strap, shoe accents and soles (smooth with finger dipped in cornstarch). Cover all remaining areas with tip 16 stars. Use tip 3 to overpipe outline eyebrows; outline and pipe in blue edging on vest front (smooth with finger). Use 2 shades of green to pipe tip 366 leaves for bottom border. Position confetti sprinkles on cake sides and background areas. Position balloon cakes; push ribbons into hand. Serves 15.

A Pal at Your Place!

Pans: Non-Stick Cookie Sheet, Cooling Grid, p. 151

Tips: 2, 3, 5, 6, p. 142

Colors: *Go, Diego, Go!* Icing Color Set (skin tone, brown, blue, black), p. 170; Royal Blue, Lemon Yellow, Leaf Green, p. 136

Candy: Candy Melts®† (White, Orange, Red, Green, Yellow), p. 166; Alphabet Candy Mold, p. 168

Recipes: Royal Icing, Roll-Out Cookies, p. 114

Also: 2008 Pattern Book (*Diego* Body, Easel Back), p. 128; *Go, Diego, Go!* Icing Decorations, p. 170; 101 Cookie Cutters Set, p. 162; Cake Boards, p. 233; Disposable Decorating Bags, p. 140; Meringue Powder, p. 137; waxed paper, knife, ruler

In advance: Make *Diego* using royal icing. Copy pattern, attach to board and cover with waxed paper. Outline and pipe in shirt, vest and shorts with tip 6, shoes with tip 5, arms and legs with tip 3, waving hand with tip 2. Pipe tip 2 dots for badge. Position icing decoration head; pipe tip 2 outline neck. Let dry. **Also:** Mold candy letters using melted candy in cut Disposable Decorating Bags. Make large initials using alphabet cutters from 101 Cutters Set; place on Non-Stick Cookie Sheet and fill ¼ in. deep. Refrigerate until firm; carefully unmold. Make remaining letters for names using Alphabet Candy Molds. Let set; unmold.

Prepare and roll out cookie dough. Cut rectangle plaques 2½ in. high, 6 in. wide for 5 letter names, adding ½ in. to width for each additional letter. Use pattern to cut 2 easel backs for each plaque. Bake and cool all cookies. Cover plaques with melted candy (p. 126); let set. Attach candy letters with melted candy. Attach *Diego* to plaque with royal icing; pipe hand and fingers on large letter with tip 2 outlines. Let set. Attach easel backs to cookies with melted candy. Each serves 1.

Diego Delivers!

Pans: 6 x 2 in. Round, p. 153; Cookie Sheet, Cooling Grid, p. 154

Tips: 2, 5, 6, 10, 233, p. 142-143

Colors:* Royal Blue, Kelly Green, Burgundy, Brown, Red-Red, p. 136

Recipes: Buttercream, Royal Icings, Roll-Out Cookies, p. 114

Also: 2008 Pattern Book (Tree Top), p. 128; *Go, Diego, Go!* Candle, p. 170; Cake Dividing Set, p. 135; 10 in. Cake Boards, Fanci-Foil Wrap, p. 233; Piping Gel, Meringue Powder, p. 137; White Candy Melts®†, p. 166; Decorator Brush Set, p. 167; pretzel rods, granulated brown sugar, knife, spatula, toothpicks

In advance: Make cookie tree for cake top. Prepare and roll out dough; trace treetop pattern with toothpick and cut with knife. Bake and cool. Using tip 10 and royal icing, pipe in treetop; let dry. Attach pretzel rod using melted candy; let set.

Ice 2-layer cake smooth and position on foil-wrapped 10 in. cake board. Using spatula, ice grassy area on cake top and random hills around bottom. Use Cake Dividing Set to divide cake into 6ths. At each division pipe a tip 6 swirl tree top; add tip 5 outline trunk and branches. Use darker green to pipe tip 2 outline flower stems and pull-out dot leaves; add tip 2 pull-out dot flowers. Sprinkle brown sugar sand on board around cake. Pipe tip 233 grass bottom border. Tint Piping Gel blue; spread on board for water. Insert tree in cake top; position candle. Serves 12.

*Combine Brown with Red-Red for brown shown.

†Brand confectionery coating.

Diego Spies a Shortcut

Pan: Standard Muffin, p. 154

Tip: 352, p. 143

Color: Kelly Green, p. 136

Recipe: Buttercream Icing, p. 114

Also: *Go, Diego, Go!* Topper, Picks, Standard Baking Cups, p. 170

Bake and cool cupcakes in *Diego* Baking Cups. Spatula ice tops; position topper and picks. Use darker green to pipe tip 352 leaves. Each serves 1.

▲ Ice and Go with *Pablo*

Pan: Standard Muffin, p. 154

Tip: 4, p. 142

Colors:* Red-Red, Christmas Red, Golden Yellow, Orange, p. 136

Recipe: Buttercream Icing, p. 114

Also: *The Backyardigans* Baking Cups, Icing Decorations, p. 171

Ice cupcakes smooth with spatula. Edge with tip 4 outlines. Position icing decoration. Each serves 1.

*Combine Red-Red with Christmas Red for red shown. Combine Golden Yellow with Orange for yellow shown.

▶ Sweet Dreams, *Dora!*

Pans: *Dora the Explorer*, p. 176; Cookie Sheet, Cooling Grid, p. 165

Tips: 2, 3, 13, 16, 21, p. 142-143

Colors: *Dora the Explorer* Icing Color Set (red, pink, brown, skin tone), p. 176; Kelly Green, Royal Blue, Orange, Lemon Yellow, Black, Copper (skin tone), Violet, p. 136

Recipes: Buttercream, Color Flow Icings, Roll-Out Cookies, p. 114

Also: 101 Cookie Cutters Set, p. 162; Star Plastic Nesting Cutter Set, p. 163; Cake Boards, Fanci-Foil Wrap, p. 233; Yellow Cake Sparkles, p. 139; Color Flow Mix, p. 137; cornstarch

In advance: Make cookie stars. Prepare and roll out dough; cut 5 stars using smallest nesting cutter and 4 stars using 3 in. nesting cutter. Bake and cool cookies. Cover cookies with thinned color flow icing (p. 126). Sprinkle small stars with Cake Sparkles. Let dry. **Also:** Use tip 3 and full-strength color flow to pipe features on large stars. Outline and flow in eyes and mouths; add dot pupils and outline eyebrows. Let dry. **And:** Make bear cookie. Cut cookie using bear from 101 Cutter Set; bake and cool. Use tip 2 and buttercream to outline all details. Pipe in eyes, eyebrows, dot nose, vest stripes, pipe in tummy, inside ears and paw pads (pat smooth with finger dipped in cornstarch). Outline and pipe in vest accents; pipe dot pupils. Outline Dora's fingers, cover body and *Dora's* fingers with tip 13 stars.

Ice cake sides and background areas smooth. Outline all details with tip 3. Use tip 3 to outline and pipe in eyes, irises, mouth and tongue (smooth with finger). Add tip 3 dot pupils and highlights. Cover *Dora* with tip 16 stars; add tip 3 dot buttons. Position bear cookie. Pipe tip 21 star bottom border. Position star cookies. Cake serves 12; each cookie serves 1.

◀ Very Important Penguin!

Pan: *The Backyardigans*, p. 171

Tips: 3, 12, 16, 21, p. 142-143

Colors:* *The Backyardigans* Icing Colors Set (yellow, blue, red, black), p. 171; Orange, Leaf Green, Sky Blue, Royal Blue, Violet, Rose, Golden Yellow, Lemon Yellow, Red-Red, p. 136

Fondant/Gum Paste: White Ready-To-Use Rolled Fondant (96 oz.), p. 130; Rolling Pin, Roll & Cut Mat, p. 133; Brush Set, Easy-Glide Fondant Smoother, p. 131

Recipe: Buttercream Icing, p. 114

Also: 2008 Pattern Book (Starburst Background Sections), p.128; Jumbo Stars Sprinkles, p. 138; Cake Boards, Fanci-Foil Wrap, p. 233; Piping Gel, p. 137; 17 x 19 in. foamcore board (¼ in. thick), knife, cornstarch, waxed paper, toothpicks

In advance: Make fondant background. Tint fondant, 6 oz. for each color, to lighter shades of blue, violet, orange, green and yellow; take 4 oz. of each color and tint to corresponding darker shades. Roll out ⅛ in. thick. Use pattern to cut stars from lighter shades and base pieces from darker shades. Let dry on cornstarch-dusted surface. **Also:** Prepare base board. Wrap foamcore in foil; brush lightly with Piping Gel. Cover board with 54 oz. white fondant; smooth with Fondant Smoother.

Position *Pablo* cake on foil-covered cake board cut slightly larger than cake. Ice sides and background areas smooth. Outline features with tip 3. Outline and pipe in eyes with tip 12 (smooth with finger dipped in cornstarch). Using tip 3, add dot pupils and highlights, outline and pipe in bow tie, beanie and propeller (shape and smooth with finger). Pipe in tongue and outline mouth with tip 3; pipe beak top and bottom; overpipe edge of top beak and indent with brush edge. Cover remainder of head and body with tip 16 stars. Overpipe tip 3 outline eyebrows and eyelids. Use toothpick to mark cake size on base board. Arrange fondant background pieces, securing to board with damp brush. Position cake; pipe tip 21 shell bottom border. Position star sprinkles. Serves 12.

*For fondant, combine Royal Blue with Sky Blue for blue shown, Violet with Rose for violet shown, Orange with Red-Red for orange shown and Leaf Green with Lemon Yellow for green shown.

Pans: 6, 8 x 2 in. Round, p. 153

Tips: 1, 3, 13, 129, 349, 352, p. 142-143

Colors:* Royal Blue, Violet, Rose, Leaf Green, Kelly Green, Teal, p. 136

Recipes: Buttercream, Royal Icings, p. 114

Also: *Disney Fairies* Candle, p. 172; Blue, Violet Color Mist™ Food Color Spray, p. 136; Meringue Powder, p. 137; Dowel Rods, Flower Spikes (4), p. 232; Cake Circles, 10 in. Silver Cake Base, p. 233; white 22-gauge florist wire (4 pieces, each 16 in. long), florist tape, waxed paper, knife

In advance: Make royal icing flowers and stars. Pipe 30 tip 129 drop flowers in dark rose with tip 3 dot centers in white. Pipe 30 each violet, light rose and teal tip 13 stars. Make extras to allow for breakage. Let dry.

Ice 2-layer cakes smooth with buttercream. Prepare for Stacked Construction (p. 112) and position on Cake Base. Spray with blue, then violet, Color Mist. Using buttercream, pipe tip 3 message, random dots and various flower stems on cake sides. Attach flowers with dots of icing. Use 2 shades of green and tips 349 and 352 to pipe assorted leaves on stems and bottom borders. Pipe random tip 1 outline and dot starbursts on cake sides. Group wires into pairs; twist both ends of each pair together. Wrap ends in florist tape; shape wires into curls. Secure both ends in Flower Spikes using royal icing. Insert spikes in cake sides and cover hole with icing. Attach stars to wires with dots of royal icing. Position candle on cake top. Serves 32.

*Combine Violet with Rose for violet shown. Combine Rose with Violet for rose shades shown.

©Disney

▼ **Wish Upon a Star**

Pans: Star Cookie Treat, p. 165; Cooling Grid, p. 154

Color: Lemon Yellow, p. 136

Recipes: Roll-Out Cookies, Poured Cookie Icing, p. 114

Also: *Disney Fairies* Icing Decorations, p. 172; White Cake Sparkles™, p. 139; 8 in. Cookie Treat Sticks, p. 165

Prepare dough. Bake and cool cookie treats on sticks. Cover with poured icing (p. 126); immediately sprinkle with Cake Sparkles. Attach Icing Decorations with icing dots. Each serves 1.

©Disney

◄ Her Garden Glistens

Pan: *Disney Fairies*, p. 172
Tips: 2, 3, 5, 16, p. 142-143
Colors:* *Disney Fairies* Icing Colors Set (blue, yellow, red, skin tone), p. 172; Violet, Rose, Leaf Green, Black, p. 136
Fondant/Gum Paste: White Ready-To-Use Rolled Fondant (48 oz.), White Pearl Dust, p. 130; Gum-Tex™, Rolling Pin, Roll & Cut Mat, p. 133; Flower, Leaf Cut-Outs™, p. 132; Fondant Shaping Foam, Confectionery Tool Set, Brush Set, Easy-Glide Fondant Smoother, p. 131
Recipe: Buttercream Icing, p. 114
Also: Lily Nail Set, Flower Former Set, p. 131; Blue, Violet Color Mist™ Food Color Spray, p. 136; Piping Gel, p. 137; aluminum foil, cornstarch, tea strainer, non-toxic pastel chalk (greens, yellows), 18 in. foamcore circle (¼ in. thick)

In advance: Make fondant flowers and leaves. Combine 1 teaspoon Gum-Tex with 12 oz. fondant. Tint 8 oz. fondant green; roll out ⅛ in. thick. Cut 30 leaves with largest cutter, 20 with medium cutter. Place each leaf on thin shaping foam and score vein lines using small veining tool from set. Let dry on flower formers dusted with cornstarch. Tint 2 oz. light and 2 oz. dark violet; roll out ⅛ in. thick. Cut 3 flowers in each color with largest cutter, 3 in each color with medium cutter. Make foil cups by pushing 4 in. foil squares halfway down into 1⅝ and 2½ in. lily cups. Shape flower in cup; roll small white ball centers and attach with damp brush. Remove and let dry. **Also:** Grate chalk in tea strainer to make "dust" in 2 shades of green and 2 shades of yellow; brush onto leaves. Brush leaves and flowers with Pearl Dust. **And:** Cover base board (p. 124). Tint 35 oz. fondant blue. Cover base board; smooth with Fondant Smoother. Spray with blue and violet Color Mist to vary shading.

Ice sides and background areas of cake smooth. Outline details and pipe in features with tip 3. Pipe in eye and mouth (smooth with finger dipped in cornstarch). Pipe in lips, irises then pupils; smooth. Add dot eye highlights. Overpipe upper eyelids (pat slightly). Cover face and hair with tip 16 stars. Pipe tip 3 strings on ponytail. Pipe tip 2 pull-out eyelashes. Position cake on base board; pipe tip 5 bead bottom border. Pipe tip 5 vines on circle. Attach leaves and flowers with icing. Pipe tip 2 outline and dot sparkles. Serves 12.

*Combine Violet with Rose for dark violet. Combine Rose with Violet for light violet.

©Disney

▲ Tink's Here in a Blink!

Pan: Standard Muffin, p. 154
Colors:* Violet, Rose, p. 136
Fondant/Gum Paste: White Ready-To-Use Rolled Fondant, p. 130; Round Cut-Outs™, p. 132; Rolling Pin, Roll & Cut Mat, p. 133; Brush Set, p. 131
Recipe: Buttercream Icing, p. 114
Also: *Disney Fairies* Baking Cups, Fun Pix®, Icing Decorations, p. 172; White Cake Sparkles, p. 139; cornstarch

In advance: Make circles. Tint portions of fondant violet and rose; roll out ⅛ in. thick. Cut circles using smallest Cut-Out. Brush with water and sprinkle with Cake Sparkles; let dry on cornstarch-dusted surface.

Ice cupcakes smooth. Position circles; insert pick or position icing decoration in center. Each serves 1.

*Combine Violet with Rose for violet shown.

©Disney

▶ Think Tink

Pans: Silicone Mini Flower Mold, p. 149; Cookie Sheet, Cooling Grid, p. 154
Tip: 8, p. 142
Colors:* Rose, Violet, p. 136
Also: *Disney Fairies* Party Toppers, p. 172; Ready-To-Use Decorator Icing, p. 137; cornstarch

Bake and cool cakes in silicone mold supported by cookie sheet. Tint a portion of icing light violet and heat to pouring consistency; cover cakes with poured icing (p. 126). Let set. Tint remaining full-strength icing darker violet; outline and pipe in teardrop-shaped petals with tip 8 (smooth with finger dipped in cornstarch). Position topper. Each serves 1.

*Combine Violet with Rose for violet shades shown.

©Disney

◀ Bright Blossoms *Pooh*

Pan: *Pooh*, p. 179

Tips: 4, 5, 8, 10, 12, 16, p. 142-143

Colors: *Pooh* Icing Color Set (*Pooh* gold, green, black), p. 179; Kelly Green, Lemon Yellow, Violet, Rose, Orange, p. 136

Fondant/Gum Paste: Neon Colors Fondant Multi Pack, p. 130; Flower Cut-Outs™, p. 132; Rolling Pin, Roll & Cut Mat, p. 133

Recipe: Buttercream Icing, p. 114

Also: Flower Plastic Cutter, p. 163; Candy Melting Plate, p. 167; Cake Boards, Fanci-Foil Wrap, p. 233; cornstarch, aluminum foil, 3½-4 in. diameter round container

In advance: Make fondant flowers. Cut 6 x 12 in. strip of foil; fold into 6 in. square. Set foil over round container; press to form shallow cup, about ¾ in. deep, and dust with cornstarch. Roll out orange fondant ⅛ in. thick. Cut large flower using cookie cutter. Set in foil cup to dry. Roll out orange and yellow fondant ¹⁄₁₆ in. thick. Cut 8 of each color using medium flower Cut-Out. Let dry in Candy Melting Plate dusted with cornstarch.

Position cake on foil-wrapped board. Ice sides and background areas smooth. Using tip 4, outline *Pooh* and pipe in nose and eyes. Cover shirt and body with tip 16 stars. Pipe tip 8 outline flower stem. Pipe elongated shell inner petals using tip 12 for large flower, tip 5 for small flowers. Add dot centers using tip 12 for large flower, tip 4 for small flowers. Add tip 10 bead bottom border. Attach flowers with icing dots. Serves 12.

▲ A Hunnysuckle from *Pooh*!

Pans: Cookie Sheet, Cooling Grid, p. 165

Tips: 8, 12, p. 142

Colors:* Violet, Rose, p. 136

Cookie: Flower Plastic Cutter, p. 163; 6 in. Cookie Treat Sticks, p. 165

Recipes: Buttercream Icing, Roll-Out Cookies, p. 114

Also: *Pooh* Icing Decorations, p. 179; Yellow Candy Melts®†, p. 166; Disposable Decorating Bags, p. 140; Cake Boards, p. 233; waxed paper

Prepare and roll out dough. Cut cookies with flower cutter; bake and cool. Cover cookies with melted candy in cut bag (p. 126). When set, attach lollipop stick to back using melted candy; let set. In buttercream, pipe tip 12 elongated shell petals. Pipe tip 8 spiral flower center. Position icing decoration. Each serves 1.

*Combine Violet with Rose for violet shown.

©Disney
Based on "Winnie the Pooh" works by A. A. Milne and E. H. Shepard.

▶ *Lightning* in Neon

Pan: *Cars*, p. 174

Tips: 3, 16, 21, p. 142-143

Colors: *Cars* Icing Color Set (yellow, blue, red, black), p. 174; additional Black and Lemon Yellow (for background), Leaf Green, Rose, Royal Blue, Orange, Violet, Red-Red, p. 136

Fondant/Gum Paste: White Ready-To-Use Rolled Fondant (96 oz.), p. 130; Easy-Glide Fondant Smoother, p. 131; Rolling Pin, Roll & Cut Mat, p. 133; Alphabet/Number Cut-Outs™, p. 132

Recipe: Buttercream Icing, p. 114

Also: 2008 Pattern Book (Background Sections), p. 128; Piping Gel, p. 137; Fanci-Foil Wrap, p. 233; 20 x 17½ x ½ in. thick foamcore board, knife, cellophane tape

One day in advance: Tint fondant for board as follows: 14 oz. gray (use a small amount of black), 36 oz. black, 10 oz. green, 8 oz. orange, 7 oz. blue, 4 oz. each rose, violet, yellow; 3 oz. brown, 1 oz. dark gray; reserve 4 oz. white. Use patterns to make fondant-covered background board (p. 121).

Bake and cool *Lightning McQueen* cake. Ice cake sides, background areas, headlights, mouth, front windshield, side windows and blue lightning bolt smooth. Using tip 3, outline car details and number; add dot rivets on hood. Pipe in eyes with tip 3 (smooth with finger dipped in cornstarch); add tip 3 dot pupils. Cover tires with tip 16 lines. Cover car, lightning bolt and number with tip 16 stars. Add tip 3 outline muffler. Pipe tip 21 shell bottom border. Position cake on fondant-covered board. Serves 12.

*Combine Leaf Green with Lemon Yellow for green shown. Combine Violet with Rose for violet shown. Combine Brown with Red-Red for brown shown. Combine Lemon Yellow with Leaf Green for yellow Piping Gel highlights shown.

©Disney/Pixar

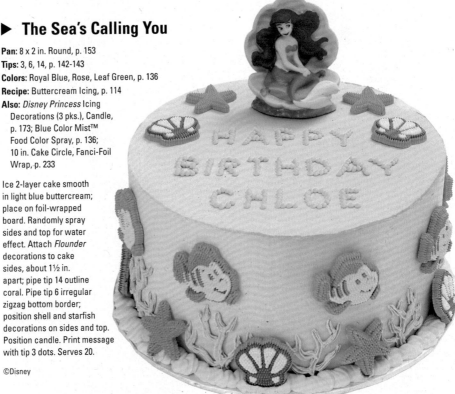

▲ Sea Snacks

Pan: Standard Muffin, p. 154
Tips: 14, 352, p. 143
Colors: Royal Blue, Rose, Kelly Green, p. 136
Recipe: Buttercream, Royal Icings, p. 114
Also: Cake Boards, Fanci-Foil Wrap, p. 233; *Disney Princess* Baking Cups, Party Toppers, p. 173; Meringue Powder, p. 137, waxed paper

In advance: Make 2 coral clusters and 1 sea plant group for each cupcake using royal icing. Cover board with waxed paper and pipe tip 14 coral branches in random shapes, approximately 1½ x 1½ in. wide. For sea plants, pipe tip 352 leaves in heights up to 2 in. Make extras to allow for breakage; let dry overnight.

Spatula ice cupcakes in buttercream, using swirl motion. Position topper and insert royal icing decorations. Each serves 1.

©Disney

▲ Adorable *Ariel*

Pan: *Disney Princess*, p. 173
Tips: 3, 6, 14, 16, 352, p. 142-143
Colors:* *Disney Princess* Icing Color Set (copper for skin tone), lavender, no-taste red, sky blue), p. 173; Rose, Lemon Yellow, Black, Royal Blue, Kelly Green, Leaf Green, p. 136
Candy: Seashells Candy Mold, 168; White Candy Melts®†, Primary and Garden Candy Colors Set, p. 166
Recipe: Buttercream Icing, p. 114
Also: Cake Boards, Fanci-Foil Wrap, p. 233; granulated brown sugar

In advance: Make 17 candies. Tint portions of melted white candy pink and orange. Make marbleized seashells (p. 125) using Seashells Mold; refrigerate until firm and unmold.

Position cake on foil-wrapped board at least 2 in. larger than cake. Ice cake sides smooth. Use tip 3 to outline all details. Pipe in eyes, lips and flower center with tip 3. Cover body, swimsuit, face and hair with tip 16 stars; pipe tip 3 eyelashes. Pipe tip 14 outline coral and tip 352 sea plants on cake sides. Spatula ice cake board around bottom border; pipe tip 6 random zigzags. Immediately cover with granulated brown sugar. Position candy shells. Serves 12.

*Combine Rose with Lemon Yellow for rose mouth.

†Brand confectionery coating.

©Disney

▶ The Sea's Calling You

Pan: 8 x 2 in. Round, p. 153
Tips: 3, 6, 14, p. 142-143
Colors: Royal Blue, Rose, Leaf Green, p. 136
Recipe: Buttercream Icing, p. 114
Also: *Disney Princess* Icing Decorations (3 pks.), Candle, p. 173; Blue Color Mist™ Food Color Spray, p. 136; 10 in. Cake Circle, Fanci-Foil Wrap, p. 233

Ice 2-layer cake smooth in light blue buttercream; place on foil-wrapped board. Randomly spray sides and top for water effect. Attach *Flounder* decorations to cake sides, about 1½ in. apart; pipe tip 14 outline coral. Pipe tip 6 irregular zigzag bottom border; position shell and starfish decorations on sides and top. Position candle. Print message with tip 3 dots. Serves 20.

©Disney

SCOOBY-DOO!

◀ Making His Presents Known!

Pans: *Scooby-Doo*, p. 178; 10 x 2 in. Square, p. 153
Tips: 3, 16, 18, p. 142-143
Colors:* *Scooby-Doo* Icing Color Set (brown, black, teal, yellow), p. 178; Red-Red, Sky Blue, Lemon Yellow, Leaf Green, Creamy Peach, Orange, Violet, Rose, p. 136
Fondant/Gum Paste: White Ready-To-Use Rolled Fondant, p. 130; Gum-Tex™, Rolling Pin, Roll & Cut Mat, p. 133; Fondant Ribbon Cutter/Embosser Set, p. 131
Recipe: Buttercream Icing, p. 114; Thinned Fondant Adhesive, p. 115
Also: 2008 Pattern Book (Hat, Package Bursts, Gift Tag, Numbers), p. 128; Circle Metal Cutter, p. 164; 4 in. Lollipop Sticks, p. 169; Flower Former Set, p. 131; Wooden Dowel Rods, p. 232; Fine Tip Primary Colors FoodWriter™ Edible Color Markers, p. 130; Cake Boards, p. 233; cornstarch, knife, ruler, facial tissue, curling ribbon

In advance: Make background decorations. Add 2 teaspoons Gum-Tex to 22 oz. fondant. Tint as follows: 5 oz. green, 5 oz. dark violet, 4 oz. blue, 3 oz. yellow, 2 oz. light violet, 2 oz. orange, 1 oz. pink. Roll out ⅛ in. thick. Use circle cutter to cut balloons. Use wide end of a decorating tip to cut confetti circles: 15 orange, 15 pink, 2 green, 2 blue, 2 light violet. Let all dry flat on cornstarch-dusted surface. Make curliques (p. 124). Use Cutter/Embosser with straight edge wheels and ¼ in. spacer to cut 8-10 thin strips. Wrap strip around dowel rod; let set 5-10 minutes then slide off rod and let dry. For curled package streamers, use Cutter/Embosser with straight edge wheels and 1 in. spacer to cut 2 strips. Use knife to cut V-shape on bottom ends. Prop with facial tissue to raise curves and let dry. **Also:** Make pattern pieces. Roll out fondant ⅛ in. thick. Use patterns to cut hat, gift tag, age number and 8 package bursts. Let bursts dry on back of large flower formers dusted with cornstarch. Cut ¼ in. wide strips and use damp brush to attach to hat for stripes; trim to fit. Let all dry flat on cornstarch-dusted surface. **And:** Attach lollipop stick to back of hat using fondant adhesive; let dry.

Bake and cool *Scooby-Doo* and 1-layer square package cakes. Trim square cake to 10 x 8 in.; on *Scooby-Doo*, trim off 1 in. of bottom plus top hand and hamburger. Use white buttercream to ice smooth sides and background areas of *Scooby-Doo* and package sides; use blue icing for top of package. Position cakes on board. For *Scooby-Doo*, use tip 3 to outline and pipe in inside ears, eyes, tongue, dog tag and ring, plus eyebrows, nose, mouth and spots (smooth with finger dipped in cornstarch). Pipe tip 3 dot pupils; flatten slightly. Cover *Scooby-Doo* with tip 16 stars. Insert hat; pipe tip 16 pull-out star pompom. Pipe tip 18 shell bottom borders. Use Cutter/Embosser with straight edge wheels and 1 in. spacer to cut 8 in. long ribbons for package; position on cake. Attach confetti circles to ribbons with damp brush. Write message on gift tag with FoodWriter. Position tag, curled package streamers, package bursts and number on cakes; outline number with tip 3. Position balloons, curling ribbon, curliques and remaining confetti around cakes. Serves 27.

*Combine Violet with Rose for violet shown.

▶ *Scooby* Pops Out

Pans: Jelly Roll, p. 154; Cookie Sheet, Cooling Grid, p. 154
Candy: White Candy Melts®† (14 oz. makes 3 treats), p. 166; Primary, Garden Candy Color Sets, p. 166
Also: *Scooby-Doo* Party Toppers, p. 178; Cake Boards, Fanci-Foil Wrap, p. 233; Flower Former Set, p. 131; Disposable Decorating Bags, p. 140; waxed paper, cellophane tape, ruler, knife

In advance: Make package bursts. Cover back of smallest Flower Former with waxed paper. Using melted candy in cut bag, pipe random bursts with 1, 2 or 3 points; bottom edge should be straight to attach to cake top. Refrigerate until firm.

Bake and cool 1 in. high cake using firm-textured batter such as pound cake. Cut one 3 in. and one 1¾ in. square for each treat (Jelly Roll Pan will make 10 treats). Cover cakes with melted candy (p. 126); refrigerate until firm. Use warm knife to even bottom edges. Place 3 in. cake on 3½ in. foil-wrapped square; attach small cake to top using melted candy. Attach topper in center using melted candy. Attach package bursts with melted candy. Using melted candy in cut decorating bags, pipe spirals, outline ribbons and dots. Each serves 1.

†Brand confectionery coating.

▶ Orbiting the Planet

Pans: 11 x 15 x 2 in. Sheet, p. 153; Cookie Sheet, Cooling Grid, p. 154
Candy: White Candy Melts®† (5 pks.), Primary, Garden Candy Color Sets, p. 166
Also: 2008 Pattern Book (Planet Ring), p. 128; Standard Cupcakes 'N More® Dessert Stand, p. 146; *Superman* Party Toppers (4 pks.), p. 178; Round Cut-Outs™, p. 132; Circle Metal Cutter, p. 164; Parchment Triangles, p. 140; Cake Boards, p. 233; Large Cake Leveler, p. 134; waxed paper, cellophane tape, paper, knife, ruler

In advance: Make candy planet, planet base and building bases. Tint Candy Melts®: 14 oz. (1 pk.) each green, blue, violet and gray. Tint 6 oz. yellow and 4 oz. black. Make planet and ring using melted yellow candy in cut parchment bag. For planet and its base, set medium and large round Cut-Outs on waxed paper-covered board. Fill ⅛ in. deep with melted candy; let set. For ring, tape pattern to board and cover with waxed paper. Outline and pipe in with candy; let set. Carefully remove from paper, turn over and overpipe back for strength; let set. Pipe letters on large round; let set. Attach large round planet to medium round base and ring to planet using melted candy. Let set. **Also:** Make building bases, 6 each in green, blue, violet and gray. Use metal cutter to trace circles on paper; tape pattern to cake board and cover with waxed paper. Outline and pipe in circles with melted candy in cut parchment bag. Let set; reserve tinted candy.

Bake and cool cake using firm-textured batter such as pound cake; level to 2 in. high. Cut into 2 in. square buildings. Cover with melted candy (p. 126); let set. Using melted candy in cut parchment bag, pipe windows and doors. Attach buildings to bases. Attach planet to top building; attach toppers to others. Position on Dessert Stand. Each serves 1.

▶ Putting Metropolis on the Map

Pan: *Superman*, p. 178
Tips: 1, 3, 16, 21, p. 142-143
Colors:* *Superman* Icing Color Set (red, yellow, blue, copper for skin tone, blue), p. 178; Royal Blue, Golden Yellow, Black, Christmas Red, p. 136
Fondant/Gum Paste: White Ready-To-Use Rolled Fondant (72 oz.), p. 130; Rolling Pin, Roll & Cut Mat, p. 133; Easy-Glide Fondant Smoother, Brush Set, p. 131
Recipe: Buttercream Icing, p. 114
Also: 2008 Pattern Book (Buildings), p. 128; 101 Cookie Cutters Set, p. 162; Cake Boards, Fanci-Foil Wrap, p. 233; Piping Gel, p. 137; 20 x 20 x ½ in. thick foamcore board, knife, cornstarch

In advance: Prepare base board. Cut foamcore quarter-circle with 19½ in. long straight sides at a 90° angle; wrap with foil. Tint 60 oz. fondant yellow and 6 oz. light blue; roll out ⅛ in. thick. Lightly brush board with piping gel; wrap with yellow fondant (p. 124). Cut 20 x 1 in. wide strips of light blue fondant; attach to straight edges with damp brush. Cut 30 x 1 in. strip; attach to curved edge. **Also:** Make letters. Tint 3 oz. fondant red; roll out ¹⁄₁₆ in. thick. Cut letters using cutters from set; attach to board with damp brush. Roll ⅛ in. diameter yellow fondant logs; attach on letters using damp brush. **And:** Make buildings. Roll out light blue and yellow fondant ⅛ in. thick. Using patterns, cut buildings; attach to board using damp brush. Cut yellow windows and details; attach to buildings using damp brush.

Position *Superman* cake on foil-wrapped cake board. Ice sides smooth. Outline and pipe in eyebrows with tip 1 (smooth with finger dipped in cornstarch). Outline nose and under eyes with tip 1. Outline all other details with tip 3. Pipe in around eyes and under eyebrows with tip 1 (smooth with finger dipped in cornstarch). Cover with tip 16 stars; add tip 16 pull-out star hair. Pipe tip 21 shell bottom border. Position cake on base board. Serves 12.

Care Bears

◄ Birthday Bear is Bearing Treats

Pan: *CareBears*™, p. 180

Tips: 2, 3, 16, p. 142-143

Colors:* *CareBears*™ Icing Color Set (teal, yellow, orange), p. 180; Rose, Violet, Sky Blue, Buttercup Yellow, Black, p. 136

Fondant/Gum Paste: White Ready-To-Use Rolled Fondant (24 oz.), p. 130; Gum-Tex™, Rolling Pin; Roll & Cut Mat, p. 133; Brush Set, p. 131

Candy: White Candy Melts®†, p. 166; 6 in. Lollipop Sticks, p. 169

Recipes: Buttercream, Royal Icings, p. 114

Also: 2008 Pattern Book (Lollipop, Ice Cream Cone), p. 128; Meringue Powder, p. 137; Flowerful Medley Sprinkles Assortment, p. 138; Cake Board, Fanci-Foil Wrap, p. 233; cornstarch, knife, toothpicks, ruler

Two days in advance: Make fondant lollipop, ice cream cone and wrapped candies (p. 121). Add 1½ teaspoons Gum-Tex to 20 oz. white fondant; tint 5 oz. each violet, rose, sky blue, buttercup yellow. Reserve remaining white.

On *Care Bears* cake, trim rainbow area above head flat. Ice cake sides, tummy and background areas smooth. Outline body, muzzle, mouth and eyes with tip 3. Cover bear with tip 16 stars. Pipe in tip 2 whites of eyes, irises, dot pupils and white highlights (smooth with finger dipped in cornstarch). Pipe in tip 3 nose (smooth); pipe tip 2 dot freckles. Outline star pattern (included on pan instruction sheet) on tummy with toothpick. Outline and pipe in stars with tip 3 (smooth); add tip 16 shooting lines. Position fondant candies around cake. Cut lollipop sticks to 2 in.; attach one each perpendicular to backs of ice cream cone and lollipop with melted candy. Also attach a 6 in. lollipop stick vertically to back of lollipop with melted candy; let set. Insert ice cream cone and lollipop. For hands, roll out white fondant ⅛ in. thick; cut 1¾ in. circles and shape with fingers. Outline hands with tip 3; cover with tip 16 stars. Position hands. Print tip 3 message. Add confetti sprinkles on cake. Serves 12.

*Combine Violet and Rose for violet shown.

†Brand confectionery coating.

► Care to Give it a Whirl?

Candy: Pinwheel Lollipop Mold, p. 168; White Candy Melts®†, Primary, Garden Candy Color Sets, p. 166; 6 in. Lollipop Sticks, p. 169

Also: *Care Bears*™ Icing Decorations, p. 180; Parchment Triangles, p. 140

Divide Candy Melts into 5 bowls. Melt and tint 1 each yellow, pink, violet and blue; reserve white. Use melted candy in cut parchment bags to pipe alternating colors into mold. Refrigerate until firm. Fill remainder of cavity with melted white candy; tap to remove air bubbles. Position lollipop stick; refrigerate until firm and unmold. Attach icing decorations with melted candy. Each serves 1.

► Strawberry Tea

Pans: *Strawberry Shortcake*, p. 180; Long Loaf , p. 154

Tips: 1, 3, 8, 16, 45, 103, 127D, 349, 352, p. 142-143

Colors: *Strawberry Shortcake* Icing Color Set (red, brown, skin tone), p. 180; Rose, Teal, Red-Red, Brown, p. 136

Fondant/Gum Paste: White Ready-To-Use Rolled Fondant (24 oz.), p. 130; Gum-Tex™, Rolling Pin, Roll & Cut Mat, p. 133

Recipes: Buttercream, Royal Icings, p. 114

Also: 2008 Pattern Book (Teacup, Teapot, Strawberries), p. 128; Meringue Powder, p. 137; 4 in. Lollipop Sticks, p. 169; 15 x 16 in. foamcore board (½ in. thick), knife, ruler, toothpicks, cornstarch

In advance: Make and decorate teapot and teacups (p. 121). **Also:** Make strawberries using royal icing (p. 121).

Bake and cool cakes. Use knife to trim loaf cake to 13 x 4 x 2½ in. high; trim arms, hands and hair off of *Strawberry Shortcake* cake. Ice loaf cake smooth with pink buttercream; position on foil-wrapped board against *Strawberry Shortcake*. Use white buttercream to fill gap and ice sides of *Strawberry Shortcake* smooth; ice eyes, hatband and bow loops smooth. Add tip 45 stripes to hatband and bow loops (smooth with finger dipped in cornstarch). Outline eyes, mouth and nose with tip 3. Pipe in tip 3 irises, dot pupils, highlights, nose, mouth, tongue and teeth (smooth with finger). Use tip 3 to outline hat, hatband, bow loops and strawberry on hat. Cover hat, strawberry on bow, dress, collar, face and neck with tip 16 stars. Pipe tip 16 pull-out star hair. Pipe tip 3 outline lashes and dot seeds on strawberry. Roll 2 fondant logs 4 in. long; taper and position on cake for arms. Roll out small amount of fondant ¼ in. thick; cut 3 circles, 1¼ in. diameter. Attach 1 circle at each shoulder to build up puff sleeves; place teapot in position on 3rd circle. Using tip 16 stars, cover sleeves and arms; pipe hand and fingers over teapot. Add tip 103 ruffle and tip 45 outline band on sleeves. Roll out small amount of fondant ⅛ in. thick; cut streamers for bow and attach. Pipe tip 352 leaves on strawberry on bow and tip 8 stripes on streamers (smooth with finger). Pipe tip 127D ruffle at bottom of table. Make fondant drapes (p. 124) using 3¼ x 2 in. strips; attach with icing. Attach royal icing berries to table and hat using buttercream. Insert teacups. Use tip 3 to outline bow streamers, add dots to tablecloth and print message. Pipe tip 8 bead bottom border. Serves 24.

◀ Party Combo

Pans: 6, 8 x 2 in. Rounds, p. 153; Standard Muffin, p. 154

Tips: 2, 5, 17, p. 142-143

Colors: Royal Blue, Red-Red, Lemon Yellow, Kelly Green, Orange, p. 136

Recipes: Buttercream, Royal Icings, p. 114

Also: 2008 Pattern Book (Musical Staff), p. 128; *Sesame Street* Icing Decorations, Standard Baking Cups, Parade Cake Top Set, p.179; Cake Boards, Fanci-Foil Wrap, p. 233; 10 in. Decorator Preferred® Scalloped Separator Plate, p. 231; Meringue Powder, p. 137; 3 in. Globe Base Set, p. 228; Dowel Rods, p, 232; Numerals Candle, p. 189; Regular Crayons Candles (2 pks.), p. 191; waxed paper, toothpick

One day in advance: Make musical notes. On waxed paper, using royal icing and tip 5, pipe 5 notes each, 1 in. and 2 in. high. On 2 in. notes, add a puddle of icing to support Elmo icing decoration; position icing decoration before icing sets. Make extras to allow for breakage and let dry.

Bake and cool cupcakes, 1-layer 6 in. and 2-layer 8 in. rounds. Ice all smooth in buttercream. Prepare rounds for Stacked Construction (p. 112), positioning 6 in. cake near back edge of 8 in. cake. Position cakes on 10 in. plate. Using pattern, mark musical staff with toothpick on sides of 8 in. cake. Pipe tip 5 lines, ½ in. apart for musical staff. Attach notes with dots of icing. Add tip 17 shell top and bottom borders. Pipe tip 2 squiggles on cupcakes; insert matching crayon candles. Position cake on pillars; position toppers and numeral candle on cake. Arrange cupcakes around cake. Cake serves 26; each cupcake serves 1.

▶ *Elmo's* Bursting to Celebrate!

Pans: *Elmo* Face, p. 179; 12, 14 x 2 in. Rounds, p. 153

Tip: 3, p. 142

Colors:* Lemon Yellow, Golden Yellow, Royal Blue, Leaf Green, Rose, Orange, Red-Red, Christmas Red, Black, p. 136

Fondant/Gum Paste: White Ready-To-Use Rolled Fondant (168 oz.), p. 130; Brush Set, Easy-Glide Fondant Smoother, p. 131; Gum-Tex™, Rolling Pin, Roll & Cut Mat, p. 133

Candy: Candy Melts ®† in Red (3 pks.), White (1 pk.); Primary, Garden Candy Color Sets, p. 166; 8 in. Lollipop Sticks, p. 169

Recipe: Buttercream Icing, p. 114

Also: 2008 Pattern Book (Paper Bursts), p. 128; Plastic Dowel Rods, p. 232; 101 Cookie Cutters Set, p. 162; Fine Tip Primary Colors FoodWriter™ Edible Color Markers, p. 130; Flower Former Set, Parchment Triangles, p. 140; 16 in. Round Silver Cake Base, p. 233; ruler, knife, waxed paper, cornstarch

In advance: Make fondant paper bursts, hands and crayon (p. 121). **Also:** Make Elmo candy plaque (p. 126).

Prepare 2-layer round cakes for Stacked Construction (p. 112) and rolled fondant (p. 115). Tint 80 oz. fondant blue and 60 oz. yellow; cover cakes and smooth with Fondant Smoothers. Draw scribbles on each cake with FoodWriter markers. For letters, tint 1½ oz. fondant each: rose, orange, green. Tint 1½ oz. of remaining blue and yellow fondant darker shades than used to cover cake. Roll out fondant ⅛ in. thick; cut message using cutters from set. Attach letters with damp brush. Pipe tip 3 lines on letters in buttercream. For borders: Roll ¼ in. diameter logs of blue and yellow fondant. Cut logs into ¾ in. pieces; roll each into a ball and attach to base of cake with dots of icing. Insert candy plaque in cake top. Insert lollipop stick into hand with crayon; insert in cake. Position other hand. Attach paper bursts with melted yellow candy. Serves 103.

*Combine Lemon Yellow with Golden Yellow for yellow covering cake. Combine Leaf Green with Lemon Yellow for green letters. Combine Christmas Red with Red-Red and a small amount of black for red hands.

©2007 JGL, LLC The name, likeness and signature of Jeff Gordon and the likeness of the #24 DuPont Chevrolet are used under license granted by HGL, LLC.

▶ Take a Victory Lap!

Products officially licensed by NASCAR®: Pan, Icing Colors Set (black, red, yellow, blue), p. 181

Pan: Long Loaf, p. 154

Tips: 2, 3, 6, 8, 12, 21, 46, 55, p. 142-143

Colors:* Royal Blue, Copper (skin tone), Kelly Green, Orange, Golden Yellow, Lemon Yellow, Brown, Black, Red-Red, Violet, Rose, p. 136

Recipes: Buttercream, Royal Icings, p. 114

Also: 2008 Pattern Book (People, Pennant), p. 128; Fine Tip Primary Colors FoodWriter™ Edible Color Markers, p. 130; Cake Boards, Fanci-Foil Wrap, p. 233; Meringue Powder, p. 137; Flowerful Medley Sprinkles Assortment, p. 138; 4 in. Lollipop Sticks, p. 169; construction paper (white and colors), tape, scissors, toothpicks, waxed paper, cornstarch, long knife

In advance: Make royal icing fans and construction paper pennants and message strips (p. 119). Position car cake on foil-wrapped board. Ice cake sides and background areas smooth with buttercream. Pipe in window areas and headlights with tip 3 zigzags (smooth with finger dipped in cornstarch). Outline car, windows, headlights, hood, detailing, number and tires with tip 3. Pipe in bumper and sides of car with tip 3 zigzags (smooth with finger). Pipe in wheel wells, rims, racing stripes and window trim with tip 3 (smooth with finger). Pipe in NASCAR® logo background with tip 1 (smooth with finger); pipe NASCAR letters with tip 1 (smooth with finger). Outline and pipe in tip 1 and tip 3 details on front bumper, tires and side panels. Add tip 3 outline spoiler. Cover car and numbers with tip 16 stars. Pipe tip 21 shell bottom border. Serves 12.

For Grandstand: Bake and cool Long Loaf cake using firm-textured batter such as pound cake. Using toothpicks, mark a line across cake front, 1 in. from bottom; also mark a line across cake top, 1 in. from back edge. Use long knife to cut off cake between marks to make grandstand rise from front to back. Ice smooth with buttercream (blue seating area, remainder white). Pipe tip 46 (smooth side up) outline front railing and vertical braces; edge sides and back with tip 55 stripes. Add confetti sprinkles; insert people and pennants, trimming sticks if needed. Position message strips in hands. Serves 24.

*Combine Violet with Rose for violet shown.

◀ *Jeff Gordon* Fast Treats

Pan: Standard Muffin, p. 154

Tip: 16, p. 143

Color: Black, p. 136

Products officially licensed by Jeff Gordon: Icing Decorations, Baking Cups, Candle, p. 181

Recipe: Buttercream Icing, p. 114

Also: 13 Count Standard Cupcakes 'N More Dessert Stand, p. 146

Cover cupcake tops with tip 16 stars in checkerboard pattern. Position cupcakes on stand. Position icing decorations and candle. Each serves 1.

▶ Sub-Tropical *SpongeBob*

Pans: 9 x 13 x 2 in. Sheet, p. 153; Cookie Sheet, Cooling Grid, p. 154

Candy: White Candy Melts®† (1 pk.), Primary Candy Color Set (orange, blue), p. 166

Also: 2008 Pattern Book (Door, Window, Smokestack), p. 128; *SpongeBob SquarePants* Party Toppers, p. 175; 101 Cookie Cutters Set, p. 162; Cake Boards, p. 233; Parchment Triangles, p. 140; Rolling Pin, p. 133; scissors, granulated sugar, waxed paper, knife, spearmint leaves

In advance: Pipe candy door, window and smokestack. Tint 2 oz. candy blue. Trace patterns and tape to board; cover with waxed paper. Pipe basic shapes using melted candy in cut parchment bag; tap to settle candy, refrigerate to set. Overpipe window center, wheel and smokestack details. Let set.

Bake and cool 1 in. high sheet cake using firm-textured batter such as pound cake (1 cake makes 10 treats). Place football cutter from set upside down on cake top; use knife to cut around outside of cutter. Make pineapple shape by trimming bottom straight and top round. Place cakes on cooling grid set over pan. Tint 10 oz. candy orange. Cover cakes with melted candy (p. 126); tap to settle candy, refrigerate until set. Tint 2 oz. candy dark orange. Use cut parchment bag to pipe lines and dots. Let set. Cut spearmint leaves in half lengthwise. Roll out on waxed paper sprinkled with sugar; cut leaves in assorted lengths. Attach door, window, smokestack and leaves with melted candy; let set. Position *SpongeBob* topper. Each serves 1.

†Brand confectionery coating.

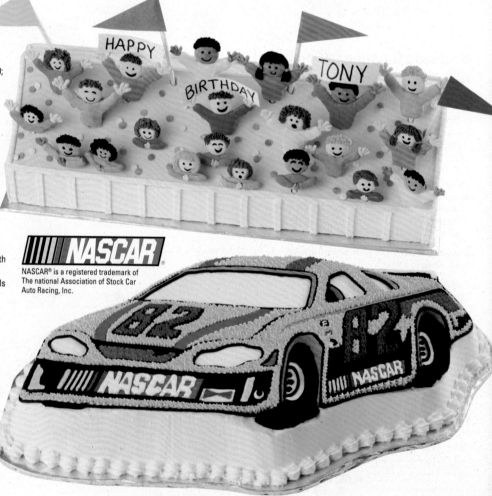

NASCAR® is a registered trademark of The national Association of Stock Car Auto Racing, Inc.

▶ Grillmaster *SpongeBob*

Pan: *SpongeBob SquarePants*™, p. 175

Tips: 3, 16, 21, p. 142-143

Colors:* *SpongeBob SquarePants* Icing Color Set (yellow, red, blue, brown), p. 175; Black, Golden Yellow, Orange, Violet, Royal Blue, Leaf Green Icing Colors, p. 136

Fondant/Gum Paste: White Ready-To-Use Rolled Fondant (24 oz.), p. 130; Gum-Tex™, Rolling Pin, Roll & Cut Mat, p. 133; Cutter/Embosser, Brush Set, p. 131

Recipe: Buttercream Icing, p. 114; Thinned Fondant Adhesive, p. 115

Also: 2008 Pattern Book (Hamburger, Spatula, Hand, Hat), p. 128; 8 in. Lollipop Sticks, p. 169; Cake Board, Fanci-Foil Wrap, p. 233; toothpick, paring knife, cornstarch

In advance: Make fondant hamburger, spatula, candle, and hat (p. 121).

Bake and cool cake. Trim off left hand and open area on left side of body; leave sleeve. Ice sides and background areas smooth. Pipe in tip 3 SpongeBob spots (smooth with finger dipped in cornstarch). Pipe tip 3 whites of eyes, irises, pupils, tongue, mouth and teeth (smooth with finger dipped in cornstarch). Outline body, face and shoes with tip 3. Cover face, right arm, legs and shoes with tip 16 stars. Using tip 3, pipe string eyelashes, stripes on socks and belt, pipe in tie and add dot freckles. Position spatula; attach hamburger and candle with dots of icing. Curve lollipop stick to make arm holding spatula and cover with fondant; insert in cake. Cut hand using pattern and white fondant; position on cake. Outline hand and arm with tip 3 and cover with tip 16 stars. To support hat, insert 2 lollipop sticks in top of head; one extended 1 in., the other 2 in. Position hat on sticks, attaching with thinned fondant adhesive; outline top and pipe anchor with tip 3. Pipe tip 21 shell bottom border. Serves 12.

*Combine *SpongeBob SquarePants* Yellow, Blue and Brown for green outlines on *SpongeBob*. Combine Royal Blue, Black and Violet for navy hat brim shown. Combine Brown with Orange for tan bun shown. Combine Red with Brown for reddish brown hamburger shown.

◀ Sling Along with *Spider-Man*!

Pans: *Spider-Man*, p. 177; Cookie Sheet, Cooling Grid, p. 154

Tips: 2, 3, 16, 21, p. 142-143

Colors:* *Spider-Man* Icing Color Set (dark blue, red, black), p. 177; Leaf Green, Lemon Yellow, Golden Yellow, Violet, Rose, p. 136

Recipes: Buttercream, Royal Icings, Roll-Out Cookies, p. 114

Also: Cake Boards, Fanci-Foil Wrap, p. 233; 101 Cookie Cutters Set, p. 162; Alphabet/Numerals Icing Decorations, p. 189; Flowerful Medley Sprinkles Assortment, p. 138; Meringue Powder, p. 137; Cake Dividing Set, p. 135; curling ribbon, toothpicks, cornstarch

In advance: Make cookie balloons. Prepare and roll out dough. Cut circles using largest round cutter from set; bake and cool cookies. Cover cookies with thinned royal icing (p. 126); let dry. **Also:** Pipe webs. Use Cake Dividing Set to divide cookies into 8 sections. Use tip 2 and darker shades of royal icing to pipe straight lines, then curves. Let dry.

Ice sides and background areas of cake smooth with buttercream. Outline details with tip 3. Outline and pipe in mask and eyes (smooth with finger dipped in cornstarch). Cover *Spider-Man* with tip 16 stars. Pipe tip 21 shell bottom border. Add confetti sprinkles on cake sides and to background areas. Attach alphabet decoration message to cookies with dots of icing. Insert one end of ribbon into cake above hand; attach other end to cookie back with icing. Curl additional ribbons and insert into cake below hand. Cake serves 12; each cookie serves 1.

*Combine Golden Yellow with Lemon Yellow for yellow shown.

Your Holidays are Hot!

Holiday traditions have their place, but it's fun to shake up the seasons too. Look what we've done with some of your favorite seasonal themes! On the night before Christmas, see inside a holiday house as the family spies Santa making his escape. For Easter, discover an explosion of eggs that pair pastels with polka dots. Here, try a new brew for your Halloween gathering, with stand-up witch cupcakes, a cauldron of candy, wacky witch cookies and pretzel pop claws. Get set for holidays that will amaze everyone!

Instructions for projects shown on these two pages are on page 38.

Closely-Witched Pot

Pans: Sports Ball Set, p. 159; Non-Stick Cookie Sheet, Cooling Grid, p. 151
Tips: 1A, 2, 4, 7, 21, 46, p. 142-143
Colors:* Orange, Lemon Yellow, Golden Yellow, Leaf Green, Violet, Rose, p. 136
Fondant/Gum Paste: White Ready-To-Use Rolled Fondant (24 oz.), p. 130; Rolling Pin, Roll & Cut Mat, p. 133; Round Cut-Outs™, p. 132
Candy: Dark Cocoa Candy Melts®† (2 pks.), Garden Candy Color Set, p. 166; 6 in. Lollipop Sticks, p. 169
Recipe: Buttercream Icing (stiff consistency), p. 114
Also: Wacky Witch Silly-Feet! Silicone Baking Cups, p. 194, assorted green candy-coated chocolates, jellies and hard candies, pretzel sticks, sugar ice cream cones, cornstarch, spatula, knife, scissors, ruler

In advance: Make candy shell (p. 125) cauldron in ball pan half using melted candy tinted black. Fill pan to ½ in. from top; reserve poured out candy for hats. Refrigerate until firm; unmold. **Also:** Make witch hats. For brim, set largest round Cut-Out on non-stick cookie sheet; fill ³⁄₁₆ in. deep with melted candy. Refrigerate until firm; unmold. Cut 2 in. off tip of ice cream cone; cover with melted candy (p. 126); let set. Attach cones to brims using melted candy. When set, use buttercream to pipe tip 46 smooth side up hat band and tip 4 outline buckle.

Bake and cool cupcakes in silicone cups supported by cookie sheet. Build up icing head with tip 1A; smooth and round with spatula. Tint 10 oz. fondant orange, 8 oz. yellow and 2 oz. green. Make 8 groups of flames. Roll out yellow and orange fondant ¼ in. thick. Use knife to cut 1 to 2½ in. long flat-bottom flames, each with one V-shaped yellow and two V-shaped orange pieces. Let dry on cornstarch-dusted board. For arms, cut lollipop sticks to 3 in. long. Roll a ½ in. ball of green fondant for each hand; flatten slightly as you insert on end of stick. Cut fingers with knife. Pipe arm using bag fitted with tip 21; insert lollipop stick, squeeze and pull out stick. Clean ½ in. icing off stick. Insert arms in cupcakes. For hair, roll out orange fondant ⅛ in. thick. Cut a 1 x 1½ in. strip; cut slits ¾ in. deep and ¹⁄₁₆ in. apart for strands of hair. Attach hair and hat. Pipe tip 7 dot eyes and cheeks (flatten with finger dipped in cornstarch) and pull-out nose. Pipe tip 2 outline eyelids and mouth. Pipe tip 2 dot tooth and pupils; flatten with finger. Position cauldron; fill with assorted candies. Position flames, pretzels and witches. Each witch serves 1.

*Combine Golden Yellow with Lemon Yellow for yellow shown. Combine Violet with Rose for violet shown.

Haunting Stares

Cookie: Witch's Hat Comfort Grip™ Cutter, Pumpkin Nesting Cutter Set, p. 196; Cookie Sheet, Cooling Grid, p. 154
Candy: White, Dark Cocoa Candy Melts®† (1 pk. white for about 4 treats), Primary, Garden Candy Color Sets, p. 166; Decorator Brush Set, p. 167; Candy Melting Plate, p. 167
Colors:* Lemon Yellow, Leaf Green, Violet, Rose, p. 136
Recipe: Roll-Out Cookies, p. 114
Also: Parchment Triangles, p. 140; rolling pin, waxed paper

In advance: Make cookies. Prepare dough and tint part green; roll out and cut heads using largest pumpkin cutter from set. Tint remaining dough violet; cut hats using hat cutter. Bake and cool cookies. **Also:** Tint portions of candy red, green, yellow, black and orange using candy colors. Mold eyeballs in melting plate cavities using melted candy in cut parchment bags. Pipe black pupil; let set. Pipe orange iris; let set. Fill remainder of cavity with white for eye; let set.

Assemble on waxed paper using melted candy in cut parchment bags. Attach hat to head. Outline and pipe in nose; let set. Attach eyeballs; let set. Outline around eyeballs. Pipe line for mouth; outline and fill in hat band; let set. Pipe outline buckle and hair. Outline and fill in tooth; let set. Each serves 1.

*Combine Leaf Green with Lemon Yellow for green shown. Combine Violet with Rose for violet shown. Use Black candy color and Dark Cocoa candy to make black candy.

Fingers of Fate

Candy: White, Dark Cocoa Candy Melts®†, Garden and Primary Candy Color Sets,* p. 166; Witch Fingers Pretzel Mold, p. 194;
Also: Parchment Triangles, p. 140; Decorator Brush Set, p. 167; pretzel rods

Tint melted white candy green and cocoa candy black using candy colors. Mold pretzel candies following mold instructions. Refrigerate until firm; unmold. Each serves 1.

*Combine Green with Yellow candy colors for green shown.

▼ Spreading Sorcery

Pan: Mini Wonder Mold, p. 155
Tips: 8, 16, p. 142-143
Colors:* Golden Yellow, Brown, Red-Red, p. 136
Recipe: Spicy Cheddar Spread, p. 114
Also: 8 oz. cream cheese (softened), pretzel rod, crackers, vegetable pan spray, plastic wrap

Prepare cheese spread and press into prepared pan. Cover and chill until firm. Shortly before serving, unmold onto plate; insert pretzel rod in center. Tint 1 oz. softened cream cheese brown; tint remainder golden yellow. Cover with tip 16 lines; pipe tip 16 pull-out stars at top. Pipe tip 8 brown band. Surround with crackers.

*Combine Brown with Red-Red for brown shown.

▲ Whiskers Whisks Away

Cookie: Halloween 4-Pc. Grippy™ Cutter Set, Halloween Metal Cutter Set, p. 196
Tip: 2, p. 142
Colors:* Orange, Leaf Green, Lemon Yellow, p. 136
Recipe: Your favorite ham salad or sandwich spread
Also: 6 in. Lollipop Sticks, p. 169; thin-sliced pumpernickel bread, block-style cheddar cheese, cream cheese, cheese slicer, knife

For each sandwich, cut 2 pumpernickel cats using Grippy Cutter. Make sandwich using your favorite filling. Slice cheddar cheese ¼ in. thick; cut broom bristle base using metal broom cutter. Insert lollipop stick; use knife to score lines. Position stick through sandwich. Tint small amounts of cream cheese. Using tip 2, pipe outline band on broom, cat whiskers and mouth; pipe bead eyes, dot nose and pupils. Each serves 1.

*Combine Leaf Green with Lemon Yellow for green shown.

†Brand confectionery coating.

▶ Creepy Sweeper

Pans: 10½ x 15½ x 1 in. Jelly Roll, Cooling Grid, p. 154

Color: Brown, p. 136

Candy: Halloween Lollipop Kit (includes 5 oz. light cocoa and 2½ oz. each white and orange Candy Melts® used), p. 194; White Candy Melts®† (14 oz. to make about 4-6 treats), Primary, Garden Candy Color Sets, p. 166; Decorator Brush Set, p. 167

Recipe: Favorite crisped rice cereal treats (1 batch will make 15-18 treats)

Also: Halloween Metal Cutter Set, p. 196; 6 in. Cookie Treat Sticks, p. 165; Parchment Triangles, p. 140; Clear Vanilla Extract, p. 139; knife, waxed paper, spatula

In advance: Make cats. Tint melted cocoa candy with black Candy Color. Mold cat from kit without lollipop stick; refrigerate until firm then unmold. Use hot knife to remove candy from between legs. Using melted candy in cut parchment bags, add white dot eyes and let set; add orange pupils, nose, mouth and whiskers. **Also:** Make broomsticks. Paint cookie sticks with mixture of brown icing color and vanilla. Let dry.

Prepare cereal treat recipe and press into pan ¾ in. thick; let set and unmold. Cut broom bristle base using candy corn cutter from set. Cover treats with yellow tinted candy (p. 126); let set. Seal back side with melted candy using a spatula; let set. Use hot knife or metal skewer to make hole in candy at pointed top; push in broomstick. Using melted candy in cut parchment bags, pipe orange band and let set; pipe yellow lines for bristles and let set. Attach cat with melted candy. Each serves 1.

▼ A Broom That Zooms!

Pan: Classic Wonder Mold, p. 155

Tip: 21, p. 143

Colors:* Golden Yellow, Lemon Yellow, Brown, Red-Red, p. 136

Fondant/Gum Paste: White Ready-To-Use Rolled Fondant (24 oz.), p. 130; Rolling Pin, Roll & Cut Mat, p. 133; Brush Set, p. 131

Recipe: Buttercream Icing, p. 114

Also: 10 in. Cake Circles, Fanci-Foil Wrap, p. 233; Plastic Dowel Rods, p. 232; masking tape, knife, ruler

In advance: Make broomstick. Tape 2 dowel rods together, end to end; cut to 16 in. long. Tint 12 oz. fondant brown; roll out ⅛ in. thick. Cut a 4 x 10½ in. rectangle; attach around end of dowel rod with damp brush. Shape to create a lumpy surface. Score woodgrain lines with knife.

Bake and cool cake using firm-textured batter such as pound cake. Position on foil-covered board. Insert broomstick. Cover cake with tip 21 lines, working from bottom up. Roll out fondant ⅛ in. thick; cut a 1¼ x ½ in. strip and attach around handle with icing. Pipe tip 21 pull-out star bristle ends. Serves 12.

*Combine Golden Yellow with Lemon Yellow for yellow shown. Combine Brown with Red-Red for brown shown.

▼ Quick Critter Cupcakes

Pan: Standard Muffin, p. 154

Tip: 1M (2110), p. 143

Color: Orange, p. 136

Recipe: Buttercream Icing, p. 114

Also: Happy Haunters Standard Baking Cups, Happy Haunters Fun Pix®, p. 194; Halloween Confetti Sprinkle Decorations, p. 195

Bake and cool cupcakes. Cover tops with tip 1M swirl. Sprinkle on confetti; insert pick. Each serves 1.

▲ Fly-By-Night Fun

Pan: Oval Pan Set (7¾ x 5⅝ in. used), p. 153
Tips: 3, 8, p. 142
Colors: Black, Rose, p. 136
Recipes: Buttercream Icing, p. 114; favorite cocoa-flavored crisped rice cereal treats (2 recipes)
Also: 2008 Pattern Book (Wing, Ear), p. 128; 13 x 19 in. Cake Board, Fanci-Foil Wrap, p. 233; toothpicks, knife, cornstarch

Prepare 2 recipes of your favorite cocoa-flavored rice cereal treats; tint marshmallow mixture black before adding cereal. For head, press into oval pan 2 in. high; unmold. Make 2 additional 1 in. high ovals; unmold. Using patterns, cut out wings and ears (reverse pattern for 2nd wing). Position wings next to head on foil-wrapped cake board; attach ears using toothpicks. Outline and fill in eyes with tip 8 (pat smooth with finger dipped in cornstarch). Pipe tip 3 dot pupils and tip 8 outline mouth. Serves 24.

▶ Eat His Dust!

Pan: Spooky Ghost, p. 193
Tips: 3, 12, 16, 18, p. 142-143
Colors:* Golden Yellow, Lemon Yellow, Rose, Brown, Red-Red, Black, p. 136
Fondant/Gum Paste: White Ready-To-Use Rolled Fondant, p. 130; Gum-Tex™, Rolling Pin, Roll & Cut Mat, 133; Brush Set, p. 131
Recipe: Buttercream Icing, p. 114
Also: 2008 Pattern Book (Broom Base), p. 128; Wooden Dowel Rod, p. 232; Cake Circles, Fanci-Foil Wrap, p. 233; ruler, knife, cornstarch

In advance: Prepare broomstick. Cut dowel rod to 10 in. long. Tint 4 oz. fondant brown; roll out ⅛ in. thick. Cut a 3 x 10 in. rectangle; attach around dowel rod with damp brush, rolling twice around. Use fingers to create a bumpy texture. **Also:** Make broom base. Tint 3 oz. fondant yellow; add ½ teaspoon Gum-Tex. Roll out ⅛ in. thick; cut broom base using pattern. For bristles, cut pointed strips ⅛ to ¼ in. wide and 4 to 4½ in. long, cutting as many as needed to cover base. Cut a ¼ x 1 in. brown strip for band. Attach broom base to stick; layer on bristle strips then wrap band over tops, attaching all with a damp brush. Let dry on cornstarch-dusted surface.

Position cake on foil-wrapped cake board. Ice mouth and eye areas smooth. Add tip 3 dot pupils. Pipe tip 16 star cheeks. Cover cake with tip 18 stars. Position broomstick. Use tip 12 to overpipe and build up arm over broomstick. Cover with tip 18 stars. Serves 12.

*Combine Golden Yellow with Lemon Yellow for yellow shown.
Combine Brown with Red-Red for brown shown.

▼ Happy Haunters Pops

Candy: Happy Haunters Lollipop Mold, p. 194; White, Light and Dark Cocoa, Yellow, Orange Candy Melts®†, Garden Candy Colors Set*, p. 166; 4 in. Lollipop Sticks, p. 169; Candy Melting Plate, Decorator Brush Set, p. 167
Also: Parchment Triangles, p. 140

Tint small amounts of melted white candy green, pink and violet using Candy Colors in Melting Plate. Tint melted dark cocoa candy black. Mold lollipops using painting method (p. 125); let set and unmold. Each serves 1.

*Combine Green candy color with Yellow Candy Melts for green shown. Combine Black candy color with Dark Cocoa Candy Melts for black shown.

†Brand confectionery coating.

◄ Crazy Crawler

Pan: Iridescents! Jack-O-Lantern, p. 193
Colors:* Leaf Green, Lemon Yellow, Black, Rose, Orange, p. 136
Fondant/Gum Paste: White Ready-To-Use Rolled Fondant (85 oz.), p. 130; Rolling Pin, Roll & Cut Mat, p. 133; Easy-Glide Fondant Smoother, Brush Set, p. 131
Recipe: Buttercream Icing, p. 114
Also: Knife, ruler

Prepare cake for rolled fondant (p. 115). Tint 38 oz. fondant green, 38 oz. orange, 8 oz. black and 1 oz. pink. Cover cake with green fondant; smooth with Fondant Smoother. Shape hat with 24 oz. orange fondant; attach to top edge of cake with damp brush. Roll out remaining orange fondant ¼ in. thick. Cut a 1 in. wide strip for base of hat; attach to cake with damp brush, shaping top of hat to curve of cake. Cut a 1½ in. wide strip for hat brim; attach with damp brush. Shape 2 in. and 3 in. white circles for eyes, 1½ in. pink circles for cheeks, ½ in. black balls for pupils; flatten then attach with damp brush. Roll out black fondant ⅛ in. thick; cut a ¼ in. wide strip for mouth and attach with damp brush. Roll ¾ in. diameter green logs for legs, from 3 to 6 in. long. Attach ends to cake with damp brush. Shape 8 shoes using 1 oz. black balls; attach with damp brush. Serves 12.

*Combine Leaf Green with Lemon Yellow for green shown.

Instructions on facing page.

► Scaredy-Cat Cake

Pan: Stand-Up Cuddly Bear Set, p. 157
Tips: 1A, 2, 3, 5, 127, 233, p. 142-143
Colors:* Orange, Violet, Rose, Black, p. 136
Recipes: Buttercream, Chocolate Buttercream Icings, p. 114
Also: Cake Circles, Fanci-Foil Wrap, p. 233; sugar ice cream cone, knife

Bake and cool cake using firm-textured batter such as pound cake. Position on covered triple-thick cake board. Trim off arms; trim ears to a point. Trim stomach area flat. Ice inside of ears, eyes, nose and cheeks smooth. Pipe tip 3 outline mouth and dot pupils. Cover cake with tip 233 pull-out fur; pipe tip 2 pull-out fur in tight spaces around facial features. Using tip 1A, overpipe and build up legs, tail and paws; cover with tip 233 pull-out fur. Ice sugar cone smooth; position on head. Pipe tip 127 ruffle brim; decorate hat with tip 5 irregular lines in a spiral pattern. Serves 12.

*Combine Violet with Rose for violet shown.

▼ He's a Ham Fan!

Pans: Mini Ball, p. 159; Cookie Sheet, Cooling Grid, p. 154
Tips: 3, 5, 16, p. 142-143
Colors:* Brown, Red-Red, Lemon Yellow, Golden Yellow, Black, p. 136
Recipes: Buttercream Icing, Roll-Out Cookies, p. 114
Also: 2008 Pattern Book (Turkey Head), p. 128; Daisy Comfort Grip™ Cutter, p. 164; Orange and Red Colored Sugars, p. 139; 4 in. Lollipop Sticks, p. 169; Light Cocoa Candy Melts®†, p. 166; Rolling Pin, p. 133; cornstarch, knife

In advance: Make cookies. Prepare and roll out dough; cut tail feathers using daisy cutter. Cut off 3 petals to make a flat edge. Place on cookie sheet and sprinkle with colored sugars. Cut head using pattern. Bake and cool cookies. **Also:** Use melted candy to attach lollipop stick to back of head cookie, leaving 2 in. extended to insert into cake; let set.

Bake and cool mini cakes; cut in half. Insert heads. Pipe tip 5 dot eyes, tip 3 dot pupils. Using tip 3, outline and fill in beak (pat smooth with finger dipped in cornstarch). Cover head and body with tip 16 stars. Add tip 16 pull-out wings. Attach tail feathers with icing. Pipe tip 5 red wattle. Each serves 1.

*Combine Brown with Red-Red for brown shown. Combine Golden Yellow with Lemon Yellow for yellow shown.

▶ Apples in Disguise

Pan: Bite-Size Gingerbread Boy, p. 197
Candy: Orange, White, Light Cocoa Candy Melts®†, Primary, Garden Candy Color Sets, p. 166
Also: 6 in. Cookie Treat Sticks, p. 165; Petite Leaves Icing Decorations, p. 213; Parchment Triangles, p. 140; 6 in. Cake Circles, Fanci-Foil Wrap, p. 233; apples (clean & dry), waxed paper

In advance: Make scarecrows. Tint melted white candy skin tone by adding a little melted light cocoa candy. Mold scarecrow in gingerbread boy pan (p. 125), filling cavities ¼ in. deep; refrigerate until firm then unmold. Tint small amounts of melted white candy yellow, blue, red, black and green (combine green and yellow). Using melted candy in cut parchment bags, pipe hat with brim; outline and fill in shirt and pants, let set. Pipe lines for hands and feet; outline and fill in eyes, nose and pocket. Pipe dot pupils and outline mouth; outline hat band. Pipe zigzag collar and outline details on shirt and pants.

Melt orange candy; add candy color for deeper orange. Insert cookie treat stick into apple and dip into melted candy, turning to cover all sides. Set on waxed paper until firm. Using melted candy in cut parchment bag, pipe lines. Place on foil-wrapped circle and secure with melted candy. Attach scarecrow to stick and leaves to board with melted candy. Each serves 1.

†Brand confectionery coating.

▲ The First Thanksgiving

Pan: 9 x 5 in. Loaf, Cookie Sheet, Cooling Grid, p. 154
Tips: 1, 2, 2A, 6, p. 142
Colors:* Black, Brown, Copper (skin tone), Golden Yellow, Lemon Yellow, Leaf Green, Kelly Green, Orange, Red-Red, Royal Blue, p. 136
Fondant/Gum Paste: White Ready-To-Use Rolled Fondant (57 oz.), p. 130; Rolling Pin, Roll & Cut Mat, p. 133; Easy-Glide Fondant Smoother, Brush Set, Confectionery Tool Set, p. 131
Recipes: Buttercream, Royal Icings, Roll-Out Cookies, p. 114
Also: Pumpkins Candy Mold, p. 212; 101 Cookie Cutters Set, p. 162; Cake Boards, Fanci-Foil Wrap, p. 233;

Meringue Powder, p. 137; craft knife, ruler, cornstarch, 20 x 10 in. triple-thick cardboard or ½ in. foamcore board

In advance: Tint fondant as follows: 3 oz. yellow, 3 oz. green, 1 oz. lighter green, 4 oz. orange, 3 oz. gray, 1 oz. light brown, 1 oz. dark brown, 2 oz. orange for yams, 3 oz. brown for turkey. Reserve remaining white fondant. Make food for table (p. 121). **Also:** Bake, cool and decorate cookie people and easel backs (p. 122). **And:** Make fondant pumpkins. Press fondant into candy mold and unmold; let dry on cornstarch-dusted board.

Bake and cool 2 loaf cakes; position end to end on foil-wrapped board. Prepare for rolled fondant (p. 115). Roll out white fondant ⅛ in. thick. Cover cake; smooth top only with

Fondant Smoother, allowing sides to drape for tablecloth effect. Roll out gray fondant ⅛ in. thick. Cut plates using smallest circle cutter from set. Use medium circle from set to cut serving plate for yams; cut a ¼ in. strip and attach for raised rim. Use football cutter from set to cut serving plate for corn; trim ends to round off. Cut a ¼ in. strip and attach for raised rim. Cut a 2 x 3½ in. rectangle for turkey platter. Position plates and food on table. Position cookie people in back, fondant pumpkins in front. Cake serves 24; each cookie serves 1.

*Combine Golden Yellow with Lemon Yellow for yellow shown. Combine Leaf Green with Lemon Yellow for lighter green in corn. Combine Orange with Red-Red and Black for yams. Combine Brown with Red-Red, Orange and Black for turkey; combine Brown with Red-Red for other browns shown.

▶ Fall Frolicking

Pans: Standard Muffin, Cookie Sheet, Cooling Grid, p. 154

Tips: 2, 3, p. 142

Colors:* Golden Yellow, Lemon Yellow, Orange, Red-Red, Christmas Red, Brown, Black, Royal Blue, Copper (skin tone), Kelly Green, p. 136

Fondant/Gum Paste: White Ready-To-Use Rolled Fondant (24 oz.), p. 130; Gum-Tex™, Rolling Pin, Roll & Cut Mat, p. 133

Recipes: Buttercream, Royal Icings, Roll-Out Cookies, p. 114

Also: 2008 Pattern Book (Easel), p. 128; Cakes 'N More 3-Tier Party Stand, p. 230; Gingerbread Boy Comfort Grip™ Cutter, p. 200; Harvest Mini Metal Cutter Set, Autumn Leaves Standard Baking Cups, p. 213; Fine Tip Primary Colors FoodWriter™ Edible Color Markers, p. 130; Flower Former Set, p. 131; Meringue Powder, p. 137; cornstarch, toothpicks, knife

In advance: Make fondant leaves. Add 2 teaspoons Gum-Tex to fondant. Divide fondant into 6ths. Tint medium and dark shades of yellow, orange and red. Roll out ⅛ in. thick and cut about 125 assorted leaves using oak and maple leaf mini cutters. Let dry on smallest flower former. When dry, use red and green FoodWriters to add veins on either side of leaves. **Also:** Make cookie people. Prepare roll-out cookie dough and tint various skin tones. Cut using Gingerbread Boy cutter; cut 1 easel for each using pattern. Bake and cool cookies. Decorate with royal icing. Use tip 3 to outline and fill in shirts, pants and shoes; pipe outline fingers (pat smooth with fingertip dipped in cornstarch). Pipe tip 2 swirl, zigzag or pull-out hair, outline eyes, outline and fill-in mouths. Let dry. Attach easel to back using royal icing. Let dry.

Bake and cool 24 cupcakes. Ice smooth using spatula. Position 2-3 leaves on each. Position people on stand and surround with cupcakes. Position additional leaves. Each cupcake or cookie serves 1.

*Combine Golden Yellow with Lemon Yellow for yellows shown. Combine Red-Red with Christmas Red for reds shown.

▶ Harvest Hero

Pans: Silicone Mini Jack-O-Lantern Mold, p. 193; Cookie Sheet, Cooling Grid, p. 154

Tips: 2, 3, 10, 44, 103, 104, p. 142

Colors:* Royal Blue, Red-Red, Christmas Red, Golden Yellow, Kelly Green, Black, Brown, p. 136

Recipes: Royal Icing, Roll-Out Cookies, p. 114

Also: 101 Cookie Cutters Set, p. 162; Meringue Powder, p. 137; White Ready-To-Use Decorator Icing, p. 137; Rolling Pin, p. 133; cornstarch, knife, waxed paper

In advance: Make cookies. Roll out dough and cut using largest boy cutter from set. Bake and cool. **Also:** Make cakes. Fill pumpkin cavities ½ full; bake and cool cakes. Unmold; trim off facial features with knife. Cover pumpkins with heated decorator icing (p. 126). Let set.

Set cookies on waxed paper; decorate using full-strength royal icing. Attach cake head to cookie with icing. Build up top of hat with tip 10 (smooth with finger dipped in cornstarch). Pipe tip 104 ruffle hat brim. Pipe tip 44 (smooth side up) stripe hat band. Add details with tip 3. Outline and fill in shirt, pants and shoes; smooth. Outline and fill in pocket; add dot buttons (flatten with finger dipped in cornstarch). Pipe pull-out hay. Outline and fill in eyes and nose; smooth. Pipe tip 2 outline mouth; add dot pupils (flatten slightly) and nose details. Pipe tip 103 ruffle collar; add tip 3 dot cheeks (flatten and smooth with finger dipped in cornstarch). Each serves 1.

*Combine Red-Red with Christmas Red for red shown.

◄ Holiday Triple Play

Pan: Oval Pan Set (7¾ x 5⅝ in. used), p. 153

Tips: 5, 8, 9, p. 142

Colors:* Leaf Green, Lemon Yellow, Black, Red-Red, Royal Blue, p. 136

Fondant/Gum Paste: White Ready-To-Use Rolled Fondant (72 oz.), p. 130; Rolling Pin, Roll & Cut Mat, p. 133; Brush Set, Easy-Glide Fondant Smoother, p. 131

Recipe: Buttercream Icing, p. 114

Also: 2008 Pattern Book (Top Hat Snowman, Stocking Cap Snowman, Earmuffs Snowman), p. 128; Cake Boards, Fanci-Foil Wrap, p. 233; 101 Cookie Cutters Set, p. 162; knife, waxed paper, ruler

Prepare 1-layer cakes for rolled fondant (p. 115). Tint 36 oz. fondant light green; divide 18 oz. fondant into 5 portions and tint bright green, red, blue and black. Reserve 6 oz. white. Cover cakes with light green; smooth with Fondant Smoother and position on foil-wrapped cake boards. Roll out white fondant ⅛ in. thick. Cut snowman bodies using medium round cutter and heads using small round cutter from set. Using small cutter, cut a ¼ in. curve at top of body to accommodate head. Position snowmen on cakes.

For details, roll out fondant colors ⅛ in. thick. Using patterns, cut clothes for all snowmen. Cut ½ in. nose, ¾ in. mouth and ¾ x ⅛ in. arms for all. Use narrow end of tip 8 to cut eyes for all. For Top Hat Snowman, use narrow end of tip 9 to cut dots for vest and scallop edge at bottom of vest. Cut a ¼ x 1 in. strip for top of scarf; roll and flatten a ¼ in. ball for knot. For Stocking Cap Snowman, use narrow end of tip 8 to cut vest buttons, tip 5 for boot buttons. With knife, cut a ¼ x 1½ in. strip for top of scarf, roll and flatten ¼ in. balls for knot and hat pompom. Cut a 1¾ x ⅛ in. strip for broomstick and a ⅝ in. wide half-oval for bristles. For Earmuffs Snowman, cut a 2 x ⅛ in. strip for earmuff band. Roll and flatten small balls for pant legs and earmuffs; score earmuff edges with knife. For scarf, cut ⅜ in. wide strips of red and green and position side by side; roll lightly to join pieces. Cut a ¼ x 1½ in. section for top and ¼ x 2 in. sections for tails. Attach all pieces using damp brush. Roll ½ in. fondant balls for bottom borders; attach with damp brush. Each cake serves 5.

*Combine Leaf Green with Lemon Yellow for greens shown.

▼ Snow Dancer

Pans: Sports Ball, Soccer Ball, p. 159
Colors:* Red-Red, Royal Blue, Leaf Green, Lemon Yellow, Black, Violet, Rose, p. 136
Fondant/Gum Paste: White Ready-To-Use Rolled Fondant (48 oz.), p. 130; Rolling Pin, Roll & Cut Mat, p. 133; Cutter/Embosser, Brush Set, p. 131
Recipe: Buttercream Icing, p. 114
Also: Holiday Cutter Set, p. 200; 13 x 19 in. Cake Boards, Fanci-Foil Wrap, p. 233; ruler, knife

Ice Sports Ball and Soccer Ball cakes smooth; position on foil-wrapped double-thick board with cake edges touching. Tint 20 oz. fondant red, 3 oz. each blue and black, 2 oz. green, 1 oz. violet; reserve 1½ oz. white. Roll white into a 4½ in. long log and position in space between head and body. For earmuffs, roll two 1½ in. balls of blue; flatten on side and position. Roll a 9 x ¼ in. black log, curve and position for earmuff band. Roll a 6 in. violet log; cut 2 in. arms and 1 in. legs and position. Roll out red fondant ¼ in. thick. Cut mitten and boot using cutters from set; reverse cutters and repeat for opposite side, then position. For scarf, roll out red ⅛ in. thick; cut 1 in. wide strips 6, 6½ and 3 in. long. Curve 6½ and 3 in. strips and position for tails; position 6 in. strip around neck. Roll out green ⅛ in. thick and cut 1 in. squares; attach to scarf, 1 in. apart, with damp brush. Shape a 1 in. ball for nose, a ⅞ in. ball for mouth and ½ in. balls for eyes; position. Shape and flatten ¾ in. balls for buttons; position. Serves 18.

*Combine Leaf Green with Lemon Yellow for green shown. Combine Violet with Rose for violet shown.

▲ The Cool Ones

Pan: Snowman Cookie Treat, p. 199
Tips: 2, 2A, 3, 4, p. 142
Colors: Red-Red, Leaf Green, Royal Blue, Black, p. 136
Recipe: Buttercream, Royal Icings, Roll-Out Cookies, p. 114
Also: 2008 Pattern Book (Boots, Shoes, Mittens), p. 128; Meringue Powder, p. 137; waxed paper, black shoestring licorice, cornstarch

In advance: Make royal icing details. Copy patterns and cover with waxed paper. Use tip 3 to pipe pull-out broom bristles, outline and pipe in mittens (smooth with finger dipped in cornstarch). Use tip 4 to outline and pipe in boots and shoes (smooth with finger). Let dry. Attach 1 in. piece of licorice to backs of all with royal icing; attach broom to mitten. Let dry.

Bake cookie treats without sticks; cool. Use knife to trim off hats for rounded snowman heads. Decorate with buttercream. Use tip 2A to outline and fill in heads and bodies (smooth with finger dipped in cornstarch). Insert licorice string arms and legs. Use tip 2 to pipe dot eyes, outline mouth and pull-out nose on all; pipe dot buttons. For Earmuff Snowman, pipe tip 3 dot earmuffs; insert 3¼ in. licorice string for band. Pipe tip 3 outline scarf (flatten with finger); overpipe with tip 2 stripes. For Top Hat Snowman, use tip 3 to pipe zigzag vest; outline and fill in scarf (smooth with finger). Outline and fill in top of hat with tip 4; add tip 3 outline brim and tip 2 outline band. For Stocking Cap Snowman, use tip 3 to outline and fill in shirt and scarf (smooth with finger). Use tip 3 to outline and fill in hat brim; pipe tip 2 stripes and dot pompom. Each serves 1.

◀ North Pole Native

Pans: Step-By-Step Snowman, p. 197; Oval Set (13½ x 9⅞ in. used), p. 153
Tips: 12, 16, 18, p. 142-143
Colors:* Black, Kelly Green, Lemon Yellow, Golden Yellow, p. 136
Fondant/Gum Paste: White Ready-To-Use Rolled Fondant (54 oz.), p. 130; Rolling Pin, Roll & Cut Mat, p. 133
Recipes: Buttercream, Chocolate Buttercream, Roll-Out Cookies, p. 114
Also: 2008 Pattern Book (Penguin Foot and Face), p. 128; Fanci-Foil Wrap, p. 233; 24 x 14 in. foamcore board (½ in. thick), 8 in. candy cane, knife, toothpicks, cornstarch, spatula

In advance: Make cookie feet. Use pattern to cut 2 cookies for each foot; reverse pattern and cut two more. Bake and cool. Stack right- and left-foot cookies with icing; let set.

Bake and cool 1-layer cakes. Use knife to trim snowman face flat and to cut holly leaf off hat; cut 2 in. from top of oval to accommodate bottom of snowman cake. Place cakes together on foil-covered board; if needed, position a 2½ oz. log of fondant at seam to level tops. Mark face using pattern; mark tummy oval 1½ in. from edge. Spatula ice tummy and build up bottom for rounded shape. For arms, use 50 oz. fondant to roll 2 logs, about 8 in. long. Position top of arms on board at shoulder; curve end of right arm onto cake top; attach with icing. For beak, shape 1½ oz. fondant into cone with 2 in. diameter base; use knife to cut slit for mouth. Attach with icing; spatula ice smooth.

Cover face and tummy with tip 16 stars; outline eyes with tip 12 and pipe in (smooth with finger dipped in cornstarch). Cover body with tip 16 stars; pipe tip 12 dot pupils. Using tip 18, cover left arm with pull-out stars; position candy cane on right arm, then pipe pull-out stars above, below and over candy cane for fingers. Position feet next to cake and secure with icing. Cover feet and hatband with tip 16 stars. Using tip 16 stars, cover hat and overpipe a 1½ in. wide scarf with ends 3½ and 5 in. long; overpipe 3½ in. overlapping end for dimension. Serves 27.

▶ Junior Reindeer

Pan: Friendly Lion, p. 157
Tips: 1, 3, 8, 12, 16, 21, p. 142-143
Colors: Royal Blue, Brown, Red-Red, Black, Rose, p. 136
Recipes: Buttercream, Royal Icings, p. 114
Also: 2008 Pattern Book (Reindeer Head and Antlers), p. 128; Cake Board, Fanci-Foil Wrap, p. 233; 4 in. Lollipop Sticks, p. 169; Meringue Powder, p. 137; waxed paper, paring knife, toothpick, cornstarch

In advance: Make 2 antlers with royal icing. Copy pattern and cover with waxed paper. Cut lollipop stick into 2 in. pieces. Position sticks on pattern, so that 1 in. extends from base. Pipe antlers with tip 8, leaving extended portion of stick bare. Let dry; carefully remove waxed paper. Turn antlers over and overpipe with tip 8. Let dry overnight.

On lion cake, trim off ears, eyes, nose and two points of mane around neck. Ice sides and background areas smooth; trace head pattern with toothpick. Outline body, head, ears and facial features with tip 3. Pipe in whites of eyes, pupils, tongue, hooves and inside ears with tip 12 (smooth with finger dipped in cornstarch). With tip 3, outline and pipe in ½ in. wide collar; add dot jingle bells. Cover reindeer with tip 16 stars. Insert antlers. Pipe tip 21 pull-out star hair. Pipe tip 1 outline and dot snowflakes. Pipe tip 21 shell bottom border. Serves 12.

◀ A Dazzling December!

Pan: Iridescents! Tree, p. 197

Tip: 2A, p. 142

Color: Kelly Green, p. 136

Fondant/Gum Paste: Primary Colors Fondant Multi Pack, p. 130; Round and Star Cut-Outs™, p. 132; Rolling Pin, Roll & Cut Mat, p. 133

Recipe: Buttercream Icing, p. 114

Also: Yellow, Red, Green and Blue Sparkle Gels, p. 137; Cake Boards, Fanci-Foil Wrap, p. 233; cornstarch, knife, spatula

In advance: Make star. Roll out small amount of yellow fondant ⅛ in. thick. Cut star with largest Cut-Out. Let dry on cornstarch-dusted surface.

Spatula ice cake fluffy. Roll out fondant colors ⅛ in. thick. For swags, cut circle with largest Cut-Out; move cutter up ½ in. and cut again. Position swags on cake, trimming at sides to fit. Cut ornaments using wide end of tip 2A; position on cake. Position star. Use Sparkle Gels in matching colors to pipe zigzags on swags and spirals on ornaments and star. Serves 12.

▶ Party with the Penguin

Pan: Stand-Up Cuddly Bear Set, p. 157

Tips: 4, 18, p. 142-143

Colors:* Black, Red-Red, Christmas Red, Lemon Yellow, Golden Yellow, Kelly Green, p. 136

Fondant/Gum Paste: White Ready-To-Use Rolled Fondant (24 oz.), p. 130; Gum Tex™, Rolling Pin, Roll & Cut Mat, p. 133

Recipe: Buttercream Icing, p. 114

Also: 2008 Pattern Book (Wing), p. 128; Cake Board, Fanci-Foil Wrap, p. 233; 8 in. Lollipop Sticks, p. 169; sugar ice cream cone, cornstarch

In advance: Make wings. Add ½ teaspoon Gum-Tex to 4 oz. fondant. Tint black. Roll out ⅜ in. thick and using pattern, cut 2 wings. Insert 2 lollipop sticks 2½ in. deep into flat edge of one wing. Let wings dry.

Prepare cake using firm-textured batter such as pound cake. Fill prepared pan and core, bake and cool following directions. Insert baked core into cake body, attaching with icing, and position on prepared board. Trim off ears, arms, muzzle, tail, back of legs. Ice head smooth. Tint 3 oz. fondant yellow; shape top and bottom beak sections. Cut two lollipop sticks to 3 in. and insert into base of beak sections; insert into cake. Using tip 4, pipe in eyes (smooth with finger dipped in cornstarch); outline eyebrows. Cover body and feet with tip 18 stars. Ice cone smooth; position on head. Cut a strip of fondant ½ in. wide and wrap around cone. Add tip 18 pull-out star fringe at tip and base of cone. Trim lollipop sticks on wing to 5 in. long, insert into cake. Attach other wing with icing. Serves 12.

*Combine Red-Red with Christmas Red for red shown. Combine Lemon Yellow with Golden Yellow for yellow shown.

▲ Santa's Surprise!

Pan: Stand-Up House, p. 158

Tips: 1, 2, 3, 4, 7, 17, 45, p. 142-143

Colors: Kelly Green, Lemon Yellow, Red-Red, Black, Rose, Royal Blue, Violet, Brown, Copper (skin tone), p. 136

Fondant/Gum Paste: White Ready-To-Use Rolled Fondant (30 oz.), p. 130; Cutter/Embosser, p. 131; Star Cut-Outs™, p. 132; Rolling Pin, Roll & Cut Mat, p. 133

Recipes: Buttercream, Royal Icings, p. 114

Also: 2008 Pattern Book (Fireplace, Staircase Riser), p. 128; Jumbo Rainbow Nonpareils Sprinkle Decorations, p. 138; Meringue Powder, Piping Gel, p. 137; Fanci-Foil Wrap, p. 233; sugar ice cream cones, knife, ruler, 18 x 13 x ½ in. thick foamcore board, jumbo spice drops, square caramels, mini jelly candies, granulated sugar, toothpick, cornstarch

In advance: Make 4 small and 2 large trees using royal icing. For small trees, cut sugar cones to 1¾ in., 2 in., 2½ in. and 3 in. high. Cover cones with tip 3 pull-out dots; attach nonpareils. For each large tree, stack 3 sugar cones and secure with royal icing. Beginning at bottom, cover trees with tip 17 pull-out stars. Attach nonpareils as you pipe branches to treetop. For stars, roll out yellow spice drop on surface sprinkled with sugar; cut 2 stars using medium Cut-Out. Attach with tip 3 dots of royal icing.

Cover foamcore base with Fanci-Foil Wrap. Using pan as a guide, mark base where house cakes will be positioned, creating a 30° angle where house fronts meet. Mark floor area by drawing a line from corner of house backs to corner of base. For floor, tint 8 oz. fondant brown; roll out ⅛ in. thick and cut an 18 x 7 in. piece. Brush base from house backs to edge of base lightly with piping gel. Attach fondant, trimming at markings. Using ruler and straight-edge wheel of Cutter/Embosser, score lines for floorboards. First, mark horizontal lines, ⅜ in. apart. Next, mark floorboards 3 and 3½ in. long to stagger joints. For snow area, roll out remaining white fondant ⅛ in. thick. Brush base from house fronts to edge of base lightly with piping gel and cover area with fondant. Trim to fit.

Bake and cool cakes using firm-textured cake batter such as pound cake. Trim bottoms of 2 house cakes to stand level on board; position on base. On both house fronts, mark with toothpick and ice smooth 1½ in. square top windows. On Door House, mark and ice smooth a 2 in. square bottom window and a 1¾ x 3¼ in. door with a ½ in. square window. On Chimney House, mark and ice smooth a 2 x 3 in. bottom window. On both house fronts and sides, pipe ½ x ¼ in. high bricks using tip 4, staggering ends to create a brickwork pattern (smooth with finger dipped in cornstarch). Pipe tip 1 outline windowpanes. Pipe tip 3 pull-out dot window and door garland trim, wreath, bushes and tree in front window. Attach nonpareils. On wreath, add tip 2 dot berries and outline bow. Pipe tip 3 dot doorknob. Add tip 3 pull-out icicles on windowsills. For chimney, cut 4 caramels on an angle to fit roof peak; attach 2 on each side of peak with buttercream. Attach a second row of 4 caramels. Ice rooftops fluffy with spatula. Pipe tip 7 icicles along eaves.

Decorate house backs (inside of houses). Ice walls on both houses smooth with spatula. Pipe tip 45 trim on peak of both houses. On Chimney House, mark a 1½ in. circle for wreath; pipe tip 3 dot wreath and bow. Mark fireplace using pattern, starting 1 in. from left edge of wall. Ice inside area smooth.

Using heavy pressure, pipe tip 3 bricks (smooth with finger dipped in cornstarch). Pipe tip 3 outline mantel; add tip 3 outline candles and dot garland, tip 2 dot flames. For Santa, outline and pipe in tip 7 head (pat smooth). Outline and pipe in tip 3 suit, hat and boots (pat smooth). Pipe tip 2 dot facial features. Add tip 3 zigzag fur trim, swirl beard and pompom, pull-out moustache and dot mittens. Pipe tip 3 dot garland along bottom of trim. On Door House, mark inside door 1¾ x 3¼ in. high; outline and pipe in (pat smooth). With tip 3, outline and pipe in a ½ in. square window; add dot doorknob. Mark upstairs railing, with top beam 2¾ in. from house peak and bottom 1 in. below top beam. Pipe tip 3 outline beams with vertical posts 1 in. apart. For staircase, mark and pipe in riser pattern; mark banister 1½ in. above riser, following angle. Pipe tip 3 outline banister with vertical posts 1 in. apart. Figure pipe family (p. 119) using tips 2, 3 and 7. Pipe tip 3 dot garland on staircase and railing. For gifts, trim jumbo spice drops into squares and roll in granulated sugar. Pipe tip 2 outline ribbons and bows. Ice white fondant-covered board fluffy with spatula, leaving walkway clean. Attach mini jelly candies for walkway. Position cone trees and packages. Serves 24.

◀ Shimmy Down the Chimney!

Pan: 9 x 13 in. Sheet, p. 154
Candy: White, Red and Light Cocoa Candy Melts®†, p. 166; Christmas Characters Lollipop Mold, p. 198; 4 in. Lollipop Sticks, p. 169
Recipe: Favorite crisped rice cereal treats
Also: Parchment Triangles, p. 140; large spice drops, ruler, knife, scissors, granulated sugar

In advance: Mold Santa lollipops using painting method (p. 125). Mix a small amount of red candy into white to make pink. Let set.

Prepare cereal treat recipe and press into pan, 1 in. deep; unmold. Cut 2 in. squares; stack 3 and press together to make 2 x 2 x 3 in. high chimney. Use melted white candy in cut parchment bag to pipe lines for 1 x ½ in. bricks. Pipe mound of candy snow on top, letting edges drip down. For arms, cut red spice drops in half lengthwise; roll out on surface sprinkled with sugar. Cut lollipop stick in half; wrap around end of lollipop stick, leaving 1 in. extended; secure with melted candy. For mittens, cut green spice drop lengthwise in half; roll out in sugar. Shape mittens by hand; attach to arms using melted candy. For body, cut spice drop in half horizontally; insert Santa lollipop stick through top half. Cut small hole in top center of chimney. Insert sticks, cut to fit, into chimney to position head and arms. Use melted candy to pipe fur trims on front and around neck and arms. Each serves 1.

▼ The Santa Squad

Pan: Cookie Sheet, p. 154
Tips: 1A, 2, 3, 4, 21, 352, p. 142-143
Colors:* Kelly Green, Red-Red, No-Taste Red, Rose, Black, Copper (skin tone), p. 136
Recipes: Buttercream Icing (stiff consistency), Royal Icing, p. 114
Also: 2008 Pattern Book (Hand), p. 128; Santa Silly-Feet! Silicone Baking Cups, p. 198; 4 in. Lollipop Sticks, p. 169; granulated sugar, sugar ice cream cones, spice drops, waxed paper, knife, cornstarch

In advance: Make hats. Trim sugar cones to 2¾ in. long. Ice smooth with spatula using royal icing; let dry.

Bake and cool cupcakes in silicone cups supported by cookie sheet. Using tip 1A and stiff consistency buttercream, pipe a mound of icing on top for head. Smooth with spatula. For arms, cut lollipop sticks to 3 in.; insert 1½ in. into cupcake. Pipe arms with buttercream, inserting tip 21 over stick and pulling out bag with even pressure. For hands, roll out spice drops on waxed paper sprinkled with sugar. Using pattern, cut hand with knife; reverse pattern for opposite hand. Attach hands to arms with dots of icing. For Santa, pipe tip 3 dot eyes and nose (flatten and smooth with finger dipped in cornstarch). With tip 2, pipe in mouth, eyebrows and dot pupils (flatten and smooth). Position hat. Pipe tip 4 zigzag pompom, fur trim, hair and beard, outline moustache. For elf, attach hat. Pipe tip 4 zigzag pompom and tip 352 pull-out trim. Pipe tip 3 dot eyes (flatten and smooth). With tip 2, pipe in mouth and add dot pupils (flatten and smooth). Pipe tip 4 pull-out dot nose and dot cheeks (flatten and smooth). Add tip 352 pull-out leaf ears. Each serves 1.

*Combine Red-Red and No-Taste Red for red shown.

▶ Starlight Pine

Tips: 4, 17, p. 142-143
Color: Kelly Green, p. 136
Candy: Yellow Candy Melts®†, p. 166; Stars Candy Mold, p. 168
Recipe: Royal Icing, p. 114
Also: Jumbo Confetti Sprinkle Decorations, p. 138; Meringue Powder, p. 137; Cake Boards, p. 233; sugar ice cream cones, waxed paper

In advance: Make star. Fill mold halfway with melted candy; refrigerate until firm and unmold.

For trees, stack 3 sugar cones, securing with icing. Place on waxed paper-covered board. Build up bottom with icing for tree shape. Cover cone with tip 17 pull-out stars, working from bottom up. Position confetti sprinkles. Pipe tip 4 pull-out snow. Attach star to treetop with icing; let set. Each serves 1.

†Brand confectionery coating.

◀ Winter Lights Display

Pans: 11 x 15 x 2 in. Sheet, Cookie Sheet, Cooling Grid, p. 154

Tips: 1, 2, 5, p. 142

Colors:* Leaf Green, Lemon Yellow, Violet, Rose, Orange, Black, Red-Red, Christmas Red, Sky Blue, p. 136

Fondant/Gum Paste: White Ready-To-Use Rolled Fondant (24 oz.), p. 130; Rolling Pin, Roll & Cut Mat, p. 133; Brush Set, p. 131

Recipes: Royal Icing, p. 114; Thinned Fondant Adhesive, p. 115

Also: Graceful Tiers Cake Stand, p. 230; Ready-To-Use Decorator Icing (4 containers), Meringue Powder, p. 137; Holiday Mini Cutter Set, p. 200; 101 Cookie Cutters Set, p. 162; Soft Yellow Sugar, p. 208; 4 in. Lollipop Sticks, p. 169; 1 in. Diameter Candy Cups, p. 167; Cake Board, p. 233; 24-gauge white florist wire (16 in.), glue gun, cornstarch, knife

In advance: Make fondant stars, trees and snowmen. Tint 3 oz. fondant yellow, 3 oz. green; reserve remaining white. Roll out fondant ⅛ in. thick. Cut 12 stars, 11 trees and 11 gingerbread boy snowmen using cutters from Holiday Mini Set. Let dry overnight on cornstarch-dusted board. When dry, brush stars with water and sprinkle with yellow sugar. **Also:** Decorate snowmen using royal icing. Pipe tip 1 dot eyes and mouth; add tip 2 pull-out nose. Pipe in tip 1 boots (pat smooth with finger dipped in cornstarch); pipe in tip 5 scarves and hats. Let dry overnight. When dry, cut lollipop sticks to 2 in. and attach to backs of trees and snowmen using royal icing; let dry.

And: Attach stars to top of stand. Cut 2 florist wires to 8 in.; wrap around top of stand so that ends face up. Secure wires with glue gun. Curve ends into a spray formation and attach 6 stars with Fondant Adhesive; let dry.

Bake and cool 2 in. high sheet cake. Mark circles on cake using medium circle cutter from 101 Cutter Set. Cut out cakes with knife. Tint a portion of Ready-To-Use Icing blue and heat to pouring consistency; cover cakes with poured icing (p. 126). Let dry. Position cakes on flattened paper candy cups. Heat reserved white icing to pouring consistency and pour over cake tops, dripping down sides for snow effect; let dry. Insert snowmen and trees. Position cakes on stand. Attach remaining stars to stand with adhesive. One sheet cake makes 22 to 24 mini cakes; each serves 1.

*Combine Violet with Rose for violet shown. Combine Red-Red with Christmas Red for red shown.

▼ Top of the Mountain

Pan: Standard Muffin, p. 154

Tips: 4, 17, p. 142-143

Colors:* Leaf Green, Lemon Yellow, Kelly Green, p. 136

Fondant/Gum Paste: White Ready-To-Use Fondant (72 oz.), p. 130; Rolling Pin, Roll & Cut Mat, p. 133; Star Cut-Outs™, p. 132; Brush Set, p. 131

Recipe: Buttercream Icing, p. 114

Also: Cakes 'N More™ 3-Tier Party Stand, p. 230; Snowman Baking Cups, Fun Pix®, p. 198; Jumbo Rainbow Nonpareils Sprinkle Decorations, p. 138; spatula, sugar ice cream cones (9), knife, cornstarch

In advance: Make stars. Tint 2 in. ball of fondant yellow; roll out ⅛ in. thick. Cut 3 stars using medium Cut-Out. Let dry on cornstarch-dusted surface.

Also: Prepare stand. Roll out fondant ⅛ in. thick. Using 8 in. plate from stand as a guide, mark a 2 in. border around plate. Use knife to cut wavy edge within border for snow. Position plate on stand and drape fondant on top, securing with damp brush. Repeat with 10 and 12 in. plates.

And: Make trees. Stack 3 sugar cones, securing with icing in between. Build up bottom with icing for tree shape; cover with tip 17 pull-out stars, working from bottom up. Sprinkle with nonpareils; add tip 4 pull-out snow. Attach star with icing. Position trees on stand.

Ice cupcakes smooth with spatula. Insert picks in cupcakes. Position cupcakes on stand. Each serves 1.

*Combine Leaf Green and Kelly Green with Lemon Yellow for green shown.

▲ Built for the Cold

Pan: Mini Ball, p. 159

Tips: 8, 12, 16, p. 142-143

Colors:* Red-Red, Leaf Green, Lemon Yellow, Violet, Rose, Black, Royal Blue, p. 136

Fondant/Gum Paste: White Ready-To-Use Rolled Fondant (24 oz.), p. 130; Gum-Tex™, Rolling Pin, Roll & Cut Mat, p. 133; Cutter/Embosser, Brush Set, p. 131; Round Cut-Outs™, p. 132

Recipe: Buttercream Icing, p. 114; Thinned Fondant Adhesive, p. 115

Also: 2008 Pattern Book (Mittens, Head & Hat), p. 128; 101 Cookie Cutters Set, p. 162; 4 in. Lollipop Sticks, p. 169; black shoestring licorice, cornstarch, waxed paper, knife, ruler, toothpicks

In advance: Make heads. Add ¼ teaspoon Gum-Tex to 2 oz. fondant; roll out ⅛ in. thick. Use Head & Hat pattern to cut stocking cap head; use medium round Cut-Out to cut other heads. Tint 1 oz. of fondant red and roll out; cut mittens using pattern. Let all dry on cornstarch-dusted surface.

When dry, cut lollipop sticks to 3½ in. long; attach to back of heads using fondant adhesive.

Ice mini cakes smooth with buttercream. Tint fondant as follows: 4 oz. green, 2 oz. red, 2 oz. black, 2 oz. blue, 1 oz. violet. Roll out ⅛ in. thick. For all, cut fondant decorations and attach with damp brush. Cut eyes with narrow end of tip 8; roll ⅛ x ½ in. long tapered logs for nose and mouth. Insert heads in cakes. For Top Hat Snowman, cut 10 x ½ in. green strip for jacket bottom; cut scallop edge using smallest round cutter. Cut 10 x ¾ in. red strip for jacket top; attach dots cut with narrow end of tip 8. Cut 5 x ½ in. green strip for collar. Cut a 1½ x ¾ in. rectangle for hat top; attach with adhesive. Roll a 2 x ¼ in. log for brim; cut a 1½ x ⅛ in. strip for hatband. Cut 8 x ¼ in. scarf and tie around neck. For Earmuff Snowman, roll and flatten ⅜ in. balls for earmuffs; attach 3½ in. licorice string for band. Cut 8 x ¼ in. green strip for scarf; attach ¼ in. red squares then wrap around neck. Cut buttons with narrow end of tip 12. For Stocking Cap Snowman, cut red hat using pattern; attach ¼ in. green strips, trimming to fit. Roll ½ in. ball for pompom; indent with tip 16 for texture. For shirt, cut 6 x 1½ in. strip and wrap around cake; smooth seam in back and use knife to cut front vent. Cut 8 x ¼ in. strip for scarf and tie around neck. For all arms, wrap 2 in. lollipop stick with 1¼ x ⅝ in. fondant strip. Attach mittens with adhesive, let set, then push arms into cakes. Each serves 1.

*Combine Violet with Rose for violet shown. Combine Leaf Green with Lemon Yellow for green shown.

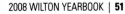

▼ Queen of Hearts

Pans: Standard Muffin, p. 154; Non-Stick Cookie Sheet, Cooling Grid, p. 151

Candy: Candy Melts®† in White (3 pks.), Light Cocoa (1 pk.), Primary, Garden Candy Color Sets, p. 166; Heart Lollipop Mold, p. 204; 4 in. Lollipop Sticks, p. 169; Decorator Brush Set, p. 167

Recipe: Buttercream Icing, p. 114

Also: Hearts Remembered Standard Baking Cups, p. 204; Standard Cupcakes 'N More® Dessert Stand, p. 146; Round Cut-Outs™, p. 132; Jumbo Hearts Sprinkle Decorations, p. 138; Girl Plastic Cutter, p. 163; Parchment Triangles, p. 140; waxed paper

In advance: Mold candies. Melt 1 pk. white candy and tint ½ pink, ½ red. Tint a small amount of melted white candy skin tone using orange and pink candy colors. Mold base for girl: Place largest round Cut-Out on cookie sheet; fill ⅛ in. deep with melted candy. Follow same procedure to mold girl using skin tone candy and girl cutter. Refrigerate candies until firm; unmold. For heart attached to wand, fill inner portion of Heart Lollipop Mold with melted red candy; refrigerate until firm and unmold. Trim lollipop stick to 2 in.; attach heart and jumbo heart sprinkle. Decorate girl using melted candy in cut parchment bag. Pipe facial features, hair, dress, shoes and belt. Pipe arms and puffy sleeves; position wand and pipe both hands. Pipe an outline crown base and attach 3 jumbo heart sprinkles. Let set completely. Make an easel for girl: cut a Candy Melts wafer in half, trim one rounded end flat; attach 2 pieces to back. Attach girl to base. **Also:** Mold 23 hearts without sticks using painting method (p. 125); mold some center heart areas with pink, others with white. Refrigerate until firm; unmold.

Ice cupcakes smooth with spatula; position sprinkles. Attach candy hearts to cupcakes with small mound of icing. Position cupcakes and girl on stand. Each cupcake serves 1.

†Brand confectionery coating.

▲ Toad-al Infatuation

Pans: Cookie Sheet, Cooling Grid, p. 154

Tips: 1, 3, 8, 12, p. 142

Colors:* Leaf Green, Lemon Yellow, Rose, Red-Red, Black, p. 136

Recipes: Royal Icing, Roll-Out Cookies, p. 114

Also: Heart Plastic Nesting Cutter Set, p. 163; Circle Metal Cutter, p. 164; Meringue Powder, p. 137; Cake Board, p. 233; waxed paper, cornstarch

In advance: Make cookies. Prepare and roll out dough. For each, cut message heart using smallest heart cutter, body using largest heart cutter and head using circle cutter. Bake and cool. **Also:** Cover cookies with thinned royal icing (p. 126). Let dry. **And:** Decorate head. Place round cookie on waxed paper-covered board. Pipe tip 12 outline eye socket (flatten with finger dipped in cornstarch). Pipe tip 8 ball eyes and flatten; pipe tip 3 dot pupils and flatten. Outline and pipe in mouth. Pipe tip 8 pull-out crown points; pipe tip 3 bead hearts on points. Let dry thoroughly.

Attach head to body with icing; if needed, prop up to maintain position until dry. Attach pink heart. Pipe tip 1 message. Pipe tip 8 outline arms and bead fingers; pipe tip 12 bead toes. Each serves 1.

*Combine Leaf Green with Lemon Yellow for green shown.

For ice cream scoop, press prepared cereal treats mixture into pan cavities sprayed with pan spray, leaving some excess on edges. Unmold immediately and cover with melted candy (p. 126); let set. Pipe topping using melted candy in cut parchment bag; let set 1 minute then add sprinkles. Print message with melted candy; let set. Attach candy heart and licorice stem with melted candy. Fill cup with conversation hearts; position scoop. Each serves 1.

†Brand confectionery coating.

◀ Love Struck

Pans: Cookie Sheet, Cooling Grid, p. 154
Tips: 1, 2, 3, 4, p. 142
Colors: Copper (skin tone), Black, Brown, Rose, Red-Red, p. 136
Recipes: Royal Icing, Roll-Out Cookies, p. 114
Also: Boy Plastic Cutter, p. 163; Fine Tip Primary Colors FoodWriter™ Edible Color Markers, p. 130; Meringue Powder, p. 137; 6 in. Lollipop Sticks, p. 169; White Candy Melts®†, p. 166; card stock, hole punch, curling ribbon (18 in. per treat), ruler, scissors, cornstarch

In advance: Make cookies. Prepare dough; tint skin tone. Roll out and cut using boy cutter. Roll a tiny ball for nose; attach. Bake and cool cookies.

Decorate using royal icing. Outline and pipe in shorts with tip 4 (pat smooth with finger dipped in cornstarch). Add tip 2 zigzag waistband. Pipe tip 3 dot eyes; add tip 2 dot pupils and zigzag hair. Build up and pipe in gloves with tip 4 (pat smooth with finger). Use tip 4 to outline and pipe in shoes (pat smooth). Use tip 1 to add outline glove laces, mouth and black eye. Let dry. Attach lollipop stick to back using melted candy; let set. Cut 1¼ x 2¾ in. tag; print message with FoodWriter. Punch hole; attach to stick with ribbon. Each serves 1.

▶ Roping Romance

Pans: Cookie Sheet, Cooling Grid, p. 154
Tips: 2, 3, p. 142
Colors:* Rose, Violet, Red-Red, Brown, Lemon Yellow, Black, Copper (skin tone), p. 136
Fondant/Gum Paste: White Ready-To-Use Rolled Fondant, p. 130; Rolling Pin, Roll & Cut Mat, p. 133
Cookie: Heart Plastic Nesting Cutter Set, p. 163; Boy Plastic Cutter, p. 163; 6 in. Cookie Treat Sticks, p. 165
Recipes: Royal Icing, Roll-Out Cookies, p. 114
Also: White Candy Melts®†, p. 166; Fine Tip Primary Colors FoodWriter™ Edible Color Markers, p. 130; Meringue Powder, p. 137; Parchment Triangles, p. 140; Cake Boards, p. 233; waxed paper, knife, cornstarch

In advance: Make cookies. Prepare and roll out dough. Cut hearts using 3½ in. heart cutter; cut cowboys using boy cutter. Bake and cool cookies. Cover hearts with thinned royal icing (p. 126). Let dry. **Also:** Attach cookie stick to back of heart with melted candy, leaving 3 in. extended at bottom.

Place cowboy on waxed paper-covered board; decorate using royal icing. Use tip 3 to outline and pipe in face, bandana, hands (not fingers), shirt, pants and shoes (pat smooth with finger dipped in cornstarch). Outline and pipe in hat, overpiping brim for dimension (smooth with finger). Use tip 2 to add pull-out hair, dot nose and mouth, outline mustache, eyes and hat band. Pipe tip 2 scallop border on heart. Print message with FoodWriter.

Tint fondant yellow. Roll 2 logs ⅛ x 6 in.; twist together for bottom rope. Use melted candy to attach over stick and cowboy. Roll 2 logs ⅛ x 4 in.; twist together. Attach over top of heart, trimming as needed. Pipe tip 2 pull-out fingers over rope. Each serves 1.

*Combine Violet with Rose for violet shown.

▼ Bowl Over Your Valentine!

Pans: Mini Ball, p. 159; Cookie Sheet, Cooling Grid, p. 154
Candy: White, Red Candy Melts®†, Garden Candy Color Set, p. 166; Hearts Candy Mold, p. 204; Peanut Butter Cups Candy Mold, p. 169
Recipe: Favorite crisped rice cereal treats
Also: Hearts Confetti Sprinkle Decorations, p. 204; Parchment Triangles, p. 140; red shoestring licorice, waxed paper, conversation hearts candies, vegetable pan spray

For each treat you will need a candy shell (p. 125) bowl, base, peanut butter cup and heart cherry. Mold shell bowl ⅛ in. thick in mini ball pan; refrigerate until firm and unmold. For base, fill pan cavities ½ in. deep; refrigerate until firm and unmold. Mold solid candy peanut butter cup and heart; refrigerate until firm and unmold. To assemble, lightly slide top of base over warm cookie sheet to slightly flatten; attach upside-down peanut butter cup to center with melted candy. Let set. Flatten bottom of bowl on warm cookie sheet as above; attach peanut butter cup with melted candy. Let set. Using melted candy in cut parchment bag, pipe bead seam around base of peanut butter cup and 8 lines on sides of shell; let set.

▼ Sweetie Pies

Pan: Mini Heart, p. 203
Recipe: Favorite pie crust mix or recipe (2-crust recipe makes 5 treats)
Also: Rolling Pin, Roll & Cut Mat, p. 133; cherry pie filling, ruler, spoon

Preheat oven to 375°F. Roll out crust. Ease dough into cavity and trim ½ in. beyond heart shape. Place crusts in alternating rows so they are not next to each other. Spoon in filling. For lattice top, roll out dough; cut ⅝ in. wide strips. Position on pie, trimming to fit. Use fingers to crimp border. Bake for 17-20 minutes or until lightly browned. Cool in pan; remove for serving. Each serves 1.

▶ Up for a Celebration!

Pans: Cookie Sheet, Cooling Grid, p. 154

Tips: 2A, 3, p. 142

Colors:* Lemon Yellow, Golden Yellow, Rose, Brown, Red-Red, p. 136

Fondant/Gum Paste: White Ready-To-Use Rolled Fondant (24 oz. for 20 treats), p. 130; Gum-Tex™, Rolling Pin, Roll & Cut Mat, p. 133; Leaf Cut-Outs™, p. 132; Brush Set, p. 131

Recipes: Buttercream Icing (stiff consistency), p. 114; Thinned Fondant Adhesive, p. 115

Also: 2008 Pattern Book (Bunny Hands, Chick Wings, Hair), p. 128; Silly-Feet! Silicone Baking Cups, p. 147; 4 in. Lollipop Sticks, p. 169; jelly beans, spice drops, granulated sugar, knife, cornstarch, waxed paper, spatula

In advance: Make fondant pieces (p. 121). Let all pieces dry on cornstarch-dusted surface. Trim lollipop sticks to 2½ in. Attach ears and wings to sticks with thinned fondant adhesive. Let set.

Bake and cool cupcakes in silicone cups supported by cookie sheet. Using stiff buttercream and tip 2A, pipe head, building up for dimension; round with spatula. For bunny: Pipe tip 3 outline mouth and dot eyes; attach jelly bean nose with icing. Insert ears. For arms, trim lollipop sticks to 3 in. long. Roll 2 fondant logs, ½ x 1 in. Push stick into log until ½ in. is exposed at top; attach hand to end with fondant adhesive. Insert arms. For chick: Pipe tip 3 dot eyes. Cut orange spice drop in half; shape and cut each half into pointed beak. Cover with granulated sugar. Attach beak; insert hair and wings. Each serves 1.

*Combine Lemon Yellow with Golden Yellow for yellow shown. Combine Brown with Red-Red for brown shown.

◀ Cheeky Chick

Pans: Decorated Egg, p. 206; Cookie Sheet, Cooling Grid, p. 154

Tips: 5, 16, p. 142-143

Colors:* Lemon Yellow, Golden Yellow, Orange, Royal Blue, p. 136

Recipes: Buttercream Icing, Roll-Out Cookies, p. 114

Also: 2008 Pattern Book (Wings, Feet), p. 128; Cake Boards, Fanci-Foil Wrap, p. 233; knife, toothpicks, cornstarch

In advance: Make cookies. Prepare and roll out dough. Use patterns to cut 4 wings and 4 feet (reverse patterns for 2 of each). Bake and cool.

Position egg cake on foil-wrapped cake board. Sandwich cookies with icing; position on board next to cake. Outline and pipe in eyes with tip 5 (pat smooth with finger dipped in cornstarch). Ice feet smooth. Build up beak with icing; shape and pat smooth. Score line for mouth with edge of knife. Cover body with tip 16 stars; cover wings with tip 16 pull-out stars. Cake serves 12; each cookie serves 1.

*Combine Lemon Yellow with Golden Yellow for yellow shown.

◀ Rabbit Nabbed It!

Pans: Bunny Cookie Treat, p. 206; Cookie Sheet, Cooling Grid, p. 154

Tips: 3, 4, 5, 16, p. 142-143

Colors:* Brown, Rose, Kelly Green, Red-Red, p. 136

Cookie: Easter 18-Pc. Cutter Collection, p. 208; 6 in. Cookie Treat Sticks, p. 165

Recipes: Royal Icing, Roll-Out Cookies, p. 114

Also: Meringue Powder, p. 137; jelly beans, waxed paper, cornstarch

In advance: Make cookies. Prepare and roll out dough. Cut basket cookies using cutter from set; bake and cool. Bake and cool bunnies in Cookie Treat Pan using cookie sticks cut to 5 in. long, leaving 3 in. extended.

For bunny: Ice area inside ears (pat smooth with finger dipped in cornstarch). Use tip 3 to pipe outline mouth and pipe in eyes. Cover remainder with tip 16 stars. Attach jelly bean nose. For basket: Pipe tip 5 basketweave base; pipe tip 4 rope handle. Attach jelly beans with icing dots. Add tip 3 pull-out grass. Attach basket to end of cookie stick with icing. Overpipe tip 16 stars for hands. Each serves 1.

*Combine Brown with Red-Red for dark brown shown.

▼ Hares to You!

Pans: Cookie Sheet, Cooling Grid, p. 154

Tip: 233, p. 142

Colors:* Leaf Green, Lemon Yellow, p. 136

Recipe: Buttercream Icing, p. 114

Also: Pastel Silicone Baking Cups, Bunnies & Chicks Fun Pix®, p. 207; Colorful Egg Mix Sprinkle Decorations, p. 208

Bake and cool cupcakes in silicone cups supported by cookie sheet. Cover tops with tip 233 pull-out grass. Add sprinkles; insert pick. Each serves 1.

*Combine Leaf Green with Lemon Yellow for green shown.

▼ Bucktooth Bunny

Pans: Step-By-Step Bunny, p. 206; Cookie Sheet, Cooling Grid, p. 154

Tips: 3, 16, p. 142-143

Colors: Rose, Royal Blue, p. 136

Recipe: Buttercream Icing, Roll-Out Cookies, p. 114

Also: 2008 Pattern Book (Hands, Feet, Tail), p. 128; Cake Boards, Fanci-Foil Wrap, p. 154; knife, toothpicks, cornstarch

In advance: Make cookies. Prepare and roll out dough. Use patterns to cut 2 hands, 2 tails and 4 feet (reverse pattern for 2 of feet). Bake and cool cookies.

Position bunny cake on foil-wrapped board. Sandwich feet and tail cookies with icing; position on board next to cake. Build up face area with icing for a flat surface. Ice inside of ears smooth. Use tip 3 to pipe outline mouth and whiskers; outline and pipe-in nose, teeth and eyes (pat smooth with finger dipped in cornstarch). Cover cake, feet and tail with tip 16 stars. Position hands; cover with tip 16 stars. Cake serves 12; each cookie serves 1.

◄ Brilliant Basket

Pans: 6 x 3, 9 x 2 in. Round, p. 153
Tip: 5, p. 142
Colors:* Lemon Yellow, Rose, Violet, Royal Blue, Orange, Leaf Green, p. 136
Fondant/Gum Paste: White Ready-To-Use Rolled Fondant (72 oz.), p. 130; Round, Leaf and Oval Cut-Outs™, p. 132; Rolling Pin, Roll & Cut Mat, p. 133; Brush Set, Easy-Glide Fondant Smoother, p. 131
Recipe: Buttercream Icing, p. 114
Also: 2008 Pattern Book (Handle), p. 128; White Candy Melts®†, p. 166; Plastic Dowel Rods, p. 232; Cake Circles, p. 233; Gum-Tex™, p. 133; Flower Former Set, p. 131; Ceramic Pedestal Cake Stand, p. 145; 6 in. Lollipop Sticks, p. 169; cornstarch, waxed paper, knife, ruler

In advance: Make fondant pieces. Tint fondant as follows: 6 oz. yellow, 4 oz. green, 2 oz. light blue, 2 oz. violet, 2 oz. rose, 2 oz. orange. Add ¾ teaspoon Gum-Tex to yellow, ½ teaspoon to green and ¼ teaspoon to all other colors. Shape 4 oz. yellow into 3 logs ⅜ x 18 in.; braid together. Cover handle pattern with waxed paper; dust with cornstarch. Curve braid over pattern; let dry. **Also:** Make leaves. Roll out green fondant ⅟₁₆ in. thick. Cut leaves using medium Cut-Out; move cutter down ⅛ in. and cut again to make leaf slightly smaller. Cut ⅛ in. off bottom to make a straight edge. Make 45-50 leaves; let dry on cornstarch-dusted medium flower formers. **And:** Make eggs. Roll out 5 fondant colors ⅛ in. thick. Use largest oval Cut-Out to cut 2-3 eggs in each color. Let dry on cornstarch-dusted surface 24 to 48 hours. Use melted candy to attach lollipop sticks to back of eggs and to each end of handle. Leave ends exposed to insert into cake.

Bake and cool 1-layer 6 in. cake (3 in. high) and 2-layer 9 in. cake (bake 2 layers 1½ in. high for a 3 in. high cake). Prepare for rolled fondant (p. 115) and Stacked Construction (p. 112). Tint 18 oz. fondant yellow, 30 oz. rose (reserve 3 oz. white). Cover cakes; smooth with Fondant Smoother. Stack cakes. Pipe tip 5 bead bottom borders. Roll out white fondant ⅟₁₆ in. thick. Use smallest round Cut-Out to cut approximately 70 dots; attach to cakes using damp brush. Insert handle into cake top; insert eggs. Use melted candy to attach 2 rows of leaves around edge of top cake. Serves 30.

*Combine Violet with Rose for violet shown.

▶ The Shell Game

Pan: Dancing Daisy Flower, p. 158
Tips: 3, 16, 233, p. 142-143
Colors:* Leaf Green, Lemon Yellow, Sky Blue, Creamy Peach, Rose, Violet, p. 136
Recipe: Buttercream Icing, p. 114
Also: Hoppy Easter Colored Metal Cutter Set, p. 208; Petite Eggs Icing Decorations (2 pks.), p. 207; Cake Boards, Fanci-Foil Wrap, p. 233

Bake and cool cake. Ice cake sides smooth. Lightly ice top; imprint center of each petal with egg cutter from set. Cover cake top with tip 16 stars. Pipe tip 3 dots on eggs. Overpipe tip 16 spiral on center. Pipe tip 233 pull-out grass bottom border. Position icing decorations to cake sides. Serves 12.

*Combine Violet with Rose for violet shown.

◀ Pearlized Posies

Pans: Dimensions® Large Cupcake, p. 150; Cookie Sheet, Cooling Grid, p. 154
Candy: White Candy Melts®† (5 pks.), Primary, Garden Candy Color Sets, p. 166; Truffles Candy Mold, 6 in. Lollipop Sticks, p. 169; Brush Set, p. 131
Recipe: Roll-Out Cookies, p. 114
Also: 2008 Pattern Book (Handle), p. 128; White Pearl Dust, p. 130; Oval Cut-Outs™, p. 132; Flower Former Set, Disposable Decorating Bags, p. 140; Fanci-Foil Wrap, p. 233; lemon leaves, pastry brush, 3½ in. craft circle (1½ in. high), knife

In advance: Make cookies. Prepare and roll out dough. Use largest oval Cut-Out to cut 8-10 egg cookies. Use pattern to cut handle. Bake cookies; recheck handle cookie against pattern; trim if necessary. Cool cookies. **Also:** Make candy shell basket. Melt 2½ pks. candy; pour 1½ cups into bottom half of cupcake pan. Tilt pan and use pastry brush to brush candy up onto sides of pan. Refrigerate until firm. Repeat with additional melted candy until you have built up a shell 3/16 in. thick. Refrigerate until firm; unmold. **And:** Make candies for handle. Using truffle mold, fill cavities 1/3 full to make 12 candies. Refrigerate until firm; unmold. **And:** Make leaves. Tint portion of melted white candy green; brush onto backs of lemon leaves. Make 15-20 leaves. Let dry in large flower formers.

To finish handle, brush back of cookie with melted candy; let set. Turn over onto cooling grid. Cover with melted candy (p. 126) in disposable decorating bag; tap grid gently to settle candy. Move to waxed paper-covered board to set completely. Attach truffle candies with melted candy; let set. Tint portions of melted white candy pink, yellow, violet and blue using candy colors. Cover egg cookies with melted candy; let set. Using melted candy in cut bag, pipe white dots; let set. Use melted candy to attach lollipop sticks to backs of eggs; let set. Wrap entire craft circle with foil; position circle inside basket. Attach handle on basket edge with melted candy. Insert eggs, trimming sticks if needed to vary heights. Peel lemon leaves off candy; attach around basket with melted candy. Use dry brush to brush Pearl Dust over all. Each egg serves 1.

†Brand confectionery coating.

▶ He Spotted More Eggs!

Pans: Oval Set (13½ x 9⅞ in. used), p. 153; 3-D Bunny, p. 206; Cookie Sheet, Cooling Grid, p. 154
Tips: 1A, 2, 3, 16, 233, p. 142-143
Colors:* Leaf Green, Lemon Yellow, Royal Blue, Violet, Rose, p. 136
Recipes: Buttercream, Color Flow Icings, Roll-Out Cookies, p. 114
Also: Hoppy Easter Colored Metal Cutter Set, p. 208; White Candy Melts®†, p. 166; 4 in. Lollipop Sticks, p. 169; Wooden Dowel Rods, p. 232; Parchment Triangles, p. 140; Color Flow Mix, p. 137; Cake Boards, Fanci-Foil Wrap, p. 233; candy-coated chocolates, jelly beans, 1 x 12 in. ribbon, cornstarch

In advance: Make cookie eggs. Prepare and roll out dough; cut 13 eggs using cutter from set. Bake and cool. Using tinted full-strength color flow, outline cookies with tip 3; let set. Flow in using thinned color flow in cut parchment bag; add dots of white color flow and let set. With melted candy, attach lollipop stick to back of 1 cookie, leaving 2 in. exposed to insert into cake.

Bake and cool bunny and 1-layer oval cakes using firm-textured batter such as pound cake. Position oval cake on foil-covered cake board. Ice smooth and prepare for Stacked Construction (p. 112). Position bunny cake over dowel rods. Ice area inside ears; smooth with finger dipped in cornstarch. Use tip 1A to build up icing for arms. Outline legs, arms and mouth with tip 3. Cover body with tip 16 stars; pipe tip 16 rosette tail. Attach jelly bean nose and candy eyes with tip 2 dots. Insert egg on stick into cake between arms. Tie ribbon into a bow; attach with icing. Attach cookies to cake sides. Pipe pull-out grass border using tip 233 and tip 2 in tight spaces. Cakes serve 27; each cookie serves 1.

*Combine Violet with Rose for violet shown.

▼ Uncle Sam & Lady Liberty

Pan: Cookie Sheet, p. 154
Tips: 2A, 3, 4, 7, 21, p. 142-143
Colors:* Royal Blue, Lemon Yellow, Golden Yellow, Red-Red, Christmas Red, Kelly Green, Copper (skin tone), Brown, Black, p. 136
Fondant/Gum Paste: White Ready-To-Use Rolled Fondant (24 oz.), p. 130; Gum-Tex™, Rolling Pin, Roll & Cut Mat, p. 133; Brush Set, p. 131
Recipes: Buttercream Icing (stiff consistency), p. 114; Thinned Fondant Adhesive, p. 115
Also: 2008 Pattern Book (Hat, Crown), p. 128; Silly Feet! Silicone Baking Cups, p. 147; Stars and Stripes Party Picks, p. 210; 4 in. Lollipop Sticks, p. 169; cornstarch, knife, waxed paper, spatula

In advance: Prepare fondant pieces. Mix 2 teaspoons Gum-Tex into 24 oz. of fondant. Tint 1¼ in. ball skin tone, 1 in. ball red, ¾ in. ball blue, 1½ in. ball green; reserve remaining white. Roll out ⅛ in. thick. Use pattern to cut crown. For hat use pattern to cut white base. Cut red and blue strips about ⅛ in. wide for stripes; attach with damp brush. Let all pieces dry on cornstarch-dusted surface. Attach lollipop stick to back of hats with thinned fondant adhesive.

Bake and cool cupcakes in silicone cups supported by cookie sheet. Pipe tip 2A head, building up for dimension; round with spatula. For arms, cut lollipop sticks to 3 in. long. Insert 1½ in. deep through tip 21 into bag of icing; squeeze as you pull out stick. For hands, divide skin tone fondant into 4ths. Roll each piece into a ball and flatten slightly. Shape hand and cut slits for fingers. Clean icing off ½ in. of iced arm; attach hand. Insert arms in cupcake. Use tip 3 to pipe dot or outline eyes; outline and pipe in mouths. Use tip 7 to pipe dot noses and tip 4 to pipe outline or pull-out hair. Insert flag picks; curl fingers around. Attach crown; insert hat. Each serves 1.

*Combine Red-Red with Christmas Red for red shown.
Combine Lemon Yellow with Golden Yellow for yellow shown.
Combine Brown with Red-Red for brown shown.

▲ Stars Bursting in Air

Pans: Standard Muffin, Cookie Sheet, Cooling Grid, p. 154
Tip: 1M (2110), p. 143
Recipes: Buttercream Icing, Roll-Out Cookies, p. 114
Also: Cupcake Party Stand, p. 146; Nesting Stars Metal Cutter Set, Patriotic Stars Standard Baking Cups, p. 210; Red, Blue Colored Sugars, p. 211

Make cookie stars. Prepare and roll out dough; cut stars using smallest cutter from set. Sprinkle with colored sugars. Bake and cool cookies and cupcakes. Ice cupcakes with tip 1M swirl. Place in stand; position star cookies. Each serves 1.

◀ Red, White and BBQ!

Pan: Mini Star, p. 209
Also: Stars Nesting Metal Cutter Set, Stars and Stripes
   Party Picks, p. 210; hot roll mix, ground beef, cheese,
   lettuce, bread knife, scissors

In advance: Make rolls following package directions
(2 stars for each sandwich). Grease Mini Star pan.
Press prepared hot roll mix into cavities. Let rise and bake
15 to 18 minutes. When cool, trim rolls to level of pan.

Season ground beef to taste. Press 3 oz. beef into
largest star cutter; remove cutter. Grill or broil until
cooked. Cut cheese stars using largest star cutter.
Build sandwich with roll, lettuce, burger and
cheese topped by roll. Trim lettuce to follow star
shape; insert pick. Each serves 1.

▶ Skyrocket Sandwich

Fondant/Gum Paste: Round and Star Cut-Outs™, p. 132
Also: Patriotic Foil Pix, p. 210; assorted sandwich
   breads, lunchmeats and cheeses

Cut bread and sandwich fixings using largest
round cutter. Stack, alternating layers and
colors; secure with pick. Use cutters to cut
additional cheese stars; arrange around
sandwich stack. Each serves 1.

▼ American Made

Pans: Stars and Stripes, p. 209; Cookie Sheet, Cooling
   Grid, p. 154
Tips: 3, 21, p. 142-143
Recipes: Buttercream Icing, Roll-Out Cookies, p. 114
Also: Red, Blue Sparkle Gel, p. 137; Star Comfort Grip™
   Cutter, p. 210; Tapered Spatula, p. 140; Cake Boards,
   Fanci-Foil Wrap, p. 233; ruler, toothpicks, waxed paper,
   cornstarch

For stars: Prepare and roll out dough; cut about 10
cookies using star cutter. Bake and cool. Decorate
with Sparkle Gel outlines in starburst pattern.

For flag: Position cake on foil-wrapped
board. Ice smooth. Mark 3½ x 4¾ in.
wide corner area; cover with blue
gel. In corner, mark 11 vertical
rows, about ⅜ in. apart; pipe tip 3
icing dots, alternating rows of
5 and 4 dots. Flatten slightly with
spatula dipped in cornstarch.
Mark 13 stripes, 1 in. wide;
outline and pipe in
alternating stripes
with red gel.
Add tip 21 star
bottom border.
Position cake
board on plate to
raise it about 1 in.;
position cookies.
Cake serves 12;
each cookie
serves 1.

The Big Event!

This isn't just any party—someone's life is changing in an exciting new way and everyone's coming to celebrate. These are the cakes to greet them with. For the mom-to-be, the sweet nursery toybox of fondant shown here, filled with candy toys. For the newly confirmed, a twist on the traditional cross cake, featuring fondant mosaic tiles in eye-pleasing colors. To honor the grad, a 2-tier cake capped by a candy mortarboard, fondant diploma and a lush rose garland. Look ahead for the perfect design to help you mark the moment.

Instructions for projects shown on these two pages are on page 62.

Toy Box Tot

Pans: 8, 12 x 2 in. Square, p. 153

Tips: 5, 8, p. 142

Colors:* Lemon Yellow, Golden Yellow, Rose, Kelly Green, Violet, Royal Blue, p. 136

Fondant/Gum Paste: White Ready-To-Use Rolled Fondant (96 oz.), p. 130; Alphabet/Number Cut-Outs™, p. 132; Brush Set, Easy-Glide Fondant Smoother, p. 131; Gum-Tex™, Rolling Pin, Rolling Pin Guide Rings, Roll & Cut Mat, p. 133

Candy: White Candy Melts®†, Primary, Garden Candy Color Sets, p. 166; 2-Pk. Baby Candy Molds, p. 168

Topper: Baby Face, p. 237

Recipes: Buttercream, Royal Icings, p. 114

Also: 2008 Pattern Book (Toy Box Lid, Base, Short Sides, Long Sides), p. 128; Parchment Triangles, p. 140; Dowel Rods, p. 232; Cake Boards, Fanci-Foil Wrap, p. 233; Meringue Powder, p. 137; cornstarch, waxed paper, tissue

In advance: Make toy box. Combine 2 teaspoons Gum-Tex with 21 oz. fondant. Roll out ³⁄₁₆ in. thick using guide rings. Using patterns, cut 2 long sides, 2 short sides, 1 lid and 2 bases; cut one base vertically in thirds. Let dry on cornstarch-dusted board. **Also:** Make puddle dots (p. 120) on waxed paper-covered board using thinned royal icing in rose, yellow, green, violet and blue. Make 7-9 puddles in each color, 1 in. diameter. Make extras to allow for

breakage and let dry. **And:** Make candy toys using painting method (p. 125); make 2-3 of each shape in molds except sun, moon and star. Refrigerate until firm; unmold.

Prepare 1-layer cakes for Stacked Construction (p. 112) and rolled fondant (p. 115). For 8 in. cake, tint 24 oz. fondant rose; for 12 in. cake, tint 48 oz. yellow. Cover cakes and smooth with Fondant Smoother; reserve remaining fondant. Position cakes on double-thick foil-wrapped boards. Pipe tip 8 bead bottom borders in buttercream. Tint 1 oz. portions of fondant pastel blue, green and violet. Separately roll out, along with reserved rose and yellow fondant, ¹⁄₁₆ in. thick using guide rings. Cut ¼ in. wide strips for toy box trim; attach to box pieces with damp brush, cutting to fit as needed. Assemble box with royal icing; let dry. Cut letters and numbers for toy box using Cut-Outs; attach to box with damp brush. Attach puddles to cake sides with buttercream. Position base pieces which were cut in thirds in box to raise baby topper. Fill box with candy toys and position topper. Attach lid with royal icing or melted candy, supporting with tissue until set. Position toy box on cake. Serves 68.

*Combine Lemon Yellow with Golden Yellow for yellow shown.

Cradled Favors

Fondant: White Ready-To-Use Rolled Fondant, p. 130; Fine Tip Primary Colors FoodWriter™ Edible Color Markers, p. 130; Brush Set, p. 131

Color: Copper (skin tone), p. 136

Also: Pink, Blue Pearlized Baby Cradles, p. 234;

candy-coated chocolates, cornstarch

Tint fondant copper. For each head, roll a ¾ in. ball of fondant; let dry on cornstarch-dusted surface. Draw facial features with black FoodWriter. Roll a tiny ball of fondant for nose; attach with damp brush. Fill cradles with chocolates; position head. Each serves 1.

Playtime Pop-Up!

Pan: Petite Loaf, p. 154

Candy: White Candy Melts®† (2 pks.), Primary, Garden Candy Color Sets, p. 166; Smiley Face Lollipop Mold, p. 168

Also: Parchment Triangles, p. 140; Mini Pacifiers Candies, p. 235; waxed paper

For toy boxes, make candy shells (p. 125) ¼ in. thick in pan cavities; refrigerate until firm and unmold. For lids, make ¼ in. thick candy plaques (p. 126) in pan cavities; refrigerate until firm and unmold. Using candy colors, tint melted candy blue and pink; pipe trim and message using cut parchment bag. Let set. For faces, tint melted white candy with orange to achieve skin tone; mold in Smiley Face Mold and refrigerate until firm. Unmold and position on waxed paper. Tint melted candy black; pipe facial features using cut parchment bag. Pipe nose and ears with melted candy; let set. Position candies in toy box; position candy face in center. Attach lid to box with melted candy; let set. Each serves 1.

◀ Stork at Your Service

Pans: Stork Express, p. 156; 11 x 15 x 2 in. Sheet, p. 153

Tips: 3, 12, 16, 17, p. 142-143

Colors:* Violet, Pink, Copper (skin tone), Kelly Green, Leaf Green, Royal Blue, Black, Lemon Yellow, Golden Yellow, p. 136

Fondant/Gum Paste: White Ready-To-Use Rolled Fondant (80 oz.), p. 130; Funny Flowers Cut-Outs™, p. 132; Cutter/Embosser, Brush Set, Easy-Glide Fondant Smoother, p. 131; Rolling Pin, Roll & Cut Mat, p. 133

Recipe: Buttercream Icing, p. 114

Also: 101 Cookie Cutters Set, p. 162; Cake Board, Fanci-Foil Wrap, p. 233; Plastic Dowel Rods, p. 232; 16 x 23 in. triple-thick cardboard or ½ in. thick foamcore board, knife, plastic ruler

Bake and cool stork cake and two 1-layer sheet cakes. Place stork cake on foil-wrapped board. Ice smooth cake sides, background areas and inside blanket. Outline body, feet, beak, cap and baby blanket with tip 3; cover all (except wings) with tip 16 stars. Add tip 16 pull-out star wings. Pipe in tip 3 eye on stork; add tip 3 dot pupil. Pipe in tip 12 ball baby head. Outline baby's eyes and mouth with tip 3.

Position sheet cakes side-by-side on base. Ice together at seam; prepare cakes for rolled fondant (p. 115). Tint 24 oz. fondant Leaf Green and 48 oz. light blue. Cover cake to form sky and grass (p. 121). For sun, tint a 2 in. ball Lemon Yellow; roll out ⅛ in. thick and cut circle using largest round cutter from set. Cut ⅛ x 1½ in. long strips for sun rays. For clouds, roll out white fondant ⅛ in. thick; cut random cloud shapes with knife. Attach sun, rays and clouds with damp brush. Position stork on sheet cake. Tint portions of fondant pink, violet and kelly green. Roll out ⅛ in. thick. Cut flowers using medium and large Cut-Outs; roll small ball centers and attach with damp brush. Attach flowers to cake with damp brush. For stems, cut ⅛ in. strips in various lengths; attach. Cut and attach grass tufts. Pipe tip 16 shell bottom border on stork and tip 17 shell bottom border on sheet cake. Serves 72.

*Combine Violet with Rose for violet shown.

▶ Bear Hugs for Baby

Pan: Teddy Bear, p. 156

Tips: 4, 5, 16, p. 142-143

Colors:* Brown, Red-Red, Black, p. 136

Fondant/Gum Paste: White Ready-To-Use Rolled Fondant (24 oz.), Pastel Colors Multi Pack Fondant (2), p. 130; Gum-Tex™, Rolling Pin, Roll & Cut Mat, p. 133; Cutter/Embosser, Brush Set, p. 131

Recipe: Buttercream Icing, p. 114

Also: Cake Board, Fanci-Foil Wrap, p. 233; Piping Gel, p. 137; 14 x 18 x ¼ in. foamcore board, spatula, knife, ruler, cornstarch

In advance: Prepare fondant blanket. Roll out pastel colors ⅛ in. thick and cut 4 in. squares, 3 in each color. Position on foil-wrapped board, beginning 1 in. from edges; secure with piping gel. Use ridged wheel of Cutter/Embosser to imprint quilting lines, 1 in. apart and at 45° angle. Add ½ teaspoon Gum-Tex to 8 oz. white fondant. Roll out ⅛ in. thick. Cut 1 in. strips and pleat to form ruffle. Attach to board with piping gel. Cover seam with tip 4 bead border.

Position bear cake on foil-wrapped cake board. Pipe in ears, eyes, paw pads and foot pads with tip 5; pipe in pupils, nose and mouth with tip 4 (smooth all with finger dipped in cornstarch). Cover bear with tip 16 stars. Serves 12.

*Combine Brown with Red-Red for brown shown.

◀ Powers Beyond Mortal Moms!

Pan: 6 x 2 in. Round, p. 153

Tips: 2, 5, 16, 17, p. 142-143

Colors: Royal Blue, Lemon Yellow, p. 136

Candy: Mini Baby Icons Mold, p. 237; White, Light Cocoa Candy Melts®† (1 pk. each), Primary, Garden Candy Color Sets, p. 166

Recipes: Buttercream, Royal Icings, p. 114

Also: Super Mom-To-Be Cake Topper, p. 237; Cake Circles, Fanci-Foil Wrap, p. 233; Meringue Powder, p. 137; waxed paper

In advance: On waxed paper, using royal icing, make 15 tip 16 drop flowers with tip 2 dot centers. Make extras to allow for breakage; let dry. **Also:** Make candies. Melt candy and tint using candy colors; lighten cocoa by mixing with white for brown shown. Mold about 15 candies, filling cavities only half full. Refrigerate until firm, unmold.

Ice 2-layer cake smooth with buttercream. Pipe tip 5 swirl clouds on cake sides. Pipe tip 17 shell bottom border. Position candies, flowers and topper. Serves 12.

†Brand confectionery coating.

▼ Your Proudest Day

Pans: Oval Pan Set (7¾ x 5⅝ in., 16½ x 12⅜ in. used), p. 153
Tips: 2, 3, 20, 129, 225, 349, p. 142-143
Colors: Rose, Kelly Green, Brown, p. 136
Fondant/Gum Paste: White Ready-To-Use Rolled Fondant (72 oz.), p. 130; Gum-Tex™, Rolling Pin, Roll & Cut Mat, p. 133; Easy-Glide Fondant Smoother, Brush Set, p. 131
Ornaments: Sweet Couple, p 226; Newborn Baby Figurines, p. 235
Recipes: Buttercream, Royal Icings, p. 114; Thinned Fondant Adhesive, p. 115
Also: Italic Make-Any-Message Press Set, p. 139; Dowel Rods, p. 232; 14 x 20 in. Show 'N Serve™ Cake Boards, Cake Circles, Fanci-Foil Wrap, p. 233; Color Tray, p. 130, Meringue Powder, p. 137; 4 in. Lollipop Sticks, p. 169; waxed paper, ruler, cornstarch, knife

In advance: Make bench. Tint 2 in. fondant ball light brown; knead in ¼ teaspoon Gum-Tex. Roll out ⅛ in. thick. Cut 1¼ x 3¼ in. rectangle for seat. For legs, trim 4 lollipop sticks to 3¼ in. Roll out fondant ¹⁄₁₆ in. thick. Cut ⅝ x 1¼ in. strip. Brush back with damp brush and wrap around one end of stick leaving 2 in. exposed to insert into cake; smooth seam. Let all pieces dry on cornstarch-dusted board. When dry, attach legs to seat using fondant adhesive; let dry at least 48 hours. **Also:** Make royal icing drop flowers. Pipe 75 with tip 225 in light rose and 75 with tip 129 in dark rose (make extras to allow for breakage). Pipe tip 2 dot centers; let dry. **And:** Use thinned royal icing to paint dress and shoes on ornament; let dry. Roll out white fondant ⅛ in. thick. Cut a 3 x 3 in. piece to wrap around baby figurine. Brush back with damp brush and position on couple ornament; let dry.

Bake and cool cakes using smallest and largest oval pans from set. Prepare cakes for rolled fondant (p. 115) and Stacked Construction (p. 112); cover and smooth with Fondant Smoother. Sponge thinned light green royal icing onto lower half of cake sides using crushed waxed paper (p. 120). Stack cakes on foil-wrapped cake board cut to fit; position bench, inserting exposed end of sticks into cake. Using buttercream, pipe tip 20 shell bottom borders. Attach flowers; pipe tip 349 leaves. Imprint message on cake using message press; write tip 3 message. Position ornament. Serves 27.

▶ Baby's Our Blessing

Pans: 6, 8 x 2 in. Round, p. 153, Decorator Preferred® 10 x 3 in. Round, p. 152
Tips: 2, 2A, 4, 8, 24, 102, 126, p. 142-143
Color: Royal Blue, p. 136
Ornament: Cradle, p. 237
Recipes: Buttercream, Royal Icings, p. 114
Also: Cake Circles, 14 in. Silver Cake Base, p. 233; Dowel Rods, p. 232; Cake Dividing Set, p. 135; Meringue Powder, p. 137; Flower Nail No. 7, p. 140; waxed paper, toothpicks, ruler

In advance: Make royal icing flowers. Make 24 tip 102 roses with tip 8 bases and 18 tip 126 roses with tip 2A bases (p. 118). Make 214 tip 24 drop flowers with tip 2 dot centers. Make extras of all to allow for breakage; let dry.

Bake and cool 2-layer 6 and 8 in. cakes 4 in. high and 2-layer 10 in. cake 5 in. high (bake two 2½ in. layers for a 5 in. high cake). Ice cakes smooth with buttercream and prepare for Stacked Construction (p. 112). Use Cake Dividing Set to mark 6 in. cake into 6ths, 8 in. cake into 8ths and 10 in. cake into 10ths. Assemble cakes on Cake Base. Using buttercream, pipe tip 2 double drop strings between division points, 2 and 1½ in. from top edge of cake. Attach drop flowers in a garland 1 in. from top edge of cake. Pipe tip 4 bead bottom borders. Attach smaller roses at division points. Attach larger roses around base. Position ornament. Serves 60.

▶ Blessings for Her

Pan: Cross, p. 209
Tip: 3, p. 142
Color: Rose, p. 136
Fondant/Gum Paste: White Ready-To-Use Rolled Fondant (48 oz.), White Pearl Dust, p. 130; Rolling Pin, Roll & Cut Mat, p. 133; Easy-Glide Fondant Smoother, Brush Set, Fondant Ribbon Cutter/Embosser Set, p. 131
Recipes: Buttercream, Royal Icings, p. 114
Also: Cake Boards, Fanci-Foil Wrap, p. 233; Meringue Powder, p. 137; knife, ruler

Prepare cake for rolled fondant (p. 115). Tint 30 oz. fondant rose and cover cake; smooth with Fondant Smoother. Roll out white fondant ⅛ in. thick and cut out cross using top of pan as pattern (sections are 2 in. wide). Position cross on cake, securing with damp brush. Cut lattice strips using Ribbon Cutter/Embosser with 2 straight-edge wheels and ¼ in. spacer. Position strips diagonally on cross, spacing ½ in. apart. Secure with damp brush. Trim off excess with a sharp knife as strips are positioned. Using royal icing, pipe tip 3 dots on lattice strips. Let dry 1 hour. Roll ½ in. flattened balls of white fondant and place in spaces between lattice, securing with damp brush. Using a dry brush, brush white areas of cake top with Pearl Dust. Roll ½ in. balls of rose fondant and attach for bottom border with damp brush. Serves 12.

◀ Faith Mosaic

Pan: Cross, p. 209
Tip: 3, p. 142
Color: Royal Blue, p. 136
Fondant/Gum Paste: White Ready-To-Use Rolled Fondant (48 oz.), White Pearl Dust, p. 130; Square Cut-Outs™, p. 132; Rolling Pin, Roll & Cut Mat, p. 133; Brush Set, Easy-Glide Fondant Smoother, p. 131
Recipe: Buttercream Icing, p. 114
Also: Communion Boy Topper, p. 192; 101 Cookie Cutters Set, p. 162; Cake Board, Fanci-Foil Wrap, p. 233; Parchment Triangles, p. 140, cornstarch

Position cake on foil-wrapped board cut 1 in. larger on each side. Prepare cake for rolled fondant (p. 115). Cover cake; smooth with Fondant Smoother. Roll out a small amount of fondant ⅜ in. thick; cut platform for topper using medium round cookie cutter. Let platform dry on cornstarch-dusted cake board. Tint 4 oz. portions of fondant light, medium and dark blue. Roll out colors ⅛ in. thick; cut mosaic squares using smallest Cut-Out. Position various color squares on cake top and board base; trim squares as needed to fit around cake and secure with damp brush. Pipe tip 3 bead bottom border. Brush squares with Pearl Dust. Position platform and topper. Serves 12.

◀ Greeting La Quinceañera

Pans: 6, 8, 10 x 2 in. Round, p. 153

Tips: 2, 3, 4, 225, p. 142

Colors:* Violet, Rose, p. 136

Ornament: La Quinceañera, p. 227

Recipes: Buttercream, Royal Icings, p. 114

Also: 2008 Pattern Book (Triple Drop Strings), p. 128; 8, 10, 12 in. Plates, 9 in. Twist Legs (2 pks.) from Crystal-Clear Cake Divider Set, p. 228; Cake Circles, Cake Boards, p. 233; Romantic Heart Base, p. 227; Flower Former Set, p. 140; 4 in. Lollipop Sticks (3 pks.), p. 169; White Pearl Dust, p. 130; Clear Vanilla Extract, p. 139; Meringue Powder, p. 137; Brush Set, p. 131; 10 x 2 in. craft foam circle, silk roses, waxed paper, ruler, paper

Two weeks in advance: Prepare royal icing decorations. Make 300 tip 225 drop flowers with tip 2 dot centers; let dry. **Also:** Make triple drop strings. Make several copies of pattern and attach to outside of largest flower former; tape waxed paper over pattern to cover. Pipe 40 tip 3 triple drop strings; make extras to allow for breakage and let dry. **And:** Prepare lollipop sticks with royal icing. On 45 sticks, pipe 4 tip 2 dots (1 at each end and two 1 in. from end); attach a drop flower at center. On 74 sticks, pipe 3 tip 2 dots (1 at each end and 1 at center); attach 2 drop flowers between center and end dots. Brush sticks with mixture of clear vanilla and Pearl Dust following package directions. Let all pieces dry thoroughly.

Ice 2-layer cakes smooth with buttercream and prepare for Push-in Pillar Construction (p. 112). Pipe tip 4 bead bottom borders.

At reception: Assemble cakes, positioning base cake on craft circle. Pipe tip 2 beads around pillars. Pipe tip 3 royal icing scallops around edge of plates, ¾ in. apart and with point ¼ in. from edge. Position prepared sticks, tilting inward from scallop points to cake top; alternate 1 single-flower stick with 2 double-flower sticks. Pipe tip 3 bead top borders with buttercream. Attach triple drop strings with tip 3 and royal icing, positioning slightly behind bead borders and between single-flower sticks. Attach flower to top border where triple strings meet. Position topper on top half of heart base; position on top tier. Position silk roses under base cake. Serves 60.

*Combine Violet with Rose for violet shown.

▶ Honoring the Heritage

Pans: 6, 10, 14 x 2 in. Square, p. 153

Tip: 3, p. 142

Fondant: White Ready-To-Use Rolled Fondant (192 oz.), p. 130; Round Cut-Outs™, p. 132; Rolling Pin, Roll & Cut Mat, p. 133; Easy-Glide Fondant Smoother, Brush Set, 131

Candy: Hanukkah Lollipop Mold, p. 202; White Candy Melts®†, 8 in. Lollipop Sticks, p. 169

Also: 2008 Pattern Book (Star-of-David), p. 128; 8, 12 and 16 in. Decorator Preferred® Smooth-Edge Square Plates, p. 231; White Pearl Dust (3 pks.), p. 130; Gum-Tex™, p. 133; Parchment Triangles, p. 140; Cake Boards, Fanci-Foil Wrap, p. 233; 9 in. Baker's Best® Disposable Pillars with Rings (2 sets), p. 229; Meringue Powder, p. 137; ⅜ in. and ⅞ in. wide ribbon (3½ yards each), double stick tape, cornstarch, knife

In advance: Make large and small stars. Knead 2 teaspoons Gum-Tex into 24 oz. fondant. Roll out ⅛ in. thick. Use pattern and knife to cut out large star. Cut ¼ in. strips for borders; brush backs with damp brush and attach to large star. Dust with Pearl Dust and let dry on cornstarch-dusted surface. When dry, turn over and attach lollipop stick to back using melted candy; leave 4 in. extended to insert into cake. Make 108 small stars (make extras to allow for breakage). Dust cavities of candy mold with Pearl Dust. To mold stars, cut fondant circles using medium round Cut-Out; press firmly and evenly into star cavities, unmold. Trim about ¹⁄₁₆ in. off 4 side points of 36 stars. Let all dry on cornstarch-dusted surface.

Prepare 2-layer cakes for rolled fondant (p. 115); cover and smooth with Fondant Smoother. Prepare for Push-In Pillar Construction (p. 112). Wrap ⅞ in. ribbon border around bottom edge of each cake; overlap ends and secure with double stick tape. Wrap ⅜ in. ribbon around cakes, allowing ½ in. space from ⅞ in. ribbon; overlap ends and secure with double stick tape.

At reception: Assemble cakes. Attach stars using melted candy in cut parchment bag or royal icing and tip 3. Use 2 trimmed stars on each side of 8 in. plate, 3 on each side of 12 in. plate and 4 on each side of 16 in. plate to fit width properly. Insert large star. Serves 113.

†Brand confectionery coating.

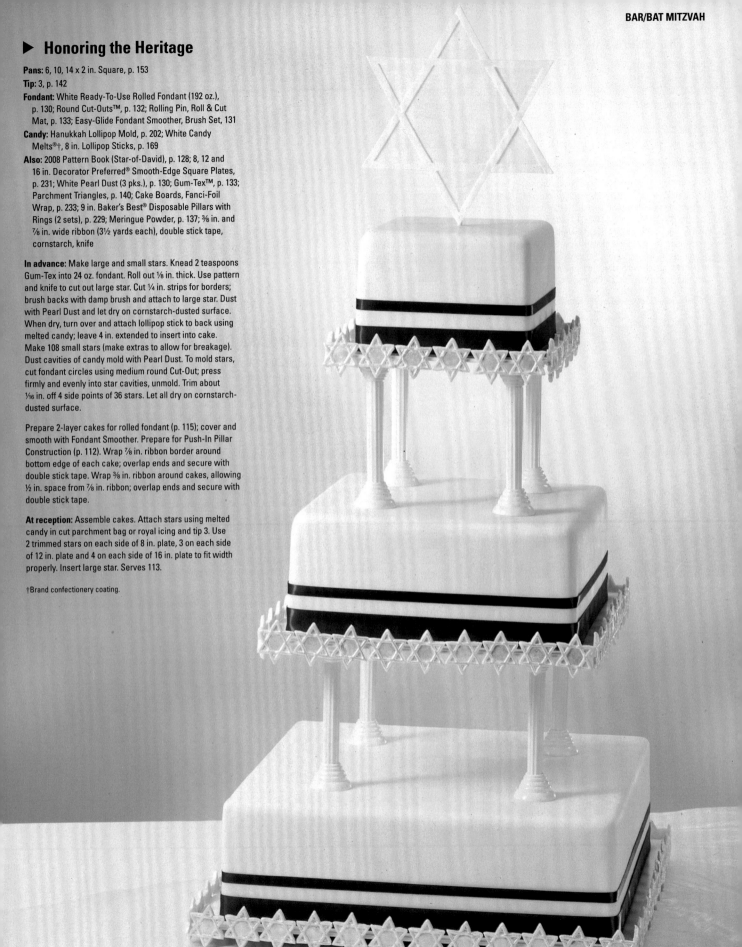

▶ The Future's in Their Hands!

Pan: Cookie Sheet, p. 154
Tips: 1, 1A, 2, 3, p. 142
Colors:* Brown, Red-Red, Copper (skin tone), Black, Brown, Royal Blue, p. 136
Fondant/Gum Paste: White Ready-To-Use Rolled Fondant, Neon Colors Fondant Multi Pack, p. 130; Square Cut-Outs™, p. 132; Brush Set, p. 131; Rolling Pin, Roll & Cut Mat, p. 133
Recipe: Buttercream Icing (stiff consistency), p. 114
Also: Silly-Feet! Silicone Baking Cups, p. 147; 6 in. Cookie Treat Sticks, p. 165, knife, cornstarch

In advance: Make arms, mortarboards and diploma (p. 122).

Bake and cool cupcakes in silicone cups supported by cookie sheet. Cover cupcake tops with tip 1A icing mound. Smooth with spatula to create a rounded head. Pipe tip 2 dot noses and tip 3 dot cheeks (flatten and smooth with finger dipped in cornstarch). Outline and pipe in tip 2 mouths. Pipe tip 3 curly hair. Pipe tip 2 outline eyes on boys and tip 3 dot eyes, tip 2 dot pupils and tip 1 pull-out eyelashes on girls. Attach mortarboards and insert arms in cupcakes. For tassel/cord, roll out yellow fondant 1⁄16 in. thick and cut a 1 x 1½ in. rectangle. Cut small slits for fringe on 1 in. side and roll up. For cord, flatten end of tassel without fringe and trim to form a thin string; attach to mortarboard top with damp brush. For top button, roll a small fondant ball and attach with damp brush. Each serves 1.

*Combine Brown with Red-Red for brown shown.

◀ Congratulate the Graduate

Pans: 8 x 2 in. Round, 12 x 18 x 2 in. Sheet, p. 153; Topping Off Success, p. 211
Tips: 1, 5, 10, 12, 18, 102, 104, p. 142-143
Colors: Royal Blue, Moss Green, Lemon Yellow, p. 136
Fondant/Gum Paste: White Ready-To-Use Rolled Fondant (66 oz.), p. 130; Brush Set, Easy-Glide Fondant Smoother, p. 131; Ready-To-Use Gum Paste (1 pk.), Rolling Pin, Roll & Cut Mat, p. 133
Candy: White Candy Melts®† (2 pks.), Primary Candy Color Set, p. 166
Recipes: Buttercream, Royal Icings, p. 114
Also: 7 in. Baker's Best Disposable Pillars with Rings, p. 229; 9 in. Decorator Preferred® Scalloped Plate, p. 231; Plastic and Wooden Dowel Rods, Flower Spikes, p. 232; Fine Tip Primary Colors FoodWriter™ Edible Color Markers, p. 130; Green Leaves (3 pks.), p. 223; Flower Nail No. 7, p. 140; Cake Boards, Fanci-Foil Wrap, p. 233; Female Grad Bobbling Topper, p. 212; Meringue Powder, p. 137; waxed paper, cornstarch, foil, 22-gauge green florist wire (55 pieces 6 in. long), 20-gauge green florist wire (30 pieces 6 in. long and 2 pieces 36 in. long), green florist tape, wire cutters, bubble wrap, craft block, knife, ruler, hot glue gun

In advance: Make royal icing floral garlands (p. 120), using 35 tip 102 apple blossoms with tip 1 dot centers and 30 tip 104 roses with tip 12 bases. **Also:** Make candy plaque (p. 126) mortarboard in Topping Off Success pan using painting method (p. 125). Refrigerate until firm; unmold. **And:** Make diploma (p. 122).

Prepare 1-layer cakes for rolled fondant (p. 115). Tint fondant blue. Cover cakes; smooth with Fondant Smoother. Prepare for Push-In Pillar Construction (p. 112). Pipe tip 18 shell bottom borders using buttercream.

At reception: Assemble cakes. Insert 1st flower spike into back of 8 in. cake; insert 1st garland section and curve around and down to bottom cake. (If needed, place a small amount of fondant in flower spike to secure garland.) Insert 2nd flower spike in back of sheet cake at end of 1st garland. Insert 2nd garland section and curve around cake to the front. Position diploma. Cut white plastic dowel rods to support candy plaque on angle. Position and attach candy plaque with melted candy. Position topper. Serves 46.

DIPLOMA

Class

of

2008

†Brand confectionery coating.

▼ A Brilliant Success

Pan: Little Hero, p. 160

Tips: 3, 8, 16, 18, p. 142-143

Colors:* Royal Blue, Copper (skin tone), Brown, Red-Red, Christmas Red, Black, Lemon Yellow, Golden Yellow, p. 136

Recipe: Buttercream Icing, p. 114

Also: 2008 Pattern Book (Mortarboard), p. 128; Cake Boards, Fanci-Foil Wrap, p. 233; cardboard, scissors, toothpicks, cornstarch

Use pattern to cut mortarboard from cardboard and cover with foil. Position cake on foil-wrapped cake board. Trim off collar and hose. Build up diploma area with icing. Ice smooth cake sides, background areas, inside of sleeve, bottom of diploma, inside mouth, whites of eyes and mortarboard. Outline all areas with tip 3. Cover with tip 16 stars; overpipe nose and cheeks. Pipe tip 3 bead heart tongue, dot pupils (flatten and smooth with finger dipped in cornstarch) and string eyebrows. Pipe tip 18 shell bottom border. Position mortarboard; pipe tip 18 swirl hair. Pipe tip 8 dot button (flatten) and tip 3 strings for tassel. Serves 12.

*Combine Brown with Red-Red for brown shown. Combine Lemon Yellow with Golden Yellow for yellow shown. Combine Red-Red with Christmas Red for red shown.

▲ A Quick Study

Pans: Classic Wonder Mold, p. 155; Decorator Preferred® 9 x 2 in. Round, p. 152

Tips: 3, 6, p. 142

Colors:* Royal Blue, Lemon Yellow, Golden Yellow, Black, Brown, Red-Red, p. 136

Recipe: Buttercream Icing, p. 114

Fondant/Gum Paste: White Ready-To-Use Rolled Fondant (24 oz.), p. 130; Rolling Pin, Roll & Cut Mat, Gum-Tex™, p. 133; Cutter/Embosser, Brush Set, p. 131

Also: 2008 Pattern Book (Head, Hand, Mortarboard), p. 128; Silly Feet! Cake Stand, p. 145; White Candy Melts®†, p. 166; Plastic Dowel Rods, p. 232; 11¾ in. Lollipop Sticks, p. 169; ruler, knife, cornstarch, cardboard

In advance: Make head and mortarboard. Tint fondant: 12 oz. blue and 6 oz. light brown. Add ½ teaspoon Gum-Tex to 4 oz. blue and ¾ teaspoon Gum-Tex to 6 oz. brown. Roll out ⅛ in. thick. Use patterns to cut out head and mortarboard. Set on cornstarch-dusted board to dry. Reserve remaining fondant.

Bake and cool Wonder Mold and 1-layer 9 in. round cakes using firm-textured batter such as pound cake. Stack cakes on stand. Using a spatula, ice shirt area smooth; ice gown, running edge of spatula vertically over icing to form pleats. Using tip 6, outline and pipe in tie. Pat smooth. Attach head to mortarboard using melted candy; let set. Using melted candy, attach 3 lollipop sticks to back of head leaving 5 in. extended; let set, then insert into cake (trim sticks as needed to fit). Pipe tip 3 outline eyes, pipe in mouth and swirl hair. Roll three ½ in. fondant balls, flatten slightly and attach for nose and cheeks using a damp brush. For tassel and string, tint fondant yellow and roll out ⅛ in. thick. Cut a 2½ x ¼ in. strip for cord; cut a 3 x 1½ in. rectangle for tassel. Fringe long side of rectangle, using knife to cut slits ⅛ in. apart to within ½ in. of top edge. Roll and smooth top for tassel. For button, roll a 1½ in. fondant ball and flatten. Attach button, cord and tassel using damp brush. Roll 5½ x 1½ in. logs for arms; position on cake. Cut dowel rod to 6½ in. long; with icing, attach between arms for diploma. Roll out fondant ⅛ in. thick; cut out hands using pattern (reverse for 2nd hand). Attach over diploma with icing. For sleeve and neckline trim, roll out fondant ⅛ in. thick; cut ½ in. wide strips and attach using damp brush. Serves 24.

*Combine Lemon Yellow with Golden Yellow for yellow shown. Combine Brown with Red-Red for brown skin tone shown.

Your Day to Shine

Choose a wedding cake to match the dazzle of diamonds and the sparkle of champagne. Start with the majestic 3-tiered cake at right, that pairs our shimmering Double Ring Topper with brilliant sugared fondant bands. Or discover the lustrous color our new Pearl Dust can bring when brushed on flowers, fondant bows and ruffles. Elsewhere, we introduce great ways to add texture and motion, with graceful curtain-look panels, scrolled stands and Victorian-inspired Lambeth.

Instructions for projects shown on these two pages are on page 72.

Banding Together

Contrasting texture is your best bet for adding excitement to an all-white wedding cake. Here, the ribbed fondant bands, swirls of gum paste roses and a sparkling sugar finish combine to create motion and drama.

Pans: 6 x 2, 8 x 2 Round, p. 153; Decorator Preferred® 10 x 3 in. Round, p. 152

Tip: 3, p. 142

Fondant/Gum Paste: White Ready-To-Use Rolled Fondant (96 oz.), p. 130; Ribbon Cutter/Embosser Set, Easy-Glide Fondant Smoother, Confectionery Tool Set, p. 131; Ready-To-Use Gum Paste (4 pks.), Rolling Pin, Roll & Cut Mat, Brush Set, p. 133; Floral Collection Flower Making Set, p. 132

Topper: Infinity Rings Cake Pick, p. 227

Recipes: Buttercream Icing, p. 114; Gum Paste Adhesive, p. 115

Also: Candlelight Cake Stand (includes 4 flameless votives shown, or use your own tea lights), p. 230; Decorator Preferred® 8, 14 in. Smooth Edge Plates, p. 231; 7½ in. Twist Legs, 10 in. Plate (from Crystal-Clear Cake Divider Set), p. 228; "Hidden" Pillars, p. 229; White Sparkling Sugar, p. 139; Piping Gel, p. 137; ruler, toothpicks, 2 in. craft block (for drying roses)

At least one week in advance: Make 16 large, 17 medium and 20 small gum paste roses (p. 123).

Prepare 2-layer 6, 8 and 10 in. cakes (for 10 in. cake, bake two 2½ in. high layers to make a 5 in. high cake) for Push-In Pillar Construction (p. 112). Prepare cakes for rolled fondant (p. 115). Cover cakes with rolled fondant; smooth with Fondant Smoother. Roll out fondant ⅛ in. thick. Using straight-edge wheels and ½ in. spacer from Ribbon Cutter/ Embosser, cut cake side strips to equal height of each cake. You will need 13 for 6 in. cake, 17 for 8 in. cake, 23 for 10 in. cake. Brush strips with thinned Piping Gel; cover with Sparkling Sugar. Shake off excess sugar. Attach strips to cake sides with damp brush, 1 in. apart. For area between strips, roll ¼ in. diameter logs of fondant to equal height of each cake; attach with damp brush.

At reception: Assemble cakes, using twist legs in 14 in. cake and hidden pillars in 10 in. cake, extending about 1½ in. above cake. Pipe tip 3 ball bottom border on all cakes. Position small roses below 6 in. cake, medium roses below 10 in. cake; insert large roses at base of 14 in. cake. Position topper.** Position votives. Serves 62.*

*The top tier is often saved for the first anniversary. The number of servings given does not include the top tier.

**Always place a separator plate, or a cake board cut to fit, on the cake where you position any figurine or topper. This protects both the cake and your keepsake. For extra stability, secure your figurine to the plate with double-stick craft tape.

That Certain Sparkle

Pan: 9 x 13 x 2 in. Sheet (makes approximately 12 gifts), p. 153

Tip: 3, p. 142

Fondant/Gum Paste: White Ready-To-Use Rolled Fondant (48 oz.), p. 130; Quick Ease Roller, Easy-Glide Fondant Smoother, Cutter/Embosser, Brush Set, p. 131; Gum-Tex™, Rolling Pin, Roll & Cut Mat, p. 133

Recipe: Buttercream Icing, p. 114

Also: Piping Gel, p. 137; White Sparkling Sugar, p. 139; Circle Metal Cookie Cutter, p. 164; ruler, waxed paper, cornstarch, knife

In advance: Make and assemble bows (p. 124) using 10 oz. fondant mixed with 1 teaspoon Gum-Tex. For each loop, cut a 3 x ½ in. strip using straight-edge wheel from Cutter/ Embosser. Fold over and attach ends with damp brush. Dry loops on side. For each knot, cut a 1¾ x ½ in. strip. Brush bows with thinned piping gel and sprinkle with Sparkling Sugar. Let dry, then assemble.

Bake and cool a 2 in. high cake using firm-textured batter such as pound cake; freeze. Use circle cutter to imprint cake top; cut individual cakes using a knife. Prepare cakes for rolled fondant (p. 115); cover and smooth with Fondant Smoother. For ribbons on cakes, roll out fondant ⅛ in. thick. Cut 3 x ½ in. strips using straight-edge wheel from Cutter/Embosser. Attach across cake top and sides using damp brush. Brush ribbons with thinned piping gel and sprinkle with Sparkling Sugar. Using tip 3, attach bow with icing. Each serves 1.

▶ Love's a Bed of Roses

Pans: Heart Pan Set (6, 8, 14 x 2 in. used), p. 153

Tips: 3, 8, 12, 46, 125, p. 142-143

Color: Rose, p. 136

Fondant/Gum Paste: White Ready-To-Use Rolled Fondant (24 oz.), p. 130; Letters & Numbers Gum Paste and Fondant Mold Set, Rolling Pin, Roll & Cut Mat, p. 133; Cutter/Embosser, p. 131

Recipes: Buttercream, Royal Icings, p. 114; Thinned Fondant Adhesive, p. 115

Also: Comfort Grip™ Round Cutter, p. 164; Flower Nail No. 7, p. 140; Cake Board, Fanci-Foil Wrap, p. 233; Meringue Powder, p. 137; Disposable Decorating Bags, p. 140; waxed paper squares, cornstarch, knife

In advance: Using royal icing, make 70 tip 125 roses with tip 12 bases. Let dry. **Also:** Make center heart plaque. Set aside 1 oz. of white fondant; tint remainder light rose. Roll out rose fondant ¼ in. thick. Using 6 and 8 in. pans as patterns, cut 1 fondant heart in each size. Let dry on waxed paper-covered board dusted with cornstarch. **And:** Make monogram. Using white and rose fondant, make 2-tone letters following mold directions. Let dry on cornstarch-dusted board. Using royal icing, attach 6 in. heart to 8 in. heart; edge hearts with tip 3 beads and let dry.

Ice 2-layer 14 in. cake smooth in buttercream, with white sides and rose top. For cake side swags, roll out remaining rose fondant ⅛ in. thick. Cut circles using cutter; cut in half with paring knife. Starting with front point of cake, attach half-circles to cake sides with buttercream, aligning straight edge with top and ending so that half-circles at front point meet. Pipe tip 46 (smooth side up) bands at swag points and at center of swag, approximately 1½ in. apart, on cake sides. Pipe tip 8 ball bottom border. In royal icing, pipe tip 3 bead garlands at bottom edge and center of fondant swags; let dry. Position roses on cake top. Position heart plaque; attach monogram with fondant adhesive. Serves 72.

The Perfect Accent: Our Graceful Cake Knife & Server is a wonderful keepsake of your special day (p. 215).

▶ Vivid Victorian

Pans: Square Set (8, 12, 16 in. needed), p. 153
Tips: 1, 2, 3, 4, 5, 14, 16, 18, 32, 131, 224, p. 142-143
Color: Ivory, p. 136
Fondant/Gum Paste: White Ready-To-Use Rolled Fondant (96 oz.), p. 130; Ready-To-Use Gum Paste, Rolling Pin, Roll & Cut Mat, Letters & Numbers Gum Paste/Fondant Mold, p. 133; Easy-Glide Fondant Smoother, p. 131
Recipes: Buttercream, Royal Icings, p. 114
Also: 2008 Pattern Book (Oval Topper, Topper Brace, Question Mark), p. 128; 2½ in. Globe Pillar Set (2), p. 228; 10, 14 in. Square Decorator Preferred® Smooth Edge Plates (1 each), p. 231; Decorator Favorites Pattern Press Set, p. 139; Piping Gel, Meringue Powder, p. 137; Fanci-Foil Wrap, p. 233; 20 in. square plywood or foamcore base board, cornstarch, toothpick, paring knife

Several days in advance: Make topper. Roll out gum paste ¼ in. thick. Use patterns to cut oval and brace; let dry overnight on cornstarch-dusted board. Imprint oval with smallest C-scroll press; pipe scrolls with tip 16 and royal icing. Tint 2 oz. gum paste ivory. Follow mold directions to make 2-tone monogram letters; let dry on cornstarch-dusted board. Use royal icing to pipe tip 2 dots around letters and tip 2 beads around oval. Attach letters. Attach brace to back of oval; let dry. **Also:** Make 68 tip 224 and 128 tip 131 drop flowers using royal icing; add tip 2 dot center. Make extras to allow for breakage and let dry.

Prepare base board. Tint 72 oz. fondant ivory and roll out. Cover 20 in. board with foil, brush with Piping Gel and cover with ivory fondant. Smooth with Fondant Smoother. Prepare 2-layer cakes for Globe Pillar Set construction (p. 113); position on separator plates or base board. Ice cakes smooth in buttercream. Mark 8 in. cake side 1¼ in. down from top; use pattern and toothpick to trace question marks pattern, 1½ in. apart. Outline patterns with tip 16 in ivory; overpipe in white with tip 5, then tip 3 in white. Mark

2¾ in. up from base of cake for triple drop strings, with points between question marks. Top strings will be 2¼ in. from base of cake at deepest point, middle strings 1⅝ in. and bottom strings 1⅜ in. At top string marking, pipe tip 16 zigzag garland in ivory; overpipe in white with tip 5 and tip 3 strings. At middle string marking, pipe tip 5 strings; overpipe with tip 3 strings. At bottom string marking, pipe tip 3 strings. Pipe tip 5 fleurs-de-lis between question marks; add tip 2 dots at drop string points. On cake top, pipe tip 14 zigzag scallop between question marks. Attach tip 224 drop flower at each scallop point. Pipe tip 18 shell bottom border.

Divide 12 in. cake side into 4ths; mark garland area 1¼ in. down from top edge. Pipe tip 16 zigzag garland in ivory; overpipe with white tip 4 drop strings, then tip 4 drop strings ¼ in. above garland. Pipe tip 4 e-motion garland ¼ in. below zigzag garland. Mark cake sides for bottom arch design, ¾ in. from base for points and 1¼ for top of arch. Cover marks with tip 3 e-motion. For middle arch, pipe tip 2 beads, ¼ in. above bottom arch. For top arch, pipe tip 1 U-motion ¼ in. above middle arch. On cake top, mark ¾ in. from edge of cake; pipe tip 4 curved outline. Add tip 3 e-motion scallops above strings. Attach a tip 131 drop flower at scallop points. Pipe tip 18 shell bottom border.

On 16 in. cake, pipe tip 18 shell bottom border. Divide cake side into 5ths; mark 2¼ in. from bottom. Pipe tip 32 upright elongated shells in ivory, 2¼ in. high. Mark 1 in. down from cake top, above each shell. Imprint large C-scroll pattern from press set at markings and on cake base around upright shells; pipe tip 32 over imprints. Mark 1 in. down from cake top; pipe tip 4 double drop strings between C-scrolls. Mark 1 in. up from bottom of cake; pipe tip 4 double drop strings to connect C-scrolls. Attach tip 131 drop flowers at all drop string points, on ends of C-scrolls and at top of elongated shells. On cake top, imprint 4 large C-scrolls on each side; pipe tip 16 zigzag over imprints. Overpipe with tip 16, then tip 5 and tip 3 outlines. At corners, pipe tip 32 fleurs de lis; attach tip 131 drop flower at point.

At reception: Assemble cakes. Position topper. Serves 200.*

The Perfect Accent:
Fluted Toasting Glasses
and Crystal-Look
Cake Knife & Server
complete the reception
table (p. 216).

▲ Garden Terraces

Pans: 3-Tier Paisley Set (all pans used), p. 153

Tips: 1, 5, p. 142

Colors:* Black, Rose, Violet, p. 136

Fondant/Gum Paste: White Ready-To-Use Rolled Fondant (180 oz.), p. 130; Round Cut-Outs™, p. 132; Ready-To-Use Gum Paste, Rolling Pin, Roll & Cut Mat, p. 133; Easy-Glide Fondant Smoother, Fondant Shaping Foam, Confectionery Tool Set, Brush Set, p. 131

Recipes: Buttercream, Royal Icings, p. 114; Gum Paste Adhesive, p. 115

Also: 2008 Pattern Book (Garden Greenery), p. 128; Piping Gel, Meringue Powder, p. 137; Plastic Dowel Rods, Flower Spikes, p. 232; Fanci-Foil Wrap, p. 233; 20 x 30 in. foamcore board (½ in. thick), 26-gauge florist wire (75 pieces, 5½ in. long), florist tape, toothpicks, waxed paper, scissors or wire cutters, cornstarch, knife

Several days in advance: Make 75 gum paste ruffled fantasy flowers (p. 123) on wires.

One day in advance: Prepare base board. Cut foamcore board 2 in. larger than largest paisley pan; wrap with foil and brush with piping gel. Tint 36 oz. fondant black; roll out

⅛ in. thick. Cut piece 2 in. larger than board. Cover board and smooth with Fondant Smoother.

Prepare 2-layer cakes for Stacked Construction (p. 112) and rolled fondant (p. 115); cover cakes with fondant and smooth with Fondant Smoother. Trace greenery pattern onto waxed paper. Hold against cake sides and use toothpick to imprint designs on fondant. Use royal icing to cover designs with tip 1 outlines; add random tip 1 dots. Pipe tip 5 bead bottom borders. Shape flowers into 2 medium (20 flowers each) and 1 large (30 flowers) crescent-shaped sprays by wrapping stems together with florist tape. Cut a plastic dowel rod to 5½ in.; insert in top cake, 1 in. from back left edge. Position 1 medium floral spray by inserting stems into dowel rod. Position remaining floral sprays using flower spikes. Serves 94.**

*Combine Violet with Rose for violet shown.

**The top tier is often saved for the first anniversary. The number of servings given does not include the top tier.

The Perfect Accent:
Celebrate the special couple
with our Bride & Groom
Toasting Glasses (p. 216).

▲ Pleated Pathways

Pans: Oval Set (all pans used), p. 153

Tips: 3, 5, p. 142

Color: Rose, p. 136

Fondant/Gum Paste: White Ready-To-Use Rolled Fondant (192 oz.), p. 130; Easy-Glide Fondant Smoother, Brush Set, Confectionery Tool Set, Flower Former Set, p. 131; Gum-Tex™, White Pearl Dust, Rolling Pin, Roll & Cut Mat, p. 133; Floral Collection Flower Making Set, p. 132

Topper: Forever In Your Eyes, p. 226

Recipes: Buttercream, Royal Icings, p. 114

Also: Piping Gel, Meringue Powder p. 137; Wooden Dowel Rods, p. 232; Cake Boards, Fanci-Foil Wrap, p. 233; ruler, knife, facial tissue, 20 in. oval foamcore board (½ in. thick), cornstarch

In advance: Prepare base board. Wrap foamcore board with foil and brush with piping gel. Tint 48 oz. of fondant rose; roll out ⅛ in. thick. Cut piece 2 in. larger than board. Cover board and smooth with Fondant Smoother. Reserve remaining rose fondant. **Also:** Make flowers. Roll out reserved rose fondant ¹⁄₁₆ in. thick. Cut 26 large flowers using pansy

cutter from Flower Making Set; cut 56 small flowers using apple blossom cutter from set. Make extras to allow for breakage and let dry on small flower formers dusted with cornstarch. When dry, attach 26 small flowers to 26 large flowers with tip 3 dots of icing. Pipe tip 3 dot centers on all flowers; let dry.

Prepare 1-layer (2 in. high) cakes for Stacked Construction (p. 112). Prepare and cover cakes with rolled fondant (p. 115); smooth with Fondant Smoother. Pipe tip 5 bead bottom borders on all cakes. Make fondant drapes (p. 124) for all tiers; drapes will be made using the following fondant strips: For 7 in. cake, cut 6 x 12 in. strip; 10 in. cake, cut 6 x 14 in. strip; 13 in. cake, cut 6 x 17 in. strip; base board, cut 6 x 20 in. strip. Attach drapes on corresponding cakes with damp brush. Before brushing drapes with Pearl Dust, cover exposed areas of cake with facial tissue, leaving only fondant drapes uncovered. Dip dry brush in Pearl Dust and apply to drapes. Attach flowers with tip 3 dots of icing.

At reception: Position topper.*** Serves 71.**

***Always place a separator plate, or cake board cut to fit, on the cake where you position any figurine or topper. This protects both the cake and your keepsake. For extra stability, secure your figurine to the plate with double-stick craft tape.

◄ Little Formalities

Pan: 9 x 13 x 2 in. Sheet, p. 153
Tip: 4, p. 142
Colors: Rose, Black, p. 136
Fondant/Gum Paste: White Ready-To-Use Rolled Fondant (24 oz. makes 4 cakes), p. 130; Letters & Numbers Gum Paste/Fondant Mold Set, Easy-Glide Fondant Smoother, Cutter/Embosser, Brush Set, p. 131; Rolling Pin, Roll & Cut Mat, p. 133
Recipes: Buttercream Icing, p. 114; Thinned Fondant Adhesive, p. 115
Also: Cake Board, p. 233; ruler, cornstarch

At least 1 day in advance: Make bow loops. Tint 1 oz. fondant rose for each cake. Roll out ¹⁄₁₆ in. thick. Using straight-edge wheel of Cutter/Embosser, cut a ½ x 3 in. long strip for each loop. Press ends together and let dry overnight on sides on cornstarch-dusted board. For knot, cut a ½ x 1¾ in. long rose strip; wrap around ends of 2 loops, then brush strip ends with water. Pinch ends together to secure. Reserve remaining rose fondant for cake top.

Bake 1-layer sheet cake. Cut cake into 3 in. squares. Prepare cakes for rolled fondant (p. 115). For each cake, tint 4 oz. fondant black. Cover cakes with black fondant; smooth with Fondant Smoother. Roll out white and rose fondant ¹⁄₁₆ in. thick. Cut a 2¾ in. white square and a 2⅜ in. rose square. Attach white, then rose square to cake with damp brush. Using narrow end of tip 4, punch out black fondant dots; attach to bow loops with damp brush. Attach bow to cake with thinned fondant adhesive. Follow package directions for molding monogram letter using black and white fondant. Attach letter with damp brush. One sheet cake makes 9-12 cakes; each serves 1.

► Double-Ring Ceremony

Pans: Hexagon Set (9, 15 x 2 in.), p. 153
Tips: 1, 3, 5, p. 142
Fondant/Gum Paste: White Ready-To-Use Rolled Fondant (30 oz.), White Pearl Dust, p. 130; Spiral Pattern Roller, Gum-Tex™, Rolling Pin, Roll & Cut Mat, p. 133; Brush Set, Confectionery Tool Set, p. 131; Floral Collection Flower Making Set, p. 132
Topper: Infinity Rings Cake Pick p. 227
Recipes: Buttercream, Royal Icings, p. 114
Also: 2008 Pattern Book (Smooth and Swirled Fondant Patterns—9, 15 in. cake sizes), p. 128; Crystal-Look Bowl, Dowel Rods, p. 232; Meringue Powder, p. 137; Cake Board, Fanci-Foil Wrap, p. 233; 3 in. craft circle, knife, silk flowers, cornstarch

Several days in advance: Make flowers. Combine ½ teaspoon of Gum-Tex with 6 oz. of fondant; roll out ⅛ in. thick. Using cutters from Floral Collection Set, cut 12 apple blossoms and 24 forget-me-nots. Place flowers on thick foam and cup centers with dog bone tool; let dry on cornstarch-dusted board. Add tip 3 dot centers in royal icing.

Ice 2-layer 9 and 15 in. cakes smooth with buttercream icing and prepare for Stacked Construction (p. 112). Roll out fondant ¼ in. thick. Using patterns, cut six each Smooth and Swirled Fondant pieces for cakes. Imprint swirled pieces using Spiral Pattern Roller. Attach a swirled piece to each smooth piece with damp brush. Position pieces on cakes. Lightly brush with Pearl Dust. Pipe tip 1 "S" scrolls around bottom edge of fondant. Attach a forget-me-not at bottom point of smooth pieces on 9 in. cake; attach an apple blossom to bottom points of smooth pieces on 15 in. cake. Pipe tip 5 bead below each flower. Pipe tip 3 beads over fondant seams on cake tops. Pipe tip 5 bead bottom borders on both cakes. With tip 3 dots, attach a cluster of 1 apple blossom and 2 forget-me-nots at each bottom corner of 15 in. cake.

At reception: Wrap craft circle in foil and place in Crystal-Look Bowl. Position silk flowers. Position pick by inserting into cake top.** Serves 70*.

▶ Touched by Romance

Pans: 6, 10, 14 x 2 in. Round, p. 153
Fondant/Gum Paste: White Ready-To-Use Rolled Fondant (180 oz.), Orchid Pink Pearl Dust, p. 130; Cutter/Embosser, Easy-Glide Fondant Smoother, Fondant Shaping Foam, Confectionery Tool Set, Brush Set, p. 131; Rolling Pin, Roll & Cut Mat, p. 133
Topper: Bianca, p. 225
Recipe: Buttercream Icing, p. 114
Also: Floating Tiers Cake Stand, p. 231; Cake Circles, p. 233; drawing compass, ⅝ in. wide pink satin ribbon (3 yards); facial tissue, ruler

Two days in advance: Make cake top flowers. For 14 in. cake, roll out a small amount of fondant ½ in. thick. Using straight-edge wheel of Cutter/Embosser, cut a 3 in. diameter circle for base; soften edge to round and taper. For petal layers, roll out fondant ⅟₁₆ in. thick. Cut a 6 in. diameter circle; position on thin foam and ruffle edges with ball tool. Attach petal layer to base with damp brush; prop up edges with pieces of crumpled tissue. Make additional petal layers as above, cutting 5¼, 4½, 3¾, 3, 2¼ and 1½ in. circles; attach in descending order with damp brush. Prop up edges with tissue as above. For 10 in. cake, make base and petals as above, using a 2 in. diameter base and 4½, 3¾, 3, 2¼ and 1½ in. circles for petal layers. Let dry overnight. Brush edges of petals with Pearl Dust.

Prepare 2-layer cakes for rolled fondant (p. 115). Cover cakes with fondant; smooth with Fondant Smoother. Make cake side ruffles. For 6 in. cake, roll out fondant ⅟₁₆ in. thick. Using straight-edge wheel of Cutter/Embosser, cut a 19 x 2¾ in. wide strip; on thin foam, ruffle one edge of strip with ball tool. Loosely roll up strip to prevent stretching, then unroll and attach to cake side with damp brush, positioning straight edge at base of cake. Follow same ruffling and rolling procedure with a 19 x 2¼ in. wide strip and a 19 x 1¾ in. wide strip; attach to cake side, positioning straight edges at base of cake. Attach satin ribbon to base of cake with dots of icing. For 10 in. cake, cut 2 each 16 x 2¾ in., 16 x 2¼ in. and 16 x 1¾ in. strips; ruffle and roll same-size strips together and attach as above. For 14 in. cake, cut 3 each 15 x 2¾, 15 x 2¼ and 15 x 1¾ in. strips; ruffle and roll same-size strips together and attach as above. Brush edges of all ruffles with Pearl Dust. Attach satin ribbons to base of 10 and 14 in. cakes.

At reception: Position cakes on stand. Position cake top flowers on 10 and 14 in. cakes. Position topper on 6 in. cake.** Serves 116.*

*The top tier is often saved for the first anniversary. The number of servings given does not include the top tier.

**Always place a separator plate, or a cake board cut to fit, on the cake where you position any figurine or topper. This protects both the cake and your keepsake. For extra stability, secure your figurine to the plate with double-stick craft tape.

The Perfect Accent:
The first toast should be in our Timeless Glasses (p. 216).

The Flower Show

Pans: 6, 8, 10 x 2 in. Round, p. 153

Tips: 1, 101, 102, 103, 352, p. 142-143

Colors:* Rose, Lemon Yellow, Golden Yellow, Moss Green, Brown, p. 136

Fondant/Gum Paste: Natural Colors Fondant Multi Pack, p. 130; Cutter/Embosser, Rolling Pin, Roll & Cut Mat, p. 133

Recipes: Buttercream, Royal Icings, p. 114

Also: 2008 Pattern Book (5-Petal Division Templates), p. 128; Graceful Tiers Cake Stand, p. 230; Flower Nail No. 7, Flower Former Set, Disposable Decorating Bags, p. 140; Meringue Powder, p. 137; Cake Circles, p. 233; waxed paper squares, ruler

Several days in advance: Make royal icing flowers using 5-petal templates as a guide. Make 50 each pink and yellow tip 101 apple blossoms. Make 40 each pink and yellow tip 102 apple blossoms. Make 25 each pink and yellow tip 103 wild roses. Make extras to allow for breakage; let apple blossoms dry in medium flower formers and wild roses dry in large flower formers. When flowers are dry, pipe tip 1 pull-out stamens at centers. **Also:** Make 100 puddle dots (p. 120), ⅜ in. diameter, on waxed paper squares using thinned pink royal icing in cut disposable bag. Make extras to allow for breakage; let dry.

Ice 2-layer cakes smooth in buttercream. Combine Light and Dark Brown fondant packets and add brown icing color to deepen. Roll out fondant ⅛ in. thick. Cut 1 in. wide strips, long enough to wrap around each cake; position around base of cakes. Attach puddle dots 1 in. apart on strips with buttercream. Mound icing at center of each cake and position various flowers; position other flowers randomly. Add tip 352 leaves. Position cakes on stand. Serves 62.**

*Combine Lemon Yellow with Golden Yellow for darker yellow shown.

**The top tier is often saved for the first anniversary. The number of servings given does not include the top tier.

The Perfect Accent:
Add the finishing touch with our Graceful Cake Knife & Server and Graceful Toasting Glasses (p. 215).

Bunches and Bows

Pans: Decorator Preferred® 8, 12, 16 x 3 in. Round, p. 152

Tips: 3, 5, p. 142

Colors:* Brown, Red-Red, p. 136

Fondant/Gum Paste: White Ready-To-Use Rolled Fondant (456 oz.), White Pearl Dust, p. 130; Gum Tex™, Rolling Pin, Roll & Cut Mat, p. 133; Brush Set, Easy-Glide Fondant Smoother, p. 131

Recipes: Buttercream, Royal Icings, p. 114

Also: Decorator Favorites Pattern Press Set, p. 139; 9 in. Twist Legs (2) and 6, 10, 14 in. Plates (from Crystal-Clear Cake Divider Set), p. 228; Meringue Powder, p. 137; Cake Board, Fanci-Foil Wrap, p. 233; plastic grape clusters (approximately 30), 20 in. diameter plywood or foamcore board, granulated sugar, cornstarch, ruler

Several days in advance: Make bow loops. Add 2 teaspoons of Gum-Tex to each 24 oz. of fondant (192 oz. will be needed). Roll out ⅛ in. thick. For 16 in. cake, make approximately 40 loops, cutting a 1⅜ in. wide x 16-18 in. long strip for each. For 12 in. cake, make approximately 30 loops, cutting a 1⅜ x 12-14 in. long strip for each. For top bow, make approximately 18 loops, cutting a 1 in. wide x 11-12 in. long strip for each. Brush one end of strips with water, fold over and secure ends to form loops. Let dry on sides for several days on cornstarch-dusted board. When dry, brush loops with Pearl Dust. On 6 in. plate, assemble top bow (p. 124) using royal icing; let dry.
Also: Prepare grape clusters. Mix Meringue Powder with a little water; brush onto grapes, then sprinkle with sugar.

Prepare 2-layer cakes (bake two 2½ in. layers to make 5 in. high cakes) for rolled fondant (p. 115) and Push-In Pillar Construction (p. 112). Cover cakes with rolled fondant; smooth with Fondant Smoother. Wrap base with foil; position 16 in. cake. Randomly imprint cake sides with large, medium and small C-scrolls from press set. Outline scrolls with tip 3 in buttercream; pipe tip 3 curls on some scrolls. Pipe tip 5 bead bottom borders.

At reception: Assemble cakes. Attach two rows of loops on 16 and 12 in. cakes with royal icing; trim loops as needed to fit. Position top bow. Position grape clusters. Serves 156.**

*Combine Brown with Red-Red for brown shown.

**The top tier is often saved for the first anniversary. The number of servings given does not include the top tier.

The Perfect Accent:
Our Crystal-Look Cake Server
is ideal in any setting (p. 216).

▶ Spirits Soaring

Pans: 8, 12, 16 x 2 in. Round, p. 153
Tips: 2, 5, 10, 13, 101, 103, 225, p. 142-143
Color: Golden Yellow, p. 136
Topper: Spring Song, p. 226
Recipes: Buttercream, Royal Icings, p. 114
Also: Kolor-Flo Fountain, Wooden Dowel Rods, p. 232;
  10, 18 in. Decorator Preferred® Smooth Edge Plates
  (2 of each size), p. 231; 13¾ in. Roman Columns (3 pks.),
  5 in. Grecian Pillars, p. 229; Cake Boards, Fanci-Foil Wrap,
  p. 233; Flower Nail No. 7, p. 140; Meringue Powder, p. 137;
  waxed paper squares, 26 in. diameter plywood base,
  8 x 4 in. high foil-wrapped round craft block, silk flowers,
  ⅜ in. ribbon (3 yds.), double-stick tape

In advance: Make royal icing flowers. Use flower nail to
make 165 tip 103 roses with tip 10 bases and 159 tip 101 roses
with tip 5 bases. Make 318 tip 225 drop flowers and 159 tip 13
drop flowers; add tip 2 dot centers. Make extras to allow for
breakage; let dry. **Also:** Prepare petal-shaped board, wrap
with foil and attach ribbon to side with tape.

Prepare seven 8 in., one 12 in. and one 16 in. 2-layer cakes
for Pillar and Stacked Construction (p. 112). Ice smooth in
buttercream with white tops and yellow sides. Position six
8 in. cakes on base board. Attach tip 103 roses at all top
borders. Attach a tip 101 rose below points where tip 103
roses meet. Attach a tip 225 drop flower, then a tip 13 drop
flower, below each tip 101 rose. Position a tip 225 drop
flower between each tip 101 rose. Pipe tip 5 bead
bottom border on all cakes.

At reception: Place foil-wrapped craft block at
center of 8 in. cakes on base board. Position
fountain and columns; assemble stacked 12
and 16 in. cakes and 8 in. top tier above the
circle of 8 in. cakes. Position 7 roses in a
cluster between Grecian Pillars on 12 in.
cake. Position silk flowers around fountain.
Position topper.** Serves 300.*

*The top tier is often saved for the first anniversary.
 The number of servings given does not include the
 top tier.

**Always place a separator plate, or cake board cut
 to fit, on the cake where you position any figurine or
 topper. This protects both the cake and your keepsake.
 For extra stability, secure your figurine to the plate with
 double-stick craft tape.

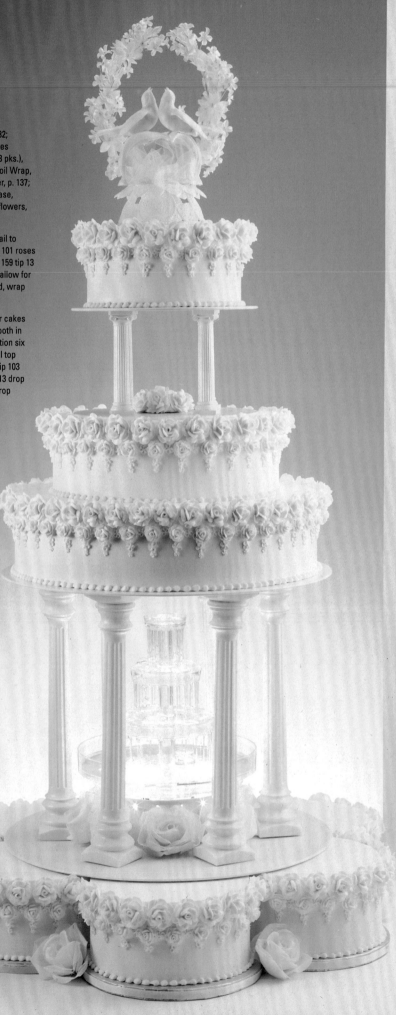

▶ # Upper Echelon

Pans: 6, 10, 14 x 2 in. Square, 12 x 18 x 2 in. Sheet, p. 153
Tips: 2, 5, p. 142
Fondant/Gum Paste: White Ready-To-Use Rolled Fondant
(24 oz.), p. 130; Gum-Tex™, Rolling Pin, Roll & Cut Mat,
p. 133
Topper: Elegance, p. 226
Recipes: Buttercream, Royal Icings, p. 114
Also: 2008 Pattern Book (Swag), p. 128; 5 in. Curved Pillars
(3 pks.), p. 229; 6, 10, 14 in. Square Smooth Edge Plates
(2 of each size), p. 231; Meringue Powder, p. 137;
Disposable Decorating Bags, p. 140; Dowel Rods, p. 232;
18 x 18 x ½ in. plywood or foamcore board, 16 x 16 x 4 in.
craft block, paring knife, cornstarch, toothpick, fresh or
silk flowers

At least 3 days in advance: Make swags. Combine 12 oz.
fondant with 2 teaspoons of Gum-Tex. Roll out ¹⁄₁₆ in. thick.
Mark pattern with toothpick and cut 96 swags. Make extras
to allow for breakage and let dry on cornstarch-dusted
board. **Also:** Make puddle dots (p. 120). Pipe 36 dots, ½ in.
diameter, using thinned royal icing in cut disposable bag.
Two days in advance: Add spikes to swags. Turn over dry
swags and pipe a tip 5 pull-out spike on each swag, ¾ in.
high, using royal icing. Let dry.

Bake three 1-layer 12 x 18 in. cakes 2 in. high; position
one 12 x 18 in. cake on foil-wrapped plywood or foamcore
board. Cut a second 12 x 18 in. cake into two 18 x 6 in.
halves. Position one half cake against 12 x 18 in. cake on
board for an 18 in. square, icing the seamed area together.
Repeat for top 18 in. layer so that seams are perpendicular
to each other. Also bake 2-layer 6, 10 and 14 in. cakes and
position on same-size separator plates. Ice cakes smooth in
buttercream. Prepare cakes for Separator Plate and Pillar
Construction (p. 112). Mark sections every 2 in. across
and every ½ in. down with toothpick. In royal icing, pipe
tip 2 drop strings, 1 in. deep, in each 2 in. section. Pipe
5 additional drop strings, 1 in. deep, beginning at each
½ in. mark. Add tip 2 dot at each drop string point.

At reception: Assemble cakes. Place 18 in. cake
on 16 x 16 x 4 in. craft block to create a space
under cake.

Attach swags to bottom of all cakes, inserting
spikes into bottom edge of cake and securing
with royal icing. Pipe 3 tip 2 drop strings on
swags. Add tip 2 dot at drop string points.
Attach puddle dots between swags on
18 in. cake to cover board. Position flowers
beneath 18 in. cake. Position topper.**
Serves 246.*

Instructions for projects shown on these two pages are on page 102-103.

Come to Camelot

When your knights gather at the round table, this bold birthday castle will make their day! It's decked out in fondant finery, including window buntings, textured stonework and an open drawbridge. It's time for a tournament, as fondant knights and horses gather around the grounds— and a dragon cake waits to light the birthday candles!

It's a Candy Kingdom

Make every kid's sweetest dreams come true—a world where your street is made of treats and your playground is filled with pinwheel pops to climb. An ice cream cone castle cake is at the center of it all, topped by a 3-D giant cupcake and surrounded by cone turrets finished with swirls of icing, sprinkles and candy. And because the best birthday parties have plenty of treats kids can grab for themselves, we've added lively lollipops and sprinkle-topped cupcakes around the main cake.

Instructions for projects shown on these two pages are on pages 103-104.

Fairyland Forest

Take the birthday girl's breath away, with an amazing woodland retreat up in a tree. Like magic, a center column is transformed into a mighty oak, which securely holds a castle cake accented by fondant flowers and royal icing shingles. The forest fantasy is completed by colorful cookie fairies and flowers every little pixie will love.

Instructions for projects shown on these two pages are on page 104.

A Fairytale Romance

Now that your prince has arrived, it's time for the romantic castle you've always dreamed about. The traditional stacked wedding cake is made fanciful and fun with pretty icing hearts and flowers adorning the high-rising palace peaks. The reception's royal treatment is heralded by heart cookie and cupcake favors and crown mini cakes.

Instructions for projects shown on these two pages are on page 105.

Instructions for projects shown on these two pages are on pages 105-106.

98 | 2008 WILTON YEARBOOK

Fun in the Dungeon!

There was always one house on the block that was the most fun to visit on Halloween.
This year, it's yours! You've brought Dracula's castle to life–a cake that captures the
ghostly glow of a Transylvanian twilight. Great details pop up from every corner,
including fondant masonry, lattice windows, hovering ghosts and bats in the belfry.
Complete the scene with a candy and cookie graveyard filled with friendly spirits.
It's the ideal way to raise the rafters on the spookiest night of the year!

The Towers of Toyland!

Imagine St. Nick chilling out here the other 364 nights of the year! It's a magnificent North Pole cake featuring dazzling fondant-striped turrets crowned with candy and a rainbow of sugars. Complete the scene by surrounding the cake with merry stand-up cookies featuring the entire Claus crew, a sleigh full of candy and snow-topped sugar cone trees. What a fitting way to start the magic at your holiday celebration.

Instructions for projects shown on these two pages are on page 106.

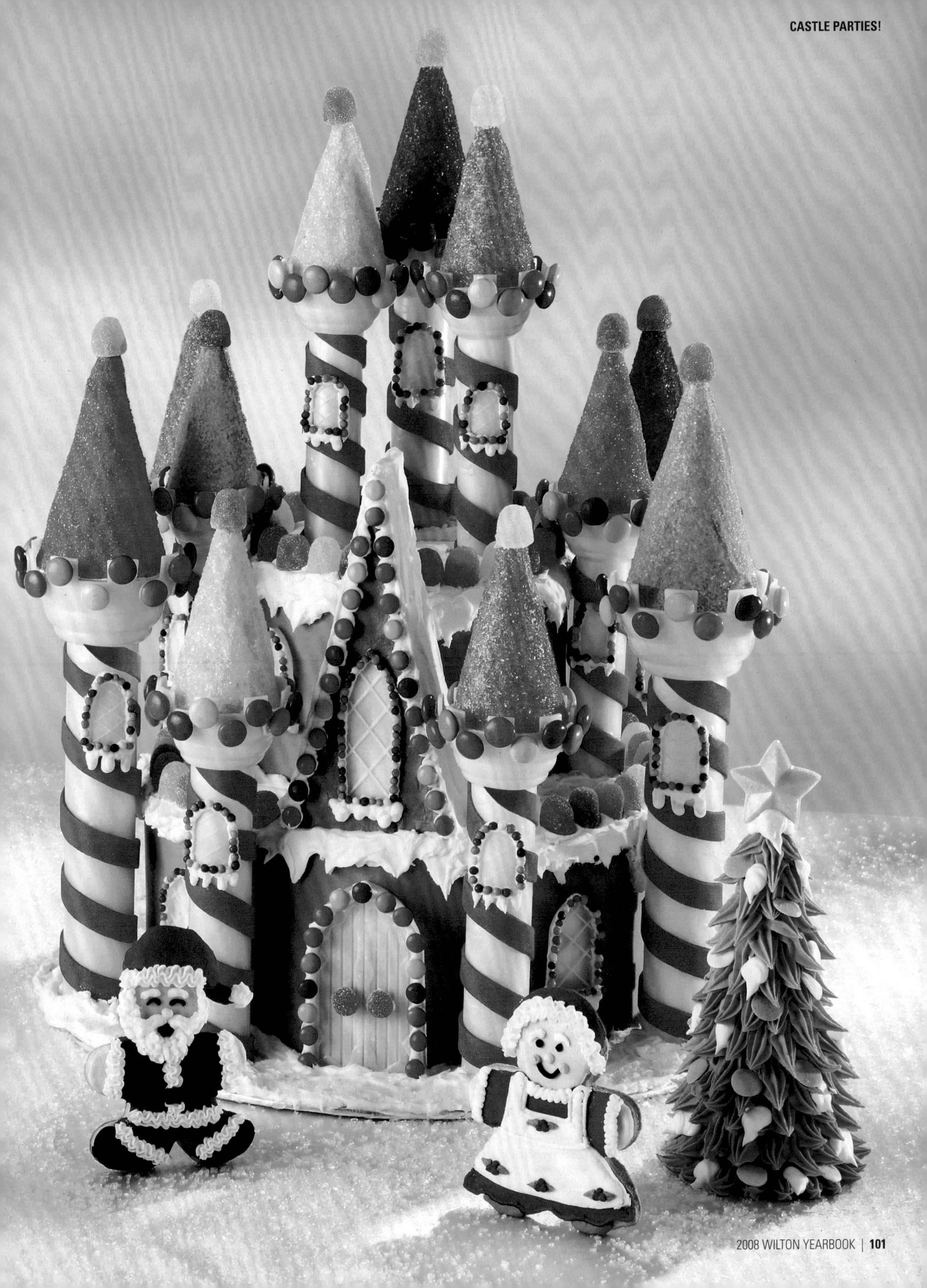

CASTLE INSTRUCTIONS

Your castle scenes come together here! When you surround your cake with single-size treats to tempt your guests, the entire presentation gains appeal. Follow our step-by-step instructions to make your kingdom come to life!

The Princess' Address

Pans: 6, 10 x 2 in. Round, p. 153
Tips: 2, 3, 5, 12, 349, p. 142-143
Colors:* Violet, Rose, Kelly Green, p. 136
Fondant/Gum Paste: White Ready-To-Use Rolled Fondant (8 oz.), p. 130; Floral Collection Flower Making Set, p. 132; Rolling Pin, Roll & Cut Mat, p. 133
Recipes: Buttercream, Royal Icings, p. 114
Also: Romantic Castle Cake Set, p. 145; 14 in. Silver Cake Base, Cake Circles, p. 233; White Candy Melts®†, p. 166; White Cake Sparkles (2 pks.), p. 139; Plastic Dowel Rods, p. 232; Meringue Powder, p. 137; cornstarch, ruler

In advance: Make flowers using Flower-Making Set. Tint 8 oz. fondant rose and roll out 1⁄16 in. thick. Cut 285 forget-me-nots; make extras to allow for breakage. Place on thick foam and cup centers using end of stick 2. Use royal icing to pipe tip 2 dot centers; let dry. **Also:** Add trims in violet royal icing. Ice turret peaks and sprinkle with Cake Sparkles. Pipe tip 3 arch around windows on towers and main roof; sprinkle with Cake Sparkles. Outline door and windows for cake sides with tip 5; sprinkle with Cake Sparkles. Ice sides of main roof and overpipe scalloped edge with tip 5; sprinkle with Cake Sparkles. Let dry. **And:** Prepare towers to insert in cake. To make 1 large, 4 medium and 2 small towers which will be inserted into cakes more stable, attach plastic dowel rods, cut 1 in. shorter than height of cake, to bottom of towers. Stand tower upside down; attach cut dowel rod to base with melted candy. Refrigerate until firm.

Ice 2-layer cakes smooth. Prepare for Stacked Construction (p. 112); position 6 in. cake 1⁄2 in. from center toward back of 10 in. cake to allow for main roof in front. Working from top to bottom, assemble and decorate using buttercream icing. Decorate 3 towers (small, medium, large) for 6 in. cake top. Attach turret peaks and flowers under windows; pipe tip 3 dots on battlements and tip 2 double drop strings above windows; add tip 349 leaves. Insert first 3 towers into cake top. Pipe tip 5 bead border around tower bases

and bottom of 6 in. cake. Attach flowers for top border; add tip 349 leaves. Insert 4 plastic windows around sides of 6 in. cake. Attach flowers under windows; pipe tip 349 leaves. Position main roof on 10 in. cake. Prepare 3 medium towers and 1 small tower as described above. Insert in 10 in. cake and pipe tip 5 bead border around bases and bottom border of 10 in. cake. Attach flowers for top border; add tip 349 leaves. Insert door at front and 2 plastic windows on sides of 10 in. cake. Attach flowers under windows and around door; pipe tip 349 leaves. Prepare 3 large and 2 small towers as described above for sides of cake; attach to cake board, touching cake sides. Pipe tip 12 random zigzag around base; position flowers and pipe tip 349 leaves. Serves 40.

*Combine Violet with Rose for violet shown.

Royal Ride

Pan: Sports Ball Set, p. 159
Tip: 3, p. 142
Colors:* Rose, Violet, p. 136
Fondant/Gum Paste: White Ready-To-Use Rolled Fondant (6 oz.), White Pearl Dust, p. 130; Gum-Tex™, Rolling Pin, Roll & Cut Mat, p. 133; Floral Collection Flower Making Set, p. 132; Brush Set, p. 131

Recipe: Royal Icing, p. 114
Also: 2008 Pattern Book (Coach Window), p. 128; Animal Pals 50-Pc. Cutter Set, 101 Cookie Cutters Set, p. 162; White Candy Melts®†, p. 166; White Cake Sparkles™, p. 138; Cake Boards, p. 233; Pastry Brush, p. 134; Meringue Powder, p. 137; knife, cornstarch, warming plate, ruler

In advance: Prepare fondant trims, coach stand. Add 1⁄2 teaspoon Gum-Tex to 6 oz. fondant; tint 2 oz. rose. Roll out rose and white fondant 1⁄8 in. thick. For stand, cut a 9 x 1 in. strip; wrap around a baking stand from Sports Ball Set. Using cutter from Animal Pals Set, cut 2 horses. Using knife, cut four 2 x 1 in. wide triangle easels to support horses. Using cutters from 101 Cutters Set, cut 4 medium circles for wheels and 1 rose heart for top of coach. Let all pieces dry on cornstarch-dusted board. **Also:** Make flowers using Flower-Making Set. Roll out rose fondant 1⁄16 in. thick. Using forget-me-not cutter, cut 16 flowers; place on thick foam and cup centers using stick 2. Add tip 3 dot centers in royal icing; let dry.

Make 2 candy shells (p. 125) for coach using bottom half of Ball Pan; refrigerate, then unmold. Smooth edges by gliding shells along warming tray; while warm, attach halves to form a ball coach. Position in stand so that seam is horizontal. Using pattern and knife, score window on each side of coach. Continue carefully scoring with warm knife to cut out windows; smooth edges with fingers. Divide and mark into 8ths; turn coach bottom side up in stand to decorate. Pipe rows of tip 3 beads on bottom half at marked sections and to create doors. Turn coach over in stand to complete decorating. Pipe tip 3 beads on top half sections. Add tip 3 outline door handles. Divide wheels into 6ths. Pipe tip 3 outline spokes. Attach flowers on edge and at center with icing. For window trim, roll out rose fondant 1⁄16 in. thick. Cut circles using wide end of tip 3; cut circles in half and attach around windows with icing. Outline window trim using tip 3. Shape a 1 in. white fondant ball; flatten and attach to top of coach. Insert fondant heart. On horses, outline and pipe in tip 3 saddle. Add tip 3 dot eyes, swirl mane, outline harness, tail and around saddle. Brush all pieces with Pearl Dust and sprinkle with Cake Sparkles. Attach wheels to coach with dots of icing. Attach 2 easels to back of each horse with icing; position horses.

*Combine Violet with Rose for violet shown.

Palace Pals

Pan: Mini Wonder Mold, p. 155
Tip: 3 (2 needed), p. 142
Colors:* Royal Blue, Violet, Rose, p. 136
Fondant/Gum Paste: White Ready-To-Use Rolled Fondant (8 oz. for each figure), p. 130; Confectionery Tool Set, p. 131; Rolling Pin, Roll & Cut Mat, p. 133

Recipes: Buttercream, Royal Icings, p. 114
Also: 2008 Pattern Book (Crown), p. 128; Mini Doll Picks, p. 155; Cake Board, p. 233; Meringue Powder, p. 137; curling ribbon, straight pins, ruler, cornstarch

In advance: Make queen's crown. Tint 1⁄2 oz. fondant rose; roll out 1⁄8 in. thick. Use pattern to cut out crown; curve into a half circle and let dry upright on cornstarch-dusted board.

Prepare mini cakes for rolled fondant (p. 115). Build up folds under skirts. Roll fondant 1⁄4 in. thick; for each skirt, cut 6 triangles, 3 x 1 in. wide at bottom and tapering to a point at top. Divide cake into 6ths and attach 1 fondant triangle at each division point, positioning wide end at bottom. Divide remaining fondant in 3rds and tint blue, rose and violet; tint a 1⁄2 ball of each color slightly darker. Roll out light fondant 1⁄8 in. thick. For each skirt, cut a 6 in. diameter circle and cover cake; smooth with fingers. Roll out fondant 1⁄16 in. thick and cut a 1 x 11⁄2 in. strip to cover bodice of doll picks. Shape two 1⁄4 in. fondant balls and attach with damp brush for puffed sleeves; imprint with small ball tool to add texture. Insert picks in cakes. In darker fondant, cut a 3⁄16 in. wide strip and attach at waist with damp brush. Position crown for queen. For princess' hats, cover tip 3 with fondant. Knot the end of a 6 in. piece of curling ribbon and thread through top of hat. Insert straight pin into top of head, leaving 11⁄2 in. extended; position hat. Each serves 1.

*Combine Violet with Rose for violet shown.

Come to Camelot

Pans: 6, 10 x 2 in. Square, p. 153
Tip: 3, p. 142
Colors: Black, Kelly Green, Royal Blue, p. 136
Fondant/Gum Paste: White Ready-To-Use Rolled Fondant (120 oz.), Primary and Natural Colors Fondant Multi Pack, p. 130; Square, Oval Cut-Outs™, p. 132; Rolling Pin, Roll & Cut Mat, p. 133; Cutter/Embosser, Brush Set, p. 131
Recipes: Buttercream, Royal Icings, p. 114
Also: 2008 Pattern Book (Small, Medium and Large Turret Peaks, Door, Window Patterns), p. 128; Romantic Castle Cake Set, p. 145; White Candy Melts®†, Garden Candy Colors Set, p. 166; 4 in. Lollipop Sticks, p. 169; Clear Vanilla Extract, p. 139; Piping Gel, Meringue Powder, p. 137; Plastic Dowel Rods, p. 232; 20 x 1⁄2 in. thick foamcore square or circle, construction paper, thin wooden skewers, wire cutters, waxed paper, cellophane tape, cornstarch, knife, shredded coconut

In advance: Make drawbridge. With wire cutters, trim off spikes from door piece. Roll out fondant ¼ in. wider than door. Cover front and side of door with brown fondant. Score wood lines with straight-edge wheel of Cutter/Embosser. Let dry on cornstarch-dusted board.

To make 4 small and 1 medium towers which will be inserted into cakes more stable, attach plastic dowel rods, cut 1 in. shorter than height of cake, to bottom of towers. Stand tower upside down; attach cut dowel rod to base with melted candy. Refrigerate until firm. Tint 96 oz. white fondant gray using black color; remove 8 oz. and tint dark gray. Tint remaining 24 oz. white fondant blue. Brush all towers lightly with Piping Gel. Cover towers with light gray fondant; smooth with fingers. For bricks, imprint towers with small square Cut-Out. Roll out blue fondant ⅛ in. thick; mark 4 small, 1 medium and 4 large turret patterns with toothpick and cut out with knife. Brush turret peaks lightly with Piping Gel; attach fondant pieces, wrapping around peaks. Roll out black fondant ⅛ in. thick. Cut out window patterns: 4 small and 17 large (used for medium and large towers); attach to towers with damp brush. For window ledges, roll out yellow fondant ⅛ in. thick; cut oval using medium Cut-Out and attach, trimming to fit. For stonework around tower windows, shape balls of dark gray fondant in various sizes; flatten and attach. For bunting beneath windows, roll out red fondant ¹⁄₁₆ in. thick. Using knife, cut a 1½ x 2 in. strip. Gather strip and form folds in fondant by placing 1 skewer under bottom edge of strip and 1 on top, next to the first skewer. Repeat with more skewers to form 3 folds. Remove skewers and gather fondant at each end. Pinch ends of fondant and taper; trim as needed. Brush back of strip with damp brush and attach below window. For battlement squares on cake top borders, roll out light gray fondant ⅛ in. thick; cut 50 squares using smallest Cut-Out. Let dry on cornstarch-dusted board. For drawbridge ropes, paint two 4 in. lollipop sticks with black color thinned with vanilla; let dry.

Prepare 3-layer 10 in. square cake (bake one 1 in. and two 2 in. layers for 5 in. high cake) and 2-layer 6 in. square cake for rolled fondant. Prepare cakes for Stacked Construction (p. 112). Cover cakes with light gray fondant. Position cake on base board. For bricks, imprint sides with smallest square Cut-Out. Roll out black fondant ⅛ in. thick. Use patterns to cut door and large window for cake sides. Attach with damp brush. Cut and attach window ledges and bunting as above. Shape and attach stonework around windows as above. Attach battlement squares with royal icing around top borders.

For flag bases, roll a ⅜ in. ball of blue fondant; flatten slightly and insert a lollipop stick cut to 2 in., supporting with royal icing if needed. Let dry. Attach towers to sides of 10 in. cake with melted gray candy. Insert medium tower at center of 6 in. cake and 4 small towers in 10 in. cake. Cut 2¼ x 1 in. flags from construction paper. Attach to sticks with icing, then attach bases to turret peaks. Ice base board fluffy in buttercream. Position drawbridge on base board. Attach ropes diagonally on each side of drawbridge. Tint coconut (p. 120) and sprinkle around base board. Serves 42.

Court Jousters

Pan: Cookie Sheet, p. 154
Color: Royal Blue, p. 136
Fondant/Gum Paste: White Ready-To-Use Rolled Fondant (24 oz.), Natural and Primary Colors Fondant Multi Packs, p. 130; Cutter/Embosser, Brush Set, p. 131; Oval Cut-Outs™, p. 132; Rolling Pin, Roll & Cut Mat, p. 133
Also: 101 Cookie Cutters Set, Animal Pals 50-Pc. Cutter Set, p. 162; White Candy Melts®†, p. 166; 4 in. Lollipop Sticks, p. 169; Cake Boards, p. 233; cornstarch, toothpicks, ruler, fork, knife

Three days in advance: Make horses and knights. For horses: Roll out fondant ⅛ in. thick; cut using horse cutter from Animal Pals set. Cut 1 horse each in white, black and brown. Let dry on cornstarch-dusted board. Tint a portion of fondant light gray by adding a little black fondant to white. Roll out different colors of fondant ⅛ in. thick for saddles and trims. Cut oval using medium Cut-Out; cut in half to form saddle. For saddle trim, cut another oval using medium Cut-Out; move cutter up ¼ in. and cut again. For harness and hooves, cut ⅛ in. wide strips. Roll small dot for eye. Attach all pieces using damp brush. Roll thin logs in various lengths for mane and tail; build-up layers, attaching with damp brush. Let dry.

For knights: Tint portion of fondant blue/gray by adding a little royal blue color to light gray fondant. Roll out ⅛ in. thick. Cut using small gingerbread boy cutter from 101 Cookie Cutter set. Cut 2 light gray and 2 blue/gray knights. Let dry on cornstarch-dusted board. Roll out fondant for trims ⅛ in. thick. For helmet, use gingerbread boy cutter to cut out just head and part of chest area; fringe bottom using fork. For mask, cut oval using smallest Cut-Out from set; cut in half and score lines using knife. Cut ⅛ in. wide strips in black for waist. Attach all pieces using damp brush. For feathers, roll a 1 in. high flat cone. Cut at wide end to form feathers; attach to toothpick. Let dry.

For easels, roll cones of fondant about 1½ in. high. Using melted candy, attach behind knight and horse legs; adjust so pieces stand properly. Roll 1 in. fondant cone for spear tip; push onto lollipop stick. Attach spear to front and feather to back of knight using melted candy.

He'll Light the Candles!

Pan: 3-D Bunny, p. 206
Tips: 3, 12, 18, p. 142
Colors:* Leaf Green, Lemon Yellow, Black, p. 136
Fondant/Gum Paste: White Ready-To-Use Rolled Fondant (48 oz.), p. 130; Rolling Pin, Roll & Cut Mat, p. 133
Recipes: Buttercream, Royal Icings, p. 114
Also: 2008 Pattern Book (Flame, Arms, Teeth, Large and Medium Spikes), p. 128; Meringue Powder, p. 137; 4 in. Lollipop Sticks, p. 169; Parchment Triangles, p. 140; Cake Board, p. 233; cornstarch, colored markers, glue stick, tape, scissors, knife

In advance: Make fondant features. Tint portion of fondant green; roll out ⅛ in. thick. Using patterns, cut 2 arms, 12 teeth, 6 large spikes and 5 medium spikes. Shape 10 small fondant logs into ⅛ x ⅝ in. long tapered claws and toenails. Let all dry on cornstarch-dusted surface. **Later:** Use royal icing to attach lollipop sticks to arms, leaving 2 in. extended to insert into cake. Use royal icing and tip 18 to build up and shape arms; attach claws and let dry. Cover one side of arm with tip 18 royal icing stars and let dry; repeat on opposite side and let dry.

Bake and cool cake using firm-textured batter such as pound cake. Cut off ears. Tint ½ oz. fondant black; shape ½ x ⅛ in. thick pupils and ⅝ x ¼ in. thick nostrils. Shape 1 x ¾ x ⅛ in. white fondant ovals for eyes. Attach eyes, pupils and nostrils to cake with buttercream. Use remaining fondant to form curved tail; attach to cake with buttercream. Using buttercream, cover belly area with tip 12 lines. Using buttercream and tip 18 stars, pipe dark green spots; cover rest of body and tail with light green. Overpipe leg areas for dimension; insert toenails. Pipe tip 3 outline eyebrows and nostrils. Insert arms, teeth and spikes.

Layer and glue 3 parchment triangles together; trace pattern and cut out flame. Use markers to draw fire and print message. Tape lollipop stick to back and insert in cake. Serves 12.

*Combine Leaf Green with Lemon Yellow for light and dark green shown.

It's a Candy Kingdom!

Pans: Dimensions® Large Cupcake, p. 150; Petal Set (12 in. pan used), p. 153
Tips: 1M (2110), 2A, 3, 32, p. 142-143
Colors:* Rose, Red-Red, Royal Blue, Kelly Green, Violet, Lemon Yellow, Golden Yellow, Ivory, p. 136
Fondant/Gum Paste: White Ready-To-Use Rolled Fondant (48 oz.), p. 130; Rolling Pin, Roll & Cut Mat, p. 133; Cutter/Embosser, Brush Set, p. 131
Recipes: Buttercream, Royal Icings, p. 114
Also: Romantic Castle Cake Set, p. 145; Flowerful Medley Sprinkle Assortment, p. 138; 14 in. Cake Circles, Fanci-Foil Wrap, p. 233; Plastic Dowel Rods, p. 232; candy-coated chocolates, mini candy-coated chocolates, pinwheel mints, spice drops, ruler, knife, 5 in. round cardboard circle, shredded coconut

In advance: Prepare small towers, medium towers and cones. Tint fondant as follows: 12 oz. dark ivory and light violet; 6 oz. each light blue, light green; 2 oz. red. For small towers: Make 2 light green and 2 light violet towers. Roll out fondant ⅛ in. thick; cut 3¾ x 4 in. strips. Wrap around 4 small turret towers and seam together in back; trim if necessary. For medium towers: Make 2 light violet and 2 light blue towers. Roll out fondant ⅛ in. thick; cut 4¼ x 5 in. strips. Wrap around 4 medium turret towers and seam together as above. For stripes on towers: Tint remaining light green, light violet, light blue fondant darker shades. Roll out fondant ⅛ in. thick and cut 14 x ¼ in. strips. Beginning at top, wrap around tower and attach with damp brush. **Note:** Make sure each strip begins and ends at back of tower.

For cones: Make 8 cones in dark ivory fondant. For bottom half, roll out fondant ¼ in. thick; cut 1¼ x 3½ in. rectangle. Wrap around tower; secure back edges with damp brush. Use edge of ruler to imprint crisscross design. For top of cone, roll out fondant ⅛ in. thick and cut 2 x 8 in. strip. Beginning at top edge of tower, wrap fondant over edge and into tower and cover remaining outside of cone; trim excess with knife. For center seam of cone, roll fondant rope ¼ x 4 in. long; attach with damp brush. For top rim of cone, roll fondant rope ¼ x 8 in. long; attach with damp brush. Repeat process on all cones. Use tip 1M and royal icing to pipe swirls in each cone; add confetti sprinkles. For cherries, roll ¾ in. balls of red fondant and position on top.

Bake and cool giant cupcake and 3-layer 12 in. petal cake (bake one 1 in. and two 2 in. layers for 5 in. high cake). Attach top and bottom cupcake pieces together with icing; position on a 5 in. cardboard circle. Pipe tip 2A vertical lines on bottom sides with buttercream. Pipe tip 1M buttercream swirl on top; add confetti sprinkles and 1 in. red fondant ball for cherry. For petal cake, ice smooth and prepare for Stacked Construction (p. 112). Position giant cupcake on petal cake. Insert door and windows. Attach candy with royal icing. Pipe tip 3 lines around window edges; add mini candy-coated chocolates. Pipe tip 3 line around door; add candy-coated chocolates. With tip 3 dots, attach mints above door and windows; attach candy-coated chocolates to center of mints. Position spice drops on top edge of petal cake. Position towers at indented areas of petal cake; secure with icing if needed. In buttercream, pipe

(continued on page 104)

(continued from page 103)

tip 32 rosettes on board between towers; add candy-coated chocolates. Position spice drops and confetti for walkway. Tint coconut (p. 120) and sprinkle around base board. (If transporting cake, add towers and rosette border at site.) Serves 50.

*Combine Ivory with Golden Yellow for dark ivory cones. Combine Violet with Rose for violet shown.

Just Lolligagging!

Candy: Pinwheel Lollipop Mold, p. 168; Candy Melts®†† in White, Red, Yellow and Blue, Garden Candy Color Set, p. 166; 6 in. Lollipop Sticks, p. 169
Tips: 1, 2, 3, 5, 8, 12, p. 142
Colors:* Copper (skin tone), Brown, Black, Royal Blue, Leaf Green, Lemon Yellow, Golden Yellow, Rose, p. 136
Recipe: Royal Icing, p. 114

Also: Meringue Powder, p. 137; Fanci-Foil Wrap, p. 233; 2 in. craft foam squares, waxed paper

In advance: Mold lollipops following package directions using melted candy in various colors (add pink candy color to white candy for pink shown) and 6 in. lollipop sticks. Refrigerate until firm; unmold.

Set lollipops on waxed paper-covered board; figure pipe kids (p. 119) using royal icing. Let dry. Wrap craft squares in foil; insert lollipops. Each serves 1.

*Combine Lemon Yellow with Golden Yellow for yellow icing shown.

†Brand confectionery coating.

Confetti Cupcakes

Pan: Cookie Sheet, p. 154
Tip: 1M (2110), p. 143
Recipe: Buttercream Icing, p. 114
Also: Pastel Silicone Baking Cups, p. 207; Jumbo Confetti Sprinkle Decorations, Sour Cherry Balls, p. 138

Bake and cool cupcakes in silicone cups supported by cookie sheet. Ice with tip 1M swirl. Position confetti and center cherry. Each serves 1.

Fairyland Forest

Pans: Classic Wonder Mold, p. 155; 8 and 14 x 2 in. Round, p. 153
Tips: 1s, 2, 3, 5, 8, 12, 21, 349, p. 142-143
Colors:* Brown, Red-Red, Lemon Yellow, Leaf Green, Kelly Green, Black, Violet, Rose, Orange, Copper (skin tone), p. 136
Fondant/Gum Paste: White Ready-To-Use Rolled Fondant (72 oz.), White Pearl Dust, p. 130; Brush Set, Easy-Glide Fondant Smoother, Fondant Shaping Foam, Confectionery Tool Set, p. 131; Floral Garland Cutter/Ejector Set, Funny Flower, Leaf Cut-Outs™, p. 132; Rolling Pin, Roll & Cut Mat, p. 133
Candy: White Candy Melts®†, p. 166; 11¾ in. Lollipop Sticks, p. 169; Candy Melting Plate, p. 167

Recipes: Buttercream, Snow-White Buttercream, Royal Icings, p. 114
Also: 2008 Pattern Book (Fairy), p. 128; Romantic Castle Cake Set, p. 145; Flower Former Set, p. 131; Meringue Powder, p. 137; Cake Circles, Fanci-Foil Wrap, p. 233; Plastic Dowel Rods, p. 232; Cake Corer Tube, Tall Tier Cake Stand (12, 16 in. Plates, 13½ in. Column, Top Column Cap Nut, Bottom Column Bolt), Glue-On Plate Legs (6), p. 230; uncooked spaghetti, glue for plastic, cornstarch, soft facial tissue, vegetable pan spray, paper, pencil

In advance: Make fondant decorations. Tint 16 oz. fondant leaf green, 2 oz. violet, 2 oz. rose, 2 oz. yellow. For leaves: Roll out green fondant ⅛ in. thick. Cut 40 medium and 20 small leaves using Cut-Outs; score vein lines using small end of veiner tool from tool set. Brush with Pearl Dust and let dry in medium Flower Former dusted with cornstarch. For cake flowers: Roll out fondant ⅛ in. thick. Use Cut-Outs to cut 6 medium flowers (3 violet, 1 rose, 2 yellow) and 2 small flowers (1 pink, 1 yellow). Roll small balls of white fondant and attach to centers with damp brush. Brush with Pearl Dust and set in Candy Melting Plate dusted with cornstarch to dry. For castle flowers: Make 15 flowers each in pink, yellow and violet using flower cutter with ejector set. Pipe tip 3 dot centers using royal icing. Let dry in small Flower Former dusted with cornstarch. For fairy wings: Roll out white fondant ⅛ in. thick; cut 3 left wings using small Leaf Cut-Out. Reverse cutter for 3 right wings. Let dry. **Also:** Figure pipe 3 fairies (p. 119) using pattern and royal icing. Let dry. **And:** Add shingles on turret peaks. Use royal icing and tip 5 for small turret peaks and tip 8 for medium turret peaks. Pipe rows of beads beginning ½ in. up from bottom edge. Flatten with finger dipped in cornstarch and overlap each row. Let dry. Glue legs on 16 in. plate.

Bake and cool 2-layer 14 in. round, 2-layer 8 in. round and Wonder Mold cake. (Use firm-textured batter such as pound cake for 8 in. round and Wonder Mold cakes.) Trim wide end of Wonder Mold cake so cake measures 4 in. high. Ice and prepare 8 in. and Wonder Mold cakes for Stacked and Center Column Construction (p. 112). On 14 in. cake and board, cut center hole large enough to fit width of 13½ in. column. Prepare double-thick foil-wrapped 8 in. cake board; cut center hole in board and position 8 in. cake. Prepare 8 in. cake for rolled fondant (p. 115). Tint 48 oz. fondant copper; cover 8 in. cake; smooth with fondant smoother. Reserve remaining copper fondant. Position 14 in. cake on plate and add column. Screw in 12 in. plate. Decorate tree: To form branches, cut lollipop sticks into 8 in. lengths. Bend sticks and attach from the middle of the column to the underside edge of the 12 in. plate using melted candy; let set. Tint Snow-White Buttercream brown. Using tip 21, pipe stripes to resemble tree trunk and branches. On 14 in. cake, pipe tip 8 bead bottom border. Pipe tip 3 message. Attach flowers and leaves with dots of buttercream. Decorate castle: To make 4 small turret towers which will be inserted in Wonder Mold cake more stable, cut plastic dowel rods in the following sizes: 3 in. for center tower, 2¼ and 1 ½ in. for side towers and ¾ in. for front tower. Stand towers upside down, attach cut dowel rod to base with melted candy; refrigerate until firm. Trace windows onto paper and cut out to make pattern. Roll out white fondant ⅛ in. thick, cut windows using patterns. Also, roll out fondant ⅛ in. thick and cut out windows for sides of door 1 x ½ in. wide. Cover 4 small and 4 medium towers with reserved copper fondant, securing with damp brush. Attach windows to towers and cake using damp brush. Outline windows with tip 5. Position door. Attach flowers to windows and around door with tip 3 dots of icing; pipe tip 349 leaves. Pipe shingles on Wonder Mold cake using buttercream icing and tip 12. **At the party:** Position castle on 12 in. plate. Insert 4 small turret towers in Wonder Mold cake; position 4 medium towers on sides of 8 in. cake. Position turret peaks. Flatten pieces of green fondant and cover plate. Attach leaves with dots of melted candy. Insert fairies on sticks. Serves 89.

*Combine Brown with Red-Red for brown shown.

Fanciful Flowers

Pans: Cookie Sheet, Cooling Grid, p. 154
Tip: 3, p. 142
Colors:* Leaf Green, Lemon Yellow, Violet, Rose, Royal Blue, p. 136
Fondant/Gum Paste: White Ready-To-Use Rolled Fondant (6 oz. for 10-12 leaves with stems), p. 130; Rolling Pin, Roll & Cut Mat, p. 133; Funny Flower, Leaf Cut-Outs™, p. 132; Brush Set, p. 131

Recipes: Color Flow Icing, Roll-Out Cookies, p. 114
Also: White Candy Melts®†, p. 166; 8 in. Lollipop Sticks, p. 169; Color Flow Mix, p. 137; White Cake Sparkles™, p. 139; Parchment Triangles, p. 140; waxed paper, knife, cornstarch, ruler, craft blocks

In advance: Prepare leaves and stems. Roll out fondant ⅛ in. thick. Cut leaves using 2 largest leaf Cut-Outs; let dry on cornstarch-dusted surface. Bend lollipop sticks to curve. Roll out fondant ¹⁄₁₆ in. thick; cut 8 x ½ in. rectangle and wrap around stick, securing with damp brush. Let dry. **Also:** Prepare and roll out cookie dough. Cut flowers using large and medium Cut-Outs; bake and cool. Outline using tip 3 and full-strength color flow; flow-in with thinned color flow (p. 126). **And:** Make dot centers on waxed paper using tip 3 and full-strength color flow. Let dry.

Using full-strength color flow and tip 3, outline petals and decorate leaves. Sprinkle with Cake Sparkles. Attach flower centers to cookies and flowers and leaves to stems using melted candy in cut parchment bag. Each serves 1.

*Combine Leaf Green with Lemon Yellow for green shown. Combine Violet with Rose for violet shown.

Sending Their Best Wishes!

Pans: Cookie Sheet, Cooling Grid, p. 154
Tips: 1, 3, 6, 125, p. 142-143
Colors:* Rose, Violet, Lemon Yellow, Orange, Brown, Royal Blue, Copper (skin tone), Red-Red, Black, p. 136
Fondant/Gum Paste: White Ready-To-Use Rolled Fondant (24 oz.), White Pearl Dust, p. 130; Rolling Pin, Roll & Cut Mat, Spiral Pattern Roller, p. 133; Heart Cut-Outs™, p. 132
Recipes: Royal Icing, Roll-Out Cookies, p. 114
Also: Girl Plastic Cutter, p. 163; Flower Former Set, p. 131; Meringue Powder, p. 137; Cake Boards, p. 233; spaghetti, mini candy-coated chocolates, waxed paper, knife, ruler, cornstarch

In advance: Prepare fondant wings. Roll out fondant ⅛ in. thick; imprint with spiral roller. Cut 2 wings for each fairy using medium heart Cut-Out. Let dry on outside of medium Flower Former; dust with Pearl Dust. Let all pieces dry for 2 days before assembling. **Also:** Make cookies. Prepare dough and tint copper. Roll out dough and cut fairies using girl cutter; cut off arms to shape bodice. Cut 2 x 1 in. triangular braces, one for each fairy. Bake and cool cookies. **And:** Decorate cookies. Ice face area; pat smooth. Ice body; pat smooth. Set on waxed paper-covered board. Pipe tip 6 outline arms and legs. Pipe tip 3 outline fingers and dot nose; outline and fill-in neck area. Pipe tip 1 dot eyes and string mouth. Pipe tip 3 swirl hair and dot cheeks. With tip 3, outline and fill in bodice area and pipe bead shoes (pat smooth with finger dipped in cornstarch). Add tip 125 ruffle skirt. Make antennae by inserting 1 in. lengths of spaghetti into icing through opening of tip 3; using gentle pressure, squeeze and remove spaghetti coated with icing. Position in hair and attach mini candy to tip with icing.

Attach wings and brace to back of each cookie with tip 3 and royal icing. Let dry. Each serves 1.

*Combine Violet with Rose for violet shown. Combine Brown with Red-Red for brown shown. Combine Orange with Red-Red for orange shown.

A Fairytale Romance

Pans: Hexagon Set (15 in. pan used), 6 in. Round, p. 153; Decorator Preferred® 18 x 3 in. Half Round, p. 152

Tips: 2, 3, 4, 16, 21, 129, 225, 349, p. 142-143

Color: Kelly Green, p. 136

Topper: Just Married, p. 226

Recipes: Buttercream, Royal Icings, p. 114

Also: 2008 Pattern Book (Heart), p. 128; Romantic Castle Cake Set, p. 145; Meringue Powder, p. 137; Cake Circles, Fanci-Foil Wrap, p. 233; Plastic Dowel Rods, p. 232; White Candy Melts®†, p. 166; Cake Dividing Set, p. 135; triple thick 20 in. round cake base or ½ in. thick plywood board, waxed paper

In advance: Make hearts and flowers using royal icing. Cover pattern with waxed paper and make 11 tip 4 hearts. Make approximately 360 tip 225 drop flowers and 770 tip 129 drop flowers. Add tip 2 dot centers to all flowers. Make extras to allow for breakage and let dry.

Ice 2-layer cakes smooth (for 18 in. cake, bake four 2 in. high half rounds to make a 4 in. high cake). Prepare cakes for Stacked Construction (p. 112). To make towers which will be inserted into cakes more stable, attach Plastic Dowel Rods to bottom of towers as follows: For 4 large and 2 medium towers in 18 in. cake, cut dowel rods to height of cake; for 4 small towers and 1 medium tower in hexagon and round cakes, cut dowel rods 1 in. shorter than height of cake. Stand towers upside down; attach cut dowel rod to base with melted candy. Refrigerate until firm. Attach turret peaks to towers. Assemble cakes. Insert plastic windows on 6 in. and hexagon cakes 1½ in. from base of cake. Insert door and position main roof. Using buttercream icing, pipe tip 4 bead hearts above windows. With tip 3, outline windows and pipe double drop strings. Attach tip 225 flowers with dots of icing; add tip 349 leaves. Insert 1 medium and 2 small towers in 6 in. cake; decorate towers with buttercream. With tip 3, outline windows and pipe double drop strings. Pipe tip 4 bead hearts above windows. Attach tip 225 flowers to windowsills with dots of icing; add tip 349 leaves. Attach tip 225 drop flowers to battlements and in a cascade from top of turret peaks; add tip 349 leaves. Pipe tip 16 rosette on turret peaks; insert royal icing hearts. Position tip 225 drop flowers around bottom of towers and on top and bottom borders. Insert 2 small towers in hexagon cake; decorate same as towers in 6 in. cake. Attach tip 225 drop flowers around door, main roof and top border of cake. Pipe tip 349 leaves.

Decorate 18 in. cake: Using Cake Dividing Set, divide cake into 12ths. Mark 1½ in. down from marks. Pipe tip 16 zigzag garland between marks. Attach tip 225 and tip 129 drop flowers on garland, pipe tip 349 leaves. Pipe tip 21 shell bottom border. Cover with tip 225 and tip 129 drop flowers, add tip 349 leaves. Pipe tip 16 shell top border. Position 4 large and 2 medium towers on side of cake, at hexagon points. Decorate towers same as 6 in. cake. Serves 216.**

**The top tier is often saved for the first anniversary. The number of servings given does not include the top tier.

Their Crowning Moment

Pans: 9 x 13 x 2 in. Sheet, p. 153; Cooling Grid, p. 154

Tips: 2, 3, 24, 26, p. 142

Recipe: Royal Icing, p. 114

Also: 2008 Pattern Book (Strings), p. 128; Round Cut-Outs™, p. 132; White Ready-To-Use Decorator Icing (1 pk. for 12-15 treats), Meringue Powder, p. 137, waxed paper

In advance: Make decorations using royal icing. On pattern, covered with waxed paper, make 6 sets of tip 3 double drop strings for each cake. Make extras to allow for breakage; let dry. Make 6 tip 24 and 6 tip 26 drop flowers for each cake; add tip 2 dot centers. Make extras to allow for breakage and let dry.

Bake and cool 1 in. high sheet cake. Cut cakes using largest round Cut-Out. Cover cakes with heated Decorator Icing (p. 126). Refrigerate to set. Using Decorator Icing, pipe tip 3 bead bottom border. Divide cakes in 6ths. Attach drop strings at marks using tip 3 dots of royal icing. Attach small flower to top and large flower to bottom. Each serves 1.

Stand Up for Love

Cookie: Cookie Sheet, Cooling Grid, p. 154; Heart Plastic Nesting Cutter Set, p. 163; 6 in. Cookie Treat Sticks, p. 165; Rolling Pin, p. 133

Tips: 2, 224, 349, p. 142-143

Color: Kelly Green, p. 136

Recipes: Buttercream, Royal Icings, Roll-Out Cookies, p. 114; favorite crisped rice cereal treats

Also: White Candy Melts®†, p. 166 (1 pk. makes 6 treats); Heart Cut-Outs™, p. 132; White Standard Baking Cups, p. 189; Meringue Powder, p. 137; ⅜ in. wide satin ribbon (16 in. per treat)

In advance: Make royal icing flowers. Pipe 32 tip 224 drop flowers for each treat; add tip 2 dot centers. Make extras to allow for breakage and let dry. **Also:** Make candy shells for bases (p. 125) in baking cups.

Prepare and roll out cookie dough; cut using 2½ in. heart cutter. Bake and cool; ice smooth with buttercream. Position flowers; add tip 349 leaves in buttercream. Attach cookie stick to back using melted candy. Prepare cereal treats recipe; fill candy shells. Insert cookies on sticks; seal top with melted candy. Refrigerate until firm; remove baking cup. Tie ribbon around stick. Each serves 1.

Fun in the Dungeon!

Pans: Decorator Preferred® 6 x 2 in. 10 x 3 in. Round, p. 152

Tips: 1A, 2, 2A, 3, 6, 125, p. 142

Colors:* Black, Violet, Rose, Lemon Yellow, Golden Yellow, p. 136

Fondant/Gum Paste: White Ready-To-Use Rolled Fondant

(144 oz.), p. 130; Rolling Pin, Roll & Cut Mat, p. 133; Brush Set, p. 131; Square Cut-Outs™, p. 132; Easy-Glide Fondant Smoother, p. 131

Candy: White Candy Melts®† (1 pk.), Garden Candy Colors Set, p. 166

Recipes: Buttercream, Royal Icings, p. 114

Also: Romantic Castle Cake Set, p. 145; Fine Tip Primary Colors FoodWriter™ Edible Color Markers, p. 130; 3 in. Metal Circle Cookie Cutter, p. 164; Halloween Mini Cutter Set, p. 196; Smiling Pumpkins Icing Decorations, p. 194; Meringue Powder, Piping Gel, p. 137; 16 in. Silver Cake Base, p. 233; Plastic Dowel Rods, p. 232; ruler, craft knife, cornstarch, shredded coconut

To make towers which will be inserted into cakes more stable, attach Plastic Dowel Rods to bottom of towers as follows: For 2 small towers, cut 2 and 2½ in. dowel rods; for 3 medium and 1 small towers, cut dowel rods 1 in. shorter than height of cake. Stand towers upside down; attach cut dowel rod to base with melted candy. Refrigerate until firm. Tint 8 oz. fondant yellow, 16 oz. violet, 1 oz. black, reserve 1 oz. white, tint remainder gray. Bake and cool 2-layer 10 in. rounds 2½ in. high; trim for 5 in. high cake. Bake and cool 2-layer 6 in. rounds for 4 in. high cake. Prepare cakes for rolled fondant (p. 115). Cover cakes in gray fondant; smooth with Fondant Smoother. Prepare cakes for Stacked Construction (p. 112); position 6 in. cake ½ in. toward back of 10 in. cake to allow for main roof. Using smallest square Cut-Out, imprint bricks on cake sides.

Make ghosts and bats. Roll out white and black fondant, ⅛ in. thick. Using Halloween Mini Cutters, cut approximately 5 ghosts, flip over cutter and cut 5 more ghosts; cut 4-5 bats. Let dry on cornstarch-dusted board. In royal icing, pipe tip 2 dot eyes and mouth on ghosts. Make fondant windows for towers. Trace patterns of windows from towers and main roof. Roll out yellow fondant ⅛ in. thick. Cut out tower windows using patterns. Draw lattice design on windows using FoodWriter. For windowsills, roll violet fondant into thin logs and attach with piping gel. Prepare towers. Roll out gray fondant ⅛ in. thick and cover turret towers, securing with damp brush. Imprint bricks with smallest square Cut-Out. Using violet fondant rolled ⅛ in. thick, cut 4 in. circles for the small towers and 6 in. circles for medium and large towers. Use the wide end of tip 125 to cut a hole in the center of circles for small and medium towers. Use the wide end of tip 1A to cut a hole in center of circles for large towers. Thread circles over the towers; attach with a damp brush. Shape and trim notches on top edge for battlements. Roll out gray fondant ⅛ in. thick and use 3 in. round cookie cutter to cut a circle of fondant for each tower. Dampen and press inside towers. Attach windows to towers with damp brush. Prepare main roof. Cover front of roof with gray fondant, secure with damp brush and trim. Cover window with fondant and decorate as for tower. For rooftop, roll out black fondant ⅛ in. thick; cut a 14 x 3 in. strip. Attach to roof with damp brush; trim. Using knife, mark sections ¾ in. wide on roof, then score to resemble wood grain. Using royal icing and tip 3, add scallops on eaves (smooth with finger dipped in cornstarch). Prepare door. Roll out gray fondant ⅛ in. thick, cut using door in set as pattern. Mark slats using ruler. Attach to door from set using piping gel. Pipe tip 2 outline door pulls.

Insert 3 small turret towers in 6 in. cake and 3 medium turret towers in 10 in. cake. Attach door and 4 large turret towers around 10 in. cake, securing with melted candy tinted gray using black candy color. Position main roof above door. Using buttercream and tip 6, pipe large and small ball stones around windows and door (flatten with finger dipped in cornstarch). Make cone-shaped spires for top borders in 2 sizes. You may either roll gray fondant into cones ¾ in. and 1 in. high, or mold fondant cones inside tips 2 and 2A, dusted with cornstarch. Attach cones to top borders with damp brush. Attach icing decorations around castle with royal icing. Tint coconut (p. 120); cover board with coconut. Attach ghosts and bats to castle with melted candy. Serves 40.

*Combine Lemon Yellow with Golden Yellow for yellow shown. Combine Violet with Rose for violet shown.

Happy Jacks

Pan: 9 x 13 x 2 in. Sheet (will make about 12 treats), p. 154

Candy: Yellow, Orange and White Candy Melts®† (1 pk. each), Garden Candy Color Set, p. 166; Candy Dipping Set, p. 167

Recipe: Favorite crisped rice cereal treats

Also: Pumpkins Nesting Cutter Set, p. 196; Parchment Triangles, p. 140; Cake Board, p. 233; spice drops, waxed paper, knife

Prepare cereal treats recipe; press into pan ½ in. deep. Cut out pumpkin shapes using smallest cutter from set. Cut off stem to make straight edge. Using dipping fork, dip pumpkins into melted orange candy to cover all sides; place on waxed paper covered board until set. Outline and pipe in facial features using melted yellow candy in cut parchment bag. When set, tint a small portion of melted white candy black using candy color. Pipe dot pupils. Trim spice drop to fit at top and attach using melted candy. For stand, attach a Candy Melt to bottom of pumpkin using melted candy; let set. Each serves 1.

Frightful Forest

Pans: Cookie Sheet, Cooling Grid, p. 154

Tip: 16, p. 142

Colors:* Brown, Red-Red, p. 136

Recipes: Royal Icing, Roll-Out Cookies, p. 114

Also: 2008 Pattern Book (Tree Trunk, Tree Support), p. 128; Petite Ghosts Icing Decorations, p. 194; Meringue Powder, p. 137; Cake Board, p. 233; Parchment Triangles, p. 140; candy corn, waxed paper

In advance: Make cookies. Prepare dough, roll out and use patterns to cut 1 tree trunk and 1 tree support for each cookie tree. Make extras to allow for breakage. Bake and cool. Place tree trunk cookies on waxed paper-covered cake board. Using tip 16 and royal icing, cover trunk with lines, extending beyond cookie to create branches. Let dry overnight.

Remove cookies from board. Attach icing decorations and candy corn using dots of royal icing. Let dry 30 minutes. Attach tree support cookie to back of tree trunk with royal icing; let dry. Each serves 1.

*Combine Brown with Red-Red for cookie dough and icing shown.

Dig These Graves!

Pan: Mini Loaf, p. 154

Candy: White (2 pks.) and Light Cocoa (1 pk.) Candy Melts®†, Garden and Primary Candy Color Sets, p. 166; Monsters Candy Mold, p. 194

Also: 9-Pc. Halloween Colorful Cutter Set, p. 196; Parchment Triangles, p. 140; Cake Board, p. 233; candy pumpkins, plastic wrap, knife, waxed paper

In advance: Mold candy plaques (p. 126) for bases in Mini Loaf Pan (mix green and yellow candy colors for green shown); refrigerate until firm, unmold. Dab tops with crumpled plastic wrap dipped in melted candy; let set.
Also: Mold monster candies following mold directions.
And: Mold tombstones. Place tombstone cutter on waxed paper-covered board. Fill with melted candy about 3/16 in. deep. Refrigerate until firm and unmold.

Assemble candies and add details using melted candy in cut parchment bags. Pipe border and message on tombstone; let set. Attach tombstone to base; pipe pull-out grass. Attach pumpkin candies. To support monster candies, cut straight edges on a Candy Melts wafer, forming a right angle. Attach monster to base; position support at a right angle and attach cut sides to monster and base. Each serves 1.

The Towers of Toyland!

Pans: 6, 10 x 2 in. Round, p. 153

Tip: 3, p. 142

Colors: Rose, Lemon Yellow, Leaf Green, Violet, Orange, Brown, Red-Red, p. 136

Fondant/Gum Paste: White Ready-To-Use Rolled Fondant, p. 130; Cutter/Embosser, p. 131; Rolling Pin, Roll & Cut Mat, p. 133

Recipe: Buttercream Icing, p. 114

Also: Romantic Castle Cake Set, p. 145; Yellow, Orange, Pink, Lavender, Light Green Colored Sugar, p. 139; Jumbo Rainbow Nonpareils, p. 138; Cake Boards, Fanci-Foil Wrap, p. 233; Plastic Dowel Rods, p. 232; White Candy Melts®†, p. 166; Decorator Brush Set, p. 167; candy-coated chocolates, mini candy-coated chocolates, spice drops

In advance: Decorate turret peaks and towers. To make 1 medium and 4 small towers which will be inserted into cakes more stable, attach a plastic dowel rod, cut 1 in. shorter than height of cake, to bottom of towers. Stand tower upside down; attach cut dowel rod to base with melted candy. Refrigerate until firm. Ice turret peaks and sprinkle with colored sugar; attach spice drop to top. Tint 8 oz. fondant red. Roll out ⅛ in. thick and cut into 20 x ½ in. strips. Wrap around turret towers and attach with damp brush. Trim strips to meet tower windows. Outline tower windows using tip 3, add nonpareils. Add tip 3 pull-out icicles below windows. Attach candy-coated chocolates to turret towers with dots of icing. Attach peaks to towers with icing. Set aside.

Ice sides of 2-layer 6 in. and 10 in. round cakes; spatula ice tops, pulling icing down from top edges to create icicle look. Prepare for Stacked Construction (p. 112). Position 6 in. tier ½ in. toward back of 10 in. cake to allow for main roof. Insert window and door pieces in cake sides. Using tip 3, outline door and position mini candy-coated chocolates. Cut spice drops in half and attach for doorknobs with dots of icing. Spatula ice top of main roof; ice background areas on front of roof smooth. Position main roof piece. Pipe tip 3 scallop on eaves and attach mini candy-coated chocolates. Outline roof window and side windows with tip 3 and attach nonpareils. Add pull-out icicles under windows. Attach spice drops on top borders of cakes, securing with dots of icing if necessary. Insert 1 medium and 2 small towers in 6 in. cake; insert 2 small towers in 10 in. cake. Attach 4 large and 2 medium towers to cake sides. Spatula ice board around castle. Serves 40.

Santa & Company

Cookie: 18 Pc. Metal Holiday Cutter Set, p. 200; Cookie Sheet, Cooling Grid, p. 154; Rolling Pin, p. 133

Tips: 1, 2, 3, 4, 5, 13, 349, p. 142-143

Colors:* Red-Red, Christmas Red, Kelly Green, Copper (skin tone), Brown, Black, Orange, p. 136

Recipes: Royal Icing, Roll-Out Cookie, p. 114

Also: 2008 Pattern Book (Sleigh Front, Back and Bottom; Large and Small Easel Backs), p. 128; Meringue Powder, p. 137; mini candy canes, assorted candies, waxed paper, cornstarch

Prepare and roll out cookie dough; cut using cutters from set. Use boy cutter for Santa and elves, girl for Mrs. Claus. Cut 2 sleighs, reversing 1 before baking. Use patterns to cut sleigh front, back and bottom plus 2 easel backs for all other cookies (small size for reindeer, large for all others). Bake and cool all cookies. Decorate all on waxed paper-covered board using royal icing. With tip 4, outline and pipe in reindeer bodies, face and hands on Santa, Mrs. Claus and elves; add tip 4 shoes on Santa and elves, tip 3 shoes on Mrs. Claus (smooth with finger dipped in cornstarch). With tip 5, outline and pipe in snowmen bodies, Santa and elf suits, Mrs. Claus' dress and all hats (smooth with finger dipped in cornstarch). Pipe tip 3 apron for Mrs. Claus. For Santa, pipe tip 13 zigzag trims and swirl pompom; add tip 2 dot and outline facial features, swirl beard and mustache and outline belt and buckle. Let dry. For Mrs. Claus, use tip 3 to outline and pipe in apron. Pipe tip 13 zigzag hat trim and tip 3 zigzag at neck and cuffs. Pipe tip 2 dot and outline facial features and belt; add tip 1 dot berries and tip 349 leaves on apron. Let dry. For elves and snowmen, pipe tip 2 pull-out noses, dot and outline facial features, outline hat band on snowman; pipe tip 3 dot buttons. Using tip 4, pipe outline hat brim and cuffs for elves, scarf for snowman; add swirl pompom to elf hat. For elf, pipe tip 349 pull-out hat detail, collar, waistband and ears. Let dry. For reindeer, pipe tip 5 outline harness. Pipe tip 2 dot eye, nose and bells on harness; add zigzag hooves, outline antlers, ear, tail and leg. Let dry.

Cover sleigh pieces with thinned royal icing (p. 126); let dry. Assemble using tip 4 and full strength royal icing; pipe icing on exposed backs of sleigh cookies (pat smooth with finger dipped in cornstarch). Attach 1 full and 1 cut candy cane to each side for runners. Cover top edge with tip 13 zigzag. Let dry. Fill sleigh with candy. Attach easel backs to cookies with icing and tip 5. Position cookies. Each serves 1.

*Combine Red-Red with Christmas Red for red shown. Combine Brown with Red-Red for brown shown.

Cone-ifer Trees

Candy: Yellow Candy Melts®†, p. 166; Stars Candy Mold, p. 168

Tips: 4, 17, p. 142

Color: Kelly Green, p. 136

Recipe: Royal Icing, p. 114

Also: Jumbo Confetti Sprinkles, p. 138; Meringue Powder, p. 137; Cake Board, p. 233; sugar cones, waxed paper

Make stars by filling mold cavities halfway with melted candy; refrigerate until firm. Make trees, using 1 cone for small, 2 stacked cones for medium and 3 stacked cones for large tree. For stacked trees, cover 1½ in. of pointed end of bottom cone with tip 17 zigzags; position next cone on top. Using spatula, widen and shape base with additional icing; let set on waxed paper-covered board. Cover trees with tip 17 pull-out stars, starting at bottom and overlapping rows as you work up to tree top. Position confetti. Pipe tip 4 pull-out snow; attach star to tree top with additional icing. Let dry.

†Brand confectionery coating.

Create the Castle of Your Dreams!

Enter the Wilton Castle Decorating Contest!

MONTHLY PRIZES:
Great Wilton decorating products!

GRAND PRIZE:
A 2-week Master Course at the Wilton School!

You've seen how much fun a castle cake can be in our *Castle Parties!* section. Now it's time for you to design and decorate your own spectacular castle in the Wilton Castle Decorating Contest! Dream up a captivating castle in any theme you like, then decorate it using the Romantic Castle Cake Set.

Upload your entry at **www.castlecontest.com** or send via mail. Each month our panel of decorators will crown a winning entry. If your design wins, you'll receive exciting Wilton products like a Cupcakes Galore Decorating Assortment, a Castle Pan and Decorating Set or our Professional Decorating Turntable.

Monthly winners qualify to win our Grand Prize— a 2-week Master Course at the Wilton School of Cake Decorating and Confectionery Arts in Darien, Illinois, including transportation and lodging. It's the ultimate decorating experience!

Visit **www.castlecontest.com** for complete contest rules and to enter. Or call **800-794-5866** for details.

Step-By-Step
Decorating Guide

Decorating help starts here! Whatever cake you want to make from this Yearbook, you'll find out how to make it happen on the following pages. Whether you're creating a cake for the first time or need a quick brush-up on a technique, it's easy when you use this handy guide as you decorate.

Want to learn more?

Find Wilton Cake Decorating Classes in your area or register for The Wilton School in Darien, Illinois on line at **www.wilton. com**. Our website is also a great place to explore decorating techniques, find recipes and chat with other decorators. Visit us regularly!

Cake Preparation

Think of your cake as the canvas on which you will create beautiful icing decorations. To achieve the masterpiece you want, it is essential that your canvas be smooth and free of crumbs. These steps for preparing and icing your cake will result in the perfect decorating surface essential for your work of art.

BAKING THE CAKE

Follow recipe directions for specific baking instructions and recommended batter amounts for the pan size you choose. Prepare the pan by generously greasing the inside using a pastry brush or paper towel and solid vegetable shortening. For best results, do not use butter, margarine or liquid vegetable oil. Spread the shortening so that all indentations are covered. Sprinkle about 2 Tablespoons of flour inside the pan and shake so that the flour covers all greased surfaces. Turn pan upside down and tap lightly to remove excess flour. If any uncovered spots remain, touch up with shortening and flour. Or use Bake Easy™ Non-Stick Spray or Cake Release (p. 134) to coat the pan—no grease or flour needed. Pour batter into pan and place in pre-heated oven.

After cake has baked the specified time, remove it from the oven and let it cool in the pan on a cake rack for 10 minutes. Run a thin knife between the cake and side of the pan. Unmold from pan by placing cooling rack against cake and turning both cooling rack and pan over. Lift pan off carefully. Cool at least one hour and brush off loose crumbs prior to icing.

CUTTING AND WRAPPING A CAKE BOARD

For round, square and sheet cakes, you don't need to cut a cake board. Simply buy a ready-made board that is 2 in. larger than your cake. (For example, if the cake is 8 in. diameter, buy a 10 in. round board.) For shaped cakes, cut a board to fit. Turn pan upside down and trace outline onto your cake board. Cut board with a craft knife, leaving 1 in. extra around outline.

To wrap, trace your cut board onto Fanci-Foil, making the outline 3-4 in. larger than the board. Cut Fanci-Foil along the outline. Place your board, white side down, on top of your cut foil. Cut deep slits at several points along foil edge, creating tabs of foil to wrap neatly around the board. Secure foil tabs to the board with tape.

LEVELING THE CAKE

After the cake has cooled at least one hour, you'll need to level the top of the cake. This can be done using a serrated knife or the Cake Leveler (p. 134).

Using a Serrated Knife

Place the cake on a cake board, then place the board on a Trim 'N Turn™ Cake Stand (p. 133). While slowly rotating the stand, move the knife back and forth across the top of cake in a sawing motion to remove the crown. Try to keep knife level as you cut.

Using the Wilton Cake Leveler

Position the ends of the cutting wire (or feet on large leveler) into the notches at the desired height. With legs standing on the work surface, cut into the crusted edge using an easy sawing motion, then proceed by gently gliding wire through the cake.

TORTING THE CAKE

Torting adds extra height, drama and taste to the cake when the layers are filled with icing, pudding or fruit filling. A serrated knife or the Cake Leveler may be used to cut a cake into multiple layers.

Using a Serrated Knife

Divide cake sides and mark equal horizontal points with dots of icing or toothpicks all around. Place one hand on top of the cake to hold it steady and rotate the stand. While slowly turning the cake, move the knife back and forth to cut the cake along the measured marks. Repeat for each additional layer.

Using the Cake Leveler

Torting is easily accomplished with the Cake Leveler. Simply follow the same directions as for leveling.

Separating the Layers

Carefully slide the top torted layer onto a cake board to keep it rigid and safe from breakage. Repeat for each additional layer.

FILLING THE LAYERS

Fill a decorating bag with medium consistency icing and use a large round tip, like tip 12. Or simply use the coupler without mounting a tip.

Starting with the bottom layer, leveled side up, create a dam of icing just inside the edge of the cake (about ¾ in. high and ¼ in. from the outside edge). Fill with icing, preserves or pudding. Place next layer on top, level; repeat. Finish with top layer leveled side down.

ICING THE CAKE

For better results, use a revolving turntable like professional decorators do…see our Revolving Cake Stand and Trim 'N Turn™ Cake Stand on p. 135.

Using a Spatula

The trick to keeping crumbs out of your icing is gliding your spatula on the icing—*never allow it to touch the surface of the cake*. Place a large amount of thin consistency icing on the center of the cake.

Spread icing across the top, pushing toward edges. Smooth the top using the edge of the spatula.

Sweep the edge of the spatula from the rim of the cake to its center then lift it off and remove excess icing.

Cover the sides with icing. Smooth sides by holding the spatula upright with the edge against the icing and slowly spinning the turntable without lifting the spatula from the icing surface. Return excess icing to the bowl and repeat until sides are smooth.

Rotate the cake slightly and repeat the procedure, starting from a new point on the rim until you have covered the entire top surface. Smooth the center of the cake by leveling the icing with the edge of your spatula. For easier smoothing, it may help to dip the spatula into hot water, wipe dry and glide it across the entire surface. Set the cake aside and allow the icing to crust over for at least 15 minutes before decorating. At that point you may also lay Non-Stick Parchment Paper (p. 134) on the iced cake top and gently smooth with the palm of your hand.

Using a Decorating Tip

Trim a 16 in. Featherweight bag to fit tip 789. Fill bag half full with icing. Hold bag at 45° angle and lightly press tip against cake. Squeeze a ribbon of icing in a continuous spiral motion to cover cake top, with last ribbon forcing icing over edge of cake top.

To ice the sides, squeeze icing as you turn the cake slowly. Repeat the process until the entire cake side is covered.

Smooth sides and top with spatula, same as above.

Icing Basics

In this section, we've listed general descriptions of icings, their uses, qualities and consistencies. Use this information to determine the right icing for your cake. Refer to our recipes for homemade icings (p. 114) along with color instructions below, to create the look and taste you want.

ICING USAGE GUIDE

Icing Type	Flavor/Description	Consistency	Best Used For...	Coloring	Storage/Freshness	Special Information
Buttercream (Wilton Mix or homemade)	Sweet, buttery flavor. Tastes/looks great for most decorating.	Thin-to-stiff depending on amount of corn syrup or sugar added (sugar stiffens).	Icing cakes smooth. Borders, writing, flowers, decorations.	Yields all colors. Most deepen upon setting. Let set 2-3 hours for deep color. Some may fade in bright light.	Can be refrigerated in airtight container for 2 weeks. Iced cake stores at room temperature for 2-3 days.	Flowers remain soft enough to be cut with a knife.
Snow-White Buttercream (homemade)	Sweet, almond flavor. Ideal for wedding cakes.	Thin-to-stiff depending on amount of corn syrup or sugar added (sugar stiffens).	Icing cakes smooth. Borders, writing, flowers, decorations.	Yields truer colors due to pure white base color. Creates deep colors. Most colors deepen upon setting.	Can be refrigerated in airtight container for 2 weeks. Iced cake stores at room temperature for 2-3 days.	Air-dried flowers have translucent look. Flowers remain soft enough to be cut with knife.
Wilton Ready-To-Use Decorator White (4½ lb. tub)	Sweet, vanilla flavor. Convenient, ready-to-spread icing. Pure white color ideal for tinting.	Thin-to-medium. No need to thin for spreading.	Spreading on cakes right from the can. Piping stars, shells, messages and more.	Yields truer colors due to pure white base color. Creates deep colors. Most colors deepen upon setting.	Leftover icing can be refrigerated for 2 weeks. Iced cake stores at room temperature for 2-3 days.	Available for purchase through Wilton Yearbook, at www.wilton.com or any authorized Wilton retailer.
Wilton Ready-To-Use Decorator White (1 lb. can)	Sweet, vanilla flavor. Convenient, ready-to-spread icing. Pure white color ideal for tinting.	Stiff. Make roses right from the can.	Shells, stars, flowers—use from container. Icing cakes, writing, leaves—thin with milk, water or corn syrup.	Yields truer colors due to pure white base color. Creates deep colors. Most colors deepen upon setting.	Leftover icing can be refrigerated for 2 weeks. Iced cake stores at room temperature for 2-3 days.	Available for purchase through Wilton Yearbook, at www.wilton.com or any authorized Wilton retailer.
Wilton Ready-To-Use Decorator Chocolate (1 lb. can)	Sweet chocolate flavor. Convenient ready-to-spread icing.	Stiff. Make roses right from the can.	Shells, stars, flowers—use from container. Icing cakes, writing, leaves—thin with milk, water or corn syrup.	Recommended when black or brown icing is needed. Add a little black icing color to chocolate for a better tasting black icing.	Leftover icing can be refrigerated for 2 weeks. Iced cake stores at room temperature for 2-3 days.	Available for purchase through Wilton Yearbook, at www.wilton.com or any authorized Wilton retailer.
Royal (made with Wilton Meringue Powder)	Very sweet flavor. Dries candy-hard for lasting decorations.	Thin-to-stiff, depending on the amount of water added.	Flower making, figure piping, making flowers on wires. Decorating cookies and gingerbread houses.	Yields deep colors. Some colors may fade in bright light. Requires more icing color than buttercream to achieve the same intensity.	Icing can be stored in airtight, grease-free container at room temperature for 2 weeks. Air-dried decorations last for months.	Bowls and utensils must be grease-free. Cover icing with damp cloth to prevent crusting.
Rolled Fondant (homemade or Wilton Ready-To-Use Rolled Fondant)	Covers cakes with a perfectly smooth, satiny surface. Easy and fast to use. Knead in flavor of your choice.	Dough-like. Fondant is rolled out before being applied to cake. Stays semi-soft on cake.	Any firm-textured cake, pound cake or fruit cake. Cutting, molding and modeling decorations.	White yields pastels to deep colors. Wilton pre-colored fondant is also available in pastel shades and in Multi Packs for fondant decorations in a variety of colors.	Excess can be stored 2 months in an airtight container. Do not refrigerate or freeze. Iced cake stores at room temperature for 3-4 days.	Prior to applying fondant, cake should be lightly covered with a glaze or buttercream icing to seal in freshness and moisture.
Whipped Icing Mix (Wilton Mix)	Light, delicate vanilla flavor. Holds shape like no other mix. **For chocolate icing,** add ½ cup of sifted cocoa powder.	Velvety, perfect for stars, roses, borders, garlands and writing.	Icing cakes. Most decorations. Toppings on pies, puddings, tarts and more.	Yields any color.	Can be refrigerated in airtight container. Iced cake stores at room temperature for 2-3 days.	Exclusive Wilton formula. Available for purchase through Wilton Yearbook, at www.wilton.com or any authorized Wilton retailer.
Fluffy Boiled Icing (homemade)	Marshmallow-like flavor. 100% fat-free.	Very fluffy. Sets quickly.	Icing cakes smooth and fluffy. Borders, figure piping, writing, stringwork.	Yields pastels to deep colors.	Use immediately. Iced cake can be stored at room temperature.	Serve within 24 hours.
Stabilized Whipped Cream (homemade)	Creamy, delicate sweetness.	Light, thin-to-medium.	All cakes but especially those decorated with fruits. Borders, large tip work, writing.	Yields pastels only.	Use immediately. Iced cake must be refrigerated.	Texture remains soft on decorated cake.

COLORING ICING

Using Color

When planning your cake, think about color. Choosing appropriate colors for your cake will help you capture the mood you want for the occasion. Gather inspiration from the theme of your celebration. The icing colors you choose should carry that theme and personalize your decorating. Look around, notice everyday objects—from a garden in bloom, to the clothes people wear. Which colors appeal to you? Use your favorite colors in your decorating. Don't be afraid to try something different. Have fun using rich, bright colors and different color combinations. Begin by making a monochromatic cake, decorated all in white or in a single, pale color. Try using decorations in contrasting colors on an all-white background. Decorate using all pastels or all primary colors. Experimenting with color will help you decide which colors work to make your cake designs spectacular!

Mixing Colors

Begin with white icing and use concentrated Icing Colors (p. 136) which will not affect your icing consistency. (Using ordinary liquid food colors can thin your icing and affect your

ability to pipe certain decorations.) If you are tinting icing dark brown or black, begin with chocolate icing—your icing will not have the aftertaste that large amounts of icing color can produce. If you are tinting a large area red, use No-Taste Red.

Dip a fresh toothpick into the color, then swirl it into the icing. Add color a little at a time until you achieve the shade you desire. Always use a new toothpick each time you add color; you want to avoid getting icing in your jar of color. Blend the icing well with a spatula.

Consider the type of icing you are using when mixing color. Icing colors intensify or darken in buttercream icing about 1-2 hours after mixing. Royal icing requires more color than buttercream icing to achieve the same color intensity.

Always mix enough of each icing color to complete your entire cake. For example, if you are going to decorate a cake with pink flowers and borders, color enough icing for both. It is difficult to duplicate an exact shade of any color, and you will want to keep your colors consistent on your cake.

Bag Striping Effects

You can easily pipe two-tone decorations just by adding a different color inside the bag before you put in your tinted icing. This is how you pipe flowers with natural light and dark tones or make a rainbow-colored clown suit to brighten up the party.

Brush Striping

Produces more intense multiple colors because it is done with straight icing color brushed into the bag. Apply one or more stripes of icing color with a decorating brush, then fill the bag with white or pastel-colored icing. As the icing is squeezed past the color, your decorations will come out striped.

Spatula Striping

Produces two-tone and realistic pastel tones for flowers and figure piping. It is done with pastel-colored icing, striped inside the decorating bag with a spatula. After striping, fill the bag with white icing or another shade of the same color as the striping. Squeeze out decorations with soft contrasts.

Brush Striping

Spatula Striping

Three Essentials of Cake Decorating

Every decoration you make is the result of three things working together: the consistency of your icing, the position of the bag (that is, the way you are holding it) and the amount and type of pressure you apply to the bag. You'll know when you have everything right because you'll get perfect results time after time. This will take practice. The more you concentrate on perfecting these three essentials, the sooner you will achieve perfect results.

ICING CONSISTENCY

If the consistency of your icing is not right, your decorations will not be right either. Just a few drops of liquid can make a great deal of difference in your decorating results. Many factors can affect icing consistency, such as humidity, temperature, ingredients and equipment. You may try using different icing consistencies when decorating to determine what works best for you. As a general guideline, if you are having trouble creating the decorations you want and you feel your icing is too thin, add a little more confectioner's sugar; if you feel your icing is too thick, add a little more liquid. In royal icing recipes, if adding more than ½ cup confectioner's sugar to thicken icing, also add 1-2 additional teaspoons of Meringue Powder (p. 137).

Stiff icing is used for figure piping and stringwork and for decorations like roses, carnations and sweet peas with upright petals. If icing is not stiff enough, flower petals will droop. If icing cracks when piped out, icing is probably too stiff. Add light corn syrup to icing used for stringwork to give strings greater elasticity so they will not break.

Medium icing is used for decorations such as stars, shell borders and flowers with flat petals. If the icing is too stiff or too thin, you will not get the uniformity that characterizes these decorations.

Thin icing is used for decorations such as printing and writing, vines and leaves. Leaves will be pointier, vines will not break and writing will flow easily if you add 1-2 teaspoons light corn syrup to each cup of icing. Thin icing is used to ice cakes smooth. Begin with your prepared icing recipe, then add small amounts of the same liquid used in the recipe (usually milk or water) until the proper spreading consistency is reached.

CORRECT BAG POSITION

The way your decorations curl, point and lie depends not only on icing consistency but also on the way you hold the bag and the way you move it. Bag positions are described in terms of both angle and direction.

Angle

Angle refers to the position of the bag relative to the work surface. There are two basic angle positions, 90° (straight up) and 45° (halfway between vertical and horizontal).

90° angle
or straight up, perpendicular to the surface.

45° angle
or halfway between vertical and horizontal.

Direction

The angle in relation to the work surface is only half the story on bag position. The other half is the direction in which the back of the bag is pointed.

Correct bag direction is easiest to learn when you think of the back of the bag as the hour hand of a clock. When you hold the bag at a 45° angle to the surface, you can sweep out a circle with the back end of the bag by rolling your wrist and holding the end of the tip in the same spot. Pretend the circle you formed in the air is a clock face. The hours on the clock face correspond to the direction you point the back end of the bag.

Back of bag at 6:00

Back of bag at 3:00

The technique instructions in this Decorating Guide will list the correct direction for holding the bag. When the bag direction differs for left-handed decorators, that direction will be listed in parentheses. For example, when a bag is to be held at 3:00 for a right-handed decorator, it should be held at 9:00 for a left-handed decorator.

One more thing…since most decorating tip openings are the same shape all the way around, there's no right side and wrong side up when you're squeezing icing out of them. However, some tips, such as petal, ruffle, basketweave and leaf have irregularly shaped openings. For those you must watch your tip position as well as your bag position. If the tip opening must be in a special position, the instructions will tell you.

PRESSURE CONTROL

In addition to having the proper icing consistency and the correct bag position, you'll need to master three types of pressure control: heavy, medium and light. The size and uniformity of your icing designs are affected by the amount of pressure you apply to the bag and the steadiness of that pressure. (In other words, how you squeeze and relax your grip on the decorating bag.) Your goal is to learn to apply pressure so consistently that you can move the bag in a free and easy glide while just the right amount of icing flows through the tip. Practice will help you achieve this control.

Heavy Pressure **Medium Pressure** **Light Pressure**

Storing Cakes

Take some final precautions and store your cake the best way possible. After all, your time, effort and creativity have made it very special! Beware of the following factors, which can affect the look of your decorated cake.

Sunlight and fluorescent lighting will alter icing colors. Keep your cake stored in a covered box and out of direct sunlight and fluorescent lighting.

Humidity can soften royal icing and gum paste decorations. If you live in a climate with high humidity, prepare your royal icing using only pure cane confectioner's sugar (not beet sugar or dextrose), add less liquid and add 1 more teaspoon Meringue Powder (p. 137) to the recipe.

Heat can melt icing and cause decorations to droop. Keep your decorated cake as cool as possible and stabilize buttercream icing by adding 2 teaspoons Meringue Powder per recipe. Protect your cake by placing it in a clean, covered cake box. Avoid using foil or plastic wrap to cover a decorated cake—these materials can stick to icing and crush delicate decorations. The icing that covers your cake determines how it should be stored—in the refrigerator, at cool room temperature, or frozen, if storing for longer than 3 days. If you want to store your iced cake in a different way than noted, make a small test cake.

Icing type determines care. See chart on p. 109 for storage information.

NOTE: Cakes with thoroughly-dried royal icing decorations should be stored according to the type of icing that covers the cake. However, if royal icing decorations are to be put on a cake that will be frozen, it is recommended that these decorations be placed on the cake after thawing so that they don't bleed from condensation or become soft.

Transporting Tiered Cakes

Moving a tiered cake from one location to another does not have to be difficult. It can be quite easy! Following some simple guidelines ensures that your cake will arrive safely—whether you are traveling hundreds of miles or just a few.

Before Moving Cakes

Be certain the cake is constructed on a sturdy base made of three or more thicknesses of corrugated cardboard. Base tiers of very heavy cakes should be placed on a foam core or plywood base, ½ in. thick. Cakes on pillars must be transported unassembled. Toppers, candles and ornaments should be removed from cakes when they are being moved. For stacked cakes, move the entire assembled cake. Or, for a larger quantity of tiers, transport unassembled and assemble at the reception. Be sure to have with you the equipment and icings you will need to finish any decorating needed after assembly at the reception.

For a cake which combines stacked and 2-plate construction, take tiers apart, keeping stacked tiers as units. Boxing the cake makes transportation easier. Not only does it protect the tiers from damage, but it keeps the tiers clean—free from dirt, dust and bugs. Place the boxes on carpet foam or a non-skid mat on a level surface in the vehicle to prevent shifting. Keep the boxes flat; never place on a car seat. Boxed cakes can also be transported in the trunk of the car, except in hot weather, because air conditioning will not reach the trunk area. It's also important to find out about the reception location before the event. Knowing what to expect when you arrive can make your delivery and setup so much easier. Call the reception hall a few days before the event to get an idea of the conditions you will encounter there. Ask whether the room is located upstairs or downstairs. Find out what is the best location for bringing the cake into the building. That way you can park in the right place the first time and minimize the distance your cake has to travel from your car. Also ask how far in advance the cake can be set up so that you can plan your day and reduce the stress.

At Your Destination

Before you bring in the cake from your car, walk the path you will have to travel to the set-up site. Be alert for any bumps along the way and note any tight spaces you will have to maneuver around. Make sure the cake table is level—it's a good idea to bring a level to check this on setup day. Request a cart on wheels to move the cake into the reception area. This is easier and safer than carrying it by hand. Remove the cakes from the boxes on the reception table by cutting the sides of the boxes and sliding the cakes out. Bring along a repair kit, including extra icing, prepared decorating bags and tips, flowers and spatulas, just in case it is necessary to make any repairs. Once the cake is assembled, take a picture to establish that the cake was in perfect condition when you left it.

In Pan

Take tiers apart if constructed in Center Column or Push-In Leg method. Leave columns or legs in place. Position the plates on crumpled foil or in shallow pans if they do not sit level. Remove pillars from tier plates; plates stay in position.

In Box

Place the cakes in clean, covered, sturdy boxes that are sized to the base board of each cake. This prevents shifting within the box and possibly crushing the sides of the cake. If the box is too big, roll pieces of masking tape sticky side out and attach to the inside bottom of the box. Position the cake base on top of the tape, securing the base in the box. For taller decorations, prop up box top and sides, secure with masking tape.

On Non-Skid Foam

If tiers cannot be boxed, they can be transported on large pieces of non-skid foam. Place the foam on the floor of the vehicle, then carefully place the tiers centered on each piece of foam. Remove any ornament or fragile decorations before transporting.

Cake Baking and Serving Guides

The charts below are based on baking recommendations from the Wilton Test Kitchen; your results may vary depending on oven performance or altitude in your area. For large cakes, always check for doneness after they have baked for 1 hour.

Serving amounts are based on party-sized portions of 1 ½ x 2 in. or smaller wedding-sized portions of approximately 1 x 2 in. Cakes from 3 to 6 in. high, baked in the same size pan, would yield the same number of servings because they follow the same pattern of cutting. Cakes shorter than 3 in. would yield half the number of servings indicated for that pan. Number of servings are intended as a guide only.

Icing amounts are very general and will vary with consistency, thickness applied and tips used. Icing amounts allow for top and bottom borders.

4 IN. HIGH CAKES (using 2 in. high pans)

The figures for 2 in. pans are based on a 2-layer, 4 in. high cake. Fill pans ½ to ⅔ full.

PAN SHAPE	SIZE	NUMBER SERVINGS PARTY	NUMBER SERVINGS WEDDING	CUPS BATTER 1 LAYER, 2 IN.	BAKING TEMP.	BAKING TIME MINUTES	APPROX. CUPS ICING TO ICE AND DECORATE
Round	6 in.	12	12	2	350°	25-30	3
	8 in.	20	24	3½	350°	30-35	4
	9 in.	24	32	5½	350°	30-35	4½
	10 in.	28	38	6	350°	35-40	5
	12 in.	40	56	7½	350°	35-40	6
	14 in.	63	78	10	325°	50-55	7½
	16 in.	77	100	15	325°	55-60	9
Square	6 in.	12	18	2	350°	25-30	3½
	8 in.	20	32	4	350°	35-40	4½
	10 in.	30	50	6	350°	35-40	6
	12 in.	48	72	10	350°	40-45	7½
	14 in.	63	98	13½	325°	45-50	9½
	16 in.	80	128	15½	325°	50-55	11
Heart	6 in.	8	14	1½	350°	25-30	3½
	8 in.	18	22	3½	350°	30-35	4½
	9 in.	20	28	4	350°	30-35	6
	10 in.	24	38	5	350°	30-35	8½
	12 in.	34	56	8	325°	45-50	9
	14 in.	48	72	10	325°	45-50	10
	15 in.	50	74	11	325°	40-45	11
	16 in.	64	94	12½	325°	40-45	12
Petal	6 in.	6	8	1½	350°	25-30	4
	9 in.	14	18	3½	350°	35-40	6
	12 in.	38	48	7	350°	35-40	9
	15 in.	48	64	12	325°	50-55	11
Hexagon	6 in.	10	12	1¾	350°	30-35	3
	9 in.	20	26	3½	350°	35-40	5
	12 in.	34	40	6	350°	40-45	6
	15 in.	48	70	11	325°	40-45	9
Oval	7¾ x 5⅝ in.	9	13	2½	350°	25-30	3
	10¾ x 7⅞ in.	20	26	5	350°	25-30	4
	13½ x 9⅞ in.	30	45	8	350°	35-40	5½
	16½ x 12⅜ in.	44	70	11	325°	40-45	7½
Sheet	7 x 11 in.	28	32	5½	350°	30-35	5
	9 x 13 in.	45	50	7	350°	35-40	6
	11 x 15 in.	60	74	11	325°	35-40	8
	12 x 18 in.	72	98	14	325°	45-50	10
Paisley	Small	9	13	3	350°	35-40	5
	Medium	28	38	7	350°	45-50	6
	Large	40	56	10½	325°	55-60	8

3 IN. HIGH CAKES (using 3 in. high pans)

The figures for 3 in. pans are based on a 1-layer cake which is torted and filled to reach 3 in. high; fill pans ½ full.

PAN SHAPE	SIZE	NUMBER SERVINGS PARTY	NUMBER SERVINGS WEDDING	CUPS BATTER 1 LAYER, 2 IN.	BAKING TEMP.	BAKING TIME MINUTES	APPROX. CUPS ICING TO ICE AND DECORATE
Round	6 in.	12	12	3	350°	35-40	3
	8 in.	20	24	5	350°	55-60	4
	10 in.	28	38	8	325°	65-75	5
	12 in.	40	56	10½	325°	60-65	6
	14 in.	63	78	15	325°	75-85	8
	16 in.	77	100	18	325°	75-85	9
	18 in. Half, 2 in. layer	110*	146*	9**	325°	60-65	10½
	18 in. Half, 3 in. layer	110*	146*	12**	325°	60-65	10½
Sheet	9 x 13 in.	45	65	11½	325°	70-75	5
	11 x 15 in.	60	90	16	325°	80-85	6½
	12 x 18 in.	72	108	20	325°	85-90	8
Square	8 in.	20	32	6½	350°	60-65	4½
	10 in.	30	50	9	325°	65-75	6
	12 in.	48	72	14	325°	65-75	7½
	14 in.	63	98	19	325°	65-75	9½
Contour	7 in.	6	11	3½	350°	45-50	2
	9 in.	11	17	5½	350°	45-50	2½
	11 in.	16	24	8	325°	80-85	3
	13 in.	22	39	13	325°	75-80	4
	15 in.	32	48	16	325°	75-80	5

For pans 10 in. and larger, we recommend using a heating core (p. 147) to insure even baking. Use 2 cores for 18-in. pans.

*Two half rounds. **For each half round pan.

For additional pan information, check out www.wilton.com

General Cake Cutting Guides

The diagrams below will give you a general plan for cutting the most popular cake shapes. They will help you serve more attractive, uniform pieces while reaching your targeted number of servings. Diagrams show only one size in each shape; you will use the same general technique to cut each size cake in that shape.

WEDDING CAKES—1 x 2 in. slices

The diagrams show how to cut popular shaped wedding tiers into slices approximately 1 x 2 in. and 2 layers high (about 4 in.) For cakes shorter than 3 in. you will need to cut wider slices to serve a proper portion; even if a larger serving size is desired, the order of cutting is still the same. Before cutting the cake, remove the top tier, which is usually saved for the first anniversary and is not included in our serving amounts for wedding cakes in this book. Begin by cutting the 2nd tier, followed by the 3rd, 4th and so on.

12 in.

Square Tiers:
Move in 2 in. from the outer edge and cut vertically, top to bottom. Slice and serve 1 in. pieces of cake. Now move in another 2 in. and repeat process until the entire tier is cut.

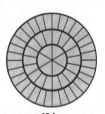
12 in.

Round Tiers:
Move in 2 in. from the tier's outer edge and cut a circle. Slice and serve 1 in. pieces from around the circle. Now move in another 2 in. and cut another circle. Repeat process until the tier is completely cut. The center core of each tier and the small top tier can be cut into 4ths, 6ths, or more, depending on size.

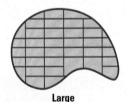
Large

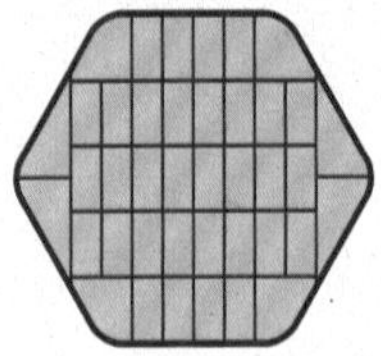

Paisley Tiers:
Move in 2 in. from the outer edge and cut across. Slice and serve 1 in. pieces of cake, similar to oval tiers as diagram shows. Now move in another 2 in., repeat process until the entire tier is cut.

12 in.

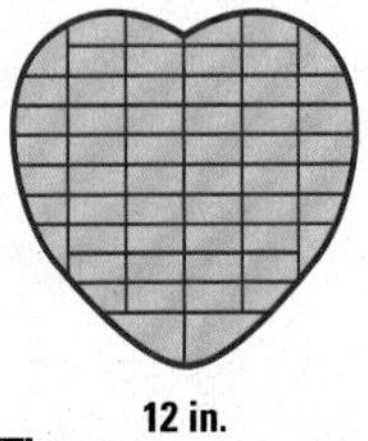

Heart Tiers:
Divide the tiers vertically into 2 in. wide rows. Within rows, slice and serve 1 in. pieces of cake.

12 in.

Hexagon Tiers:
Move in 2 in. from the outer edge and cut across. Slice and serve 1 in. pieces of cake. Now move in another 2 in., repeat process until the entire tier is cut.

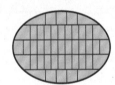
13½ x 9¾ in.

Oval Tiers:
Move in 2 in. from the outer edge and cut across. Slice and serve 1 in. pieces of cake. Now move in another 2 in., repeat process until the entire tier is cut.

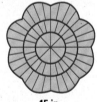
15 in.

Petal Tiers:
Cut similar to round tiers as diagram shows.

PARTY CAKES—1½ x 2 in. slices

Follow the diagrams above to cut party cakes (from 3 to 6 in. high), but adjust for the larger party-size slices. For cakes shorter than 3 in. you will need to cut wider slices to serve a proper portion; even if a larger serving size is desired the order of cutting is still the same.

Rounds:
To cut round cakes, move in 2 in. from the cake's outer edge; cut a circle and then slice approximately 1½ in. pieces within the circle. Now move in another 2 in. and cut another circle; slice approximately 1½ in. pieces. Continue until the cake is completely cut. Note: 6 in. diameter cakes should be cut in wedges, without a center circle. Cut petal and hexagon cakes similar to round cakes.

Squares:
To cut square cakes, move in 2 in. from the outer edge and cut top to bottom, then slice approximately 1½ in. pieces. Now move in another 2 in. and continue until the entire cake is cut.

Sheets: Cut sheet cakes similar to square cakes.

Tiered Cake Construction

There are many methods of constructing tiered cakes. Here are some used in this book. Visit www.wedding.wilton.com for more construction methods.

TO PREPARE CAKE FOR ASSEMBLY

Place base tier on a sturdy base plate of 3 or more thicknesses of corrugated cardboard. For heavy cakes, use foam core or plywood. Base can be covered with Fanci-Foil Wrap and trimmed with Tuk-'N-Ruffle or use Ruffle Boards® (p. 233). Each tier of your cake must be on a cake circle or board cut to it. Place a few strokes of icing on boards to secure cake. Fill and ice layers before assembly.

Adding Dowel Rods to Tiered Cakes

Use the upper tier for size reference when determining dowel rod placement. All the dowel rods must be placed within the area you will mark (see steps below) to provide adequate support.

1. Center a cake board the same size as the tier above it on base tier and press it gently into icing to imprint an outline. Remove. Use this outline to guide the insertion of the dowel rods.

2. Insert one dowel rod into cake straight down to the cake board. Make a knife scratch on the rod to mark the exact height. Pull dowel rod out.

3. Cut the suggested number of rods (see note below) the exact same length, using the mark on the first one as a guide.

4. Insert rods into tier, spacing evenly 1½ inches in from the imprinted outline. Push straight down until each touches the cake board. Repeat this procedure for every stacked or pillared tier on the cake.

NOTE: The larger and more numerous the tiers, the more dowels needed. If the tier above is 10 in. or less, use six ¼ in. wooden dowels. Use 8 dowel rods for 16 in. and 18 in. cakes; on these larger tiers, use ½ in. plastic dowel rods in the base tier. When using white plastic dowel rods that are wider and provide more support, the number needed may be less.

Stacked Construction

Stacking is the most architectural method of tiered cake construction. Tiers are placed directly on top of one another and pillars are not used. Cakes are supported and stabilized by dowel rods and cake boards.

1. Dowel rod all tiers except top tier.

2. Position the middle tier on the base tier, centering exactly.*

3. Repeat with the top tier.

4. To stabilize tiers further, sharpen one end of a long dowel rod and push it through all tiers and cake boards to the base of the bottom tier. To decorate, start at the top and work down.

*Finely shredded coconut or confectioner's sugar, placed in area where cake circles or plastic plates will rest, helps prevent frosting on the cake from sticking.

Separator Plate (2-Plate) and Pillar Construction

This most dramatic method features 2, 3 or more single cakes towered together. Use separator plates and pillars (p. 229, 231).

1. Set cake tiers on separator plates 2 in. larger in diameter than cakes.

2. Dowel rod cakes and position separator plates on tiers with feet up. (Note: Connect only same size separator plates with pillars.)

3. Position pillars over feet on separator plates.

4. Carefully set cake plate on pillars. Continue adding tiers this way.**

**Assemble cakes when you arrive at the reception or party.

Push-In Pillar Construction

Simple assembly—no dowel rods needed! Use any type of Wilton push-in pillars (p. 229) and plates (p. 231).

1. Mark tier for push-in pillar placement. Use the separator plate for the next tier above, gently pressing it onto the tier, feet down, making sure it is centered. Lift plate away. The feet will leave marks on the icing to guide the position of pillars when you assemble the tier. Repeat this process for each tier, working from largest to smallest tier. The top tier is left unmarked.

2. Place each tier on its separator plate, securing with icing.

3. Position push-in pillars at marks, and insert into tiers. Push straight down until pillars touch the cake plate.

4. To assemble, start with the tier above the base tier. Place the feet of the separator plate on the pillar openings. Continue adding tiers in the same way until the cake is completely assembled.**

Center Column Construction (Tall Tier Stand) (p. 230)

1. Use boards the same size as tiers, or if tiers are shaped, cut boards to fit. Make a waxed paper pattern for each tier except the top tier in order to find the exact center for the columns. Fold the pattern in quarters. Snip the point to make a center hole. Test the hole for size by slipping it over a column, adjust size if necessary. Trace hole pattern on prepared cake board and cut out. Also cut a hole in the top tier board to allow for the column cap nut. Save patterns for marking cake tops later.

2. The base tier of the cake will rest on a 14, 16 or 18 in. plate. (18 in. plate is footed. Do not use a bottom plate smaller than 14 in.) To add legs to bottom plate, turn it upside down; using extra strength glue designed for plastic, attach the six legs, positioning the legs over each of the ribs on the plate.

3. Prepare and ice tiers and position on prepared cake boards. Make the center holes for the columns in all tiers except the top tier. Mark the top of the cakes with corresponding waxed paper pattern. Cut the hole by pressing the Cake Corer Tube (p. 230) through the tier right down to the bottom. Hold the corer upright, remove cake corer and push the upper part down to eject the cake center.

4. Screw in a column to the prepared base plate and bottom column bolt from underneath the plate. Slip the next size tier on its plate over the column.

5. Add a second column and position the next size tier on its plate, slipping it over the column. Finally, add on the top plate only, securing the top column nut. Place the top tier on the plate and decorate bottom border.**

Globe Pillar Set Construction

These elegant pearl-look globes (p. 228) are available in separate sets of four 2 in., 2½ in. or 3 in. globes. The 3 in. globes are to be used to support the base cake only. They have a reinforced center channel which eliminates the need for pillars. The 2 and 2½ in. sets should be used with 9 in. "Hidden" Pillars (included in set); do not use these sets to support the base cake. Your cake design may use a base board instead of the 3 in. globes to support the base cake as shown below.

1. Position separator plate holding base cake on 3 in. Globe Base Set or a thick base board. Using the separator plate which will hold the cake above, mark base cake for pillar placement (see Push-In Pillar construction, p. 112). Lift plate away.

2. Insert pillars through cake centered over marked area to rest on its separator plate or base board. Place the correct size globe (2½ in. for cake shown here) over the pillars. Mark pillars where they extend above markings. The cut pillars should be equal to the height of the base cake plus the height of each globe.

3. Trim pillars at markings with craft knife or serrated edge knife.

4. Insert pillars in base cake. Position globes over pillars.

5. Position the tier above on globes.

6. Add additional sets for more tiers.

Tailored Tiers Construction

Our Tailored Tiers Cake Display Set (p. 228) features fabric-wrapped separators which add great texture to your tiered design. The top 2 tiers are decorated on same-size boards, then transported to the reception on larger boards, so that cakes can be easily transferred to the separator plates during assembly. Bottom borders are then added to these tiers. The recommended display for Tailored Tiers separators includes a 14 in. base cake, a 10 in. center cake and a 6 in. top cake.

1. Ice cakes; place 14 in. base cake on 16 in. base board wrapped in foil or 16 in. Silver Cake Base (p. 233). Place 10 in. center and 6 in. top cakes on same size boards. Mark 14 in. and 10 in. cakes for placement of dowel rods. Center the 8 in. plate from the Tailored Tiers set on top of the 14 in. cake and press it gently into icing to imprint an outline. Remove. Use this outline to guide the insertion of dowel rods.

2. Dowel rod 14 in. cake (see page 112). Place the 6 in. plate from set on top of the 10 in. cake and repeat process for marking and inserting dowel rods. Complete decorating on cakes, except bottom borders of 10 in. center and 6 in. top cakes, which will be done at reception. Attach 10 in. and 6 in. cakes to larger boards before transferring to reception.

3. Place the 12 in. plate (spikes up) on table. Center the large (7¼ in.) separator over the plate and press down over the spikes. Position one 8 in. plate (spikes down) on top of the large separator. Place the second 8 in. plate (spikes up) on table. Center the small (4¼ in.) separator over the plate and press down over the spikes. Position the 6 in. plate (spikes down) on top of the small separator.

4. At reception: Position the large separator, with 8 in. plate on bottom and 12 in. plate on top, on the base cake. Remove 10 in. and 6 in. cakes from their larger boards. Position 10 in. cake on large separator.

5. Add bottom border to 10 in. cake. Position the small separator, with 6 in. plate on bottom and 8 in. plate on top, on the 10 in. cake. Position 6 in. cake on small separator. Add bottom border.

To Use Acetate Wrap for Tailored Tiers

1. Insert photos, patterned paper or fabric in pockets of acetate wrap. Trim inserted items as needed to fit.
2. Wrap acetate around separator and fasten Velcro® ends.

Alternate 2-Plate Set-Ups

The Fluted Bowl and Spiral Separator Sets shown below are assembled similar to 2-Plate and Pillar Construction (p. 112)—the separators provide support instead of pillars; each set includes 2 separator plates. Cakes must still use dowel rods to support cakes and secure the separators.

Fluted Bowl Separator Set (p. 228)

Spiral Separator Set (p. 228)

Dowel rod base cake as for 2-Plate & Pillar Construction. Position smaller plate from set on base cake (spikes up). Position Fluted Bowl or Spiral Separator over spikes. Position next tier on larger plate from set. Position plate (spikes down) on separator.

Recipes

The cakes, cookies and other desserts in this Yearbook were made using our favorite kitchen-tested recipes. Follow these instructions for decorated desserts that look and taste their best!

ICING RECIPES

*Buttercream Icing (Medium consistency)

½ cup solid vegetable shortening
½ cup butter or margarine, softened
1 teaspoon Clear Vanilla Extract
4 cups sifted confectioners' sugar (about 1 lb.)
2 tablespoons milk

In large bowl, cream shortening and butter with electric mixer. Add vanilla. Gradually add sugar, one cup at a time, beating well on medium speed. Scrape sides and bottom of bowl often. When all sugar has been mixed in, icing will appear dry. Add milk and beat at medium speed until light and fluffy. Keep bowl covered with a damp cloth until ready to use. For best results, keep icing bowl in refrigerator when not in use. Refrigerated in an airtight container, this icing can be stored 2 weeks. Rewhip before using.

Makes about 3 cups.

For thin (spreading) consistency icing, add 2 tablespoons light corn syrup, water or milk.

For Pure White Icing (stiff consistency), omit butter; substitute an additional ½ cup vegetable shortening for butter and ½ teaspoon No-Color Butter Flavor (p. 139). Add up to 4 tablespoons light corn syrup, water or milk to thin for icing cakes.

Chocolate Buttercream Icing

Add ¾ cup cocoa powder (or three 1 oz. squares unsweetened chocolate, melted) and an additional 1-2 tablespoons milk to buttercream icing. Mix until well blended. For a unique change of pace, substitute ⅛ to ¼ teaspoon Wilton Candy Flavors (p. 166) for vanilla extract.

Chocolate Mocha Icing: Substitute brewed strong coffee for milk in Chocolate Buttercream recipe.

Darker Chocolate Icing: Add an additional ¼ cup cocoa powder (or 1 additional 1 oz. square unsweetened chocolate, melted) and 1 additional tablespoon milk to Chocolate Buttercream Icing.

*Snow-White Buttercream Icing (Firm consistency)

⅔ cup plus 3 tablespoons water, divided
¼ cup Meringue Powder
12 cups sifted confectioners' sugar (about 3 lbs.), divided
1¼ cups solid vegetable shortening
3 tablespoons light corn syrup
¾ teaspoon salt
¾ teaspoon No-Color Almond Extract
¾ teaspoon Clear Vanilla Extract
½ teaspoon No-Color Butter Flavor

In large bowl, combine ⅔ cup water and meringue powder; whip with electric mixer at high speed until peaks form. Add 4 cups sugar, one cup at a time, beating at low speed after each addition. Add remaining 8 cups sugar and 3 tablespoons water, shortening and corn syrup in 3 additions, blending well after each. Add salt and flavorings; beat at low speed until smooth.

Makes about 7 cups icing.

For thin (spreading) consistency icing, add up to 4 more tablespoons each water and corn syrup.

NOTE: Recipe may be doubled or halved.

Royal Icing

3 tablespoons Meringue Powder (p. 137)
4 cups sifted confectioners' sugar (about 1 lb.)
6 tablespoons water [1]

Beat all ingredients at low speed for 7-10 minutes (10-12 minutes at high speed for portable mixer) until icing forms peaks. Makes 3 cups.

[1] When using large countertop mixer or for stiffer icing, use 1 tablespoon less water.

Thinned Royal Icing:
To thin for pouring, add 1 teaspoon water per cup of royal icing. Use grease-free spoon or spatula to stir slowly. Add ½ teaspoon water at a time until you reach proper consistency.

Stabilized Whipped Cream Icing

½ pint (1 cup) heavy whipping cream
2 tablespoons confectioners' sugar
2 tablespoons Piping Gel (p. 137)
½ teaspoon Clear Vanilla Extract (p. 139)

Combine whipping cream and sugar in mixing bowl. Whip to soft peak stage. Add Piping Gel and vanilla, then continue to whip until stiff peaks form. Do not overbeat. Makes 1½ to 2 cups.

As an alternative, you can use frozen non-dairy whipped topping or packaged topping mix. Thaw frozen whipped topping in refrigerator before coloring or using for decorating. Use packaged topping mix immediately after preparing. Do not allow either to stay at room temperature, as it becomes too soft for decorating. Store decorated cake in refrigerator until ready to serve.

Heated Wilton Ready-To-Use Decorator Icing (p. 137)

Open icing container, remove foil. Microwave at 30% (Defrost) Power for 20-30 seconds, stirring at least once, until ready to pour. If a microwave is unavailable, icing container can be heated on a warming tray or in a pan of hot water on a stove.

Color Flow Icing Recipe (full-strength for outlining)

¼ cup + 1 teaspoon water
4 cups sifted confectioners' sugar (about 1 lb.)
2 tablespoons Color Flow Mix (p. 137)

With electric mixer, using grease-free utensils, blend all ingredients on low speed for 5 minutes. If using hand mixer, use high speed. Color flow icing "crusts" quickly, so keep bowl covered with a damp cloth while using. Stir in desired icing color. Makes approx. 2 cups color flow icing.

Thinned Color Flow: In order to fill an outlined area, the recipe above must be thinned with ½ teaspoon of water per ¼ cup of icing (just a few drops at a time as you near proper consistency). Use grease-free spoon or spatula to stir slowly. Color flow is ready for filling in outlines when a small amount dropped into the mixture takes a count of ten to disappear.

NOTE: Color flow designs take a long time to dry, so plan to do your color flow piece up to 1 week in advance.

Poured Cookie Icing

This icing dries to a shiny, hard finish. Great to use as icing or to outline and fill in with tip 2 or 3.

1 cup sifted confectioners' sugar
2 teaspoons milk
2 teaspoons light corn syrup

Place sugar and milk in bowl. Stir until thoroughly mixed. Add corn syrup; mix well. For filling in areas, use thinned icing (add small amounts of light corn syrup until desired consistency is reached).

COOKIE RECIPES

Roll-Out Cookies

1 cup (2 sticks) unsalted butter, softened
1½ cups granulated sugar

1 egg
1½ teaspoons Clear Vanilla Extract (p. 139)
½ teaspoon No-Color Almond Extract (p. 139)
2¾ cups all-purpose flour
2 teaspoons baking powder
1 teaspoon salt

Preheat oven to 400°F. In large bowl, cream butter with sugar with electric mixer until light and fluffy. Add egg and extracts; mix well. Combine flour, baking powder and salt; add to butter mixture 1 cup at a time, mixing after each addition. Do not chill dough. Divide dough into 2 balls. On a floured surface, roll each ball into a circle approximately 12 in. wide and ⅛ in. thick. Dip cookie cutter in flour before each use. Bake cookies on ungreased cookie sheet 6-7 minutes or until cookies are lightly browned. Makes about 3 dozen cookies. Recipe may be doubled.

Chocolate Roll-Out Cookies

¾ cup (1½ sticks) butter or margarine, softened
1 cup granulated sugar
2 eggs
1 teaspoon vanilla extract
3 squares (3 oz.) unsweetened chocolate, melted and cooled
3 cups all-purpose flour
1 teaspoon baking powder

Preheat oven to 375°F. In large bowl, cream butter with sugar using mixer until light and fluffy. Add eggs and vanilla; mix well. Blend in chocolate. Combine flour and baking powder; add to butter mixture, 1 cup at a time, mixing after each addition. Cover and chill until firm, about 1 hour.

Roll out dough approximately ⅛ in. thick. Dip cookie cutter in flour before each use. Bake cookies on ungreased cookie sheet 8-10 minutes or until cookies are lightly browned. Remove to rack and cool thoroughly. Makes 2-2 ½ dozen cookies.

Grandma's Gingerbread

5 to 5½ cups all-purpose flour
1 teaspoon baking soda
1 teaspoon salt
2 teaspoons ground ginger
2 teaspoons ground cinnamon
1 teaspoon ground nutmeg
1 teaspoon ground cloves
1 cup solid vegetable shortening
1 cup granulated sugar
1¼ cups unsulphured molasses[2]
2 eggs, beaten

Preheat oven to 375°F. Thoroughly mix flour, soda, salt and spices. Melt shortening in large saucepan. Cool slightly. Add sugar, molasses and eggs to saucepan; mix well. Add 4 cups dry ingredients and mix well.

Turn mixture onto lightly floured surface. Knead in remaining dry ingredients by hand. Add a little more flour, if necessary, to make firm dough.

On floured surface, roll ¼ in. thick for cut-out cookies. Bake on ungreased cookie sheet. Small and medium-sized cookies for 6-10 minutes, large cookies for 10-15 minutes. Makes 40 medium-sized cookies.

NOTE: If you're not going to use your gingerbread dough right away, wrap in plastic and refrigerate. Refrigerated dough will keep for a week.

[2] Substitute 1¼ cups light corn syrup for molasses to make Blonde Gingerbread.

SPECIALTY RECIPES

Strawberry Mousse

1 package (8 oz.) cream cheese, softened
1 jar (18 oz.) seedless strawberry jam or preserves
1 box Wilton Whipped Icing Mix (p. 137)

In large bowl, beat cream cheese with electric mixer at medium speed until smooth and creamy. Beat in jam; blend well.

Prepare Whipped Icing Mix according to package directions. Fold into cream cheese mixture; blend well. Use immediately or store covered in refrigerator up to 5 days. Makes 6 cups.

Cream Cheese Mousse

2½ cups whipping cream
4 envelopes (.25 oz. ea.) unflavored gelatin
1 cup cold water
2 packages (8 oz. ea.) cream cheese, softened
1¾ cups granulated sugar
1 tablespoon vanilla extract
2 tablespoons lemon juice
1½ tablespoons lemon zest

Spray pan with vegetable pan spray; if desired, line with plastic wrap and spray wrap.

In large bowl, whip cream with electric mixer until soft peaks form; chill until ready to use. In medium saucepan, combine gelatin with water; let stand 5 minutes. Cook on low heat 5 minutes, stirring constantly, or until gelatin is completely dissolved. In large bowl, beat cream cheese and sugar with electric mixer until light and fluffy; add vanilla, lemon juice and zest, mixing well. Beat in dissolved gelatin; immediately fold in whipped cream. Pour into prepared pan. Refrigerate until firm, at least 6 hours or overnight.

Makes 18-20 servings.

Spicy Cheddar Spread

4 cups (16 oz.) medium sharp cheddar cheese, shredded
2 packages (8 oz. each) cream cheese, softened
4 tablespoons packaged taco seasoning mix
1 can (4 oz.) chopped green chilies, well drained

Lightly spray pan with vegetable pan spray; line with plastic wrap. With electric mixer or food processor fitted with metal blade, blend all ingredients except chilies. Stir in chilies. Press into prepared pan. Cover and chill until firm, several hours or overnight. Unmold shortly before serving. Makes about 5 cups (enough to fill 4 Mini Wonder Molds).

*Changes in Wilton's traditional recipes have been made due to Trans Fat Free Shortening replacing Hydrogenated Shortening

ROLLED FONDANT AND GUM PASTE RECIPES

Fondant is rolled out and used as a covering for any firm-textured cake, pound cake or fruit cake, which is traditionally first covered with a layer of marzipan to seal in flavor and moistness of the cake. A light layer of buttercream icing or apricot glaze may also be used. Cakes covered with rolled fondant can be decorated with royal or buttercream icing. Wilton also offers convenient Ready-To-Use Rolled Fondant (p. 130) for easy-to-handle fondant with no mixing.

Rolled Fondant

1 tablespoon plus 2 teaspoons
  unflavored gelatin
¼ cup cold water
½ cup Wilton Glucose (p. 133)
2 tablespoons solid vegetable shortening
1 tablespoon Wilton Glycerin (p. 133)
Icing color and flavoring, as desired
8 cups sifted confectioners' sugar
  (about 2 lbs.)

Combine gelatin and cold water; let stand until thick. Place gelatin mixture in top of double boiler and heat until dissolved. Add glucose, mix well. Stir in shortening and just before completely melted, remove from heat. Add glycerin, flavoring and color. Cool until lukewarm. Next, place 4 cups confectioners' sugar in a bowl and make a well. Pour the lukewarm gelatin mixture into the well and stir with a wooden spoon, mixing in sugar and adding more, a little at a time, until stickiness disappears. Knead in remaining sugar. Knead until the fondant is smooth, pliable and does not stick to your hands. If fondant is too soft, add more sugar; if too stiff, add water (a drop at a time). Use fondant immediately or store in airtight container in a cool, dry place. Do not refrigerate or freeze. When ready to use, knead again until soft. This recipe makes approx. 36 oz., enough to cover a 10 x 4 in. round cake.

Extra-Firm Rolled Fondant

Use this recipe for a fondant with the extra body and pliability ideal for making drapes, swags and elaborate decorations.

1 to 2 teaspoons Gum-Tex™ (p. 133)
24 oz. Ready-To-Use Rolled Fondant (p. 130)

Knead Gum-Tex™ into fondant until smooth. Store in an airtight container or tightly wrapped in plastic.

Gum Paste

Clay-like gum paste can be rolled thinner than fondant for finer detail. Gum paste dries hard and is meant for decoration only; remove from cake before serving. For perfectly mixed gum paste whenever you need it, try Wilton Ready-To-Use Gum Paste (p. 133).

1 tablespoon Gum-Tex™ (p. 133)
3 cups sifted confectioners' sugar
  (about ¾ lb.)
1 heaping tablespoon Glucose (p. 133)
4 tablespoons warm water
1 cup sifted confectioners' sugar
  (about ¼ lb.; save until ready to use)

In a large bowl, mix Gum-Tex™ into 3 cups confectioners' sugar. Make a well in the center and set aside. Mix water and glucose in a glass measuring cup and blend; heat in microwave on high for about 30 seconds until mixture is clear. Pour into well of 3 cups confectioners' sugar and mix until well blended (mixture will be very soft). Place mixture in a plastic bag and seal tightly; let mixture rest at room temperature for 8 hours or overnight. Knead remaining confectioner's sugar into gum paste when you are ready to use it. As you work it in, gum paste will whiten and soften.

Apricot Glaze

Ideal for preparing a cake for fondant or for crumb-coating cakes before icing.

1 cup apricot preserves

Heat preserves to boiling, strain. Brush on cake while glaze is still hot. Let dry. Glaze will dry to a hard finish in 15 minutes or less. Makes enough to cover a 10 x 4 in. cake.

Thinned Fondant Adhesive

Use this mixture when attaching dried fondant to other fondant decorations or for attaching freshly-cut fondant pieces to lollipop sticks or florist wire.

1 oz. Wilton Ready-To-Use Rolled Fondant (p. 130)
  (1½ in. ball)
¼ teaspoon water

Knead water into fondant until it becomes softened and sticky. To attach a fondant decoration, place mixture in decorating bag fitted with a small round tip, or brush on back of decoration. Recipe may be doubled.

Gum Paste Adhesive

1 tablespoon Wilton Meringue Powder (p. 137)
1 tablespoon water

This easy-to-make "glue" will hold your gum paste flowers and other decorations together. Mix Meringue Powder and water together; add more water if mixture is too thick. Brush on decorations.

Chocolate Fondant

1 pk. (14 oz.) Dark Cocoa Candy Melts®* (p. 166)
½ cup light corn syrup
24 oz. White Ready-To-Use Rolled Fondant (p. 130)
Brown or Black Icing Color (p. 136, optional)

Melt Candy Melts® following package directions. Add corn syrup; stir to blend. Turn out mixture onto waxed paper; let stand at room temperature to dry and harden several hours. Wrap well and store at room temperature until ready to continue with recipe.

Knead small portions of candy mixture until soft and pliable. Knead softened mixture into fondant until smooth and evenly colored. If darker color is desired, knead in icing color.

Quick-Pour Fondant Icing

6 cups sifted confectioners' sugar (about 1½ lbs.)
½ cup water
2 tablespoons light corn syrup
1 teaspoon Almond Extract (p. 139)
Wilton Icing Colors (p. 136)

Cakes should be covered with apricot glaze (see recipe above) or a thin coating of buttercream icing. Let set 15 minutes before covering with fondant.

Place sugar in saucepan. Combine water and corn syrup. Add to sugar and stir until well mixed. Place over low heat. Don't allow temperature of fondant to exceed 100°F. Remove from heat, stir in flavor and icing color. To cover, place cake or cookies on cooling grid over a drip pan. Pour fondant into center and work towards edges. Touch up bare spots with spatula. Let set. Excess fondant can be reheated. Makes 2½ cups.

*Brand confectionery coating.

Using Rolled Fondant

The dough-like consistency of fondant makes it the perfect medium for creating ruffles and braids, stately molded accents, distinctive borders, fun trims and beautiful flowers. Decorators agree that fondant is an icing that is truly easy to work with. It's even easier with Wilton Ready-To-Use Rolled Fondant (p. 130)—no mixing, no mess!

COVERING THE CAKE

How do you cover a cake with fondant that's perfectly smooth, without wrinkles or air bubbles? The flexibility of fondant is your secret weapon. Just follow our instructions for the right ways to knead, roll out and lift the fondant, and you'll find that covering a cake is easy. For instructions on covering Square, Petal and other cake shapes, see the *Celebrate® With Fondant* book, p. 128.

1. Prepare cake by lightly covering with buttercream icing.

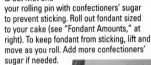

2. Before rolling out fondant, knead it until it is a workable consistency. If fondant is sticky, knead in a little confectioners' sugar. Lightly dust your smooth work surface or the Roll & Cut Mat and your rolling pin with confectioners' sugar to prevent sticking. Roll out fondant sized to your cake (see "Fondant Amounts," at right). To keep fondant from sticking, lift and move as you roll. Add more confectioners' sugar if needed.

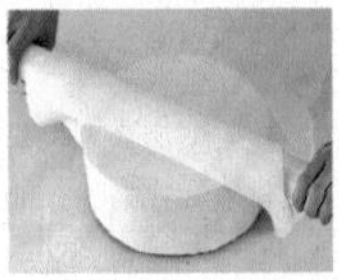

3. Gently lift fondant over rolling pin and position on cake.

4. Shape fondant to sides of cake with Easy-Glide Smoother. We recommend using the Smoother because the pressure of your hands may leave impressions on the fondant. Use the straight edge of the Smoother to mark fondant at the base of cake. Trim off excess fondant using a spatula or sharp knife.

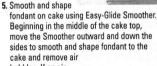

5. Smooth and shape fondant on cake using Easy-Glide Smoother. Beginning in the middle of the cake top, move the Smoother outward and down the sides to smooth and shape fondant to the cake and remove air bubbles. If an air bubble appears, insert a pin on an angle, release air and smooth the area again.

COVERING LARGE CAKES

In most cases, the smaller your cake, the easier it will be to cover with rolled fondant. However, there is an easy way to position and smooth fondant on cakes that are 12 in. diameter or larger. Follow the steps below to lift fondant onto the cake without tearing.

1. Cover cake lightly with buttercream icing. Roll out fondant sized to fit your cake.

2. Slide a large cake circle that has been dusted with confectioners' sugar under the rolled fondant. Lift the circle and the fondant and position over cake. Gently shake the circle to slide the fondant off and into position on the cake. Smooth and trim as described at left.

FONDANT AMOUNTS

Use this chart to determine how much Ready-To-Use Rolled Fondant to buy. Wilton Fondant is available in 24 oz. (1 lb., 8 oz.) and 80 oz. (5 lb.) packages. Amounts listed do not include decorations.

Cake Shape	Cake Size	Fondant
Rounds 4 in. high	6 in.	18 oz.
	8 in.	24 oz.
	10 in.	36 oz.
	12 in.	48 oz.
	14 in.	72 oz.
	16 in.	108 oz.
	18 in.	140 oz.
Rounds 3 in. high	6 in.	14 oz.
	8 in.	18 oz.
	10 in.	24 oz.
	12 in.	36 oz.
	14 in.	48 oz.
	16 in.	72 oz.
	18 in.	108 oz.
Sheets 2 in. high	7 x 11 in.	30 oz.
	9 x 13 in.	40 oz.
	11 x 15 in.	60 oz.
	12 x 18 in.	80 oz.
Ovals 4 in. high	7¾ x 5⅝ in.	24 oz.
	10¾ x 7⅞ in.	36 oz.
	13 x 9⅞ in.	48 oz.
	16½ x 12⅜ in.	72 oz.
Hearts 4 in. high	6 in.	18 oz.
	8 in.	26 oz.
	9 in.	32 oz.
	10 in.	36 oz.
	12 in.	48 oz.
	14 in.	72 oz.
	16 in.	96 oz.
Petals 4 in. high	6 in.	18 oz.
	9 in.	30 oz.
	12 in.	48 oz.
	15 in.	72 oz.
Squares 4 in. high	6 in.	24 oz.
	8 in.	36 oz.
	10 in.	48 oz.
	12 in.	72 oz.
	14 in.	96 oz.
	16 in.	120 oz.
Hexagons 4 in. high	6 in.	18 oz.
	9 in.	36 oz.
	12 in.	48 oz.
	15 in.	84 oz.
Paisley 4 in. high	6 x 9 in.	20 oz.
	9 x 12¾ in.	48 oz.
	12 x 17 in.	72 oz.

HOW TO COLOR AND FLAVOR FONDANT

You can easily tint our White Ready-To-Use Rolled Fondant (p. 130) or the Rolled Fondant recipe (above) using Wilton Icing Colors (p. 136). Using a toothpick, add icing color, a little at a time, and knead into fondant until color is evenly blended. Wilton Ready-To-Use Rolled Fondant has a mellow flavor which can be enhanced using Wilton Butter Flavor, Clear Vanilla Extract or Almond Extract (p. 139). Knead flavor into fondant until well blended.

Tip Techniques

Your icing turned out great—now you're ready to learn how to pipe beautiful shapes on your cake. Stars, shells, dots, lines and other techniques are the foundation of your decorating knowledge. We'll tell you step-by-step how to pipe each one, including the angle, pressure and movement to use for a uniform look. With practice, you can build on these basics to create many other impressive designs.

ROUND TIPS

Dot

Pipe dots for flower centers, faces, figure piping and border effects. When making large dots, lift the tip as you squeeze to allow icing to fill out completely.

Practice With: Tip 3
Icing Consistency: Medium
Bag Position: 90°
Hold Tip: Slightly above surface

1. Hold the bag straight up with the tip slightly above the surface. Squeeze the bag and keep point of the tip in icing until the dot is the size you want.
2. Stop squeezing the bag completely before you lift the tip from the dot.
3. Lift tip up and pull away from piped dot.

Ball

An important technique to master, the ball shape makes bold borders and is the first step to learn for figure piping. Vary the basic look by adding stars, dots or spirals on the ball shapes.

Practice With: Tip 9
Icing Consistency: Medium
Bag Position: 90°
Hold Tip: Slightly above surface

1. Squeeze the bag, applying steady even pressure. As the icing begins to build up, raise the tip with it, but keep the tip end buried in the icing.
2. Stop squeezing as you bring the end of the tip to the surface.
3. Lift the tip up and pull away from your piped ball. Use the edge of the tip to shave off any point so that your ball is nicely rounded.

Bead

If you can pipe a shell, you can pipe a bead—the movements are similar. To pipe a bead heart, simply pipe one bead, then a second, joining the tails. Smooth together using a decorator's brush.

Practice With: Tip 5
Icing Consistency: Medium
Bag Position†: 45° at 3:00 (9:00)
Hold Tip: Slightly above surface

1. Squeeze as you lift tip slightly so that icing fans out.
2. Relax pressure as you draw the tip down and bring the bead to a point.
3. To make a bead border, start the end of your next bead so that the fanned end covers the tail of the preceding bead to form an even chain.

Cornelli Lace

The lacy design of this freehand technique depends on continuous curving strings that do not overlap or touch.

Practice With: Tip 1 or 2
Icing Consistency: Thin
Bag Position: 90°
Hold Tip: Close to cake so icing attaches without scraping cake with tip and without flattening icing strings

Beginning and ending at edges, pipe a continuous string of icing, curve it up, down and around until area is covered. Make certain strings never touch or cross. Don't leave any loose ends! Stop pressure; pull tip away.

Printing

Practice With: Tip 3 with message press
Icing Consistency: Thin
Bag Position†: 45° at 3:00 (9:00)
Hold Tip: Lightly touching surface

You may pipe letters freehand, pipe over a pattern traced with a toothpick, or pipe after imprinting letters with a pattern press. If you are using a pattern press, let icing crust slightly, then imprint the message. With a steady, even pressure, squeeze out a straight line, lifting the tip off the surface to let icing string drop. To prevent tails from forming, be careful to stop squeezing before you touch tip to surface and pull away. Be sure the end of the tip is clean before you go on to another line.

Writing

Practice With: Tip 5
Icing Consistency: Thin
Bag Position†: 45° at 3:00 (9:00)
Hold Tip: Lightly touching surface

You may pipe letters freehand, pipe over a pattern traced with a toothpick, or pipe after imprinting letters with a pattern press. If you are using a pattern press, let icing crust slightly, then imprint the message. Steadily squeeze, gliding along the surface in a smooth, continuous motion. Use your arm, not your fingers, to form each line, letter or word. Keep your wrist straight, moving your entire forearm as a single unit. After you begin to master the curves and swings of the letters, lift the tip up slightly as you write. You'll find you have more control if you let the icing draw out slightly over the surface as you write.

Outline

Characters or designs are often outlined first, then piped in with stars or zigzags. Outlines are used for facial features, too. Color Flow plaques are also outlined before icing is flowed into the shape.

Practice With: Tip 3
Icing Consistency: Thin
Bag Position: 45° at 3:00 (9:00)
Hold Tip: Slightly above surface

1. Touch tip to surface. Raise the tip slightly and continue to squeeze.
2. The icing will flow out of the tip while you direct it along the surface.
3. To end, stop squeezing, touch tip to surface and pull away.

To Pipe-In
After outlining, using the same tip, squeeze out rows of lines to fill area. Pat icing down with fingertip dipped in cornstarch or smooth with dampened art brush.

Drop Strings

These flowing strings are a beautiful way to adorn the sides of a cake. The trick to making drop strings is to pull the bag toward you as the string drapes down. If you "draw" the string with the tip, you won't achieve a pretty curve and your strings will tend to break. Pipe at eye level to your cake so that strings line up evenly. The Cake Dividing Set (p. 135) is a great help in accurately dividing and marking your cake for even drop strings.

Single Drop Strings

Practice With: Tip 3
Icing Consistency: Stiff
Bag Position†: Shoulder level at 4:30 (7:30)
Hold Tip: Lightly touching surface to attach

1. With a toothpick, mark horizontal divisions on cake in the width you desire. Touch tip to first mark and squeeze, pausing momentarily so that icing sticks to surface.
2. While squeezing, pull the bag toward you. Continue squeezing to allow the icing to drape naturally into an arc. Icing will drop by itself—do not move the tip down with the string. The end of the tip should be the same distance from the surface as the width from point to point on your cake.
3. Stop pressure before you touch tip to second mark to end string. Repeat, keeping drop strings uniform in length and width.

Multiple Drop Strings

Try a different color for each row of multiple drop strings—put holiday colors together to really dress up your cake.

To add multiple rows of strings, mark the cake for the deepest row and pipe that row. Return to the first drop string point, squeeze the bag, and drop a string with a slightly shorter arc than in the first row. Join the end of this string to the end of the corresponding string in the first row. Repeat the process for a third row of drop strings above the second.

STAR TIPS

Star

Practice With: Tip 16
Icing Consistency: Medium
Bag Position: 90°
Hold Tip: Between ⅛ and ¼ in. above surface

1. Hold the decorating bag straight up, with the tip between ⅛ and ¼ in. above the surface, while using your other hand to hold the tip steady. Squeeze the bag to form a star. Increasing or decreasing the pressure changes the size of the star.
2. Stop squeezing the bag completely before you lift the tip from the star.
3. Lift the tip up and pull away from piped star.

Pull-out stars add even more dimension to your cake. To make them, hold bag at a 45° angle to surface. As you squeeze out icing, pull tip up and away from cake. When your mound is high enough, stop pressure and pull tip away. Work from bottom to top of area to be covered with pull-out stars.

Star Fill In

Because these close-together stars require so much piping from the same bag, it's a good idea to keep replenishing the icing. Replenish icing when it gets soft or stars will be poorly defined.

Practice With: Tip 16
Icing Consistency: Medium
Bag Position: 90°
Hold Tip: ¼ in. above surface

1. Pipe a row of stars evenly and close together, adjusting the tip position slightly each time so that the points of the stars interlock and cover the area without gaps.
2. Pipe a row of stars beneath the first, again adjusting tip position to close any gaps.
3. Continue to fill in entire area.

Zigzag

A quick and popular way to fill in outlined areas, perfect for ribbed sweater and cuff effects. You can use tight zigzags to cover the entire side of your cake—they look great!

Practice With: Tip 16
Icing Consistency: Medium
Bag Position†: 45° at 3:00 (9:00)
Hold Tip: Lightly touching surface

1. Steadily squeeze and move your hand in a tight up and down motion.
2. Continue piping up and down with steady pressure. To end, stop pressure and pull tip away. For more elongated zigzags, move your hand to the desired height while maintaining a steady pressure. For a more relaxed look, just increase the width as you move the bag along.
3. Repeat as you move in a straight line with consistent up/down motion.

†The technique instructions in this Decorating Guide will list the correct direction for holding the bag. When the bag direction differs for left-handed decorators, that direction will be listed in parentheses. For example, when a bag is to be held at 3:00 for a right-handed decorator, it should be held at 9:00 for a left-handed decorator.

116 | 2008 WILTON YEARBOOK

Zigzag Puff

This is the fluffy look you want for making clouds or smoke and to add dimension as a side border.

Practice With: Tip 17
Icing Consistency: Medium
Bag Position†: 45° at 3:00 (9:00)
Hold Tip: Lightly touching surface

1. Begin to pipe with a light pressure, then use heavier pressure toward the center of the puff, then return gradually to a light pressure to form the tapered end.
2. To end each puff, stop pressure and pull tip away.
3. Repeat as you move in a straight line to form a row of puffs.

Shell

Most popular icing technique of all, the shell is the basis for many borders. Lift tip slightly when piping shells to avoid a bumpy look.

Practice With: Tip 21
Icing Consistency: Medium
Bag Position: 45° at 6:00
Hold Tip: Slightly above surface

1. Hold the bag in the 6:00 position so that you can pull the bag toward you. The tip should be slightly above the surface.
2. Squeeze hard, letting the icing fan out generously as it lifts the tip—do not lift the bag. Gradually relax your pressure as you lower the tip until it touches the surface.
3. Stop pressure and pull the tip away, without lifting it off the surface, to draw the shell to a point.
4. To make a shell border, start the end of your next shell so that the fanned end covers the tail of the preceding shell to form an even chain.

Reverse Shell

Opposite-facing shells look spectacular as top and bottom borders and as framed areas on your cake—they add a wonderful motion effect. The look is even fancier finished with a dot or a star at the center of each shell curve.

Practice With: Tip 21
Icing Consistency: Medium
Bag Position: 45° at 6:00
Hold Tip: Slightly above surface

1. As you begin to form a shell, squeeze hard, letting the icing fan out.
2. Form a curve, moving the tip from 9:00 (3:00) to 12:00 to 6:00. Relax pressure and lower the tip, pulling straight toward you at 6:00 to form a tail.
3. Repeat with another shell, curving from 3:00 (9:00) to 12:00 to 6:00.
4. To make a reverse shell border, pipe a chain of swirling reverse shells, with the fan end of each new shell covering the tail of the previous shell. If you are making the border on a round cake, turn the cake as you go so that the back of the bag is at 6:00 and you are working toward yourself.

Rope

Finish your piped baskets with pretty edging and handles. Excellent for western or nautical themed cakes. You can make a great-looking rope with star or round tips (or basketweave tips, ridged or smooth side up).

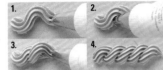

Practice With: Tip 21
Icing Consistency: Medium
Bag Position: 45° at 4:30 (7:30)
Hold Tip: Lightly touching surface

1. Using a steady, even pressure, move the tip in a gentle sideways "S" curve. Stop pressure and pull tip away.
2. Insert tip under the bottom curve of the "S" shape.
3. Squeeze the bag with steady pressure as you pull down, then lift the tip. Move up and over the tail of the "S" as you continue to squeeze and form a hook.
4. Keep spacing as even as possible and "S" curves uniform in thickness, length and overall size. Be sure to tuck the tip into the bottom curve of the previous "S" before you begin squeezing to insure the clean, continuous look of a rope.

e-Motion

These continuous e-shaped loops work best on a bottom border, or as a western lariat. If you have to stop on your border to change positions, push in your tip at the end of the "e" and continue piping to keep a smooth look.

Practice With: Tip 16
Icing Consistency: Medium
Bag Position†: 45° at 3:00 (9:00)
Hold Tip: Slightly above surface

1. Starting with bag at a 45° angle, and at bottom edge, squeeze out icing with even pressure, moving tip up to the right…
2. …and around as if writing the letter "e."
3. Repeat to complete the border, using a steady, even pressure. To end, stop pressure, pull tip away. You can vary the look of the e-motion border by making tight e's or stretched e's.

Rosette

Practice With: Tip 16
Icing Consistency: Medium
Bag Position: 90°
Hold Tip: Lightly touching surface

1. Keeping the tip slightly above the surface, squeeze out icing to form a star and, without releasing pressure, move the tip in a tight, complete rotation, starting at 9:00 (3:00), moving to 12:00. . .
2. then to 3:00 (9:00) and 6:00. . .
3. and ending back at 9:00 (3:00).
4. Stop pressure and lift tip away.

MULTIPLE TIPS

Swirl Drop Flower

The swirled look adds a nice motion effect to the cake. You must squeeze and turn at the same time.

Practice With: Tips 2D, 3; use Large Coupler
Icing Consistency: Use royal icing: medium for flower, thin for center
Bag Position: 90°
Hold Tip: Slightly above surface

1. Turn your wrist in toward you before piping. Hold bag straight up, just touching the surface. You will turn wrist a full twist. Starting with the flat of your knuckles at 9:00 (3:00), as you squeeze out the icing, slowly turn your hand, with knuckles ending at 12:00.
2. Stop squeezing and lift the tip away.
3. Make a tip 3 dot flower center, holding your bag straight up and keeping the tip buried as you squeeze. Stop squeezing, then pull your tip up and away.

BASKETWEAVE TIPS

Try using different tips to vary the woven effects.

Practice With: Tip 47
Icing Consistency: Medium
Bag Position: 45° at 6:00 for vertical stripes; at 3:00 (9:00) for horizontal bars
Hold Tip: Lightly touching surface, serrated side up

1. Squeeze out a vertical stripe of icing from top to bottom (shown ridged side up).
2. Squeeze out short horizontal stripes of icing across the vertical stripe starting at the top. Spacing between stripes should be the same as the width of the tip opening. Squeeze next vertical stripe over ends of horizontal stripes. Start next set of horizontal stripes by burying the tip under the first vertical stripe.
3. Repeat vertical lines then horizontal lines until you achieve basketweave effect. Each new set should fit between the previous set.

PETAL TIPS

Ruffle

Everyone loves a ruffle's graceful motion—ruffles always add interest to your cake. Use them as a top border, to frame a plaque or to trim doll dresses and baby bonnets.

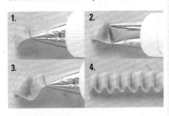

Practice With: Tip 104
Icing Consistency: Medium
Bag Position†: 45° at 3:00 (9:00)
Hold Tip: Wide end lightly touching surface with narrow end facing down and away from surface

1. Keep the wide end of your tip touching the cake with the narrow end down. Move wrist up to pull up icing.
2. Move wrist down to complete one curl of the ruffle.
3. Repeat up and down motion.
4. Raise and lower the narrow end as you move around the cake. Repeat this motion for the entire ruffle.

Bow

The bow has many uses. Create a different look by using a different tip: round, star and petal will work.

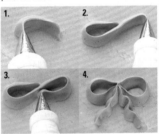

Practice With: Tip 104
Icing Consistency: Medium
Bag Position: 45° at 6:00
Hold Tip: Wide end touching surface, narrow end straight up

1. With narrow end of tip pointing straight up, squeeze, moving the tip up and around to the left and back to the starting point.
2. Continue around, making a second loop on the right.
3. The two loops will form a figure 8.
4. While holding bag in the same position, return to the center and squeeze out two streamers.

DECORATING WILTON SHAPED CAKES STEP-BY-STEP

When decorating a cake that's simply covered with stars, here are the easy steps involved.

1. Ice sides and other areas smooth per instructions.

2. Outline details.

3. Pipe in facial features, small details.

4. Cover areas with stars, stripes, zigzags or dots.

5. Add message. Edge top and base with borders. Attach flowers or trims.

Flower-Making Techniques

Explore beautiful flowers like the sweet pea or carnation, which add lovely color to your cake design. Create the magnificent rose—the most popular icing flower of all. With practice, your flowers will have the just-picked look of real garden flowers.

FLOWER NAIL FLOWERS

Using a Flower Nail

The nail is a revolving platform you hold in your hand to conveniently build roses and other flowers. It allows you to work close up, to turn for easy piping and to remove your completed flowers without damage, to dry.

The key to making the flower on the nail is to coordinate the turning of the nail with the formation of each petal.

Attach a square of waxed paper on the flat surface of the flower nail using a dot of icing. Pipe your flower directly on the waxed paper. Hold the flower nail between the thumb and forefinger of your left (right) hand (use other fingers to support nail) and roll it slowly counterclockwise (clockwise for lefties) as you press out icing with the decorating bag held in the right (left) hand. Your right (left) hand moves in and out, or up and down, as it holds the decorating bag and tip at just the right angle (in most cases 45°) and keeps the icing flowing at an even speed. After piping, slide the waxed paper

The Wilton Rose

NOTE: If you are going to be placing your roses on your cake immediately, waxed paper squares are not needed. To remove finished roses, use the Flower Lifter (p. 140). Slide flower from lifter onto cake, using a spatula.

Practice With: Tips 104, 12
Icing Consistency: Royal or stiff buttercream
Bag Position†: Base 90° (straight up); petals 45° at 4:30 (7:30)
Hold Tip: For base, slightly above nail; for petals, wide end touching base
Flower Nail: #7

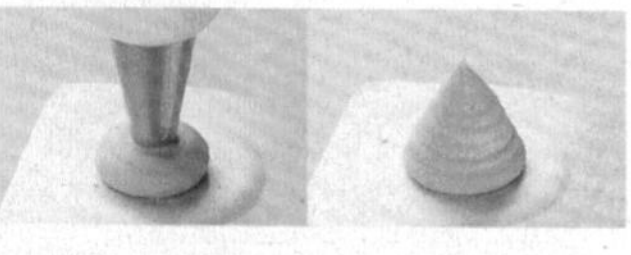

1. Make the rose base, using tip 12 and flower nail #7. Hold the bag straight up, the end of tip 12 slightly above the center of your waxed paper-covered flower nail, which is held in your other hand. Using heavy pressure, build up a base, remembering to keep your tip buried as you squeeze. Start to lift the tip higher, gradually raise the tip, and decrease the pressure.
2. Stop pressure, pull up and lift away. The rose base should be 1 1/2 times as high as the rose tip opening.

3. Make the center bud, using tip 104. Hold nail containing base in your left (right) hand and bag with rose tip 104 in right (left) hand. Bag should be at a 45° angle to the flat surface of the nail and in the 4:30 (7:30) position. The wide end of the tip should touch the cone of the icing base at or slightly below the midpoint, and the narrow end of the tip should point up and angled in over top of base.
4. Now you must do 3 things at the same time: squeeze the bag, move the tip and rotate the nail. As you squeeze the bag, move the tip up from the base, forming a ribbon of icing. Slowly turn the nail counterclockwise (clockwise for lefties) to bring the ribbon of icing around to overlap at the top of the mound, then back down to starting point. Move your tip straight up and down only; do not loop it around the base.
5. Now you have a finished center bud.

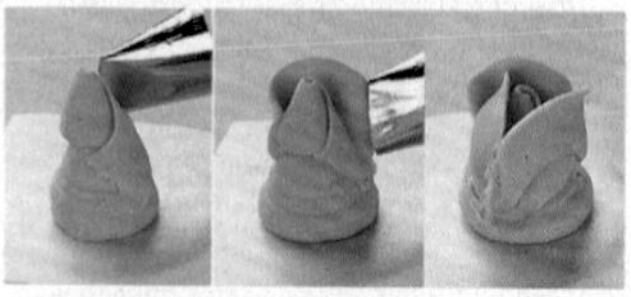

6. Make the top row of 3 petals. Touch the wide end of tip to the midpoint of bud base, narrow end straight up.
7. Turn nail, keeping wide end of tip on base so that petal will attach. Move tip up and back down to the midpoint of mound, forming the first petal.
8. Start again, slightly behind end of first petal, and squeeze out second petal. Repeat for the third petal, ending by overlapping the starting point of the first petal. Rotate the nail 1/3 turn for each petal.

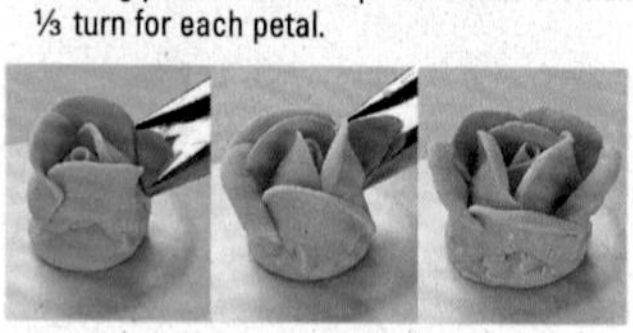

9. Make the middle row of 5 petals. Touch the wide end of tip slightly below center of a petal in the top row. Angle the narrow end of tip out slightly more than you did for the top row of petals. Squeeze bag and turn nail moving tip up, then down, to form first petal.
10. Repeat for a total of 5 petals, rotating the nail 1/5 turn for each petal.
11. The last petal end should overlap the first's starting point.

12. Make the bottom row of 7 petals. Touch the wide end of tip below the center of a middle row petal, again angling the narrow end of tip out a little more. Squeeze bag and turn nail to end of fingers, moving tip up, then down to form first petal.
13. Repeat for a total of 7 petals, rotating the nail 1/7 turn for each petal.

14. The last petal end should overlap the first's starting point.
15. Slip waxed paper and completed rose from nail. This is the completed Wilton Rose.

†The technique instructions in this Decorating Guide will list the correct direction for holding the bag. When the bag direction differs for left-handed decorators, that direction will be listed in parentheses. For example, when a bag is to be held at 3:00 for a right-handed decorator, it should be held at 9:00 for a left-handed decorator.

Rosebud

Finish your petit fours or cupcakes with one pretty rosebud. Made in buttercream, this flat flower can be piped directly on the cake.

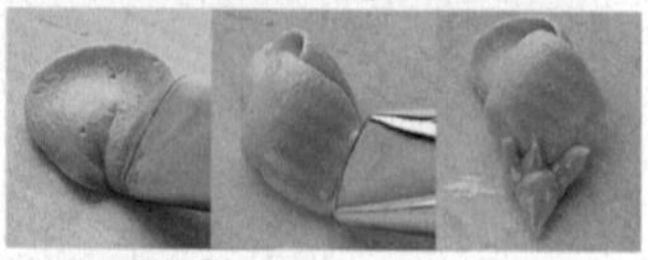

Practice With: Tips 104, 3
Icing Consistency: Stiff consistency buttercream for petals, thin consistency for sepals and calyx
Bag Position†: 45° at 4:30 (7:30) for petals; 45° at 6:00 for sepals and calyx

1. Using tip 104, make the base petal. Keep the narrow end of the tip raised up and slightly to the right (left for lefties). While squeezing, move the tip along the surface away from you in a straight line about 1/4 in. long. Pause, then continue squeezing as the icing fans out. Returning the tip to the original position and halfway back, start to release pressure, move tip to starting point, stop pressure and pull tip away.
2. Using tip 104, make the overlapping petal. Touch the wide end of the tip to the outside edge of completed petal. The bag is positioned as for the base petal, at 4:30 (7:30); hold it steady in this position until the second petal is completed. As you continue squeezing, the icing will catch the edge of the base petal and roll over it naturally. When the second petal looks complete, stop pressure completely, touch the tip back down to the surface and pull tip away.
3. Using tip 3, make the sepals and calyx. Form the middle sepal first by squeezing and letting icing build up. Lift the bag up and away from the flower. Stop pressure as you pull away to form the point of the sepal. Repeat, making a sepal on the left and right sides. For the calyx, insert tip into the base of the center sepal. Squeeze, letting the icing build up. Slowly draw the tip toward you, relaxing pressure as you move away from the flower. Stop pressure, pull away. You may want to blend the calyx into the stem using a damp brush.

Sweet Pea

One of the fastest, easiest-to-make flowers; works beautifully as part of a floral cascade. Try piping them in variegated shades.

Practice With: Tips 104, 3
Icing Consistency: Buttercream—stiff for petals, thin for calyx
Bag Position†: For center petal and calyx 45° at 6:00; for left petal 45° at 4:30 (7:30); for right petal, 45° at 7:30 (4:30).
Hold Tip: Wide end touching surface; narrow end straight up

1. Make the center petal. Squeeze the bag and lift the tip slightly off the surface (about 1/4 in.) as the icing moves forward and curls. Continue to squeeze without changing position. Relax pressure and return the tip to the surface. Stop squeezing, pull tip away.
2. Make the side petals. Position your bag slightly to the left of the center petal. Follow the same procedure as you did for the center petal—squeeze, and while the petal curls, lift the tip, relaxing your pressure and lowering the tip back to the surface. Stop squeezing and pull away. Repeat for the right side petal, holding the tip to the right of the center petal.
3. Make the calyx as above with tip 3.

Apple Blossom

Pipe apple blossoms about the size of a penny and dry them on Flower Formers (p. 140).

Practice With: Tips 101, 1
Icing Consistency: Stiff royal icing
Bag Position: 45° for petals; 90° for dots
Hold Tip: Wide end touching surface, with narrow end pointed out.
Flower Nail: #7

1. Use tip 101 and hold bag at a 45° angle to flower nail with wide end of tip touching nail center, narrow end pointed out 1/8 in. away from nail surface.
2. Squeeze bag and turn nail as you move tip 1/8 in. out from nail center and back, relaxing pressure as you return to starting point.
3. Repeat procedure to make 4 more petals. Add 5 tip 1 dots for center.

Wild Rose

A pretty year-round flower piped about the size of a flower nail. If you prefer a more cupped shape, increase the angle of the tip.

Practice With: Tips 103, 1
Icing Consistency: Medium royal icing
Bag Position: For petals 45° at 3:00 (9:00); for center 90°
Hold Tip: For petals, wide end lightly touching center of nail, narrow end pointing out and raised 1/8 in. above nail surface; for centers, slightly above flower
Flower Nail: #7

1. Use tip 103 at a 45° angle. Touch nail with wide end of tip, keeping narrow end just slightly above nail surface. Begin at center of flower nail and squeeze out first petal, turning nail 1/5 turn as you move tip out toward edge of nail. Relax pressure as you return to center of nail, curving tip slightly upward to create a cupped shape. Stop squeezing as wide end touches center of nail and lift up.
2. Repeat step 4 more times.
3. Pipe tiny pull-out dot stamens with tip 1.

Daisy

Practice with Tips: #104, 5
Icing Consistency: Medium Royal Icing
Bag Position: For Petals, 45° at 3:00 (9:00); For Center, 90°
Hold Tip: For Petals, Wide End Lightly Touching 1/4 Inch Away From Center Of Nail, Narrow End Pointing Out To Outer Edge; For Center, Hold Slightly Above Flower
Flower Nail: #7

1. Dot center of flower nail with icing as guide for flower center. Starting at any point near outer edge of nail, squeeze and move tip towards center icing dot. Stop pressure, pull tip away.
2. Repeat for a total of 12 or more petals.
3. Add tip 5 flower center and press to flatten. For pollen effect, dampen your finger, dip in crushed Cake Sparkles™, then press on center.

LILY NAIL FLOWERS

Using a Lily Nail

The lily nail helps you achieve deeply cupped flowers. You use different size nails for small and large flowers—nails range from ½ to 2½ in. in diameter. To produce flowers in your lily nail, it must first be lined with aluminum foil. This makes removal of the flower from the nail possible. To prevent the foil in your lily nail from moving when piping flowers, squeeze a dab of icing in the nail before adding the foil. Place a 2 in. square of aluminum foil in bottom half of the lily nail. Gently press the top half down into the foil, lift off.

Some flowers require a shallower foil cup. For those flowers, push foil halfway into the nail. Hold the lily nail between the thumb and forefinger on your left (right) hand and roll it slowly counterclockwise (clockwise) as you press out icing with the decorating bag held in the right (left) hand. Remove the foil cup with flower and set aside to dry.

Lily

If petals split while piping, widen tip slightly by inserting a thin spatula into the opening.

Practice With: Tips 68, 14
Icing Consistency: Stiff royal icing
Bag Position†: For petals 45° at 3:00 (9:00); for center 90°
Hold Tip: For petals, lightly touching surface of nail, wide opening parallel to surface; for center, slightly above flower line.

1. Line 1⅝ in. lily nail with foil. Use tip 68. Touch center well of nail with tip and squeeze, pulling petal up and over edge of foil cup. Decrease pressure as you reach end of petal and hesitate before you stop pressure and pull tip away, drawing petal to point.
2. Pipe 2 more petals.
3. Pipe 3 more petals between open spaces.
4. Add tip 14 star center and push in stamens.

NOTE: Stamens are not to be eaten.

FLORAL GREENERY

Leaves

Practice With: Tips 352, 67, 366
Icing Consistency: Buttercream thinned with corn syrup
Bag Position: 45° at 6:00
Hold Tip: Lightly touching surface; wide opening parallel to surface

Basic Leaf	Veined	Large Leaf
Tip 352	Leaf	Tip 366
	Tip 67	Use large coupler

1. Squeeze hard to build up the base and, at the same time, lift the tip slightly.
2. Relax pressure as you pull the tip toward you, drawing the leaf to a point.
3. Stop squeezing and lift away.

Vines

Practice With: Tip 3
Icing Consistency: Thin
Bag Position: 45° at 3:00 (9:00)
Hold Tip: Lightly touching surface

1. Touch your tip lightly to the surface as you start to squeeze, then lift slightly above the surface as you draw out the stem.
2. Move tip gently up and down to form "hills and valleys." To end the line, stop squeezing and pull the tip along the surface.
3. Add secondary curved stems, starting at main stem, stopping pressure as you pull to a point.

Figure Piping

Figure piping is a way to really add personality to your cake. Your figures can be as lifelike or cartoonish as you want them to be. Begin with a base, then add familiar shapes such as dots, balls and strings to give the figure personality.

Fairies
(see Fairyland Forest, p. 104)

Make 3 Fairies on lollipop sticks. Use Fairy Pattern and royal icing. Copy patterns, reverse one, and tape patterns to cake board. Cover with waxed paper, spray lightly with vegetable pan spray. With tip 5, pipe log body, outline legs and arms, ball head. Overpipe blouse with tip 5; add tip 5 bead skirt and outline shoes. Pipe tip 2 dot hands, nose and swirl hair. Pipe tip 1s dot eyes and outline mouth. Make antenna by inserting ¾ in. lengths of spaghetti into opening of tip 3; using gentle pressure, squeeze and remove spaghetti coated with icing. Insert in hair. Let dry, remove from waxed paper and attach wings (prepared in advance) using dots of melted candy. Attach 11 ¾ in. lollipop stick to back of fairy to be positioned at top of castle. Attach 4 in. lengths of lollipop sticks to backs of remaining 2 fairies; vertically for fairy on 14 in. cake top, horizontally for fairy on 14 in. cake side. Let all set.

Family
(see Santa's Surprise, p. 48)

Figure pipe on cake using buttercream icing. Pipe in robes and pajamas with tip 7 (pat smooth with finger dipped in cornstarch). Add tip 7 ball head (flatten and smooth with finger dipped in cornstarch). Add tip 7 outline arms and tip 3 dot hands. Pipe tip 3 swirl hair, dot eyes and mouth.

Lollipop Kids
(see Just Lolligagging, p. 104)

Set lollipops on waxed paper-covered board. Using royal icing, pipe tip 12 ball head, tip 8 outline arms and legs. Add tip 3 pull-out dot hands and fingers. Add tip 5 dot shoe. Use tip 2 for dot eyes, outline details on shirts and ears (where needed) and for swirl, pull-out and outline hairdos. Use tip 1 for dots on blouse and pupils, string mouths and bows in hair. Let dry. Each serves 1.

Racing Fans, Pennants and Message Strips
(see Take a Victory Lap, p. 34)

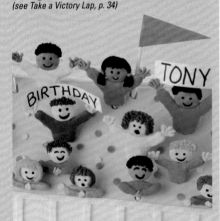

For fans, copy patterns and tape to boards; cover with waxed paper. Using royal icing, pipe tip 12 ball heads (flatten and smooth with finger dipped in cornstarch). **For smaller fans,** use tip 6 to pipe outline arms, shoulders and body; **for larger fans,** use tip 8. Pipe smaller fans hands and fingers with tip 2, larger fans with tip 3. **For all fans,** add tip 2 pull-out, outline and zigzag hairdos. Let dry. Draw facial features with black FoodWriter. Carefully remove from waxed paper. Cut lollipop sticks to 2½ in.; attach to fans' backs using royal icing, leaving 1¼ in. extended to insert into cake. Let dry. **For pennants,** cut shapes from construction paper using pattern. Tape to 4 in. lollipop sticks. **For message,** cut 1 in. wide strips; print message with FoodWriter.

Other Decorating Techniques

Combing

Practice With: Icing Sculptor™, Decorating Comb or Triangle, Trim 'N Turn™ Cake Stand (p. 135)
Icing Consistency: Medium-to-thin buttercream

Cover the cake with a slightly thicker coating of icing so the comb's ridges will not touch the cake. Hold comb at 45° angle. Comb immediately after icing cake, while icing is soft. Using a turntable helps to keep the movement smooth. Use the Icing Sculptor™, Decorating Comb or Decorating Triangle to add different contoured effects to your iced cake. Choose the type of effect you want—wide or narrow—then run that edge around your cake to form ridges. Ridges will be deep or shallow depending on the Icing Sculptor™ blade or the side of Decorating Comb or Triangle you use.

Icing Sculptor™

Select the sculpting blades you want and slide into holder. Press sculptor into iced cake as you rotate cake on turntable. Mix and match between the 64 blades to achieve the perfect look for your cake.

Pattern Press

The trick to uniform designs and steady writing and printing is using a pattern press (p. 139). Simply imprint the press on any icing, including fondant. Use the vine pattern press on cake sides for a beautiful botanical effect

Practice With: Tips 3, 16
Icing Consistency: Medium
Bag Position: 45° at 3:00
Hold Tip: Slightly above surface

1. Lightly press pattern onto your iced cake to imprint the design.
2. Outline the imprinted design with icing, using the tip of your choice. Change the tip to change the look of each pattern.

Tinting Shredded Coconut

Place desired amount of coconut in plastic bag, add a few drops of color and knead until color is evenly blended. Dry on waxed paper.

Coating Spaghetti

Break pieces of uncooked spaghetti into desired lengths. Use decorating bag with specified tip, and royal or buttercream icing as specified in cake directions. Insert a piece of spaghetti into open end of tip, then as you squeeze bag, pull spaghetti out of tip, coating spaghetti with icing. Push uncoated end into craft block to dry.

Pilgrim and Indian Cookies

(see The First Thanksgiving, p. 42)

Prepare roll-out cookie dough. Cut figures using large Gingerbread Boy cutter from 101 Cutters set (p. 162); use large Christmas tree from 101 Cutters set to cut 2 easel backs for each. Cut one large tree; trim off trunk and cut in half to form 2 triangle easels. Bake and cool cookies. **For all:** Decorate with royal icing. Use tip 6 to outline and fill in clothes and faces (pat smooth with finger dipped in cornstarch). Pipe tip 2A arms with tip 6 hands. Pipe tip 2 swirls and lines for hair, tip 6 dot nose and tip 1 line mouth and eyes.

For Indians: Cut ¼ in. fondant strips for headbands and 1 in. fondant feathers; attach with royal icing. Use royal icing and tip 2 to add feather details, hair ties and stripes on shirts. **For Pilgrim Woman:** Shape top of hat and brim from fondant; attach. Pipe tip 2 collar and cuffs with icing. **For Pilgrim Man:** Use fondant to make top of hat; attach. Cut ¼ in. fondant strips for hat band, small yellow square for buckle and smaller white square for center; attach all. Cut ¼ in. fondant strip for hat brim; attach. Use icing to outline and fill in collar. **For all:** When dry, attach easel to back with royal icing. Let dry.

Sponging

1. Pour Icing Writer or thinned royal or buttercream icing into Color Tray. Dip crumpled waxed paper or paper towel in the color. Test on parchment paper or a paper towel.
2. Lightly press against iced cake surface.
3. Continue sponging on color until surface is covered. If some areas look too light, fill in with a little more color.

Puddle Dots

Thin royal icing, adding ½ teaspoon water per ¼ cup of icing. Icing is ready for flowing when a small amount dripped back into mixture takes a count of 10 to disappear. On waxed paper, pipe a ball, ¾ to 1¼ in. diameter, depending on project instructions, using thinned royal icing in a cut parchment bag. Let dry 48 hours. Decorate following project instructions.

Floral Garlands

(see Congratulate the Graduate, p. 69)

Make 30 wired calyxes for roses using 6 in. lengths of 20-gauge wire. On waxed paper square, using royal icing, pipe a tip 10 cone. Make a ⅛ in. hook on one end of wire. Insert hook into cone. With slightly moistened brush, smooth and taper icing on the wire. Insert other end of wire into a craft block to dry. Make 35 tip 5 wired calyxes for apple blossoms using 6 in. lengths of 22-gauge wire; follow same procedure as for rose bases and let dry in craft block.

Attach apple blossoms to calyxes with royal icing; let dry. Prepare 20 tendrils by curling 6 in. pieces of 22 gauge wire around wooden dowel rod, leaving about 1½ in. straight. For garlands, wrap 36 in. lengths of 20-gauge wire with florist tape. When all flowers have dried, assemble floral garlands by attaching flowers to 36 in. wires with florist tape. Alternate apple blossoms and roses, positioning them about 1½ in. apart. Attach Wilton Green Leaves and tendrils with florist tape; bend stems for a natural look.

BRUSHING DECORATIONS WITH PEARL DUST™

It's easy to add a shimmering touch to fondant and candy decorations with Wilton Pearl Dust (p. 130). This **food-safe** powder creates rich, lustrous highlights on flowers, bows, letters and more. To apply, just brush onto your decoration with a soft artist brush. Or, to paint decorations, pour a small amount of clear vanilla, lemon juice or vodka into a Candy Melting Plate cavity; stir in a small amount of Pearl Dust and brush onto your decoration.

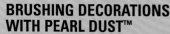

Fondant/Gum Paste Techniques

Fondant Lollipop, Ice Cream Cone and Wrapped Candies
(see Birthday Bear™ is Bearing Treats, p. 32)

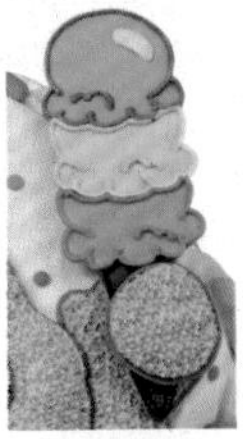

Roll out fondant colors ⅛ in. thick. Using pattern, cut violet cone with scoops. Use pattern to cut separate scoop colors; attach to violet base with damp brush. Using tip 2 and royal icing, outline ice cream cone, scoops and add white highlight to rose scoop; let dry.

For lollipop, roll a ¼ x 9 in. log for each color; place logs side by side. Pinch logs at one end and twist together from other end. Roll blended logs into a ⅜ in. diameter rope; shape into a spiral for lollipop, securing with damp brush. Let dry.

For fondant wrapped candies: Roll 4 round candies each in violet and rose using 1 in. balls flattened to ¼ in. thick. Roll 4 rectangle candies each in blue and yellow, shaping 1 x ½ in. diameter logs. **For wrappers,** roll out white fondant ¹⁄₁₆ in. thick and cut 1 x ½ in. rectangles. Brush 1 long edge with water, then form pleats by pinching side together. Attach wrappers to ends of candies with damp brush; let dry.

Fondant Paper Bursts, Crayon and Hands
(see Elmo's Bursting to Celebrate!, p. 33)

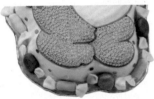

For paper bursts: Add ¾ teaspoon Gum-Tex to 8 oz. fondant; tint Lemon Yellow. Roll out ⅛ in. thick; using pattern, cut 24 bursts. Let dry on large flower formers dusted with cornstarch. **For crayon:** Add ¼ teaspoon Gum-Tex to 2 oz. fondant; tint Lemon Yellow/Golden Yellow combination. Roll a ¾ in. diameter log and form top end into cone shape. With edge of knife, score top of log ¾ in. from tip. Tint 1 oz. of fondant black, roll out ¹⁄₁₆ in. thick. Cut 2 strips ¹⁄₁₆ x 2 ½ in. long; wrap around scored area of crayon and attach with damp brush. **For hands:** Add 1 teaspoon Gum-Tex to 12 oz. fondant and tint Red-Red/Christmas Red combination. Divide in half; roll each half into a ball. Using lollipop stick, indent to form three fingers on each; shape and smooth. **For left hand,** cut slit in back with knife and separate slightly to fit crayon. Let all pieces dry overnight.

Fondant Teapot and Teacups
(see Strawberry Tea, p. 32)

Add ¼ teaspoon Gum-Tex to 4 oz. fondant; roll out ⅛ in. thick. Use pattern to cut teapot and 2 teacups (reverse pattern for second). Let dry on cornstarch-dusted surface. Decorate teapot and teacups with royal icing. Pipe tip 1 outlines, strawberries and vines; let dry. Cut lollipop stick to 3 in.; attach to back of teacups, leaving 1 in. exposed to insert in cake.

Strawberries
(see Strawberry Tea, p. 32)

Using waxed paper-covered pattern, tip 8 and royal icing, outline and pipe in 14 berries (smooth with finger dipped in cornstarch). Add tip 1 dot seeds and tip 349 leaves (use dark pink on 5 for table, teal on 9 for hat). Make extras to allow for breakage and let dry.

Fondant Hamburger, Spatula, Candle and Hat
(see Grillmaster SpongeBob, p. 35)

Combine 2 teaspoons of Gum-Tex with 24 oz. of fondant and tint as follows: 2 oz. each: navy blue, black, tan (for bun), reddish brown (for burger), Leaf Green (for lettuce), gray (use a small amount of black), light blue; tint 1 oz. yellow. Reserve 6 oz. white. Roll out fondant ⅛ in. thick on cornstarch-dusted surface. Using patterns, cut entire hat and hamburger/spatula/candle in white to use as base; cut color sections using patterns and attach to white base with damp brush. Marbleize yellow and brown fondant from burger; roll out ⅛ in. thick and cut flame shape. Let dry.

Bug Fondant Pieces
(see They're Guests, Not Pests, p. 19)

Tint fondant as follows: 2 oz. dark blue, 3 oz. orange, 3 oz. yellow, 5 oz. rose, 6 oz. black, 6 oz. violet, 12 oz. green. Add ¼ teaspoon Gum-Tex to the blue, orange and yellow fondant, ½ teaspoon to rose and violet. Add a little Gum-Tex to a 1 in. ball of black for small bug antennae. Make 2 wings for candy bee and all winged insects: Roll out fondant ⅛ in. thick. For candy bee, use largest heart cutter from

Plastic Nesting Hearts set, for butterfly use third smallest heart cutter, for spotted bug and blue bugs, use smallest heart cutter. Let all wings dry. **For candy bee:** Make 1 in. balls for antenna tips and 1 in. cone for nose. **For butterfly,** roll 1¼ , 1 and ¾ in. diameter balls for body; position on toothpick. Roll very thin 1 in. long logs for antennae and small balls for tips. **For spotted bug,** roll 2 and 1¼ in. balls for body; position on toothpick. Roll and flatten small balls for spots; attach to body with damp brush. Roll ¾ in. cone for stinger. **For blue bug,** roll 1 and 1¼ in. diameter balls for body; position on toothpick. Roll very thin 1 in. long logs for antennae and small balls for tips. When pieces are dry, complete small bugs. **For spider,** roll 2¼ and 1¼ in. balls for body; position on toothpick. Roll 3 x ¼ in. logs for legs; shape with a 45° angle. Roll small balls for feet. **For inchworm,** roll balls for body in graduating sizes, ½, ¾, 1, 1¼, 1 and ¾, in. diameter. Insert spider legs in body. Where used, insert wings and attach stinger and spider feet with damp brush. Roll and flatten small balls of fondant for eyes and pupils; roll thin logs for mouths. Attach features using damp brush. Use a toothpick to poke holes in head and ball tips for antennae. Assemble and position antennae; secure with melted candy.

Sky and Grass
(see Stork at Your Service, p. 62)

Roll out blue fondant ⅛ in. thick and cover top ¾ of cake; smooth with Fondant Smoother. Roll out green fondant ⅛ in. thick and cover lower ¼ of cake, overlapping 2 in. from edge of blue. With straight-edge wheel of Cutter/Embosser, cut a wavy line above overlap point. Remove excess green from top; lift remaining green edge to remove excess blue below, so that just 1 layer of fondant remains over cake. Smooth seam with Fondant Smoother.

Background Board
(see Lightning in Neon, p. 28)

Roll out black fondant ⅛ in. thick. Wrap foamcore board with foil. Lightly brush board with Piping Gel and cover with black fondant; smooth with Fondant Smoother. Make copies of pattern sections and tape together to form background scene. Roll out remaining fondant ⅛ in. thick and cut pattern pieces in corresponding colors. Attach pieces with damp brush as follows: gray road, violet curb, orange building, yellow windows, blue sign, brown sign post. **For V-8 sign,** position green oval first, then add rose V-8 sign. Attach brown signpost, light posts and yellow bulbs. Position green building; using pattern cut additional front peak of roof and side panel with post; attach to building for dimension. Cut ⅛ in. wide strips of white fondant for accent lines; attach to building, V-8 sign, birthday sign and around windows. Cut out message with Alphabet/Number Cut-Outs and attach to sign. Pipe tip 2 outlines using tinted Piping Gel as follows: yellow for green building and streetlights; blue for V-8 sign and birthday message; rose around birthday sign; orange around windows. Roll out yellow fondant ⅛ in. thick; cut ¼ x ½ in. strips and attach with damp brush for lane lines. Highlight lines and light post bulbs with yellow Piping Gel.

Fondant Foods
(see The First Thanksgiving, p. 42)

Yams: Using 2 oz. orange fondant, shape ½ in. balls into random ovals. Make indentations with small end of veining tool.

Corn: For ears, roll 1½ x ⅜ in. yellow logs. Score kernel lines with small paring knife. For corn husks, knead together small portions of yellow, light and dark green and brown to marbleize. Roll out marbleized fondant ⅛ in. thick. Cut various size elongated husk strips and attach with damp brush to each ear, pinching together at bottom to shape. For corn silk, cut ¼ x ¾ in. strips in brown; cut partial slits ¹⁄₁₆ in. apart. Roll and attach to top of corn. Cut some very thin strips to randomly tuck inside husks.

Turkey: Roll brown fondant into teardrop shape about 2¼ x 1¾ x 1 in. high. Flatten bottom; use small end of veining tool to score top and add dots for texture. Roll 1 x ¼ in. logs and shape into wings. Marbelize brown with white; shape a 1 x ¼ in. log for bone. Flatten end and score with tool. Wrap with a 1 x ½ in. brown log and taper for drumstick. Attach pieces with damp brush.

Bench
(see Your Proudest Day, p. 64)

Tint 2 in. fondant ball light brown; knead in ¼ teaspoon Gum-Tex. Roll out ⅛ in. thick. Cut 1¼ x 3¼ in. rectangle for seat. For legs, trim 4 lollipop sticks to 3¼ in. Roll out fondant ¹⁄₁₆ in. thick. Cut ⅝ x 1¼ in. strip. Brush back with damp brush and wrap around one end of stick, leaving 2 in. exposed to insert into cake; smooth seam. Make 4. Let all pieces dry on cornstarch-dusted board at least 48 hours. When dry, attach legs to seat using fondant adhesive; let dry.

Bunny and Duck Fondant Pieces
(see Up for a Celebration!, p. 54)

Add ½ teaspoon Gum-Tex to 6 oz. fondant. Tint ¾ in. ball rose; tint 1¼ in. ball yellow. Roll out fondant ⅛ in. thick. Use patterns to cut chick hair and 2 wings (reverse pattern for 2nd wing). Use pattern to cut bunny hands (reverse pattern for 2nd hand). For bunny ears, cut 2 white bases with medium leaf Cut-Out. Cut 2 pink insides with smallest leaf Cut-Out; attach to base with damp brush (reverse both pieces for 2nd ear). Let all pieces dry on cornstarch-dusted surface.

Head and Hands
(see They're All Big Fans, p. 67)

Add ½ teaspoon Gum-Tex to each 4 oz. of skin tone fondant. Roll out ⅛ in. thick. Use smallest round cutter from set to cut heads. Roll tiny ball for nose and attach using damp brush. Use pattern to cut 2 hands for each figure (reverse pattern for 2nd hand). Cut Lollipop Stick to 3 in. long; wrap 1 hand around stick. Let dry on cornstarch-dusted surface. Decorate heads. Place on waxed paper. Use royal icing and tip 2 to pipe swirls, lines or pull-outs for hair. Use FoodWriter to draw eyes and mouths. Use royal icing to attach 3 in. lollipop stick to back of head, leaving 2 in. exposed to insert into cupcake. Let dry.

Diploma
(see Congratulate the Graduate, p. 68)

Roll out Gum Paste ⅛ in. thick. Cut a 11 x 5½ in. rectangle; lay on waxed paper-covered board dusted with cornstarch. Roll 1 end up and around plastic dowel rod dusted with cornstarch. Roll opposite end under and around another dowel rod dusted with cornstarch. Cut a 4½ x 3 in. piece for diploma braces. Cut on a diagonal to form 2 triangles. Let pieces dry on board dusted with cornstarch. When dry attach braces to back of diploma using a glue gun to secure. Print message with black FoodWriter.

Arms, Mortarboards and Diplomas
(see The Future's in Their Hands, p. 68)

For each arm, cut a cookie stick to 3 in. Tint portions of fondant blue and yellow; roll out blue, yellow, violet, and orange fondant ¹⁄₁₆ in. thick. Wrap fondant around cookie sticks, leaving ¾ in. exposed at each end; attach with damp brush. Reserve remaining fondant. For mortarboards, roll out reserved fondant ⅛ in. thick; cut top using largest square Cut-Out. For mortarboard base, cut a 3½ x ⅛ in. fondant strip. Attach ends of strip with damp brush to form a circle. Attach base to top with damp brush. Let dry overnight. For hands, tint portions of fondant copper and brown; roll ¾ in. balls of fondant and insert on one end of fondant-wrapped cookie sticks with damp brush. Slightly flatten fondant ball and cut fingers and thumb on each hand with knife. **For diploma**, roll out white fondant ¹⁄₁₆ in. thick; cut a 1½ in. x 1 in. rectangle and roll up. Position diplomas in hands and wrap fingers around, securing with damp brush; let dry.

Bench
(see Sitting Pretty, p. 82)

Tint ¼ package Gum Paste yellow; tint ½ package Gum Paste and 2½ oz. fondant red. Roll out red Gum Paste ⅛ in. thick. Cut 2 strips 4½ x ½ in.; set on edge in "L" shape for support brackets. Use patterns to cut out bench seat and heart. Immediately use straight-edge wheel of Cutter/Embosser to score heart with quilting lines ½ in. apart. Shape 2 fondant ropes 8 x ¼ in. thick (reserve remaining fondant). Use damp brush to attach ropes to outer edge of heart, leaving ⅛ in. at bottom uncovered. Roll out yellow gum paste ⅛ in. thick. Cut 2 strips 4 x ¼ in.; set on edge and use pattern to shape bench arms. Cut 2 strips 3 x ¼ in.; set on edge and use pattern to shape bench legs. Allow all pieces to dry for several days. Roll out reserved red fondant ⅛ in. thick. Cut pads same width as arms, 1 in. long; attach to arms using damp brush.

Assemble bench using red fondant adhesive. Attach heart to seat; prop to maintain right angle and let dry for about 15 minutes. Attach "L" brackets to back of heart and under seat; let dry. Attach legs; when dry, attach arms. Finish heart with tip 2 dots of royal icing at quilting intersections. Let all dry. Brush arms and legs with Gold Pearl Dust.

Bridesmaids
(see She's Getting Hitched, p. 83)

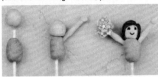

Tint 3 in. balls of fondant copper (skintone) and rose. For body, roll a ¾ in. ball and insert damp lollipop stick, leaving ¼ in. extended at top; shape into body. For head, roll a ⅝ in. ball and position on tip of lollipop stick; shape into head. Push stick into craft block and let dry. For arms, cut 2 in. lengths of spaghetti; wrap with fondant, leaving ⅜ in. exposed. For hands, roll small amount of fondant ⅛ in. thick. Cut circle using tip 10; press brush handle into fondant to indent for fingers and attach to arm. Attach arms by inserting bare spaghetti end into body slightly behind lollipop stick. Draw facial features using black FoodWriter. Pipe tip 2 pull-out hair with royal icing. Stand figures in craft block to dry. Lay flat; attach drop flowers for bouquet using royal icing; add tip 349 leaves. Let dry.

Ruffled Fantasy Flowers
(see Garden Terraces, p. 74)
Prepare Gum Paste Adhesive (p. 115). Bend 1 end of each wire to form a small hook. Tint gum paste violet; roll out ¹⁄₁₆ in. thick. Cut circle using largest round Cut-Out.

Set circles on shaping foam and use veining tool from Confectionery Tool Set to frill edges by pressing down and pulling out. Fold circle in half and brush center area with glue. Place

hook end of wire in glue and fold circle in half again. Open edges slightly and curl to randomly shape flowers. Make 75 flowers. Insert in craft block to dry.

Gum Paste Roses
(see Banding Together, p. 72)

1. Make 53 rose bases in gum paste. Roll a ⅝ in. ball of gum paste and form into a teardrop shape, 1¼ in. high. Dip toothpick in adhesive and insert in bottom of base. Insert in craft block and let dry 48 hours.

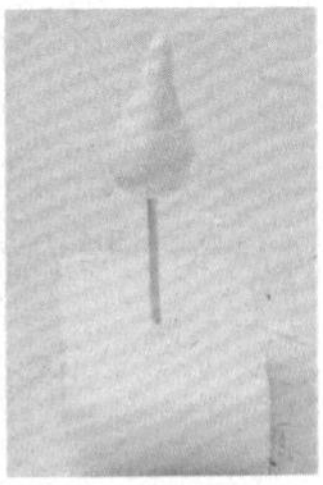

2. Roll out gum paste ¹⁄₁₆ in. thick. For 20 small roses, use tulip petal cutter from Flower Making Set to cut 1 petal for each; cut petal into 3 separate petals.

3. Place petals horizontally on thin foam dusted with cornstarch. Soften top petal edge with medium ball tool from Confectionery Set.

4. Brush back of petals from midpoint down with adhesive. Wrap petals around base to form the bud for each rose.

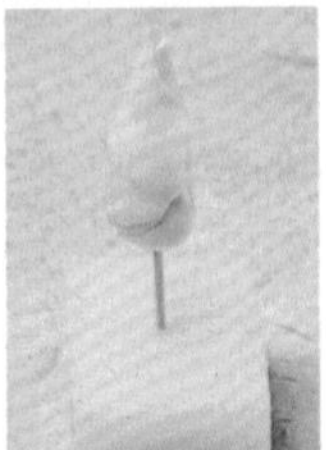

5. Cut a row of 3 petals to add to each base. Slightly widen and elongate each petal using modeling stick. Turn petals so the rounded end is the top of petal and the point is the bottom. Soften top half of petal edge with ball tool on thin foam. Turn petals over. Add adhesive to bottom half of petals; position and press into rose base. This completes the small rose.

6. For medium and large roses, cut and attach a second row of 5 petals. For large roses, cut and attach a third row of 7 petals.

Cake Top Flowers
(see Touched by Romance, p. 77)

1. **For 14 in. cake**, roll out a small amount of fondant ½ in. thick. Using straight-edge wheel of Cutter/Embosser, cut a 3 in. diameter circle for base. Soften edge to round and taper.

2. **For petal layers**, roll out fondant ¹⁄₁₆ in. thick. Cut a 6 in. diameter circle; position

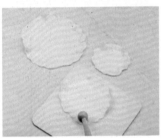

on thin foam and ruffle edges with ball tool. Attach petal to base with damp brush; prop up edges with pieces of crumpled tissue.

3. Make additional petal layers as above, cutting 5¼, 4½, 3¾, 3, 2¼ and 1½ in. circles; attach in descending order with damp brush. Prop up edges with tissue as above. For 10 in. cake, make base and petals as above, using a 2 in. diameter base and 4½, 3¾, 2¼ and 1½ in. circles for petal layers. Let dry overnight.

4. Remove tissue pieces. Brush edges of petals with Pearl Dust.

Cake Side Ruffles
(see Touched by Romance, p. 77)

1. Roll out white fondant ¹⁄₁₆ in. thick. **For 6 in. cake**, using straight-edge wheel of Cutter/Embosser, cut a 19 x 2¾ in. strip. On thin foam, ruffle one edge of strip with ball tool. Loosely roll up strip to prevent

stretching, then unroll and attach to cake side with damp brush, positioning straight edge at base of cake.

2. Follow same ruffling and rolling procedure for a 19 x 2¼ in. wide strip.

3. Follow same ruffling and rolling procedure for a 19 x 1¾ in. wide strip. Attach strips to cake side, positioning straight edge at base of cake. Brush edges of ruffles with Pearl Dust.

4. For 10 in. cake, cut 2 each 16 x 2¾ in. 16 x 2¼ in. and 16 x 1¾ in. strips; ruffle, roll same-size strips together and attach as above. For 14 in. cake, cut 3 each 15 x 2¾, 15 x 2¼ and 15 x 1¾ in. strips; ruffle, roll same-size strips together and attach as for 6 in. and 10 in. cakes. Brush edges of ruffles with Pearl Dust.

Curved Panels
(see Pure Gold, p. 87)

Add 2 teaspoons Gum-Tex™ to 24 oz. White Rolled Fondant. Tint fondant in desired shade. Roll out ¹⁄₁₆ in. thick. Cut panels 2½ in. wide x 4 in. high, or height of your cake. Lightly imprint vine pattern press on each panel, being careful not to cut through panels. Turn panels over and let dry in medium flower formers, away from direct fluorescent or natural light, at least 48 hours before decorating.

When panels are dry, outline center stem of vine imprints with tip 3 and royal icing. Add tip 2 side stems and dot flowers. Let dry.

Top Bow
(see Bunches and Bows, p. 79)

1. This bow can be assembled directly on the cake or ahead of time, using a 2 to 2½ in. fondant circle as a base. Cut strips for bow loops using dimensions listed in project instructions. Your bow may use more loops than shown here. Fold strips over to form loops. Brush ends lightly with damp brush. Align ends and pinch slightly to secure. Stand loops on side to dry.

2. Position 6 or 7 bow loops in a circle to form base of the bow. Attach to fondant circle with thinned fondant adhesive or melted candy.

3. Attach remaining loops, filling in center area of bow. Trim loop ends, if needed, to fit.

Covering Base Boards with Fondant

Cut cake boards 2 in. larger in diameter than your cake, unless otherwise directed, then roll out fondant about 1 in. larger than board size. Wrap board with foil.

1. Lightly coat board with piping gel to help the fondant stick to the foil.

2. Roll out fondant to desired size, ¼ in. thick. Position over board using a rolling pin, draping fondant over edge.

3. Trim excess fondant from edges under bottom of board. Smooth top and sides with Easy-Glide Smoother.

Fondant Leaves
(see Brilliant Basket, p. 56)

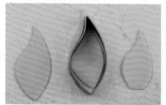

Roll out green fondant ¹⁄₁₆ in. thick. Cut leaves using medium Leaf Cut-Out. Move cutter down ¹⁄₈ in. and cut again to make leaf slightly smaller. Cut ¹⁄₈ in. off bottom to make a straight edge. Let dry on cornstarch-dusted medium flower formers.

Curliques
(see Making His Presents Known, p. 30)

Roll out fondant ¹⁄₁₆ in. thick on Roll & Cut Mat lightly dusted with cornstarch. Cut into thin strips.

Loosely wrap strips around a dowel rod several times to form curls. Let set 5 to 10 minutes. Slide curl off dowel rod and let dry. Attach to cake with Fondant Adhesive.

Fondant Drapes and Swags
(see Pleated Pathways, p. 75; Strawberry Tea, p. 32)

Roll out fondant ¹⁄₈ in. thick on Roll & Cut Mat lightly dusted with cornstarch. Cut strips as follows:

Pleated Pathways: For 7 in. cake, cut a 6 x 12 in. strip; For 10 in. cake, cut a 6 x 14 in. strip; For 13 in. cake, cut a 6 x 17 in. strip; For base board, cut a 6 x 20 in. strip.

Strawberry Tea: Cut 3 ¼ x 2 in. strips.

For both cakes: Form pleats in fondant by placing a dowel rod under bottom edge of fondant strip and one on top, next to the first dowel rod. For looser pleats, use wooden or plastic dowel rods. For tighter pleats, use wooden skewers or lollipop sticks. Repeat with more dowel rods to form pleats. Remove dowel rods, gather ends together and brush with water to secure.

Bow Loops
(see Little Formalities, p. 76)

Tint 1 oz. fondant rose for each cake. Roll out fondant ¹⁄₁₆ in. thick. Using straight-edge wheel of Cutter/Embosser (p. 131), cut a ½ x 3 in. long strip for each loop. Press ends together and let dry overnight on sides on cornstarch-dusted board. For knot, cut a ½ x 1¾ in. long rose strip; wrap around ends of 2 loops, then brush strip ends with water. Pinch ends together to secure.

Fondant Ribbon Roses

Roll out fondant ¹⁄₈ in. on Roll & Cut Mat lightly dusted with cornstarch. Cut strip following dimensions stated in project instructions. Begin rolling from one end of strip, gradually loosening roll as flower gets larger, attaching with damp brush. Use veining tool between spirals to open up petals; let dry on cornstarch-dusted board or candy melting plate.

Brush Embroidery

Add textured flowers and leaves with the soft look of lace using this easy icing technique. Works best using the square tip brush from the Wilton Brush Set (p. 131).

1. Imprint shape on freshly rolled fondant (or on your covered cake) using a Cut-Out™ or cookie cutter.

2. Thin royal or buttercream icing with Piping Gel. Using tip 2 or 3, outline shape. For large designs, outline one section of the design, brush out lines following step 3, then continue with the next design section.

3. Before each outline can dry, immediately brush out lines of icing toward center of pattern area with damp brush. Work in quick, short strokes. Clean brush with water after brushing each design to create distinct lines of icing.

SUGAR MOLDING TECHNIQUE

Sugar Mold Recipe

2 cups granulated sugar
4 teaspoons water

Place sugar in a large mixing bowl. Mix sugar, making sure there are no lumps. Make a well in sugar and add water (if you are tinting sugar, blend icing color into water at this point). Rub mixture in hands and knead for about 1 minute or until well-blended and mixture packs like wet sand. Be sure there are no lumps in mixture.

NOTE: Keep sugar mixture covered with a damp cloth when not in use.

Hollowed Sugar Mold

Mix a triple batch of the sugar mold recipe. Dust half Sports Ball Pan (p. 159) with cornstarch to prevent sticking. Fill pan to ½ in. from top. Press firmly with heel of hand; scrape a small angled spatula at a 45° angle to remove excess sugar. Cut a board to 5½ in. to fit over bottom side of mold; place board on top of sugar and unmold. With knife remove ¼ in. from bottom and ⅛ in. from top of sugar molds. For Mini Ball molds, fill cavities. Follow instructions above.

For window, immediately after unmolding, cut 2 circles of plastic wrap to the size of a large round cookie cutter. Place circles on sugar mold in window area. Position cutter on wrap. Window area will remain wet. Let mold dry 3 to 4 hours. Remove cutter and gently scoop out wet sugar, leaving a ¼ in.

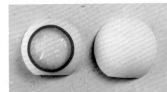

thick shell. Smooth inside and edge with your fingers. Place molded sugar, round side down, on cardboard circle to finish drying for about 24 hours, or place on cookie sheet in 200°F oven for 20 minutes. Let cool to room temperature before touching.

CANDY RECIPES

Basic Ganache and Truffles

14 oz. Candy Melts®* (p. 166)
½ cup heavy whipping cream

Chop candy (you can use a food processor). Heat whipping cream in saucepan just to boiling point. Do not boil. Remove from heat and add chopped candy, stir until smooth and glossy.
Ganache Glaze: If mixture is too thick, add 1 to 2 tablespoons whipping cream. Position cake on wire rack over drip pan. Pour glaze onto center and work out toward edges.
NOTE: Cake may be iced first in buttercream. Let icing set, then pour on ganache glaze. If cake has a perfect surface, no other icing is needed.
Whipped Ganache: Follow recipe above, using 1 cup whipping cream. Allow mixture to set and cool to room temperature (mixture will have the consistency of pudding; this may take 1-2 hours). Whip on high speed with an electric mixer until light and soft peaks form.
Truffles: Add 1 tablespoon liqueur for flavor, if desired. Stir until smooth and creamy. Refrigerate until firm. Roll into 1 in. diameter balls. Can be used as center for dipped candies, served plain or rolled in nuts, coconut or cocoa powder. Store truffles in refrigerator up to 3 weeks. Makes about 2 dozen (1 in.) balls.

Candy "Clay"

14 oz. package of Candy Melts®† (p. 166)
⅓ cup light corn syrup

Melt candy following package directions. Add corn syrup and stir to blend. Turn out mixture onto waxed paper and let set at room temperature to dry. Wrap well and store at room temperature until needed. Candy clay handles best if hardened overnight.

To Use
Candy clay will be very hard at the start; knead a small portion at a time until workable. If candy clay gets too soft, set aside at room temperature or refrigerate briefly. When rolling out candy clay, sprinkle work surface with cornstarch or cocoa (for cocoa clay) to prevent sticking; roll to approximately ⅛ in. thick.

To Tint
White candy clay may be tinted using Candy Color or Icing Color. Knead in color until well blended.

To Store
Prepared candy clay will last for several weeks at room temperature in an airtight container.

Peanut Butter Filling

1½ tablespoons butter, softened
½ cup chunky style peanut butter, room temperature
¾ cup sifted confectioners' sugar

Cream butter with peanut butter. Stir in confectioners' sugar, blending well. Add more confectioners' sugar as necessary to make thick enough to form into a ball. Use filling as a candy center for dipping, or as a center between 2 layers of coating. Makes approximately 30 candy centers.

Ready-In-Minutes Cocoa Fudge

20 oz. (approximately 4 ½ cups) Dark Cocoa Candy Melts®* (p. 166)
1 can (14 oz.) sweetened condensed milk (not evaporated)

Melt Candy Melts in microwave-safe container using microwave on low power. Add milk; stir until blended. Microwave an additional 2 to 3 minutes on medium power; stir until fudge develops a sheen. Pour mixture into buttered 7 x 11 in. non-stick Biscuit/Brownie pan and refrigerate until firm.

Cream Cheese Mints

2 oz. cream cheese, softened
¼ teaspoon peppermint candy flavor
Desired icing color
2 cups confectioners' sugar
Granulated sugar

Blend cheese with flavoring and color; mix in sugar. Knead until mixture is firm, adding more sugar if needed. Roll mixture into balls. Dip one side in a small amount of granulated sugar. Press, sugar side down, in candy mold. Unmold immediately onto waxed paper. Makes approximately 12-15 mints.

Candy Making Techniques

USING CANDY MELTS®*

Fast-melting confectionery coating wafers are the key to easy candy making. Smooth texture and great taste make Candy Melts® your most convenient option for molding. Check out all the great colors on p. 166.

To Melt
Chocolate Pro® Electric Melting Pot (p. 166): The most convenient way to melt—no microwave or double boiler needed! Melts large amounts of Candy Melts® in minutes.

Double boiler method: Fill lower pan with water to below level of top pan. Bring water to simmer, then remove from heat. Put Candy Melts® in top pan and set in position on lower pan. Stir constantly, without beating, until smooth and completely melted.

Microwave method: In microwave-safe container, microwave 1 package Candy Melts® at 30% power or defrost setting for 1 minute. Stir thoroughly. Continue to microwave and stir at 30 second intervals until smooth and completely melted. Candy Melts® may also be melted in a disposable decorating bag. Melt as described above, squeezing bag between heating intervals to blend Candy Melts® together. When completely melted, snip off end of bag and squeeze melted Candy Melts® into molds. Throw away bag when empty.

NOTE: Confectionery coating will lose its pouring and dipping consistency if overheated, or if water or other liquid is added. If coating is overheated, add 2 teaspoons hydrogenated vegetable shortening per 14 oz. Candy Melts®.

To Mold (1 color candies)
Pour melted candy into clean dry mold; tap lightly to remove air bubbles. Place mold on level surface. Refrigerate until bottom of mold appears frosty or until candy is firm. Pop out candy. For lollipops, fill molds, tap to remove air bubbles, position sticks in mold. Rotate sticks to thoroughly cover with candy so they remain securely in place. Refrigerate to set, pop out lollipops.

To Color
Add Candy Colors (p. 166) to melted Candy Melts® a little at a time. Mix thoroughly before adding more color. Colors tend to deepen as they're mixed. Pastel colored candies are most appetizing, so keep this in mind.

To Flavor
The creamy, rich taste of Candy Melts® can be enhanced by adding approx. ¼ teaspoon oil-based Candy Flavor (p. 166) to 14 oz. (one pack) of melted Candy Melts®. Never use alcohol based flavorings; they will cause candies to harden.

Multicolored Candy
Painting Method
It's easy to mold with different areas of color—just use a decorator brush to "paint" the mold with melted Candy Melts®. Refrigerate a few seconds until coating hardens, then fill mold to top with melted candy. Remember, only fill in one section of mold at a time and let it harden before adding more colors. Look for other ways to color and flavor your candy in our *Candy Making Beginner's Guide* (p. 129).

Marbleizing Method

Separately melt 2 different colors of Candy Melts®. Stir colors together, using a lollipop

stick to draw lines in mixture. Do not overmix. Quickly spoon or place into molds while mixture is still soft. Tap. Refrigerate until firm; unmold.

Layering Method
Pour melted Candy Melts® into dry molds to desired height. Refrigerate until partially set. Pour melted contrasting color to desired height. Refrigerate until partially set. Repeat until desired number of layers are formed; refrigerate until firm and unmold.

SPECIALTY TECHNIQUES

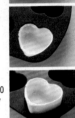

Candy Shells

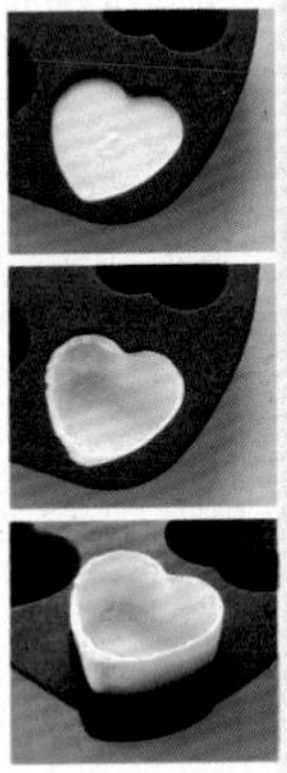

Fill pan or mold to the top edge with melted candy. Tap on counter to remove air bubbles. Let chill in refrigerator for 10-15 minutes or until a ¼ in. shell has formed. Pour out excess candy, smooth top edges with spatula and chill for 15-20 minutes longer. Carefully unmold candy shells (if you have difficulty removing shells, place in freezer for 2-3 minutes, then unmold). Excess candy can be reheated and reused. For unmolding shells from silicone molds, peel mold back, pushing candy shell out from bottom of mold.

Candy Shells in Baking Cups

Add 1 to 2 tablespoons of melted candy in the bottom of a standard baking cup. Brush candy slightly up sides, about halfway to top, forming an even edge. Refrigerate 5 to 8 minutes. Repeat process if desired, for a thicker shell. Refrigerate until firm. Carefully peel baking cup off candy shell.

Candy Faces

Make faces in the Candy Melting Plate (p. 167); fill cavities with melted Candy Melts® using a cut decorating bag. Refrigerate until firm and unmold.

Place faces on waxed paper-covered board and decorate facial features using melted candy in cut bag.

*Brand confectionery coating

Candy Plaques

Use pans as molds when making solid decorative plaques. If your pan has detail, it may be painted in desired colors as you would for any candy mold.

Pour melted candy into center of pan cavity. Tap pan gently on counter to eliminate bubbles. Candy should be about ¼ to ½ in. thick. Place pan in refrigerator for approximately 10-15 minutes until firm (check occasionally; if coating becomes too chilled, it will crack). Unmold onto hand or soft towel (tap gently, if necessary).

Elmo Candy Plaque

(see Elmo's Bursting to Celebrate, p. 33)

1. Divide and melt 1 pk. white candy: reserve 2 oz. white for eyes, tint 1 ½ oz. orange for nose, 1 oz. black for mouth and pupils; tint remainder yellow. In pan, mold mouth, nose and pupils; refrigerate until firm. Mold whites of eyes; refrigerate.

2. Mold remainder of face using 2 pks. of melted red candy. Refrigerate until firm; unmold. Cut plastic dowel rod to 10 in.; position on back of plaque, with 4 in. extended below neck. Melt remaining red candy; pour into pan to cover dowel rod. Let set completely, then unmold. Attach fondant crayon to hand with melted candy.

Candy Bases

(see Remembering the Romance, p. 84)

1. For bottom base, place Comfort Grip Cutter on pan and fill ¼ in. deep with melted candy; refrigerate until firm and unmold.

2. For upper base plate, fill muffin pan cavity ¼ in. deep with melted candy. Refrigerate until firm; unmold.

Candy Leaves

(see Fluffy Flower, p. 21)

Clean lemon leaves with damp cloth. Tint melted white candy green. Brush onto back of lemon leaf; let dry in medium flower former. When dry, peel off leaf. Paint vein lines on candy using fine tip brush and green candy color or using FoodWriters.

COLOR FLOW

Working With Color Flow

1. Trace your design pattern onto parchment paper, then tape paper onto a cake circle or the back of a cookie pan. Cover with waxed paper; smooth and tape. Using tip 2 and parchment bag half-filled with full strength Color Flow, squeeze, pull and drop icing string following pattern outline. Stop, touch tip to surface and pull away. If you will be using the same color to fill in, let outline dry a few minutes until it "crusts." To prevent bleeding of different colors, let outline dry 1-2 hours before filling in.

2. Thin Color Flow mixture with water. Cut opening in parchment bag to the size of tip 2. Fill in design with thinned Color Flow.

3. Let decorations air dry thoroughly, at least 48 hours. To remove, cut away waxed paper from board, then turn over and peel waxed paper off the Color Flow piece.

Hint: For curved decorations, dry pieces on flower formers.

To easily remove dried Color Flow, pull waxed paper backing over the edge of a table with one hand, while holding decoration with other hand. Waxed paper will pull off naturally. Or, with dried Color Flow resting on cookie sheet, place cardboard sheet over Color Flow, lift and turn over so that top of decoration rests on cardboard. Lift off waxed paper.

Since any moist icing will break down Color Flow, either position Color Flow decorations on cake shortly before serving or place on sugar cubes attaching with full-strength Color Flow.

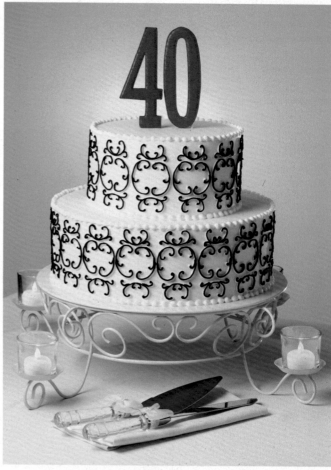

COVERING CAKES AND COOKIES WITH CANDY MELTS®* OR POURED ICINGS

A quick and easy way to give a professional-looking finish to all your baked goods! For Candy Melts®, melt following package directions. For icing recipes, follow recipe directions to reach pouring consistency. For canned icing, heat in microwave at Defrost setting for 20-30 seconds; stir. Place cooled cakes or cookies on cooling grid positioned over cookie sheet or pan. Pour or pipe candy or icing on center of item, spreading to edges with a spatula so that candy or icing drips down and covers sides. Let dry.

*Brand confectionery coating

2008 PRODUCT SHOPS

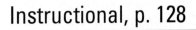

Instructional

Find inspiration with Wilton how-to books and videos. There's something perfect for your next celebration, from kids' birthday cakes to multi-tiered wedding designs.

Specialty Publications

Cupcake Fun!

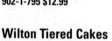

Wilton presents today's hottest party dessert like you've never seen it before. This all-new collection features over 150 exciting cupcake and treat ideas for all occasions, with complete baking and decorating instructions to make them easy. Discover captivating new shapes from coffee cups to flying saucers, plus a great recipe section with delicious surprises like Key Lime Cupcakes, Mocha Icing and more. Great baking and decorating products, too, like our Silly-Feet footed silicone cups! Cupcake Fun! is the book you need to create the ultimate cupcake celebration. See it up close in our special Cupcake Fun! section on page 146. Look for many more great cupcake ideas and recipes at www.cupcakefun.com.
902-T-795 $12.99

Wilton Tiered Cakes

If you are planning a wedding, a shower or any big event, Wilton Tiered Cakes will show you the perfect way to top it off. Experience today's most contemporary looks in reception cakes! See how exciting it can be to mix colors on a wedding cake using textured fondant or floral accents. Find an anniversary cake that's as much fun as a scrapbook, with tiers surrounded by family photos. Discover creative new construction ideas like our cute teddy bear tower with fondant baby blocks used as separators. It's all here—38 amazing cake designs—along with complete instructions, techniques, construction and cutting guides, plus great Wilton products. Soft cover, 128 pages.
902-T-1108 $14.99

Celebrate! With Fondant

It's the first book to feature fondant done the Wilton way—using our exciting cake designs, step-by-step instructions and convenient fondant products. Celebrate! with Fondant makes fondant cakes easy and fun for everyone. See how to make more than 40 terrific cakes, along with alternate ways to decorate every design and suggestions for the perfect occasions to serve them.
Soft cover, 120 pages.
902-T-911 $14.99

2008 Yearbook of Cake Decorating

Find the perfect cake for any celebration in our most exciting collection ever! You'll discover over 180 amazing all new designs in tune with today's favorite themes and colors. Our Castle Magic special section shows you how to transform an ordinary tiered cake into a captivating castle centerpiece. From a princess birthday palace to Santa's toy tower, you'll find an incredible castle cake that will be the hit of your party! You can also enter your own spectacular castle design and win great prizes in our Castle Decorating Contest. As always, you'll find the best in traditional and contemporary wedding designs, festive holiday desserts, today's hottest character cakes, wonderful cupcake creations and more. Featuring step-by-step instructions, technique resource guide, complete product section and a website link to more great designs. Soft cover; 240 pages.
English 1701-T-2026 $10.99
Spanish 1701-T-2028 $10.99

2008 Pattern Book

Duplicate many of the beautiful cake designs featured in the 2008 Yearbook and on the Wilton website. Includes over 100 decorating outlines to transfer to your cake. Easy-to-follow instructions. Soft cover, 47 pages of patterns.
408-T-2008 $7.99

Wilton Wedding Cakes— A Romantic Portfolio

Our exciting collection of tiered cakes makes the romantic wedding of every bride's dreams a reality. *A Romantic Portfolio* sets the bride's imagination free, with 38 exquisite cakes that express love in many ways. It's all here—beautiful seasonal designs, elegant shapes, classic and contemporary looks. There is a cake for every taste—along with coordinating ornament, favor suggestions and tiered cake accessories.

A Romantic Portfolio will inspire decorators as well as brides. Every design includes step-by-step decorating instructions, product checklists and serving amounts. Used with our comprehensive construction guide, patterns, techniques and recipes, *A Romantic Portfolio* has everything decorators need to recreate each cake to perfection. Soft cover, 144 pages.
902-T-907 $16.99

The Wilton School— Decorating Cakes

- 30 exciting cakes with complete instructions and product listings
- 103 technique instructions, shown step-by-step, including borders, flowers, fondant and more
- Helpful recipes, tip chart, serving and cutting guides, glossary of terms
- In-depth sections on baking cakes, preparing icing, using decorating tips, cutting and transporting cakes
- Product guide, which shows and explains the equipment and ingredients required for decorating

This exciting book presents what Wilton has learned in 79 years of teaching cake decorating, in an easy-to-follow format that reflects today's lifestyles. *Decorating Cakes* is designed to appeal to anyone who wants to make great-looking cakes for families and friends. Soft cover, 116 pages.
902-T-904 $14.99

Uses of Decorating Tips

Valuable quick reference and idea book for any decorator. Features five of the most popular decorating tip families and explains what each does. Shows the versatility of many tips by presenting varied cake designs. Soft cover, 48 pages.
902-T-1375 $9.99

Cake Decorating Beginner's Guide

- How to bake and ice perfect cakes
- How to mix any color icing with ease
- 15 fantastic cake ideas to decorate in 6 steps or less
- Step-by-step decorating instructions for stars, rosettes, drop flowers and more

Wilton, the #1 name in cake decorating, shows beginners everything they need to know, step-by-step. The *Beginner's Guide* makes decorating easy to learn and fun to do for everyone!
Soft cover, 40 pages.
902-T-1232 $3.99

Candy Making Beginner's Guide

- 20 incredible candy ideas—all made in a few easy steps
- Easy ways to melt perfectly every time
- Painting color details in candy
- How to make classic creme-filled and dipped candies
- Great candy gift and favor ideas

You'll be amazed at the fantastic candies you can make using this book. The possibilities are endless, using the great selection of Wilton Candy Melts®* and Candy Molds. The *Beginner's Guide* shows you how, step-by-step, so you will make great-looking candies your very first time. The *Beginner's Guide* has the information you need to start making candy like a pro.
Soft cover, 40 pages.
902-T-1231 $3.99

*Brand confectionery coating.

Instructional Videos

BAKE DECORATE CELEBRATE!™ Seasons 1-3 on DVD!

It's the ultimate introduction to cake and dessert decorating on video! Each boxed set includes a complete 13-episode season of the popular Telly Award-winning PBS series, which makes it easy for anyone to create something great to serve. In every episode, hosts Nancy Siler and Melanie Glasscock focus on a specific theme, such as Kids Birthdays, Shaped Pans or Whimsical Cupcakes. They'll decorate specialty projects based on that theme and give you related decorating ideas to make the celebration complete. Special segments in each episode include *Decorating Basics*, featuring essential techniques, and *Decorating Tips*, with a variety of designs made using one specific tip. Each set includes 4 discs, approx. 6 hours total.

WINNER OF 2 TELLY AWARDS!

Season 1
Garden Party Desserts, Chocolate Treats, Fruits, Easy Flowers and more.
DVD 901-T-121 Set/4 $39.99

FOUR DVDS!

Season 2
Roses, Tarts, Pool & Beach, Patriotic and more. Closed captioned.
DVD 901-T-131 Set/4 $39.99

NEW!

Season 3
Apples, Apples, Apples, Tropical & Tasty, Critters You Can Eat, Quick Change Cakes and more. Closed captioned.
DVD 901-T-132 Set/4 $39.99

NEW!

Cake Decorating Basics

See and learn the essentials of creating amazing cakes and desserts, step by step! Everything from tools to icings, baking perfect cakes, decorating stars, shells, flowers and more, is covered in this 60-minute program.
DVD 901-T-120 $19.99

How to Make Wedding Cakes

Invaluable lessons on how to design and assemble tiered cakes for weddings, showers, anniversaries and other special occasions. Hints for transporting and serving are also included in this 60-minute video. DVD material matches VHS.
DVD 901-T-256 $19.99
VHS 901-T-128 $19.99

How to Make Icing Flowers

Learn how to make roses, Easter lilies, violets, pansies, daisies, poinsettias and more! Five cake designs incorporate all the flowers included in this 60-minute video. DVD material matches VHS.
DVD 901-T-258 $19.99
VHS 901-T-119 $19.99

Wilton
Cake Decorating
Create your greatest cakes with the essentials decorators count on. Time-saving tools.
Precise tips. Quality icings. Plus, the most exciting new products for fondant decorating!

fondant fun!™

Wilton presents the easy system for fondant decorating! Convenient, Ready-To-Use Rolled Fondant. Cut-Outs™ to create fun shapes. Icing Writer™ to add vivid designs. Easy-to-use tools that help you roll, cut and color to achieve exciting new decorations!

White Ready-To-Use Rolled Fondant

Fondant has never been more convenient and easy to use for decorating! With Wilton Ready-To-Use Rolled Fondant, there's no mess, no guesswork. The 24 oz. (1½ lbs.) package covers an 8 in. 2-layer cake plus decorations; the 80 oz. (5 lbs.) package covers a 2-layer 6 in., 8 in. and 10 in. round tiered cake plus decorations. Pure white. Certified Kosher.

Color Fondant Multi Packs

Convenient four-pouch assortments of primary, neon, pastel or natural colors are perfect for making multicolored decorations. The color is already mixed in. . . no kneading, no mess, no guesswork. Great for flowers, borders and fun shapes. Each 17.6 oz. package contains four 4.4 oz. packs. Certified Kosher.
$9.99

Primary Colors
Green, Red, Yellow, Blue
710-T-445

Neon Colors
Purple, Orange, Yellow, Pink
710-T-446

Pastel Colors
Blue, Yellow, Pink, Green
710-T-447

Natural Colors
Light Brown, Dark Brown, Pink, Black
710-T-448

1. Roll out.

2. Layer over cake.

3. Trim and decorate.

24 oz. (1½ lbs.) Pk.
710-T-2076 $6.49

80 oz. (5 lbs.) Pk.
710-T-2180 $21.99

FoodWriter™ Edible Color Markers

Use like ink markers to add fun and dazzling color to countless foods. Kids love 'em! Decorate on fondant, color flow, royal icing, even directly on cookies. Brighten everyday foods like toaster pastries, cheese, fruit slices, bread and more. Each set includes five .35 oz. FoodWriter markers. Certified Kosher.

Primary Colors Sets

Yellow Green Red Blue Black

Fine Tip
609-T-100
Set/5 $7.99

Bold Tip
609-T-115
Set/5 $7.99

Fine Tip Neon Colors Set

Purple Orange Pink
Light Green Black

609-T-116
Set/5 $7.99

FINE TIP

BOLD TIP

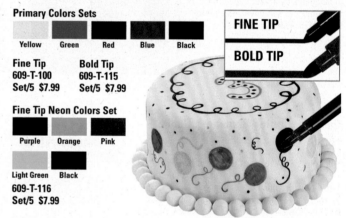

PEARL DUST™ NEW!

Give your fondant and gum paste decorations a beautiful, glittering finish! Wilton Pearl Dust creates rich, lustrous highlights on flowers, bows, letters and more. Add sparkle and fun to candy too. Easy to use, just brush onto your decoration with a soft artist brush. Or, to paint decorations, pour a small amount of clear vanilla, lemon juice or vodka into a Candy Melting Plate cavity; stir in Pearl Dust and brush onto your decoration. Edible; FDA-approved. Certified Kosher (except Orchid Pink). 0.1 oz. bottle. **$3.99**

Yellow
703-T-213

Bronze
703-T-214

Gold
703-T-216

Orchid Pink
703-T-217

Silver
703-T-218

White
703-T-219

Color Tray

Become a true fondant artist with this convenient tray! Pour in Icing Writer™ and use with the Brush Set (p.131) to add vivid designs to your fondant cakes.
1907-T-1208 $2.99

Icing Writer™

Squeeze on colorful accents —flowers, swirls, messages and more—with this ready-to-use icing! It's easy to control for precise decorating; just squeeze the bottle and icing flows smoothly from the built-in round tip. Trace imprinted shapes made with Cut-Outs or draw dazzling freehand designs. Dries to a smooth, satin finish. 3 oz. bottle. Certified Kosher. **$2.49**

Blue
710-T-2227

Red
710-T-2225

Yellow
710-T-2226

White
710-T-2228

Green
710-T-2229

Pink
710-T-2230

Violet
710-T-2231

Fondant Tools and Accessories

Flower Stamen Assortment

Finish your royal icing or gum paste flowers with a beautiful, natural look using one of these 3 lovely stamen styles. Just pipe a dot of icing for your flower center, cut stamens to desired size, insert and let dry. Includes 60 each in Pearl, Glitter and Fluffy styles. May be tinted (except Pearl) with Wilton Icing Colors added to vanilla extract. 2½ in. long with stamen on each end.
1005-T-410 Pk./180 $2.99

Fondant Shaping Foam

Thick and thin squares are the ideal soft surface for shaping flowers, leaves and other fondant or gum paste cutouts. Use the thin square for thinning petal edges with a ball tool, carving vein lines on leaves and making ruffled fondant strips. Use the thick square for cupping flower centers. Thin: 4 x 4 x ⅛ in. Thick: 4 x 4 x 1 in.
1907-T-9704 Set/2 $2.99

Confectionery Tool Set

Invaluable tools for shaping and imprinting, helping you achieve lifelike fondant or gum paste flowers. Ideal for marking patterns in fondant cakes, shaping marzipan fruits. Includes plastic Dogbone, Umbrella, Shell, Ball and Veining tools.
1907-T-1000 Set/5 $9.99

Quick Ease Roller

Makes it easy to prepare small pieces of fondant and gum paste for cutting flowers and designs. Wooden roller fits comfortably in palm of hand. 4⅛ in. wide.
1907-T-1202 $4.99

Brush Set

Add a special touch of color to your fondant-covered cake! It's easy and fun with these fine-bristle brushes and Icing Writer™. Three tip designs (round, square and bevel) help you achieve different painted effects. Also great for applying water or adhesive to attach fondant decorations.
1907-T-1207 Set/3 $2.99

Fondant Ribbon Cutter/Embosser Set

This easy-to-use tool is the perfect way to add beautiful textured fondant ribbons, stripes and bows to your cake. Just choose the cutting and embossing wheel designs you want, slide the washer, core, wheels and spacers on the roller handle, and roll on top of your fondant. (We suggest brushing the assembled roller with shortening for easy release.) The perfectly cut ribbon strips are ready to place right on your cake! Produces ribbon widths from ¼ in. to 3¾ in. when combining spacers. Complete set includes: 8 embossing wheels (4 beaded, 4 striped); 9 spacers (one ⅓ in., two each ¼, ½, ¾ and 1 in. wide); 9 cutting wheels (3 straight, 3 zigzag, 3 wavy); roller handle with detachable core; assembly hardware.
1907-T-1203 Set/26 $14.99

Embossing Wheels		Spacers					Cutting Wheels		
4 Beaded	4 Striped	| 1"	¾"	½"	⅓"	¼" | Use spacers to create the perfect ribbon width!	3 Straight	3 Zigzag	3 Wavy

Fondant Decorative Punch Set

Add exciting 3-dimensional decorations in fondant with this easy-to-use tool. In seconds, you can punch out fondant accents with elegant openwork shapes like diamonds and flowers. As you punch, the disk imprints a detailed design that adds a pretty touch of texture to any cake. The comfortable angled handle holds your choice of 8 design disks. Also great for adding fondant detail to cupcakes and cookies. Disks turn to lock into place.
1907-T-1204 Set/9 $8.99

Large Tulip with Leaves   Dutch Blossom   Paisley with Dots   Wide Diamond with Scrolls   Small Tulip with Leaves   Snapdragon with Leaves   4-Leaf Clover with Dots   Narrow Diamond with Scrolls

Flower Former Set

Dry fondant or icing leaves and flowers in a convex or concave shape. Three each of 1½, 2 and 2½ in. wide holders, all 11 in. long.
417-T-9500 Set/9 $5.99

Easy-Glide Fondant Smoother

Essential tool for shaping and smoothing rolled fondant on your cake. Works great on top, edges and sides! Shapes fondant to sides of cake so that no puffed areas appear. Trim any excess with a sharp knife. 6¼ x 3¼ in. wide.
1907-T-1200 $4.99

Cutter/Embosser

Three detachable wheels (straight, wavy and ridged) for cutting and for embossing patterns on fondant. Light, easy-rolling design cuts at the perfect angle. Comfortable handle also stores wheels.
1907-T-1206 $3.99

Candy Melting Plate

Microwave-melt up to 11 Candy Melts®* colors at one time with less mess. Plastic with non-slip grip edge. Includes decorating brush. Great for drying fondant flowers, too.
1904-T-8016 Set/2 $2.99

*Brand confectionery coating.

Fondant Tools and Accessories

Cut-Outs ™

- Fast, fun way to brighten any fondant cake!
- Great assortment of shapes for any occasion.

With Cut-Outs, it's easy to make fun 3-D shapes for your fondant cakes and cupcakes. Just roll out fondant, press down with Cut-Out and lift away. Remove shapes with a small spatula. Stainless steel (except for plastic Daisy) shapes range from ⅝ in. to 2½ in.

 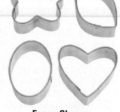 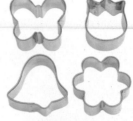 

Crinkle Shapes
Circle, Square, Triangle, Heart
417-T-444 Set/4 $2.99

Fancy Shapes
Flower, Leaf, Oval, Heart
417-T-445 Set/4 $2.99

Garden Shapes
Butterfly, Tulip, Bell, Flower
417-T-443 Set/4 $2.99

Daisy
Durable plastic.
417-T-439 Set/3 $2.49

Oval
417-T-438
Set/3 $2.49

Round
417-T-432
Set/3 $2.49

Square
417-T-431
Set/3 $2.49

People
417-T-441
Set/6 $3.99

Heart
417-T-434
Set/3 $2.49

Star
417-T-433
Set/3 $2.49

Flower
417-T-435
Set/3 $2.49

Funny Flower
417-T-436
Set/3 $2.49

Leaf
417-T-437
Set/3 $2.49

Alphabet/Number
417-T-442
Set/37 $14.99

FONDANT AND GUM PASTE DECORATING SETS

Floral Collection Flower Making Set
Make incredibly lifelike gum paste flowers. Full-color how-to book includes many arranging ideas and step-by-step instructions. Kit includes 24 plastic cutters, 1 leaf mold, 3 wood modeling tools, protector flap, 40-page instruction book and 2 foam squares for modeling.
1907-T-117 Set/32 $19.99
Book only 907-T-117 $9.99

Stepsaving Rose Bouquets Flower Cutter Set
Create gorgeous fondant and gum paste roses and forget-me-nots using book and cutters in this set. Cutters include large and small rose, rose leaf, calyx and forget-me-not.
1907-T-1003 Set/6 $7.99

Floral Garland Cutter/Ejector Set
Quickly and easily cuts and positions fondant or gum paste flowers on cakes. Includes ejector, 5 cutters and instructions.
1907-T-1001 Set/7 $9.99

ORDER TOLL FREE: 800-794-5866

LETTERS & NUMBERS GUM PASTE & FONDANT MOLD SET

With this set, it's easy to put the finishing touches on your cakes with a beautiful 3-dimensional message or monogram. Just fill molds with a 50/50 gum paste and fondant blend, press and smooth with tool included and release. Great for 2-tone letters and numbers, a perfect way to personalize cake and cupcakes. Includes 11 mold sheets with 52 alphabet molds (upper and lower case A-Z), 3 punctuation marks and 10 numeral molds, stainless steel smoothing/releasing tool, molding instructions.
2104-T-3070 Set/13 $19.99

ROLLING PINS AND MAT

Spiral Pattern Roller

This easy-to-use roller adds an exciting swirled texture to fondant cake decorations. Its lightweight design makes it easy to imprint evenly, creating a perfect look for your cake. Sized just right for preparing small amounts of fondant to create bow loops, swags, flat flowers and more. Perfect for use with Wilton Ready-To-Use Rolled Fondant, Fondant Multi Packs and Cut-Outs™. Just roll out fondant with a smooth rolling pin, then re-roll with the Spiral Pattern Roller to imprint incredible texture. Imprint width is 9¼ in.; 2 in. diameter.
1907-T-1224 $9.99

20 in. Rolling Pin

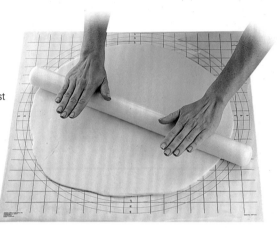

Its extra-wide, smooth design is perfect for covering cakes with rolled fondant. The non-stick surface makes handling large pieces of fondant easy—just dust the surface with confectioner's sugar and roll out fondant to the size you need, then use the Rolling Pin to lift the fondant from your work surface to the cake. Great for rolling out pastry dough and pie crusts too. 20 x 1½ in. diameter. (Mat sold below.)
1907-T-1210 $19.99

9 in. Rolling Pin

Roll out fondant evenly, in the perfect thickness for easy cutting and shaping, with this 3-piece non-stick roller. Roll to the perfect ⅛ or 1⁄16 in. height used for cutting many fondant decorations, using the slide-on guide rings. Easy to handle—just the right size for preparing small amounts of fondant to place on your cake. Perfect for use with Fondant Multi Packs and Cut-Outs™. 9 x 1 in. diameter. Includes ⅛ and 1⁄16 in. rings.
1907-T-1205 $5.99

NEW!

20 in. Rolling Pin Guide Rings

Eliminate the guesswork when you roll out fondant! Slip these easy-to-use guide rings onto the ends of your 20 in. rolling pin to achieve the perfect thickness every time. Includes 1⁄16 in. (blue) for flower petals and leaves, 3⁄16 in. (gold) for letters, numbers and appliqué shapes, ⅛ in. (orange) for shapes cut with Wilton Cut-Outs™ or cookie cutters and for covering cakes with fondant.
1907-T-1010 Set/3 $3.99

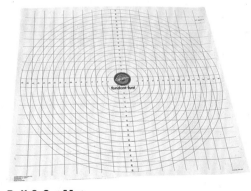

Roll & Cut Mat

For precise measuring, rolling and cutting of fondant or dough. Pre-marked circles for exact sizing. Square grid helps you cut precise strips. Non-stick surface for easy release. 20 in. square with circles from 3 in. to 19 in. diam.
409-T-412 $8.99

Gum Paste and Ingredients

Create beautiful handmolded flowers right from the package.

Ready-To-Use Gum Paste

Now you can have gum paste on hand whenever you need it! With Ready-To-Use Gum Paste, there's no mixing, no mess—just tint, roll out and cut to create incredible floral bouquets for your cakes. Follow the easy instructions included and use with Wilton Gum Paste Decorating Sets to make roses, daisies, apple blossoms, tulips and many more beautiful blooms. 1 lb. Certified Kosher.
707-T-130 $8.99

Gum Paste Mix

Just add water and knead. Workable, pliable dough-like mixture molds into beautiful flowers and figures. 1 lb. Certified Kosher.
707-T-124 $5.99

Gum-Tex™

Makes fondant and gum paste pliable, elastic, easy to shape. Plastic resealable lid. 6 oz. Certified Kosher.
707-T-117 $7.99

Glucose

Essential ingredient for making fondant and gum paste from scratch. Use with Wilton Gum-Tex™. 12 oz. Certified Kosher.
707-T-107 $3.99

Glycerin

Stir into dried out fondant, gum paste or icing color to restore consistency. 2 oz. Certified Kosher.
708-T-14 $1.99

Kitchen Tools

Make decorating and kitchen tasks easier! Lightweight, comfortable tools with contoured handles and quality blades of stainless steel and silicone heads suited for the task.

Pastry Brush
Flexible silicone bristles are great for brushing on Cake Release, shortening or hot glazes. More durable than nylon bristles. Comfortable ergonomic handle; 8½ in. long.
409-T-6056
$5.99

Cake and Pie Server
Slice and serve with greater control. The comfortable ergonomic handle with thumb rest and angled blade makes lifting every slice easier. Serrated stainless steel blade cuts even the first slice cleanly. 9 in. long.
409-T-6058 $6.99

Cookie Spatula
Angled stainless steel blade moves cookies from pan to plate with ease. Slides easily under cookies—great for serving brownies and bar cookies too. Comfortable ergonomic handle with thumb rest. 9 in. long.
409-T-6054 $6.99

All-Purpose Spatulas
Blend and mix with greater comfort, more control and less fatigue, thanks to the contoured Comfort Grip™ handle. Flexible silicone blade is ideal for blending and removing icing from bowls or containers—great for all-around kitchen use. Stain and odor resistant.
9 in.
409-T-6050 $7.99
12 in.
409-T-6052 $8.99

Cake Knife/Spatula
This stainless steel knife is perfect for torting cakes—it cuts layers cleanly and has the width you need to transfer layers without breakage. Use the smooth edge for spreading icing or filling on cake layers. It's easy to control, with a lightweight nylon handle that is comfortable in any hand. 15 in. long
409-T-6048 $9.99

Baking Accessories

Bake Easy!™ Non-Stick Spray
For cakes that turn out beautifully every time, start by spraying pans with Bake Easy. This convenient non-stick spray helps your cakes release perfectly with fewer crumbs for easier icing and a flawless look for decorating. Just a light, even coating does the job. Use Bake Easy for all mixes and recipes—cupcakes, brownies, breads and more. Versatile for all types of baking and cooking. 6 oz.
702-T-6018 $2.99

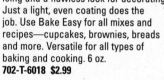

Cake Release
No need to grease and flour your baking pan—Cake Release coats in one step. Simply spread Cake Release lightly on pan bottom and sides with a pastry brush and add batter. Cakes release perfectly every time without crumbs, giving you the ideal surface for decorating. In convenient dispensing bottle. 8 oz. Certified Kosher.
702-T-6016 $3.49

Bake-Even Strips
Cakes bake perfectly level and moist, without cracking, when you wrap these strips around the pan before baking. Oven-safe, instructions and clips included.

Small Set
Two 1½ in. high strips, 30 in. long. Enough for two 8 or 9 in. round pans.
415-T-260 Set/2 $7.99

Large Set
Four 1½ in. high strips, 36, 43, 49 and 56 in. long. Enough for one each: 10, 12, 14, 16 in. round pans.
415-T-262 Set/4 $16.99

Cake Leveler
Make your cake top perfectly level for precise decorating—just place adjustable wire in notches to desired height up to 2 in. and glide through the cake. Makes torting easy, too! For cakes up to 10 in. wide.
415-T-815 $2.99

Non-Stick Parchment Paper
Use Wilton silicone-treated non-stick parchment to line baking pans and cookie sheets—a non-fat alternative that saves cleanup time. Roll out cookie dough between 2 sheets, dough won't stick and will easily transfer to your cookie sheet. You can even reuse it for the next batch. Oven-safe to 400°F, parchment is great for conventional ovens, microwaves and the freezer. Double roll is 41 square feet, 15 in. wide. Certified Kosher.
415-T-680 $4.99

Large Cake Leveler
Blade easily levels and torts cakes up to 18 in. wide. Adjusts up to 3 in. high—just twist feet to lock into notch at desired height then glide the stainless steel blade through your cake.
417-T-1198 $21.99

6-Piece Covered Mixing Bowl Set
Perfect for preparing decorating icings—clear lids snap on tight to keep icing the right texture. Includes one each 1, 2 and 3 quart nesting bowls with easy-grip handles and easy-pour spouts for better control. Rubberized base keeps bowls from sliding on countertops. Measurements clearly marked for precise mixing. Dishwasher safe.
417-T-469 Set/6 $12.99

CAKE STENCILS VARIETY PACK

Our collection of 4 stencil designs gives you several ways to make birthday and everyday cakes more festive. Decorating with stencils is so easy—just place on your iced cake, then sprinkle away with Wilton Cake Sparkles™, add exciting Wilton Sugars in a rainbow of colors or use Color Mist™ Food Color Spray. Also works beautifully with Wilton Rolled Fondant—fill in designs with sugars or decorate with FoodWriter™ Markers. Includes Happy Birthday, Flower, Swirl and Heart designs.
417-T-148 Pk./4 $6.99

ORDER TOLL FREE: 800-794-5866

Decorating Stands

A quality cake stand is a must for easy decorating. Stands lift your cake off the work surface so you can create borders conveniently. And they rotate, allowing you to decorate all the way around the cake without straining.

Tilting Cake Turntable

It tilts! Decorate any part of your cake conveniently!

The Tilting Cake Turntable moves to 3 preset angles (12°, 24°, and level) and locks in place, making every decorating technique easier! 6 in. high turntable smoothly rotates in any of the angled positions for effortless decorating of top borders, stringwork, lettering on top and sides of cake, more. Includes lock to prevent rotation. Non-slip bottom, 12 in. diameter.
307-T-894 $59.99

Professional Turntable

Extra strength and effortless turning for decorating tiered wedding cakes. Heavy-duty aluminum stand is 4½ in. high with 12 in. diameter plate. Holds cakes up to 16 in. diameter.
307-T-2501 $59.99

Revolving Cake Stand

Turns in either direction on easy-rotating ball bearings. 3 in. high, 11 in. diameter plate is white molded plastic. Holds cakes up to 10 in. diameter.
415-T-900 $11.99

Trim 'N Turn™ Cake Stand

Turns smoothly on hidden ball bearings for easy decorating and serving. Flute-edged 12 in. plate is white molded plastic. Holds cakes up to 10 in. diameter.
2103-T-2518 $7.99

ORDER ONLINE: WWW.WILTON.COM

Decorating Tools

ICING SCULPTOR®

Now your cakes can have an elegant sculpted finish that will give them a beautiful professional look. It's easy with the Icing Sculptor. Just insert any combination of the 64 design blades—mix and match between the 14 sculpting edges to create your favorite customized effects. Then glide the comb over the iced cake sides to create attractive ridges that will beautifully frame your design. Create hundreds of pattern combinations—wide or narrow ridges, dramatic swirls and vertical designs too. Includes sculptor handle, 64 design blades and complete instructions. This versatile tool has a patent pending.
2104-T-12 Set/66 $12.99

So Easy!
Select the sculpting blades you want and slide into handle. Press sculptor into iced cake as you rotate cake on turntable.

So Versatile!
Mix and match between the 14 edge designs on 64 blades to achieve the perfect look for your cake.

Includes 8 of each 2-Sided Design Blade

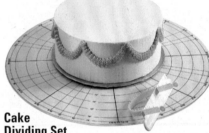

Decorating Comb

Run edge across your iced cake to form perfect ridges. Plastic, 12 x 1½ in.
417-T-156 $1.49

Decorating Triangle

Each side adds a different contoured effect to iced cakes. Easy to hold. Plastic, 5 x 5 in.
417-T-162 $1.09

Garland Marker

Adjusts to 7 preset widths and varying depths to easily mark perfectly uniform garlands on cake sides. Instructions included.
409-T-812 $3.99

Hand & Wrist Support Gloves

Makes decorating and other creative tasks more comfortable! Use whenever you work with your hands. Their exclusive Spandex and nylon construction supports vital areas of the hand and wrist to help you work more comfortably, while the breathable fabric reduces perspiration. Hand & Wrist Support Gloves promote circulation and massage muscles to reduce fatigue. Lightweight, fingerless design gives you the freedom of motion you need for all kinds of tasks including computer work, painting, sewing, knitting, quilting, crocheting and more. Machine or hand wash.
417-T-488 Pk./2 $19.99

Cake Dividing Set

Measures equal sections of your cake for precise placement of garlands, stringwork and other designs. Cake Dividing Wheel marks up to 16 divisions on cakes up to 20 in. diameter. Garland Marker adjusts to 7 widths. Instructions included.
409-T-806 Set/2 $8.99

Practice Board with Patterns Set

Includes stand and 20 full-size patterns. 9 x 6 in.
406-T-9464 $6.99

All-Purpose Decorating Gloves

Food-safe disposable gloves keep your hands clean, odor-free and protected in and out of the kitchen. Prevent color stains when tinting fondant, keep fingerprints off homemade candy, eliminate burning of skin when cutting spicy foods. Great when working with craft paint and glue too. Easy to slip-on, gloves fit either hand.
417-T-1642 Pk./20 $2.99

Icing Colors

Wilton colors are made to produce deeper, richer color by adding just a small amount. Our concentrated gel formula helps you achieve the exact shade you want without thinning your icing. You'll find a rainbow of colors, ready to blend together to create your own custom shades.

*Note: Large amounts of these colors may affect icing taste.

Use No-Taste Red for large areas of red on a cake. When using Black, start with chocolate icing to limit the amount of color needed.

‡Daffodil Yellow is an all-natural color. It does not contain Yellow #5. The color remains very pale.

Single Bottles
1 oz. Certified Kosher.
$1.99

Ivory 610-T-208	Daffodil Yellow‡ 610-T-175	Buttercup Yellow 610-T-216	Golden Yellow 610-T-159	Lemon Yellow 610-T-108	Copper (skin tone) 610-T-450	Creamy Peach 610-T-210	Rose Petal Pink 610-T-410	Terra Cotta 610-T-206	Orange 610-T-205

Red-Red* 610-T-906	Christmas Red* 610-T-302	Red (no-taste) 610-T-998	Rose 610-T-401	Burgundy 610-T-698	Pink 610-T-256	Violet 610-T-604	Delphinium Blue 610-T-228	Cornflower Blue 610-T-710	Royal Blue 610-T-655

Sky Blue 610-T-700	Teal 610-T-207	Kelly Green 610-T-752	Leaf Green 610-T-809	Moss Green 610-T-851	Juniper Green 610-T-234	Brown 610-T-507	Black* 610-T-981

Primary 4-Icing Colors Set
Lemon Yellow, Sky Blue, Christmas Red, Brown in .5 oz. jars. Certified Kosher.
601-T-5127 Set/4 $4.99

8-Icing Colors Set
Lemon Yellow, Sky Blue, Christmas Red, Brown, Orange, Violet, Pink and Leaf Green in .5 oz. jars. Certified Kosher.
601-T-5577 Set/8 $9.99

12-Icing Colors Set
Our most popular collection creates the spectrum of primary colors plus skin tones, teal and burgundy. Lemon Yellow, Teal, No-Taste Red, Brown, Copper (skin tone), Violet, Pink, Burgundy, Golden Yellow, Royal Blue, Black, Kelly Green in .5 oz. jars. Certified Kosher.
601-T-5580 Set/12 $13.99

White-White Icing Color
Stir in to whiten icing made with butter or margarine. Perfect for wedding cakes. 2 oz. Certified Kosher.
603-T-1236 $2.99

Glycerin
Stir into dried out icing color to restore consistency. 2 oz. Certified Kosher.
708-T-14 $1.99

Pastel 4-Icing Colors Set
Willow Green, Cornflower Blue, Creamy Peach, Rose Petal Pink in .5 oz. jars. Certified Kosher.
601-T-25588 Set/4 $4.99

Garden Tone 4-Icing Colors Set
Buttercup Yellow, Delphinium Blue, Aster Mauve, Juniper Green in .5 oz. jars. Certified Kosher.
601-T-4240 Set/4 $4.99

Color Mist™ Food Color Spray

This easy-to-use spray gives decorators the versatility and dazzling effects of an airbrush in a convenient can! Creates a rainbow of excitement on so many desserts. Use it to transform a plain iced cake with sensational color, add splashes of holiday color to iced cookies and cupcakes. Great for party desserts—highlighting whipped topping or ice cream with color. No mess, taste-free formula; add a little color or a lot.

Colors match Wilton Icing Colors above. 1.5 oz. Certified Kosher. $2.99

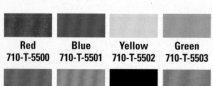

Red 710-T-5500	Blue 710-T-5501	Yellow 710-T-5502	Green 710-T-5503
Violet 710-T-5504	Pink 710-T-5505	Black 710-T-5506	Orange 710-T-5507

Icings

All Wilton icings are formulated for easy decorating as well as great taste. Our convenient ready-to-use icings are the perfect medium consistency icing for decorating, so you don't need to worry about mixing or measuring.

TUBE ICINGS, GELS

Tube Decorating Icings
The same high quality as our Ready-To-Use Decorator Icing, in a convenient tube. Create flowers, borders and more. Ideal for small areas of color on character cakes. Use with the Tip and Nail Set or Coupler Ring Set (below) and any standard-size Wilton metal tip (not included). Colors match Wilton Icing Colors shown at right. 4.25 oz. Certified Kosher. $1.99

Red 704-T-218	Royal Blue 704-T-248
Violet 704-T-242	Leaf Green 704-T-224
Lemon Yellow 704-T-236	Kelly Green 704-T-227
Orange 704-T-212	Chocolate 704-T-254
Pink 704-T-230	White 704-T-200

Black 704-T-206

Coupler Ring Set
Attach Wilton standard size metal decorating tips onto Wilton tube icings to create any technique.
418-T-47306 Set/4 $1.99

Tip and Nail Set
Tips easily twist onto Wilton tube icings to create many decorating techniques. Includes Star, Round, Leaf and Petal Tips, Flower Nail.
418-T-47300 Set/5 $1.99

Tube Decorating Gels
Add shimmering accents, colorful highlights and sparkle to your decorating with these transparent gels. Create a beautiful stained-glass effect and add distinctive writing and printing. Great for cakes and cookies. Colors match Wilton Icing Colors shown at left. .75 oz. Certified Kosher. $1.49

Red 704-T-318	Orange 704-T-312	
Pink 704-T-330	Royal Blue 704-T-348	
Violet 704-T-342	Leaf Green 704-T-324	White 704-T-302
Lemon Yellow 704-T-336	Brown 704-T-354	Black 704-T-306

Tube Icing and Gel Color Chart

Lemon Yellow	Orange	Red	Pink
Violet	Royal Blue	Leaf Green	† Kelly Green
† Chocolate	Brown	White	Black

†Not available in gel.

ORDER TOLL FREE: 800-794-5866

SPARKLE GEL

NEW!

Make your cake decorations more dynamic! Squeeze on sparkling color effects with our ready-to-use gel. Great for dots, messages, water effects and fondant accents. Try it on cookies, cupcakes, ice cream and more! Resealable 3.5 oz. tubes. Certified Kosher.
$2.99

Yellow 704-T-108

Blue 704-T-110

Green 704-T-111

Red 704-T-112

READY-TO-USE DECORATOR ICINGS

Wilton makes the only ready-to-use icing that is the perfect consistency for decorating. The pure white color is best for creating true vivid colors using Wilton Icing Colors. Rich and creamy, with a delicious homemade taste.

Large Tub

Ideal thin-to-medium consistency for use in Wilton Method Cake Decorating Classes in a convenient easy-carry tub. Great for icing cakes, making borders, messages and more. Contains 9 cups—enough to decorate ten 8 or 9 in. round cake layers. Certified Kosher.
White 704-T-680 $13.99

1 lb. Can

Ideal stiff consistency for making roses and flowers with upright petals. One 16 oz. can covers two 8 or 9 in. layers or one 9 x 13 in. cake.
White
710-T-118 $2.99
Chocolate
710-T-119 $2.99

Creamy White Buttercream Icing Mix

Our convenient mix has the delicious taste and creamy texture of homemade buttercream icing. Use just as you would your favorite buttercream recipe. Makes 1½ to 2 cups. Enough to ice a 2-layer 8 in. cake. Certified Kosher.
710-T-112 $2.99

Vanilla Whipped Icing Mix

Our light, whipped icing provides the ideal texture for decorating in an easy-to-make, delicious mix. Just add ice water and it whips up velvety-smooth for icing or decorating. Light and delicate flavor. Makes 4 cups. Certified Kosher Dairy.
710-T-1241 $4.99

Meringue Powder

Primary ingredient for royal icing. Stabilizes buttercream, adds body to boiled icing and meringue. Replaces egg whites in many recipes. Resealable top opens for easy measuring. 4 oz. can makes 5 recipes of royal icing; 8 oz. can makes 10 recipes. 16 oz. can makes 20 recipes. Certified Kosher.
4 oz. can 702-T-6007 $4.99
8 oz. can 702-T-6015 $7.99
16 oz. can 702-T-6004 $15.99

Color Flow Mix

Create dimensional flow-in designs for your cake. Just add water and confectioner's sugar. 4 oz. can makes ten 1½ cup batches. Certified Kosher.
701-T-47 $7.49

Piping Gel

Pipe messages and designs or glaze cakes before icing. Use clear or tint with icing color. 10 oz. Certified Kosher.
704-T-105 $3.99

Ready-To-Decorate Icing

Add an exciting finishing touch to treats, without mixing or mess. Just slip one of the four free tips over the nozzle and start the fun. Colors match Wilton Icing Colors (p. 136). 6.4 oz. Certified Kosher. **$3.99**

Red 710-T-4400	Green 710-T-4401	White 710-T-4402
Black 710-T-4404	Pink 710-T-4406	Blue 710-T-4407
Violet 710-T-4408	Yellow 710-T-4409	Orange 710-T-4410

Four FREE decorating tips included:

Small Round Tip For dots and outlining

Leaf Tip For basic and ruffled leaves

Large Round Tip For writing and printing

Star Tip For stars, swirls and pretty borders

Cookie Icing

Use this quick-setting microwavable icing to cover your cookies with a shiny finish—perfect for decorating with colorful Wilton Icing Writer™ accents! Easy to use—just heat and squeeze onto cookies using the convenient cap. Sets smooth in just 45 minutes. 10 oz. bottle covers 12 (3 in.) cookies. White. Certified Kosher.
704-T-481 $4.49

Icing Writer™

Squeeze on colorful accents —flowers, swirls, messages and more—with this ready-to-use icing! It's easy to control for precise decorating, just squeeze the bottle and icing flows smoothly from the built-in round tip. Trace imprinted shapes made with Cut-Outs™ or draw dazzling freehand designs. Dries to a smooth, satin finish. 3 oz. bottle. Certified Kosher.
$2.49

	Blue 710-T-2227
Red 710-T-2225	Yellow 710-T-2226	White 710-T-2228
Green 710-T-2229	Pink 710-T-2230	Violet 710-T-2231

Sprinkles

NEW!

JUMBO SHAPED SPRINKLES

Give your cakes and cupcakes a big finish! Top them with our new Jumbo Sprinkles in exciting shapes and colors. These big and bold decorations are also perfect for brownies and cookies, great for birthdays, holidays and celebrations of all kinds. Certified Kosher. **$3.99**

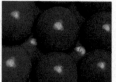

Sour Cherry Balls
4.4 oz. **710-T-034**

Heart Drops
5.25 oz. **710-T-035**

Jumbo Stars
3.25 oz. **710-T-026**

Jumbo Diamonds
3.5 oz. **710-T-027**

Jumbo Daisies
3.25 oz. **710-T-028**

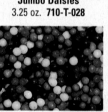

Jumbo Confetti
3.25 oz. **710-T-029**

Jumbo Hearts
3.25 oz. **710-T-032**

Jumbo Rainbow Nonpareils
4.8 oz. **710-T-033**

SHAPED SPRINKLES

Pour on the fun! Great shapes and colors add a dash of excitement to cakes, cupcakes, ice cream and more. Certified Kosher. **$2.29**

NEW!

Chocolate Hearts
2.5 oz. **710-T-622**

White Nonpareils
3 oz. **710-T-773**

Cinnamon Drops
3 oz. **710-T-769**

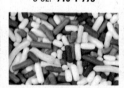

Rainbow Nonpareils
3 oz. **710-T-772**

Rainbow Jimmies
2.5 oz. **710-T-776**
6.25 oz. **710-T-994** **$4.49**

Chocolate Jimmies
2.5 oz. **710-T-774**

CAKE SPARKLES™

Add shimmering color to cakes, cupcakes, cookies and ice cream! Brilliant edible glitter in a great variety of colors, great for stencilling, highlighting messages, snow scenes. .25 oz. Certified Kosher. **$2.89**

Silver
703-T-1285

White
703-T-1290

Yellow
703-T-1272

Purple
703-T-1266

Blue
703-T-1314

Red
703-T-1284

Green
703-T-1278

Pink
703-T-1260

Orange
703-T-1308

Black
703-T-1302

6-MIX ASSORTMENTS

They're so convenient! Assorted fun shapes in an easy-pour flip-top bottle. Top cupcakes, ice cream and other goodies. Certified Kosher. **$4.99**

Flowerful Medley
Includes Confetti, Colorful Leaves, Daisies, Pastel Hearts, Wild Flowers, Butterflies. 2.23 oz. total.
710-T-4122

Animals and Stars
Includes Cows, Stars, Dinosaurs, Stars and Moons, Bears, Dolphins. 2.1 oz. total.
710-T-4123

Nonpareils
Includes Pink, Orange, Green, Red, Yellow, Purple. 3 oz. total.
710-T-4125

Jimmies
Includes Pink, Orange, Green, Red, Yellow, Blue. 2.52 oz. total.
710-T-4127

ORDER TOLL FREE: 800-794-5866

SPARKLING SUGARS

 NEW!

Put that extra dazzle in your decorating! These easy-pour sugars have a coarse texture and a brilliant sparkle that makes cupcakes, cookies and cakes really shine. 5.25 oz. bottle. Certified Kosher. **$3.99**

Yellow
710-T-036

Blue
710-T-039

Lavender
710-T-037

Pink
710-T-038

8 oz. bottle. Certified Kosher. **$4.49**

White
710-T-992

Lavender/ White
710-T-993

Rainbow
710-T-991

COLORED SUGARS

Extra-fine sugar is excellent for filling in brightly colored designs on cakes, cupcakes and cookies. 3.25 oz. bottle. Certified Kosher. **$2.29**

Blue
710-T-750

Yellow
710-T-754

Orange
710-T-759

Pink
710-T-756

Red
710-T-766

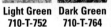

Lavender
710-T-758

Light Green
710-T-752

Dark Green
710-T-764

Black
710-T-762

4-MIX ASSORTMENTS

They're so convenient! Assorted sugars in an easy-pour flip-top bottle. Top cupcakes, ice cream and other goodies. 4.4 oz. total. Certified Kosher. **$4.99**

 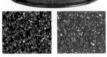

Bright Sugars
Includes Yellow, Light Green, Lavender, Pink.
710-T-651

Primary Sugars
Includes Red, Dark Green, Blue, Yellow.
710-T-650

Flavorings

Decorators trust Wilton flavorings for great taste that won't change icing consistency. Wilton flavors are concentrated—only a drop or two adds delicious taste to icings, cakes, beverages and other recipes.

Pure Vanilla Extract

The world's finest vanilla is from Madagascar. Unmatched flavor and aroma to enhance cakes, puddings, pie fillings, custards, salad dressings and more. 4 oz. Certified Kosher.
604-T-2270 **$7.99**

Clear Vanilla Extract
2 oz.
604-T-2237
$1.99
8 oz.
604-T-2269
$4.99

No-Color Butter Flavor
2 oz.
604-T-2040
$1.99
8 oz.
604-T-2067
$4.99

No-Color Almond Extract
2 oz.
604-T-2126
$1.99

NO-COLOR FLAVORINGS

Recommended by and used in Wilton Method Classes, these delicious flavors won't change your icing color. Essential for making pure white icings for wedding cakes and maintaining vibrant colors in all your decorating. Certified Kosher.

Press Sets

Block Message Press Set

Includes Best, Happy, Wishes, Anniversary, Birthday and Congratulations. Message holder. Word height 7/8 in.
2104-T-2077
Set/6 **$3.69**

Italic Make-Any-Message Press Set

Pretty and sophisticated letters for a custom message. Press words up to 10½ in. wide, letters ¾ in. high. Includes letter holder.
2104-T-2277
Set/58 **$7.99**

Make-Any-Message Letter Press Set

Imprint the perfect sentiment! Press words up to 10½ in. wide, letters ¾ in. high. Includes letter holder.
2104-T-10
Set/56 **$7.99**

Decorator Favorites Pattern Press Set

Includes: fleur de lis; double heart; medallion; open heart; closed scroll; heart; large, medium and small C-scrolls; crest; double scroll; vine.
2104-T-3160 Set/12 **$5.99**

Designer Pattern Press Set

Imprints elegant designs for easy overpiping. Includes: symmetrical swirl; small and large fleurs de lis; corner flourish; flower; heart bow; scroll; curlicues.
2104-T-3112
Set/8 **$5.99**

Script Message Press Set

Combine the words Best, Happy, Wishes, Birthday, Anniversary, and Congratulations. Word height 7/8 in.
2104-T-2061 Set/6 **$3.69**

Decorating Bags

Featherweight® Decorating Bags

Use these easy-handling bags over and over. Lightweight, strong and flexible polyester will never get stiff. Coated to prevent grease from seeping through. May be boiled; dishwasher safe. Instructions included. Sold singly.

8 in. 404-T-5087 **$2.99**
10 in. 404-T-5109 **$4.49**
12 in. 404-T-5125 **$5.49**
14 in. 404-T-5140 **$6.49**
16 in. 404-T-5168 **$7.99**
18 in. 404-T-5184 **$8.99**

Disposable Decorating Bags

Just use, then toss. Strong, flexible plastic. 12 in. size fits standard tips and couplers. Also perfect for melting Candy Melts®* in the microwave. Instructions included.

2104-T-358 Pk./12 **$3.99**
2104-T-1358 Pk./24 **$6.49**

*Brand confectionery coating.

50 Pack

Disposable Decorating Bag Dispenser Box

Now in convenient Value Packs! Dispenser boxes make it easy to pull out one bag at a time, so you can keep your decorating space uncluttered. Instructions included.

2104-T-1273 Pk./50 **$12.49**
2104-T-1249 Pk./100 **$19.99**

Parchment Triangles

Make your own disposable decorating bags with our grease-resistant vegetable parchment triangles. The professional's choice for convenience and quick bag preparation. Instructions included.

15 in. 2104-T-1508 Pk./100 **$5.99**

Icing Bag Ties

Convenient bands wrap around the twist of your decorating bag, then lock to prevent icing from oozing out of the top. As you squeeze out icing, slide the tie down to maintain the pressure.

417-T-173 Pk./12 **$3.99**

NEW!

Spatulas
ROSEWOOD HANDLES

Quality rosewood handle spatulas have been favorites for years. They have strong, flexible stainless steel blades and sturdy riveted handles.

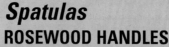

Straight Blade
11 in.; 6 in. blade.
409-T-7695 $4.99
8 in.; 4¼ in. blade.
409-T-6044 $2.99

Angled Blade
12 in.; 6¼ in. blade.
409-T-135 $5.99
8 in.; 4½ in. blade.
409-T-739 $2.99

Tapered Blade
8 in.; 4 in. blade.
409-T-518 $2.99

CONTOURED HANDLES

Decorate with greater comfort, more control and less fatigue, thanks to contoured handle with finger pad. Flexible stainless steel blade is perfect thickness for gliding over icing.

Straight Blade
15 in.; 10⅛ in. blade.
409-T-6030 $9.99
11 in.; 6 in. blade.
409-T-6018 $5.99
9 in.; 4½ in. blade.
409-T-6006 $3.99

Angled Blade
15 in.; 9⅞ in. blade.
409-T-6036 $9.99
13 in.; 7¾ in. blade.
409-T-6024 $6.49
9 in.; 4½ in. blade.
409-T-6012 $4.49

Tapered Blade
9 in.; 4 in. blade.
409-T-6003 $3.99

Tip Accessories

Maintain the quality of your Wilton metal decorating tips with these tools.

Tip/Coupler Dishwasher and Storage Bag

Place nylon mesh bag in dishwasher silverware rack for easy tip and coupler cleaning. Tips not included. 5¾ x 6 in.
417-T-1640 Pk./2 $2.99

Decorating Couplers

Couplers make it easy to change decorating tips on the same icing bag.

Standard
Fits all decorating bags and standard tips.
411-T-1987 $0.59

Large
Use with large decorating tips and 14 to 18 in. Featherweight Bags.
411-T-1006 $1.49

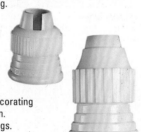

Tip Saver
Restores bent tips to their proper shape; opens clogged tips. Place tip over pointed or cone-shaped end, put on cover and twist back and forth to reshape. Heavy-duty plastic.
414-T-909 $2.79

Tip Covers
Take filled bags along for touch ups—just slip over tip and go. Plastic.
414-T-915 Pk./4 $0.99

Tip Brush
Great for cleaning small tip openings. Plastic bristles. ¼ x 4 in. long.
418-T-1123 $1.39

Tipsaver Cases
Small case holds 26 tips; large case holds 52 tips Tips not included.
Small 405-T-8773 **$5.99**
Large 405-T-7777 **$7.49**

Flower-Making Accessories

Flower Lifter
Easily transfers buttercream flowers from nail to cake without damage. Angled design keeps your hands from touching the cake. Detachable blades for easy cleaning. Plastic. 5¼ in. long.
417-T-1199 $2.99

Flower Nail No. 7
For basic flower making. Provides the control you need when piping icing flowers. Just rotate the nail between your thumb and fingers as you pipe a flower on the head. Stainless steel. 1½ in. wide.
402-T-3007 $1.09

Lily Nail Set
Essential for making cup flowers. Includes ½, 1¼, 1⅝ and 2½ in. diameter cups.
403-T-9444 Set/8 $1.99

Flower Former Set
Dry icing leaves and flowers in a convex or concave shape. Three each of 1½, 2 and 2½ in. wide holders, all 11 in. long.
417-T-9500 Set/9 $5.99

ORDER TOLL FREE: 800-794-5866

101 Piece Tool Caddy Collection

This convenient caddy contains our most complete collection of tools, colors and flavors for the cake decorator. It's a great way to organize, carry and store the essentials—tips, couplers, colors, spatulas and more. Lift-out tray holds tips, couplers, brushes and colors securely. Upright storage prevents spills and makes it easy to find what you need. Generous storage area keeps books, spatulas, bags and other large supplies neatly organized.

**2109-T-861
Set/101 $129.99**

Save over $30
Compared to individual prices

Includes These Tools:
- Eight .5 oz. Icing Colors: Golden Yellow, No-Taste Red, Brown, Violet, Pink, Royal Blue, Black, Kelly Green
- 3 Couplers (2 standard, 1 large)
- 2 Tip/Coupler Dishwasher and Storage Bags
- Tip Cleaning Brush
- 24 Disposable 12 in. Decorating Bags
- 3 Professional Reusable Decorating Bags (8, 10 and 16 in.)
- 4 Tip Covers
- Tip Saver
- 1½ in. Flower Nail No. 7
- 3 Spatulas (8 and 13 in. Angled, 8 in. Tapered)
- Flower Lifter
- Garland Marker
- *Decorating Cakes* Book
- 20 All-Purpose Disposable Decorating Gloves
- Practice Board with Patterns
- 2 Bake-Even Strips
- 8 oz. Clear Vanilla and No-Color Butter Flavors
- Cake Leveler
- Quick Ease Roller
- Easy-Glide Fondant Smoother
- Decorating Brush

Plus 18 Tips:
- Round: 1, 2, 2A, 3, 12
- Star: 16, 18, 21, 32
- Basketweave: 48
- Leaf: 67, 352
- Petal: 102, 103, 104, 125
- Drop Flower: 2D
- Cake Icer: 789

50 Piece Tool Caddy Decorating Set

We've put together the perfect set for both beginning and advanced decorators. The generous selection of tips, colors and tools gives you the flexibility to decorate virtually any kind of cake. There's also plenty of room to add new items and keep everything organized to save you time. Set includes all tools specified as needed in our Course I class.

2109-T-859 Set/50 $54.99

Save $22
Compared to individual prices

Includes These Tools:
- Tip Brush
- Decorating Brush
- 1½ in. Flower Nail No. 7
- 2 Standard Couplers
- 18 Disposable 12 in. Bags
- One 10 in. Professional Bag
- 8 in. Angled Spatula
- Four .5 oz. Icing Colors: Lemon Yellow, Christmas Red, Royal Blue, Leaf Green
- Practice Board with stand
- *Cake Decorating Beginner's Guide*

Plus 19 Tips:
- Round: 2, 3, 5, 7, 12
- Leaf: 67, 352
- Drop Flower: 225
- Closed Star: 133
- Basketweave: 47
- Open Star: 16, 18, 21, 32
- Petal: 101, 103, 104
- Large Drop Flower: 2004 (2D)
- Multi-Opening: 233

Tool Caddy Only

Lift out tray keeps 48 tips and 12 color jars within reach (tips and colors not included). Stores colors upright to prevent spilling. Plastic.
409-T-860 $24.99

Deluxe Tip Set

Includes: 26 metal decorating tips (2, 4, 7, 13, 16, 17, 18, 30, 42, 46, 47, 61, 65, 66, 67, 74, 78, 97, 98, 101, 102, 103, 104, 106, 107 and 199); 1¼ in. flower nail No. 9; tip coupler; plastic tipsaver case.
**2104-T-6666
Set/29 $25.99**

Master Tip Set

Includes: 52 metal decorating tips (1, 2, 3, 4, 6, 7, 12, 13, 16, 17, 18, 22, 24, 27, 30, 31, 32, 42, 45, 46, 47, 48, 54, 59, 61, 65, 66, 67, 68, 69, 70, 73, 74, 78, 96, 97, 98, 101, 102, 103, 104, 106, 108, 109, 123, 124, 129, 134, 136, 195, 199 and 2C); two standard tip couplers; two 1¼ in. flower nails No. 9; plastic tipsaver case.
2104-T-7778 Set/57 $44.99

Decorating Sets **NEW!**

12 Piece Cupcake Decorating Set

Create all kinds of fun cupcake designs perfect for celebrations or everyday treats! Includes star tips 1M (rosettes, stars, drop flowers), star tip 22 (zigzags, pull-out stars), round tip 12 (outlines, dots, messages) and Bismarck tip 230 for exciting filled cupcakes, plus 8 disposable bags, instruction booklet.
2104-T-6667 Set/12 $7.99

53 Piece Cake Decorating Set

The works! Decorate many advanced wedding, floral and basketweave cakes as well as basic cakes. Set includes: metal decorating tips 2, 3, 5, 7, 12, 16, 18, 21, 32, 48, 67, 101, 103, 104, 129, 225, 349 and 352; 24 disposable 12 in. decorating bags, two tip couplers; 5 icing colors (.5 oz. each: Golden Yellow, Moss Green, Rose Petal, Cornflower Blue); one 1¼ in. flower nail No. 9; 8 in. angled spatula; storage tray; and 40-page *Cake Decorating Beginner's Guide*.
2104-T-2546 Set/53 $29.99

25 Piece Cake Decorating Set

A solid foundation set for decorating. Set includes: metal decorating tips 3, 16, 32, 104 and 352; 12 disposable 12 in. decorating bags; two tip couplers; 4 icing colors (.5 oz. each: Lemon Yellow, Pink, Sky Blue, Leaf Green); 1¼ in. flower nail No. 9; instruction booklet.
2104-T-2536 Set/25 $11.99

18 Piece Cake Decorating Set

Perfect for Wilton character cakes! Set includes: metal decorating tips 4, 12, 18 and 103; 6 disposable 12 in. decorating bags; 2 tip couplers; 5 liquid color packets (.067 fl. oz. each: Yellow, Red, Green, Orange, Blue); instruction booklet.
2104-T-2530 Set/18 $6.99

Decorating Tips

All tips work with standard bags and couplers, unless otherwise indicated. Nickel-plated brass. Dishwasher safe.

ROUND TIPS
Outline, lettering, dots, balls, beads, stringwork, lattice, lacework.

 #1
402-T-1 $0.89

 #1L
402-T-901** $1.69

 #1s
402-T-1009 $1.39

 #2
402-T-2 $0.89

 #3
402-T-3 $0.89

 #4
402-T-4 $0.89

 #5
402-T-5 $0.89

 #6
402-T-6 $0.89

 #7
402-T-7 $0.89

 #8
402-T-8 $0.89

 #9
402-T-9 $0.89

 #10
402-T-10 $0.89

 #11
402-T-11 $0.89

 #12
402-T-12 $0.89

  #2A
Smaller version of 1A.
402-T-2001* $1.49

 #1A
Bold borders, figure piping.
402-T-1001* $1.69

 #230
Fill eclairs and bismarcks.
402-T-230** $1.99

#55
402-T-55 $0.89

#57
402-T-57 $0.89

#301
For flat lettering.
402-T-301 $0.89

DROP FLOWER TIPS
Small (106-225); medium (131-194); large (2C-1G, great for cookie dough).

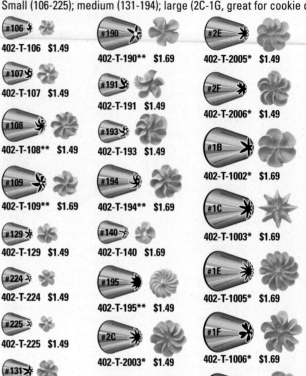

#106
402-T-106 $1.49

#107
402-T-107 $1.49

#108
402-T-108** $1.49

#109
402-T-109** $1.69

#129
402-T-129 $1.49

#224
402-T-224 $1.49

#225
402-T-225 $1.49

#131
402-T-131 $1.49

#190
402-T-190** $1.69

#191
402-T-191 $1.49

#193
402-T-193 $1.49

#194
402-T-194** $1.69

#140
402-T-140 $1.69

#195
402-T-195** $1.49

#2C
402-T-2003* $1.49

#2D
402-T-2004* $1.49

#2E
402-T-2005* $1.49

#2F
402-T-2006* $1.49

#1B
402-T-1002* $1.69

#1C
402-T-1003* $1.69

#1E
402-T-1005* $1.69

#1F
402-T-1006* $1.69

#1G
402-T-1007* $1.69

PETAL TIPS
Realistic flower petals, dramatic ruffles, drapes, swags and bows.

   #59s/59
402-T-594 $0.89

 #59
402-T-59 $0.89

 #60
402-T-60 $0.89

 #61
402-T-61 $0.89

 #62
402-T-62 $0.89

 #64
402-T-64 $0.89

 #97
402-T-97 $0.89

 #101s
402-T-1019 $1.39

 #101
402-T-101 $0.89

 #102
402-T-102 $0.89

 #103
402-T-103 $0.89

 #104
402-T-104 $0.89

 #150
402-T-150 $1.49

 #116
402-T-116* $1.49

 #121
402-T-121* $1.49

  #123
402-T-123* $1.49

  #124
402-T-124* $1.49

 #125
402-T-125* $1.49

 #126
402-T-126* $1.49

 #127
402-T-127* $1.49

  #127D
Giant Rose
402-T-1274 $1.69

BASKETWEAVE TIPS
Tips 44, 45 make only smooth stripes; rest of basketweave tips and Cake Icer make both smooth and ribbed stripes.

 #44
402-T-44 $0.89

 #45
402-T-45 $0.89

   **#46**
402-T-46 $0.89

 #47
402-T-47 $0.89

#48
402-T-48 $0.89

#1D
402-T-1004** $1.69

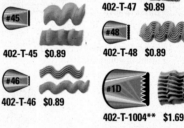 **#2B**
402-T-2002* $1.49

 **#789**
Cake Icer**
409-T-789 $2.99

MULTI-OPENING TIPS
Rows and clusters of strings, beads, stars, (Use 233 for grass).

 #42
402-T-42 $0.89

 #89
402-T-89 $0.89

 #134
402-T-134** $1.69

 #233
402-T-233 $1.49

#234
402-T-234 $1.69

 #235
402-T-235* $1.49

  Triple Star
Triple Star*
402-T-2010 $2.59

---

*Fits large coupler.   **Tip does not work with coupler. Use with parchment or uncut bags only. Cake Icer Tip should be used with bags 14 in. or larger.

ORDER TOLL FREE: 800-794-5866

OPEN STAR TIPS

Star techniques, drop flowers; the finely cut teeth of 199 through 364 create decorations with many ridges; use 6B and 8B with pastry dough too.

 #13
402-T-13 $0.89

 #14
402-T-14 $0.89

 #15
402-T-15 $0.89

 #16
402-T-16 $0.89

 #17
402-T-17 $0.89

 #18
402-T-18 $0.89

 #19
402-T-19 $0.89

 #20
402-T-20 $0.89

 #21
402-T-21 $0.89

 #22
402-T-22 $0.89

#32
402-T-32 $0.89

 #199
402-T-199 $1.49

 #362
402-T-362 $1.49

 **#363**
402-T-363 $1.49

 #364
402-T-364 $1.49

#172
402-T-172** $1.49

 **#1M (2110)**
402-T-2110* $1.49

#4B
402-T-4400** $1.49

#6B
402-T-6600** $1.49

#8B
402-T-8800** $1.69

SPECIALTY TIPS

Shells, ropes, hearts, Christmas trees, ring candle holders!

#98
402-T-98 $0.89

#347
402-T-347 $1.49

#136
402-T-136 $1.69

#77
402-T-77 $0.89

#78
402-T-78 $0.89

#83
402-T-83 $0.89

#96
402-T-96 $0.89

#79
402-T-79 $0.89

#105
402-T-105 $0.89

#80
402-T-80 $0.89

#81
402-T-81 $0.89

#250
402-T-250* $1.69

#252
402-T-252* $1.69

#95
402-T-95 $0.89

CLOSED STAR TIPS

Create deeply grooved shells, stars and fleurs de lis.

#24
402-T-24 $0.89

#26
402-T-26 $0.89

#27
402-T-27 $0.89

#28
402-T-28 $0.89

#29
402-T-29 $0.89

#30
402-T-30 $0.89

#31
402-T-31 $0.89

#33
402-T-33 $0.89

#35
402-T-35 $0.89

#133
402-T-133 $0.89

#54
402-T-54 $0.89

LEFT-HANDED TIP SETS

Now left-handers can achieve the same beautiful flowers as right-handed decorators! Nickel-plated brass tips fit standard bags and couplers.

 LEFT-HAND

 **#106L**

 **#107L**

#59°L

#97L

#116L

Drop Flower Set
Includes Left tips 106 and 107 for making small swirled flowers.
418-T-613† Set/2 $2.99

Petal Set
Includes Left tip 59° for violets, Left tip 97 for Victorian roses and Left tip 116** for large Wilton roses.
418-T-612† Set/3 $2.99

LEAF TIPS

So realistic! Ideal for shell-motion borders too.

 #65s
402-T-659 $1.39

#66
402-T-66 $0.89

 #68
402-T-68 $0.89

 #73
402-T-73 $0.89

 #75
402-T-75 $0.89

 #352
402-T-352 $1.39

 #70
402-T-70 $0.89

#65
402-T-65 $0.89

#67
402-T-67 $0.89

 #69
402-T-69 $0.89

 #74
402-T-74 $0.89

 #349/352s
402-T-349 $1.39

 #326
402-T-326 $1.39

#112
402-T-112** $1.49

 #113
402-T-113* $1.49

 **#115**
402-T-115* $1.49

 #366
Makes leaves for larger flowers.
402-T-366* $1.69

RUFFLE TIPS

Plain, fluted, shell-border, special effects.

 #86
402-T-86 $0.89

 #87
402-T-87† $0.89

 #88
402-T-88† $0.89

 #100
402-T-100 $0.89

 #353
402-T-353 $1.39

 #340
402-T-340 $1.39

#401
402-T-401 $1.39

#402
402-T-402* $1.49

#406
402-T-406* $1.69

#403
402-T-403** $1.69

†For left-handers.   *Fits large coupler.

Dessert decorator Pro™

It's easy to add beautiful decorations to any dessert or appetizer in minutes! Designed for comfortable one-hand decorating and effortless tip positioning, this is the most convenient dessert tool you'll ever use. Create beautiful decorations—shells, stars, rosettes, leaves. The great recipe book included is filled with fabulous ideas to tempt your family and friends. Decorate desserts with elegant whipped cream or icing designs. Dress up pastry shells with dramatic swirls of mousse. With Dessert Decorator Pro, you can do it all!
415-T-850 $29.99

Rotating Cylinder
Just turn to place the tip in the correct position for any decoration.

Ergonomic Design
Easy, comfortable grip for right or left hand. Outer sleeve fits your fingers like a glove.

Stainless Steel Cylinder
Preferred by pastry chefs because stainless won't transfer flavors and it maintains temperature of fillings.

Fits Virtually Any Tip/Coupler
Use with the tips included or with most other Wilton tips.

Pull-Out Plunger
Inner ring pushes filling smoothly through cylinder.

Convenient Thumb Lever
The ideal distance from cylinder for comfortable one-handed decorating.

Durable Construction
Cylinder and plunger are housed in an impact-resistant sleeve for years of great decorating performance.

Easy To Fill and Clean
Most parts detach with ease; wash in warm, soapy water.

Dessert Decorator Pro includes all this:

Two Tip Couplers
Two sizes to hold standard (small) and large tips.

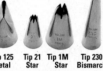

Tip 366 Leaf | Tip 4B Star | Tip 125 Petal | Tip 21 Star | Tip 1M Star | Tip 230 Bismarck

Six Durable Nickel-Plated Tips
Quality metal tips produce perfectly-shaped decorations every time.

Tips in bag for size reference only. Tips included are shown at left.

Tip/Coupler Dishwasher and Storage Bag
Just place nylon mesh bag with tips and couplers in your dishwasher silverware rack for easy tip and coupler cleaning.

Recipes and Instructions
Includes delicious recipes and easy decorating instructions for elegant desserts and appetizers.

Basic Dessert Decorator
Give your cakes and pastries a beautiful finishing touch in seconds. The easy-to-control lever helps you fill and decorate all kinds of desserts. The 4 decorating nozzles included let you pipe stars, rosettes, shells and many other accents. Works great with Wilton Icing Mixes (p. 137).
415-T-825 $10.99

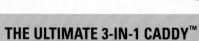

Cake Caddy™
Carry decorated desserts with ease! The 6 in. high see-through plastic dome has 3 locking latches that hold the base securely in place wherever you go. Convenient handle gives you a firm grip for a safe trip from home to car to party. The elegant base is approximately 13 in. diameter and holds and stores up to 10 in. round cake or pie, cupcakes, cookies and more.
2105-T-9952 $14.99

THE ULTIMATE 3-IN-1 CADDY™
The world's most versatile and safest cake carrier.

- Reversible, removable tray holds 12 standard cupcakes/ muffins or 24 minis
- Roomy base holds a 9 x 13 in. decorated cake when used without tray
- Textured base resists scratches when cutting cakes
- 4 locking latches keep baked goods secure
- Extra-thick walls provide the ultimate protection
- Wide, comfortable handle is easy to grab and go
- Sleek see-through design presents desserts at their best

It's the most convenient way to take along cakes, cupcakes, muffins and more! The Ultimate 3-In-1 Caddy features an exclusive reversible cupcake tray which holds 12 standard or 24 mini cupcakes. Or, remove the tray to carry up to a 9 x 13 in. decorated cake on the sturdy locking base. The see-through cover has higher sides to protect icing flowers and tall decorations. You can also use the caddy at home, to keep pies, cookies and brownies fresh for days after baking. 18 x 14⅛ x 5½ in. high.
2105-T-9958 $19.99

ROMANTIC CASTLE CAKE SET

NEW!

FEATURED ON COVER AND IN SPECIAL SECTION!

Create a fairy tale for your special celebrations, with an enchanting castle cake every guest will love. Everything you need to transform your tiered cake into a fantasy castle is included: 3 sizes of detailed turret towers with removable peak pieces, 6 lattice windows, a paneled door and main roof peak.

To assemble: Bake the cake and frost. Position the turrets, door, windows and roof. Add additional decorating detail as you want! Complete assembly and decorating ideas included for medieval, candy and princess castle designs. See additional exciting castle ideas in our Castle Parties special section (p. 88) and many more designs on-line at www.wilton.com!
301-T-910 Set/32 $19.99

NEW!

Silly Feet! Cake Stand

Everyone will get a kick out of your cake when it's served on this fun, footed stand. Just insert the plate onto the foot support, add your decorated cake, cupcakes or other desserts. Then, watch your friends make tracks to your treats! Take the fun a step further—bake and serve cupcakes in Silly-Feet! Silicone Baking Cups (p. 147). 10 in. cake plate holds an 8 in. or 9 in. round cake.
307-T-878 $14.99

Ceramic Pedestal Cake Stand

Present your cake with elegance on this classic ceramic stand. Its white pillar design features a gracefully sculpted base and a smooth attached 12 in. plate. Also use it to serve pies, brownies, cookies, candies and other special desserts. Holds cakes up to 10 in. diameter; stand is 4 in. high.
307-T-873 $29.99

Cupcake Fun!

*What makes Wilton cupcakes more fun? It's our exciting products, which make baking, decorating and serving one-of-a-kind cupcakes a pleasure! See **www.cupcakefun.com**, for more great products and ideas!*

Cupcake Fun! **NEW!**

Wilton presents today's hottest party dessert like you've never seen it before. This all-new collection features over 150 exciting cupcake and treat ideas for all occasions, with complete baking and decorating instructions to make them easy. Discover captivating new shapes from coffee cups to flying saucers, plus a great recipe section with delicious surprises like Key Lime Cupcakes, Mocha Icing and more. Great baking and decorating products, too, like our Silly-Feet! footed silicone cups! Cupcake Fun! is the book you need to create the ultimate cupcake celebration. Look for many more great cupcake ideas and recipes at www.cupcakefun.com. Soft cover, 128 pages.
902-T-795 **$12.99**

6-Cup King-Size Muffin Pan **NEW!**

Create extra-tall treats! Great for cupcakes, ice cream, molded gelatin, mini angel food cakes, and mousse. Heavy-gauge premium non-stick for quick release and easy clean-up.
2105-T-9921 **$7.99**

Jumbo Muffin Pan

Make super-size cupcakes and muffins. Six cups, each 4 x 2 in.
2105-T-955 **$5.49**

NEW!

Cupcake Pedestals

Give your cupcakes a lift and show off your desserts with these fun plastic display pedestals! Perfectly display cupcakes, muffins, party favors and more—or turn the pedestal over for the perfect ice cream cone holder! 5⅛ in. high.
307-T-839 Pk./4 **$6.99**

The Ultimate 3-In-1 Caddy™

It's the most convenient way to take along cakes, cupcakes, muffins and more! The Ultimate 3-In-1 Caddy features an exclusive reversible cupcake tray which holds 12 standard or 24 mini cupcakes. Or, remove the tray to carry up to a 9 x 13 in. decorated cake on the sturdy locking base. The see-through cover has higher sides to protect icing flowers and tall decorations. You can also use the caddy at home, to keep pies, cookies and brownies fresh for days after baking. 18 x 14 x 6¾ in. high.
2105-T-9958 **$19.99**

CUPCAKES 'N MORE® DESSERT STANDS

Individually decorated cupcakes are the perfect way to add a personal touch to celebrations. Now, with Cupcakes 'N More, you have the perfect way to serve them! The look is fresh and fun, featuring bold silver-finished wire spirals to securely hold each cupcake. The twisting, towering design is perfect for any setting—showers, kids' birthdays, weddings, holidays and more.

NEW!

13 Count Standard
9¼ in. high x 9 in. wide.
Holds 13 standard cupcakes.
307-T-831 **$12.99**

NEW!

NEW!

24 Count Mini
10½ in. high x 9 in. wide.
Holds 24 mini cupcakes.
307-T-250 **$14.99**

23 Count Standard
12 in. high x 13 wide.
Holds 23 standard cupcakes.
307-T-826 **$29.99**

19 Count Standard
18 in. high x 12 in. wide.
Holds 19 standard cupcakes.
307-T-666 **$19.99**

38 Count Standard
15 in. high x 18 wide.
Holds 38 standard cupcakes.
307-T-651 **$39.99**

ORDER TOLL FREE: 800-794-5866

JUMBO SPRINKLES

Give your cupcakes a big finish! Top them with our new Jumbo Sprinkles in exciting shapes and colors. These big and bold decorations are perfect for cupcakes, mini cakes, jumbo and king-size cupcakes, brownies and cookies. Innovative shapes for birthday, holiday or any celebration. Certified Kosher. **$3.99**

Jumbo Stars
3.25 oz. **710-T-026**

Jumbo Confetti
3.25 oz. **710-T-029**

Jumbo Diamonds
3.5 oz. **710-T-027**

Jumbo Daisies
3.25 oz. **710-T-028**

Jumbo Hearts
3.25 oz. **710-T-032**

Jumbo Rainbow Nonpareils
2.5 oz. **710-T-033**

Heart Drops
2.5 oz. **710-T-035**

Sour Cherry Balls
4.4 oz. **710-T-034**

12-Piece Cupcake Decorating Set

Wait until you see how much fun cupcakes can be using the decorating tips in this set! You¹ll create all kinds of fun designs perfect for celebrations or everyday treats! Includes star tip 1M (rosettes, stars, drop flowers), star tip 22 (zigzags, pull-out stars), round tip 12 (outlines, dots, messages) and Bismarck tip 230 for exciting filled cupcakes; 8 disposable bags, instruction booklet.
2104-T-6667 Set/12 $7.99

SILICONE BAKING CUPS

Discover the convenience and easy release of flexible silicone! Reusable oven-safe cups in fun colors and exciting shapes are perfect for baking and serving. All have convenient batter fill line.

Silly-Feet!
Orange, Yellow, Blue, Purple. Cups are 2 in. diameter. 2⁵⁄₁₆ in. high with feet.
415-T-9428 Pk./4 $9.99

Heart
6 Pink, 6 Red. 2 in. wide.
415-T-9409 Pk./12 $9.99

Diamond
6 Yellow, 6 Red. 3 in. wide.
415-T-9419 Pk./12 $9.99

Triangle
6 Pink, 6 Purple. 2⅜ in. wide.
415-T-9423 Pk./12 $9.99

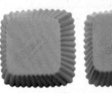
Square
6 Blue, 6 Green. 2 in. wide.
415-T-9424 Pk./12 $9.99

Add-A-Message Fun Pix®

Serve party cupcakes in an exciting new way—clip on messages, pictures and more with these colorful plastic picks! Great for place markers, announcing awards at banquets and favorite sayings. Four fun colors to go with your favorite baking cups. 3 in. high.
2113-T-7611 Pk./12 $1.99

CUPCAKE BOXES

Brightly-patterned window boxes are the perfect way to hold and display your cupcakes! Each box includes an insert with recessed space to hold standard cupcakes safely in place. Easy folding assembly; great for gifts and favors! Choose single, 4-cupcake size or 6-cupcake size.

Cupcake Heaven

Holds 1 standard cupcake.
415-T-289
Pk./3 $2.99

Holds 6 standard cupcakes.
415-T-1207
Pk./2 $4.99

Holds 4 standard cupcakes.
415-T-1206
Pk./3 $4.99

Snappy Stripes

Holds 1 standard cupcake.
415-T-1205
Pk./3 $2.99

Holds 6 standard cupcakes.
415-T-1209
Pk./2 $4.99

Holds 4 standard cupcakes.
415-T-948
Pk./3 $4.99

Baking Cups

Microwave-safe paper. Standard size, 2 in. diam., Mini size, 1¼ in. diam.

Cupcake Heaven $1.99
Standard
415-T-422 Pk./75
Mini
415-T-426
Pk./100

Snappy Stripes $1.99
Standard
415-T-5381 Pk./75
Mini
415-T-5380
Pk./100

White $1.99
King-Size
415-T-2118
Pk./24
Jumbo
415-T-427
Pk/75

Bakeware

Wilton is the #1 bakeware brand in America. From fun novelty shapes for birthday cakes to dramatic cast aluminum styles for elegant desserts, count on Wilton for the best results.

EASY-Flex
SILICONE BAKEWARE

Flexible pans and tools for great baking performance

NEW! Silicone Bakeware

Discover the convenience and easy release of flexible silicone bakeware!

- Exceptional baking performance for your favorite recipes
- Freezer, refrigerator, oven, microwave and dishwasher safe*
- Resists stains and odors
- Oven safe to 500°F
- Easy and convenient storage
- Limited lifetime warranty

Fluted Tube Pan
2105-T-4806 $12.99

9 in. Round Pan
2105-T-4800 $9.99

8 in. Square Pan
2105-T-4801 $9.99

9 x 5 in. Loaf Pan
2105-T-4804 $9.99

6 Cup Muffin Pan
2105-T-4802 $9.99

12 Cup Mini Muffin Pan
2105-T-4829 $9.99

Baking Mat

Line cookie sheets—protects against burned bottoms and cleans up with ease! Or, use as a pastry mat to roll out dough without sticking.
10 x 15 in. **2105-T-4808 $9.99**
11 x 17 in. **2105-T-4809 $12.99**

Standard Baking Cups

2 in. diameter. Convenient fill line.
415-T-9400 Pk./12 $9.99

Silicone Oven Mitt

Silicone provides better protection from oven heat! Flexible design with interior and exterior textured grip for better control.
570-T-1127 $9.99

Trivet

An excellent hot pad for tables or buffets; also great as a jar opener.
570-T-1111 $4.99

NEW! Non-Stick Liners

Never Scrub Ovens or Baking Pans Again!

- **EASY TO CLEAN**
  Spills or burned-on foods wipe away with a soft, damp cloth.

- **CUT TO FIT**
  Use as is or trim with scissors to custom fit ovens, microwaves and baking pans.

- **OVEN-SAFE UP TO 500°F**
  Withstands high baking temperatures while maintaining non-stick performance.

Keeps oven clean!

Releases food with ease!

16 x 10 in. Baking Pan Liner with Non-Slip Grip (fits 11 x 17 in. pans)
2102-T-1026 $12.99

23 x 16¼ in. Oven Liner
2102-T-1021 $14.99

16 x 16 in. Microwave Liner
2102-T-1025 $14.99

*Always place silicone bakeware on a cookie sheet for easy removal from oven.

ORDER TOLL FREE: 800-794-5866

Silicone Molds

Make treats in favorite party shapes using these colorful, easy-release molds!
Great for baking mini cakes and brownies, molding ice cream, gelatin and more.

Silicone Mini Star Mold
One cake mix makes 20 to 24 mini stars. Six-cavity pan is 10⅝ x 7 in.; individual cavities are 2½ x 2½ x 1¼ in. deep.
2105-T-4819 $9.99

Silicone Mini Rounds Mold
One cake mix makes 20 to 24 mini rounds. Six-cavity pan is 10⅝ x 7 in.; individual cavities are 2½ in. diameter x 1⅝ in. deep.
2105-T-4832 $9.99

Silicone Mini Heart Mold
One cake mix makes 20 to 24 mini hearts. Six-cavity pan is 10⅝ x 7 in.; individual cavities are 2½ x 2½ x 1¼ in. deep.
2105-T-4824 $9.99

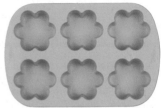

Silicone Mini Flower Mold
One cake mix makes 20 to 24 mini flowers. Six-cavity pan is 10⅝ x 7 in.; individual cavities are 2½ x 2½ x 1¼ in. deep.
2105-T-4825 $9.99

Filled Cake Pan Sets

Serve delicious filling in every slice! Create filled cakes and entrees with incredible flavor combinations using these convenient non-stick pans. The patented recessed design creates a contour you can fill with ice cream, fruit, mousse and more—just bake, fill, flip and frost! The premium non-stick coating provides easy release so cakes unmold perfectly from the pan. Also great for pasta and potato entrees, molded salads and appetizers.

NEW!

Fanci-Fill™ Cake Pan Set
Set includes two 8¾ x 2 in. non-stick pans, bonus recipe booklet with 12 delicious ideas and complete instructions. Non-stick steel.
2105-T-150
Set/2 $14.99

Mini Tasty-Fill™ Cake Pan Set
Set includes four 4 x 1¼ in. non-stick pans, bonus recipe booklet with 12 delicious ideas and complete instructions. Non-stick steel.
2105-T-155
Set/4 $9.99

Mini Shaped Pans

Mini Tiered Cakes
One cake mix makes 10-15 mini tiered cakes, perfect for individual wedding, shower and birthday desserts. Six cavity pan is 14 x 10¾ in.; individual cavities are 4 x 4¾ x 1¼ in. deep. Aluminum.
2105-T-3209 $12.99

Mini Fluted Mold Pan
One cake mix makes 12-14 mini fluted molds. Six cavity pan is 14¾ x 9¾ in.; individual cavities are 4 x 1¼ in. deep. Aluminum.
2105-T-2097 $18.99

Mini Star Pan
One cake mix makes 12-14 mini stars. Six cavity pan is 14½ x 11 in.; individual cavities are 4¾ x 1¼ in. deep. Aluminum.
2105-T-1235 $12.99

Dimensions ®
DECORATIVE BAKEWARE

Heavyweight cast aluminum conducts heat extremely evenly and allows for uniquely sculpted shapes you will be proud to serve. Bake in non-stick cast aluminum as you would in any aluminum pan. Cakes and breads rise high and bake evenly. The premium non-stick surface means foods release perfectly and cleanup is a breeze. Lifetime Warranty.

NEW!

Large Cupcake
Creates a big 3-D cupcake for the whole party to share! Assemble top and bottom cake halves with a thin layer of icing. 15½ in. x 8¼ in. x 3¾ in.; 10 cup capacity.*
2105-T-5038 $27.99

Antoinette
9 in. diameter x 4 in.;
11 cup capacity.*
2105-T-1189 $27.99

Snowflake
12 in. diameter x 10⁹⁄₁₆ in.x 2¾ in.;
11 cup capacity.*
2105-T-5030 $27.99

4 Cavity Mini Snowflakes
Each cavity 5 in. x 2¼ in. deep;
7 cup capacity.*
2105-T-5028 $27.99

Gift
11⅛ in. x 9⅝ in. x 1½ in.;
11 cup capacity.*
2105-T-5027 $27.99

Perennial
9⅝ in. diameter x 3⅛ in.;
9½ cup capacity.*
2105-T-5031 $27.99

Tulip
9½ in. diameter x 4 in.;
11 cup capacity.*
2105-T-5032 $27.99

Crown of Hearts
11 in. wide x 2½ in.;
11 cup capacity.*
2105-T-5011 $27.99

6 Cavity Mini Hearts
Each cavity 4 in. x 2 in.;
7 cup capacity.*
2105-T-5012 $27.99

Queen of Hearts
9 in. diameter x 3¼ in.;
11 cup capacity.*
2105-T-5001 $27.99

Cascade
9½ in. diameter x 4¾ in.;
11 cup capacity.*
2105-T-1199 $27.99

Belle
9 in. diameter x 3¾ in.;
11 cup capacity.*
2105-T-1186 $27.99

Marquise
8¾ in. diameter x 4 in.;
11 cup capacity.*
2105-T-1188 $27.99

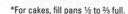
*For cakes, fill pans ½ to ⅔ full.

ORDER TOLL FREE: 800-794-5866

CHECKERBOARD CAKE SET

With this unique baking set, you'll create cakes with an exciting multi-colored pattern—there's style in every slice! Baking is easy with the Batter Dividing Ring included. Just place the Dividing Ring in one of the three 9 x 1½ in. pans in the set and follow instructions for adding dark and light colors of batter in the divisions. Repeat for 2 more layers, pouring the dark and light batters in opposite sections for the middle layer. Use the Dividing Ring's easy-lift handles to lift out ring before baking, then stack cakes to form the checkerboard. Enjoy two tastes in one cake—try the Golden Yellow/Chocolate recipe on the package. Great for colorful holiday cakes, too! Three pans feature oversized handles for safe lifting from the oven; each takes 5½ cups batter. Non-stick steel pans; plastic Dividing Ring.
2105-T-9961 Set/4 $12.99

Non-Stick Bakeware

Our premium non-stick bakeware combines superior non-stick performance, serving convenience and elegant design, to provide the highest level of baking satisfaction.

- Oversized handles for safe lifting of the pan
- Pan dimensions permanently stamped into handles
- Heavy-duty steel construction prevents warping
- Durable, reinforced non-stick coating offers superior release and easy cleanup
- 10-Year Warranty

Cake and Pie Pans

9 x 1½ in. Round Cake
2105-T-408 $7.99

9 x 9 x 2 in. Square Cake
2105-T-407 $8.99

11 x 7 x 1½ in. Biscuit/Brownie
2105-T-443 $9.99

13 x 9 x 2 in. Oblong Cake
2105-T-411 $11.99

13 x 9 x 2 in. Oblong Cake w/Plastic Cover
2105-T-423 $15.99

9 x 1½ in. Pie w/Fluted Edges
2105-T-438 $7.99

2105-T-408

2105-T-411

Cookie Pans and Sheets

Small Cookie
13¼ x 9¼ x ⅝ in.
2105-T-436 $10.99

Medium Cookie
15¼ x 10¼ x ¾ in.
2105-T-412 $11.99

Large Cookie/Jelly Roll
17¼ x 11½ x 1 in.
2105-T-413 $13.99

Jumbo Air Insulated Sheet
18 x 14 in.
2105-T-422 $19.99

2105-T-412

2105-T-422

Specialty Pans

Fluted Tube
9¾ x 3⅜ in.
2105-T-416 $13.99

6 Cavity Mini Fluted Tube
4⅛ x 2 in.
2105-T-445 $16.99

Angel Food
9⅜ x 4¼ in.
2105-T-415 $15.99

14 in. Pizza Crisper
14 x ⅝ in.
2105-T-420 $13.99

2105-T-445

2105-T-420

Muffin and Loaf Pans

6 Cup Regular Muffin
2105-T-405 $9.99

12 Cup Mini Muffin
2105-T-403 $6.99

12 Cup Regular Muffin
2105-T-406 $13.99

Large Loaf
9¼ x 5¼ x 2¾ in.
2105-T-402 $7.99

4 Cavity Mini Loaf
5¾ x 3 x 2⅛ in.
2105-T-444 $16.99

2105-T-405

2105-T-402

Springform Pans

4 x 1¾ in. Round
2105-T-453 $5.49

6 x 2¾ in. Round
2105-T-447 $9.99

9 x 2¾ in. Round
2105-T-414 $13.99

10 x 2¾ in. Round
2105-T-435 $14.99

4 x 1¾ in. Heart
2105-T-457 $7.99

9 x 2¾ in. Heart
2105-T-419 $16.99

2105-T-435

2105-T-419

Cooling Grids

10 x 16 in. Rectangle
2305-T-228 $8.99

14½ x 20 in. Rectangle
2305-T-229 $12.99

13 in. Round
2305-T-230 $9.49

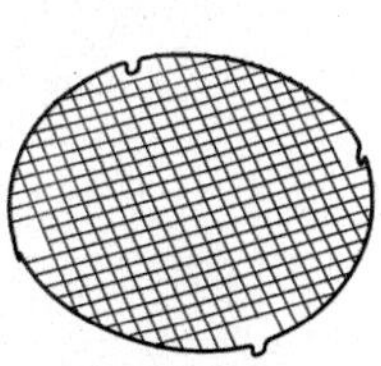

3-Tier Stackable
15⅞ x 9⅞ in.
2105-T-459 $10.99

2305-T-228

2305-T-230

2105-T-459

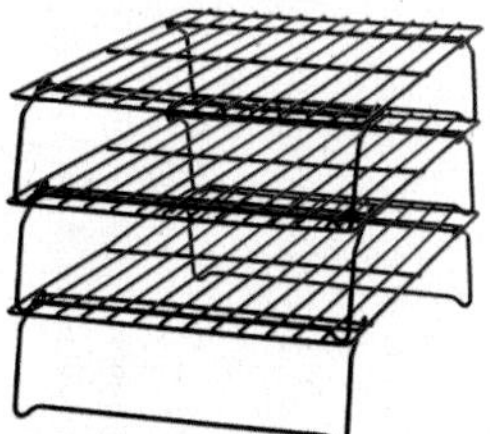

Tart/Quiche Pans

9 x 1⅛ in. Round
2105-T-442 $9.99

11 x 1⅛ in. Round
2105-T-450 $10.99

10 x 1⅛ in. Heart
2105-T-452 $9.99

Round 3-Pc. Set
8 x 1⅛ in., 9 x 1⅛ in., and 10 x 1⅛ in.
2105-T-451 Set/3 $21.99

Brioche 6-Pc. Set
3¼ x 1¼ in.
2105-T-6762 Set/6 $6.99

Tartlet 6-Pc. Set
4¾ x 1⅞ x ½ in.
2105-T-6761 Set/6 $6.99

4 in. Tart 4-Pc. Set
4 x ¾ in. with removable bottom.
2105-T-466 $9.99

4 in. Tart/Quiche 6-Pc. Set 4 x ¾ in. with removable bottom.
2105-T-441 $14.99

2105-T-450

2105-T-452

2105-T-6762

Decorator Preferred®

Professional Aluminum Bakeware

Built with the most features to help decorators bake their best! Compare these benefits to any brand:

STRAIGHT SIDES

Bake perfect 90° corners for the precise look wedding cakes require. Ordinary bakeware has rounded corners, giving cakes rounded edges.

GRIP LIP EDGES

Extra-wide rims make heavy filled pans easy to handle.

PURE ALUMINUM

The best material for baking cakes—creates a light, golden brown cake surface, beautiful for decorating.

SUPERIOR THICKNESS

Thicker than ordinary bakeware, built to distribute heat evenly for more consistent baking.

HANDCRAFTED CONSTRUCTION

Sheets and squares are handwelded for excellent detail and durability.

LIFETIME WARRANTY

Superior construction and performance designed and guaranteed to last a lifetime.

Rounds

What a selection of sizes—including the hard-to find 18 in. Half Round, which lets you bake and ice two halves to create one 18 in. round cake.

6 x 2 in.
2105-T-6122 $6.99

8 x 2 in.
2105-T-6136 $7.99

9 x 2 in.
2105-T-6137 $8.99

10 x 2 in.
2105-T-6138 $10.99

12 x 2 in.
2105-T-6139 $12.99

14 x 2 in.
2105-T-6140 $17.99

16 x 2 in.
2105-T-6141 $19.99

6 x 3 in.
2105-T-6106 $8.99

8 x 3 in.
2105-T-6105 $9.99

10 x 3 in.
2105-T-6104 $11.99

12 x 3 in.
2105-T-6103 $14.99

14 x 3 in.
2105-T-6102 $17.99

16 x 3 in.
2105-T-6101 $20.99

18 x 3 in.
Half Round
2105-T-6100 $23.99

3-Pc. Round Set

6, 10 and 14 in. diameter x 3 in. deep.
**2105-T-6114
Set/3 $36.99**

Hearts

Ultimate heart cake is beautiful for showers, weddings, more!

6 x 2 in.
2105-T-600 $6.49

8 x 2 in.
2105-T-601 $7.49

10 x 2 in.
2105-T-602 $9.99

12 x 2 in.
2105-T-607 $11.99

14 x 2 in.
2105-T-604 $13.99

16 x 2 in.
2105-T-605 $15.99

4-Pc. Heart Set

Now redesigned for a perfect fit when used with our Decorator Preferred® Heart Separator Plates shown on page 231. Includes 6, 10, 12 and 14 in. pans. Aluminum.
2105-T-606 Set/4 $37.99

Contour

Create cakes with an elegant, rounded top edge. This is the perfect shape for positioning rolled fondant. 9 x 3 in. deep.
2105-T-6121 $12.99

Heating Core

Distributes heat to bake large cakes evenly. Recommended for pans 10 in. diameter or larger. Releases easily from cake. 3½ x 3½ x 4 in. diameter.
417-T-6100 $7.49

Sheets

Extra-thick aluminum distributes heat efficiently on these large pans.

9 x 13 x 2 in.
2105-T-6146 $16.99

11 x 15 x 2 in.
2105-T-6147 $18.99

12 x 18 x 2 in.
2105-T-6148 $22.99

Squares

Perfect 90° corners give you the flawless look necessary for wedding tiers.

8 x 2 in.
2105-T-6142 $10.99

10 x 2 in.
2105-T-6143 $14.99

12 x 2 in.
2105-T-6144 $17.99

Springform Pans

When shopping for a springform pan, you want strong construction and an easy-release design that will let you remove a perfect cheesecake every time. Wilton springform pans are built tough, with strong springlocks that hold up year after year. The removable waffle-textured bottom design keeps crusts from sticking while distributing heat evenly. Springlock releases sides. Aluminum.

6 x 3 in.
2105-T-4437 $11.99

8 x 3 in.
2105-T-8464 $12.99

9 x 3 in.
2105-T-5354 $13.99

10 x 3 in.
2105-T-8465 $13.99

ORDER TOLL FREE: 800-794-5866

Performance Pans™

The classic aluminum pans—durable, even-heating and built to hold their shape through years of use. We named them Performance Pans because they perform beautifully. These are great all-purpose pans. You'll use them for casseroles, entrees, baked desserts and more. Wilton has sold millions of Performance Pans because decorators and bakers know they can depend on them.

SweetHeart Pan

A gently curving shape gives the classic heart a more romantic flair. Whether you accent it with pretty icing flowers or pair it with bold fondant decorations, this cake will charm guests for birthdays, Mother's Day, Valentine's Day, showers and more. Takes 1 standard mix. 10¼ x 11 x 2 in. Aluminum.
2105-T-1197 $11.99

Squares

6 x 2 in.
507-T-2180 $6.99

8 x 2 in.
2105-T-8191 $8.99

10 x 2 in.
2105-T-8205 $10.99

12 x 2 in.
2105-T-8213 $14.99

14 x 2 in.
2105-T-8220 $18.99

16 x 2 in.
2105-T-8231 $20.99

Rounds

6 x 2 in.
2105-T-2185 $6.99

8 x 2 in.
2105-T-2193 $7.99

10 x 2 in.
2105-T-2207 $8.99

12 x 2 in.
2105-T-2215 $11.99

14 x 2 in.
2105-T-3947 $14.99

16 x 2 in.
2105-T-3963 $17.99

2-Pan Round Set

9 x 2 in. deep
2105-T-7908 $12.99

Sheets

9 x 13 x 2 in.
2105-T-1308 $11.99

11 x 15 x 2 in.
2105-T-158 $15.99

12 x 18 x 2 in.
2105-T-182 $17.99

Covered Baking Pan

Clear, durable cover makes it easy to transport desserts and keep them fresh at home. 11 x 15 x 2 in.
2105-T-3849 $20.99

PERFORMANCE PANS™ SETS

These are the classic shapes every baker needs. Wilton has them in convenient graduated-size sets, to help you create fabulous tiered cakes or individual cakes in exactly the size you want. Quality aluminum holds its shape for years. Each pan is 2 in. deep, except where noted.

NEW!

3-Pc. Paisley Pan Set

Create a beautiful tiered cake with graceful curves unlike any other. Ideal for cascading floral arrangements—perfect for weddings, showers and more. Includes 9 x 6 in., 12¾ x 9 in. and 17 x 12 in. pans.
2105-T-4039 Set/3 $42.99

Round Pan Set

Includes 6, 8, 10, 12 in. pans.
2105-T-2101 Set/4 $31.99

Round Pan Set, 3 in. Deep

Includes 8, 10, 12, 14 in. pans.
2105-T-2932 Set/4 $42.99

Oval Pan Set

Includes 7¾ x 5⅝ in.; 10¾ x 7⅞ in.; 13½ x 9⅞ in. and 16½ x 12⅜ in. pans.
2105-T-2130 Set/4 $37.99

 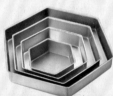

Square Pan Set

Includes 8, 12, 16 in. pans.
2105-T-2132 Set/3 $42.99

Hexagon Pan Set

Includes 6, 9, 12, 15 in. pans.
2105-T-3572 Set/4 $37.99

Petal Pan Set

Includes 6, 9, 12, 15 in. pans.
2105-T-2134 Set/4 $37.99

Specialty Pans

Classic Angel Food

If you're looking for a healthy dessert, you can't do better than angel food! It's delicious with a simple fresh fruit topping. Removable inner core sleeve, cooling legs. Aluminum.

Fancy Ring Mold

Beautiful sculpted pan, ideal for pound cakes, mousse and more! Takes 1 standard mix. 10 in. diameter x 3 in. Aluminum.
2105-T-5008 $11.99

7 x 4½ in. deep
Takes ½ standard mix.
2105-T-9311 $13.99

10 x 4 in. deep
Takes 1 standard mix.
2105-T-2525 $16.99

Ring Mold

Turn out spectacular cakes, gelatin molds and more. Takes approx. 1½ standard cake mixes. 10½ x 3 in. Aluminum.
2105-T-4013 $11.99

Cookie Sheets and Pans

A warped sheet can ruin a batch of cookies. With Wilton Cookie Sheets, you won't worry about warping. The extra-thick aluminum heats evenly for perfectly browned bottoms. Versatile sheets are great for baking appetizers, turnovers and more.

Aluminum
Extra-thick construction heats evenly for perfectly browned bottoms.

Jumbo 14 x 20 in.
2105-T-6213 **$17.99**

12½ x 16½ in.
2105-T-2975
$13.99

Insulated Aluminum
Two quality aluminum layers sandwich an insulating layer of air for perfect browning without burning.
14 x 16 in.
2105-T-2644
$18.99

Jelly Roll and Cookie Pans
Wilton pans are 1 in. deep for fuller-looking desserts.

10½ x 15½ x 1 in.
2105-T-1269 **$12.99**

12 x 18 x 1 in.
2105-T-4854 **$14.99**

Muffin Pans

With so many great Wilton muffin pans to choose from, you'll be making muffins —and cupcakes —more often. You'll love our mini pans for the perfect brunch muffins and the jumbo size pan for bakery-style muffins and cupcakes.

Standard Muffin Pan
Most popular size for morning muffins, after-school cupcakes and desserts. Twelve cups, each 3 in. diameter x 1 in. Aluminum.
2105-T-9310 **$16.99**

White Standard Baking Cups (shown on p. 189)
Microwave-safe paper. 2 in. diameter.
415-T-2505 **Pk./75 $1.49**

Mini Muffin Pans
Great for mini cheesecakes, brunches, large gatherings. Cups are 2 in. x ¾ in. Aluminum.
12 Cup 2105-T-2125 **$11.99**
24 Cup 2105-T-9313 **$17.99**

White Mini Baking Cups (shown on p. 189)
Microwave-safe paper. 1¼ in. diameter.
415-T-2507 **Pk./100 $1.49**

Jumbo Muffin Pan
Make super-size cupcakes and muffins. Six cups, each 4 x 2 in. Aluminum.
2105-T-1820 **$16.99**

White Jumbo Baking Cups (shown on p. 189)
Microwave-safe paper. 2¼ in. diameter.
415-T-2503 **Pk./50 $1.49**

Loaf Pans

It's all in the crust. Wilton Loaf Pans bake bread with hearty, crisp crusts and soft, springy centers. Our superior anodized aluminum promotes better browning, resulting in the perfect texture for all your breads.

Petite Loaf Pan
Great for single-size dessert cakes, frozen bread dough. Nine cavities, each 2½ x 3⅜ x 1½ in. Aluminum.
2105-T-8466 **$10.99**

Mini Loaf Pan
Everyone loves personal-sized nut breads or cakes. Six cavities are 4½ x 2½ x 1½ in. Aluminum.
2105-T-9791 **$10.99**

9 x 5 in. Loaf Pan
Favorite size for homemade breads and cakes. 2¾ in. Aluminum.
2105-T-3688 **$7.49**

Long Loaf Pan
Legs provide support for cooling angel food cakes, breads or classic cakes. 16 x 4 x 4½ in. deep. Aluminum.
2105-T-1588 **$13.99**

Chrome-Plated Cooling Grids

Sturdy design will never rust. Great selection of popular sizes.

13 in. Round
2305-T-130 **$7.99**

10 x 16 in. Rectangle
2305-T-128 **$5.99**

14½ x 20 in. Rectangle
2305-T-129 **$8.99**

3-Tier Stackable
Use singly or stack to save space while cooling three cake layers or batches of cookies at the same time. Individual grids are 13½ x 9¾ x 3 in. high; stacked grids are 9¾ in. high.
2305-T-151 **$12.99**

ORDER TOLL FREE: 800-794-5866

Wonder Mold Pans

Mini Wonder Mold
Use with Mini Doll Picks for a quartet of party treats. Great with the Wilton Classic Wonder Mold (at right) for a color-coordinated bridal party centerpiece. One cake mix makes 4 to 6 cakes. Pan is 10 x 10 x 3 in. deep. Individual cakes are 3½ x 3 in. Aluminum.
2105-T-3020 $11.99

Mini Doll Picks
4¼ in. high with pick.
1511-T-1019 Pk./4 $5.99

Classic Wonder Mold
Creates an elegant 3-D shape for decorating fabulous dress designs. Use with our Teen Doll Pick to make the doll of your dreams. Pan is 8 in. diameter and 5 in. deep; takes 5–6 cups of firm-textured batter. Heat-conducting rod assures even baking. Kit contains pan, rod, stand, 7 in. brunette doll pick and instructions. Aluminum/plastic.
2105-T-565 $17.99

Teen Doll Picks
Her hair and face are prettier than ever to give your Wonder Mold cakes a realism and sophistication unlike anything you've seen. 7¼ in. high with pick.
$2.99
Brunette
2815-T-101
Blond
2815-T-102

Ethnic Doll Pick
Beautiful face for realistic doll cakes. 7¾ in. high with pick.
2815-T-103 $2.99

Novelty Shaped Pans

DECORATING WILTON SHAPED CAKES STEP-BY-STEP

When decorating a cake that's simply covered with stars, here are the easy steps involved.

1. Ice sides and other areas smooth per instructions.
2. Outline details.
3. Pipe in facial features, small details.
4. Cover areas with stars, stripes, zigzags or dots.
5. Add message. Edge top and base with borders. Attach flowers or trims.

 NEW!

Pennant Pan
It's the perfect pennant to have on hand for every flag-waving occasion! Great for team sports, birthday greetings, tailgate parties and homecomings. One-mix pan is 12 ½ x 8 ½ x 2 in. deep. Aluminum.
2105-T-1190 $11.99

NEW!

Sunflower Pan
There's no better way to spread sunshine at the celebration! Ideal for cakes, mousse, gelatin and salad molds. Center can be filled with fruit and whipped topping. One-mix pan is 10 in. round x 2 in. deep. Aluminum.
2105-T-1019 $11.99

NEW!

#1 Pan
Add the #1 cake to all the important first celebrations. Great for kids' birthdays, first anniversary, contest winners, first place teams—or just to let someone know they're #1 with you! One-mix pan is 12 ¾ x 8 ½ x 2 in. deep. Aluminum.
2105-T-1194 $11.99

Novelty Shaped Pans **NEW!**

Teddy Bear Pan
Everybody just loves teddy bears. This cutie will be busy all year 'round with birthdays, school parties and baby showers. No time for hibernating with all these fun events on the agenda. One-mix pan is 13½ 12¼ x 2 in. deep. Aluminum.
2105-T-1193 $11.99

NEW!

Purse Pan
Fun is in the bag with a cake that carries excitement galore for birthday parties, showers and school celebrations. Accessorize the event with custom colors and designs. One-mix pan is 10½ x 8 x 2 in. deep. Aluminum.
2105-T-1192 $11.99

Palm Tree Pan
With this easy-to-decorate shape, you'll have your party dessert made in the shade! Whether you're celebrating a summer birthday, a retirement or a bon voyage, the Palm Tree pan is the perfect spot for colorful cakes, molded gelatin, rice cereal treats and more. One-mix pan is 14¼ x 12 x 2 in. deep. Aluminum.
2105-T-1013 $11.99

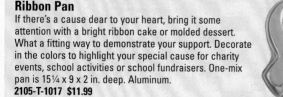

Ribbon Pan
If there's a cause dear to your heart, bring it some attention with a bright ribbon cake or molded dessert. What a fitting way to demonstrate your support. Decorate in the colors to highlight your special cause for charity events, school activities or school fundraisers. One-mix pan is 15¼ x 9 x 2 in. deep. Aluminum.
2105-T-1017 $11.99

NEW!

Stork Express Pan
This smiling stork always brings a bundle of joy to showers and baby welcome celebrations. Perfect as a colorful cake, creamy mousse or glittering gelatin mold. One-mix pan is 13 x 9 ½ x 2 in. deep. Aluminum.
2105-T-1191 $11.99

Baby Buggy Pan
These wheels will bring squeals of delight from shower and christening guests. It's a precious carriage design fit for royalty and ready to dress up for colorful cakes or elegant salads and gelatins. One-mix pan is 11¼ x 11¼ x 2 in. deep. Aluminum.
2105-T-3319 $11.99

Pineapple Pan
You can almost feel the soft, tropical winds blowing and hear island music playing when you bring this festive treat to the table. Great for backyard luaus, barbeques and pool parties. Try it with gelatin salads, pineapple upside-down cake and more. One-mix pan is 14¾ x 8¼ x 2 in. deep. Aluminum.
2105-T-1018 $11.99

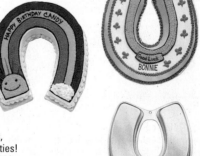

Horseshoe Pan
Say "good luck" at birthdays, graduations, bon voyage parties! One-mix pan is 11½ x 12 x 1¾ in. deep. Aluminum.
2105-T-3254 $11.99

ORDER TOLL FREE: 800-794-5866

Novelty Shaped Pans

Mini Stand-Up Bear Pan Set
Includes baking stand, four clips and instructions. Two-piece pan takes 1 cup of batter; standard pound cake mix makes about 4 cakes. Assembled cakes are 4 x 3¼ x 4¾ in. high. Aluminum.
2105-T-489 Set/8 $12.99

Stand-Up Cuddly Bear Set
Five decorating ideas on the box! Two-piece pan takes 6⅔ cups of firm textured batter. Includes 6 clips, heat-conducting core and instructions. Pan is 9 x 6¾ x 8⅝ in. high. Aluminum.
2105-T-603 Set/10 $23.99

Friendly Lion Pan
He'll be the pride of all your celebrations! Kids will just love this furry, adorable creature for birthdays, school parties and special events. He's sure to please animal-lovers of all ages. One-mix pan is 12¾ x 10¾ x 2 in. deep. Aluminum.
2105-T-1012 $11.99

Animal Crackers Pan
Make a zoo full of fun animals with this versatile pan! Pick your favorite from the menagerie of critters on the box—pig, cat, giraffe or panda bear—or create a furry face of your own. One-mix pan is 10¾ x 9¼ x 2 in. deep. Aluminum.
2105-T-4945 $11.99

Tropical Fish Pan
Everyone at the party will be hooked by this fish! Catch it at kids' celebrations and school events—it's a great cake for that special fisherman's birthday. It's a keeper! One-mix pan is 12½ x 11½ x 2 in. deep. Aluminum.
2105-T-1014 $11.99

3-D Rubber Ducky Pan
This bathtime favorite will make the biggest splash for birthdays, baby showers and school celebrations. Five adorable designs included. Two-piece pan takes 5½ cups batter, 9 x 5 x 7 in. high. Aluminum.
2105-T-2094 $14.99

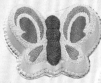

Butterfly Pan
A butterfly cake or molded salad is the perfect way to captivate! Go wild with fun colors. One-mix pan is 11 x 8½ x 2 in. deep. Aluminum.
2105-T-2079 $11.99

Lady Bug Pan
These critters are so cute, you'll want them dropping in at all your celebrations. It's a pan that adapts to any environment—try it as a birthday bee, a Valentine love bug or even a friendly fly for that special gardener in your life. One-mix pan is 12 x 10 x 2 in. deep. Aluminum.
2105-T-3316 $11.99

Novelty Shaped Pans

Topsy Turvy Pan
Our topsy turvy "tiered" cake is just the right look for wacky birthdays, wild parties or special occasions. One-mix pan is 10¼ x 12 x 2 in. deep. Aluminum.
2105-T-4946 $11.99

Cupcake Pan
Here's a "cupcake" cake that's big enough for the whole crowd to eat. Bake and decorate it to look like your favorite party cupcake—only bigger! Create endless color and flavor combinations, including the luscious Chocolate Supreme design on the label. One-mix pan is 9¾ x 9½ x 2 in. deep. Aluminum.
2105-T-3318 $11.99

Ice Cream Cone Pan
You'll find room for this cone at any celebration, from birthdays to backyard barbecues. Like a real ice cream cone, create endless flavor and color combinations. One-mix pan is 13¾ x 9¼ x 2 in. deep. Aluminum.
2105-T-2087 $11.99

Dancing Daisy Flower Pan
One perfect flower makes bunches of great desserts! It's a big, bouncy blossom that's the perfect shape for cakes, molded gelatin and ice cream, brunch breads and more. Pick this daisy for Mother's Day, wedding showers and birthdays for any garden-lover. One-mix pan is 12 x 12 x 2 in. deep. Aluminum.
2105-T-1016 $11.99

Enchanted Castle Pan
Royal treat for little girls' birthdays or any event. Wonderful for molded sugar or ice cream. One-mix pan is 11½ x 11¾ x 2 in. deep. Aluminum.
2105-T-2031 $11.99

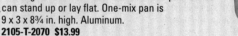

Stand-Up House Pan
A delightful "welcome home". Haunted houses, Easter hutches, Christmas cottages, school houses and dog houses are a few ideas for this pan. Cakes can stand up or lay flat. One-mix pan is 9 x 3 x 8¾ in. high. Aluminum.
2105-T-2070 $13.99

One-Mix Book Pan
This open book details life's important chapters—birthdays, baby showers, graduations and more. Five ways to decorate included. 13 x 9½ x 2 in. deep. Aluminum.
2105-T-972 $11.99

Two-Mix Book Pan
Serves up to 30. 15 x 11½ x 2¾ in. deep. Aluminum.
2105-T-2521 $15.99

Novelty Shaped Pans

Crown Pan

Treat your little princess (or prince) like royalty at their next celebration! This majestic crown cake is a fun way to honor both kids and adults alike—perfect for birthdays, school parties, Mother's and Father's Day, more! One-mix pan is 14¼ x 10½ x 2 in. deep. Aluminum.
2105-T-1015 $11.99

Party Hat Pan

When you put on this party hat, you know you're headed for fun! Customize cakes with your favorite colors and fun designs—ideal for molded desserts and salads too. What a great way to cap off any celebration, from birthdays to that New Year's Eve bash! One-mix pan is 10 x 13½ x 2 in. deep. Aluminum.
2105-T-3317 $11.99

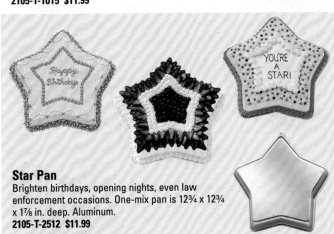

Star Pan

Brighten birthdays, opening nights, even law enforcement occasions. One-mix pan is 12¾ x 12¾ x 1⅞ in. deep. Aluminum.
2105-T-2512 $11.99

Guitar Pan

Whatever your musical choice, a guitar cake sets the tone for fun at your next party! Celebrate school band concerts, kid and adult birthdays! One-mix pan is 16½ x 8½ x 2 in. deep. Aluminum.
2105-T-570 $11.99

Sports Ball Pan Set

Use this four-piece set to create a perfect sports cake centerpiece. Includes two 6 in. diameter half-ball pans and two metal baking stands. Each pan half takes 2½ cups batter. Aluminum.
2105-T-6506 Set/4 $11.99

Soccer Ball Pan

A great way to reward a season or a game well done! One-mix pan is 8¾ x 8¾ x 3½ in. deep. Aluminum.
2105-T-2044 $11.99

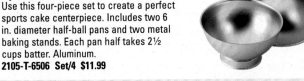

Mini Ball Pan

Ice two mini balls and push together for a 3-D effect. One cake mix makes 10–12 mini balls. Six cavities, each 3½ x 3½ x 1½ in. deep. Aluminum.
2105-T-1760 $11.99

First and Ten Football Pan

Touching down at Super Bowl parties, homecomings, award dinners and much more. One-mix pan is 12 x 7¾ x 3 in. deep. Aluminum.
2105-T-6504 $11.99

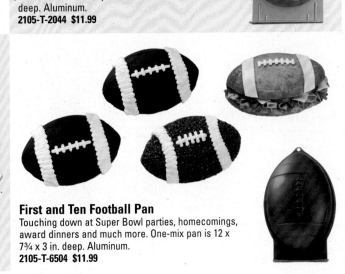

Novelty Shaped Pans

Little Hero Pan
Bring their favorite figures to life! One-mix pan is 13¼ x 6½ x 2 in. deep. Aluminum.
2105-T-2077 $11.99

Little Pirate Pan
Cute pirate-in-training design is easy to transform into just about any character. One-mix pan is 9 in. x 14¼ in. x 2 in. deep. Aluminum.
2105-T-2078 $11.99

Train Pan
Load with delicious cargo! One-mix pan is 14 x 7¼ x 2 in. deep. Aluminum.
2105-T-2076 $11.99

Choo-Choo Train Pan Set
Two-piece pan snaps together to create a cake 10 x 4 x 6 in. high. Takes 6 cups batter. Aluminum.
2105-T-2861 Set/2 $12.99

3-D Cruiser Pan
Bake exciting 3-D cakes, ready to customize for all occasions. One-mix pan is 11 x 6¾ x 4 in. deep. Aluminum.
2105-T-2043 $11.99

Race Car Pan
Customize it with your favorite colors and racing team identification. One-mix pan is 12½ x 9½ x 2 in. deep. Aluminum.
2105-T-1350 $11.99

Tractor Pan
Down on the farm has never been so much fun. One-mix pan is 13½ x 9½ x 2 in. deep. Aluminum.
2105-T-2063 $11.99

Firetruck Pan
When the occasion calls for a five-alarm celebration. One-mix pan is 15½ x 8½ x 2 in. deep. Aluminum.
2105-T-2061 $11.99

Cookie Making

Wilton has just what you need to make cookies fun! Easy-to-use presses, colossal cutter sets, fun stencils, colorful icings and unique toppings sure to create unforgettable cookies!

Cookie Presses

Wilton has the best selection of feature-packed presses anywhere! From our Comfort Grip™ Press, designed for easy handling and filling, to our powerful cordless Cookie Master™ Plus, spritz cookie-making has never been easier!

Deluxe Cookie Press

Making traditional spritz cookies has never been so easy! Cookie Pro™ Ultra II is designed to be the easiest to fill, most comfortable press you've ever used. And, with 12 terrific shapes, plus 4 fun mini cookie designs, your holiday cookie assortments will be more festive than ever! Includes complete instructions and delicious recipes.
2104-T-4018 Set/17 $24.99

- Arrow pointed toward the handle means press is in proper position.
- Soft-grip trigger for comfortable pressing, batch after batch.
- Ergonomic barrel designed for outstanding comfort and control.
- See-through barrel lets you know when to refill with dough.
- Non-slip bottom ring keeps press securely on cookie sheet for evenly shaped cookies.
- Twist-off ring with finger grips makes changing disks a breeze.

- 12 full-sized shaping disks in favorite basic and holiday shapes.
- Plus 4 BONUS mini shaping disks for making fun bite-sized cookies.

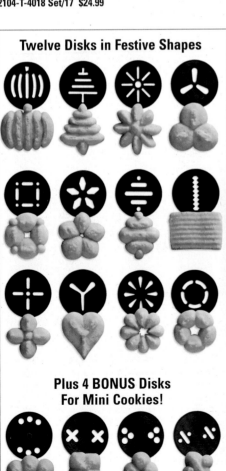

Twelve Disks in Festive Shapes

Plus 4 BONUS Disks For Mini Cookies!

Cookie Presses

COOKIE MASTER™
Plus
Cordless Cookie Press

Distinctive Cookies

Snacks & Appetizers

Desserts & More!

Our cordless cookie press is so powerful and easy to operate, you'll use it all year to create cookies, appetizers, desserts and more. Exclusive patented reverse action means there's no need to take press apart for refilling. Ergonomic design is shaped to fit in your hand for excellent comfort. Includes 12 aluminum disks in classic and seasonal shapes, 4 accent tips for decorating and filling and 2 bonus recipe booklets—sweet and savory. Uses 4 AA batteries, not included.
2104-T-4008 Set/19 $39.99

Cordless, Battery Operated
No cord means no need to be near an outlet.

Patented Reverse Action
No need to take press apart to refill—just press a button to raise the piston.

Ergonomic Design
Shaped to fit your hand for excellent comfort and ease of use. Sealed buttons keep food out.

Unique Dough Guard™
Keeps the dough away from the motor.

See-Through Barrel
Check progress and see how much dough is left.

Fluted Bottom
Raises press off of the cookie sheet for well-formed designs.

Twelve Disk Designs

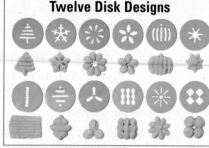

Twelve aluminum disks in classic & seasonal shapes let you create distinctive snacks, appetizers, cookies, desserts and pastries.

Four Accent Tips

Four multi-purpose accent tips make it easy to fill pastries, garnish appetizers and decorate elegant desserts.

COMFORT GRIP™
Cookie Press

Experience a classic press that is truly comfortable. Its ergonomic handle feels great in any hand—the easy-squeeze action releases perfectly shaped dough. The clear barrel takes the guesswork out of refilling. Fluted bottom raises the press off the cookie sheet to help you create better shapes. Includes 12 plastic disks in a variety of shapes plus our classic spritz recipe.
2104-T-4011 Set/13 $12.99

Twelve Disk Designs

Cookie Cutters

PLASTIC CUTTER SETS

101 Cookie Cutters
With this set, you're covered! Make cookies featuring popular holiday and theme shapes like sports, flowers, animals and more. Or use the complete alphabet and numeral collections included to create the perfect cookie message. Great for cutting all kinds of food into fun shapes—perfect for crafting, too. Average cutter size approx. 3½ x 3½ in. Recipe included.
2304-T-1050 Set/101 $14.99

A-B-C and 1-2-3
50-Pc. Cutter Set
Complete alphabet and numeral collection, great for cookies, brownies, gelatin treats, learning games, crafts and more. Average cutter size approx. 3½ x 3½ in. Recipe included.
2304-T-1054 Set/50 $8.99

Animal Pals
50-Pc. Cutter Set
Everyone will go wild for cookies, foods and crafts made with this menagerie of favorite animal shapes. Shapes include fish, dog, cat, birds, butterflies, reptiles and more. Average cutter size approx. 3½ x 3½ in. Recipe included.
2304-T-1055 Set/50 $8.99

FOODWRITER™ EDIBLE COLOR MARKERS

Use like ink markers to add fun and dazzling color to countless foods. Kids love 'em! Decorate on cookies, fondant, color flow and royal icing designs. Brighten everyday foods like toaster pastries, cheese, fruit slices, bread and more. Each set includes five .35 oz. FoodWriter pens. Certified Kosher.

Primary Colors Sets

| Yellow | Green | Red | Blue | Black |

Bold Tip 609-T-115 Set/5 $7.99
Fine Tip 609-T-100 Set/5 $7.99

Neon Colors Set

| Purple | Orange | Pink | Light Green | Black |

Fine Tip 609-T-116 Set/5 $7.99

FINE TIP
BOLD TIP

WHITE COOKIE ICING

Use this quick-setting microwavable icing to cover your cookies with a shiny finish—perfect for decorating with colorful Wilton Icing Writer™ (p. 130) accents! Easy to use—just heat and squeeze onto cookies using the convenient cap. Sets smooth in just 45 minutes. 10 oz. bottle covers approximately 12 (3 in.) cookies. Certified Kosher.
704-T-481 $4.49

Push 'N Print!

NEW!

Push 'N Print Cutter Set

Serve cookies that make a great impression—use Push 'N Print Cutters to emboss a fun message before baking! It's so easy! Load one of the 3 cutter disk designs in the press, cut the cookie, then press the plunger with disk in place to imprint the design. Bake, cool and serve a treat that's perfect for celebrations and cookie gift baskets. Great for embossed fondant decorations, too! Disks are 3 in. diameter. Recipe included.
2308-T-4004 Set/4 $6.99

Plastic Cutters

With our large variety of brightly-colored cutter shapes, the making is as much fun as the eating! Child-safe design means kids can help. Each approx. 3 x 4 in. **Each $0.69**

| **Fish** 2303-T-128 | **Dinosaur** 2303-T-112 | **Teddy Bear** 2303-T-133 | **Butterfly** 2303-T-116 | **Puppy** 2303-T-137 |

| **Star** 2303-T-135 | **Hand** 2303-T-147 | **Foot** 2303-T-113 | **Girl** 2303-T-120 | **Boy** 2303-T-124 | **Dog Bone** 2303-T-123 |

| **Locomotive Engine** 2303-T-139 | **6 Pt. Star** 2303-T-122 | **Heart** 2303-T-100 | **Cat** 2303-T-118 | **Duck** 2303-T-148 |

| **Cross** 2303-T-141 | **Ice Cream Cone** 2303-T-111 | **Sailboat** 2303-T-129 | **Airplane** 2303-T-101 | **Flower** 2303-T-117 | **Four-Leaf Clover** 2303-T-134 |

Plastic Nesting Cutter Sets

Your favorites in child-safe, graduated shapes. Discover all the fun ways to use our cutters—for bread shapes, stencils, sun catchers and so much more.

Teddy Bear
1¾ to 6⅜ in.
2304-T-1520
Set/4 $2.99

Blossom
1⅛ to 4½ in.
2304-T-116
Set/6 $2.99

Heart
1½ to 4⅛ in.
2304-T-115
Set/6 $2.99

Star
1⅝ to 4⅝ in.
2304-T-111
Set/6 $2.99

Cookie Cutters
These versatile designs are sure to spark your creativity!

COMFORT GRIP™ CUTTERS

Easy-grip stainless steel cutters with extra-deep sides are perfect for cutting so many favorite foods into spectacular shapes. Ideal for brownies, biscuits, sandwiches, sheet cakes, cheese, crispy rice treats, fudge and much more. The cushion grip gives you comfortable control even when cutting into thick desserts. Each approximately 4 x 4 x 1¾ in. Recipe included. **Each $2.99**

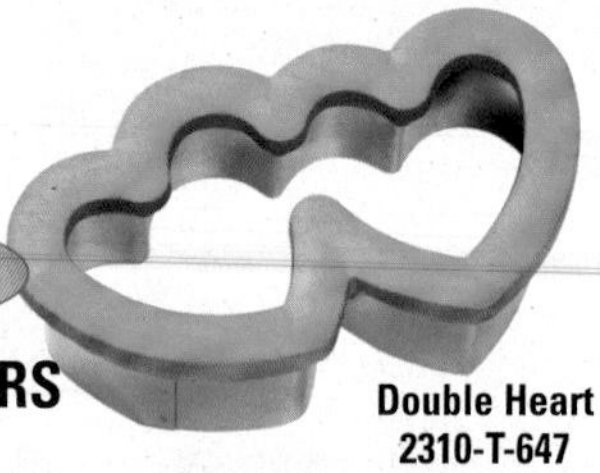

Double Heart
2310-T-647

Round
2310-T-608

Star
2310-T-605

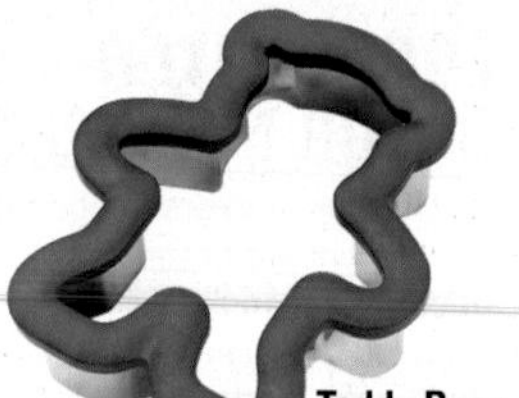

Teddy Bear
2310-T-609

Heart
2310-T-616

Butterfly
2310-T-614

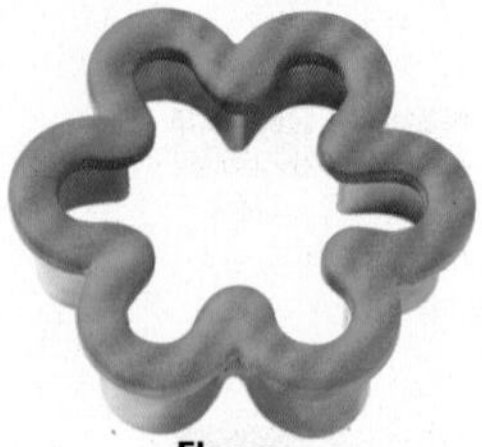

Flower
2310-T-613

Daisy
2310-T-619

METAL CUTTER SETS
Multi-piece sets add variety. Built to last, they cut cleanly and release easily. Recipe included.

Basic
Geometric, crinkle diamond, heart, half moon, star and flower. Each approx. 3 in.
2308-T-1235
Set/6 $4.99

Animals
Horse, dove, lion, duck, pig and cat. Each approx. 3 in.
2308-T-1236
Set/6 $4.99

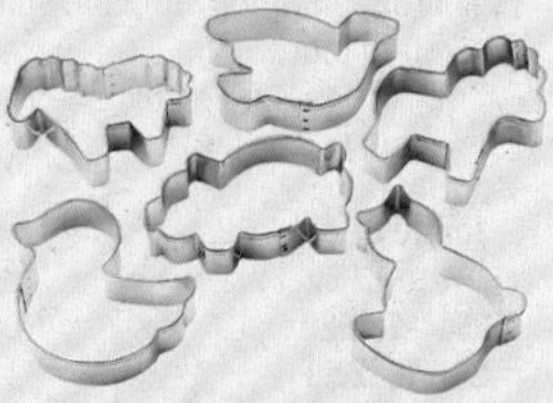

Hearts
Seven different heart cutter designs from stylized to traditional. Sizes range from 1½ to 3 in.
2308-T-1237
Set/7 $4.99

Bug Buddies
Butterfly, caterpillar, bee, ladybug, dragonfly and spider. Each approx. 3 in.
2308-T-1245 Set/6 $4.99

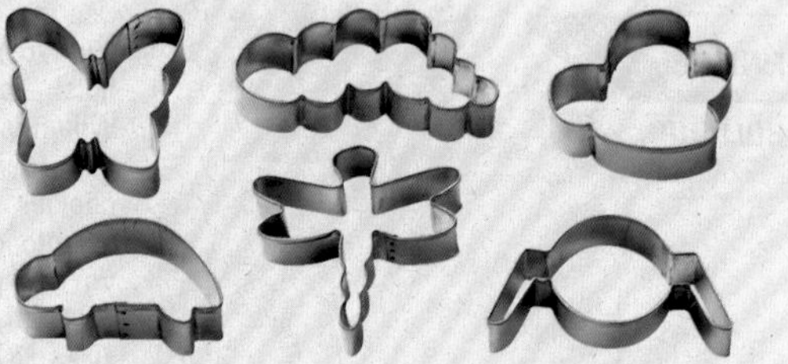

Nesting From The Heart
Two crinkled and two smooth. Largest is approx. 5 in.
2308-T-1203
Set/4 $4.49

Nesting Stars
For holidays and more! Largest is approx. 5 in.
2308-T-1215
Set/4 $4.49

Nesting Blossoms
Pretty flowers in four sizes. Largest is approx. 5 in.
2308-T-1204
Set/4 $4.49

Mini Romantic
Butterfly, heart, bell, crinkled heart, tulip, and blossom. Each approx. 1½ in.
2308-T-1225
Set/6 $2.99

Mini Noah's Ark
Horse, ark, elephant, bear, giraffe and lion. Each approx. 1½ in.
2308-T-1206
Set/6 $2.99

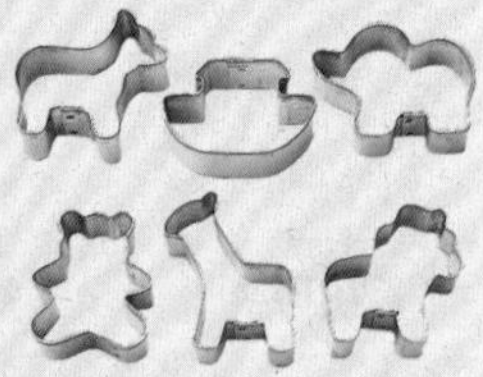

Mini Geometric Crinkle
Square, circle, heart, diamond, oval and triangle. Each approx. 1½ in.
2308-T-1205
Set/6 $2.99

METAL CUTTERS
The classic metal cutter was Grandma's favorite but she never had all these fun shapes! Metal cutters from Wilton are built to last through years of cookie making; they cut cleanly and release with ease. Each shape is approximately 3 in. **Each $0.69**

Star
2308-T-1008

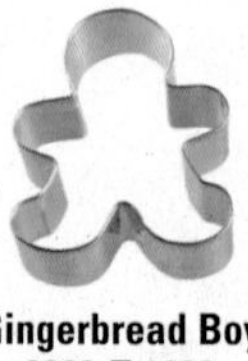

Gingerbread Boy
2308-T-1002

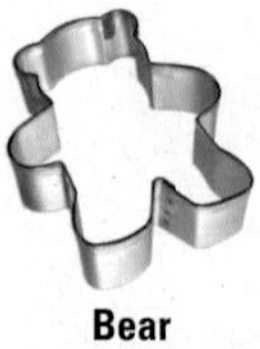

Bear
2308-T-1009

Heart
2308-T-1003

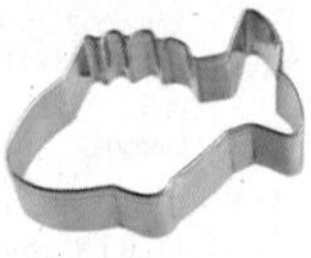

Fish
2308-T-1017

Cross
2308-T-1018

Daisy
2308-T-1007

Acorn
2308-T-1020

Maple Leaf
2308-T-1021

Oak Leaf
2308-T-1013

Butterfly
2308-T-1015

Chick
2308-T-1000

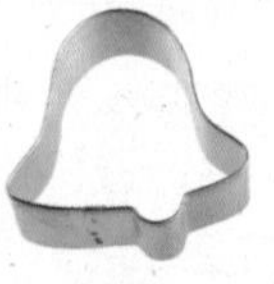

Bell
2308-T-1006

Circle
2308-T-1010

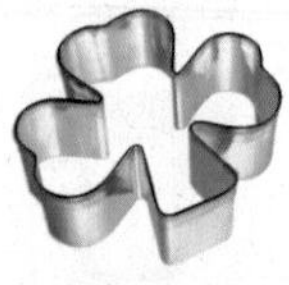

Shamrock
2308-T-1011

ORDER TOLL FREE: 800-794-5866

Cookie Bakeware and Accessories

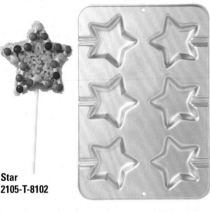

Star
2105-T-8102

Round
2105-T-8105

Blossom
2105-T-8109

Heart
2105-T-8104

Cookie Treat Pans

Cookie treats on a stick are so easy! Just press cookie dough into pan, insert a cookie stick, then bake, cool and decorate. Create your own cookie blossoms for that special someone; also great for rice cereal treats and candy. Recipe included. Each pan makes 6 individual treats, 3½ in. x ¼ in. deep. Aluminum. **Each $8.99**

Cookie Treat Sticks
For fun cookie pops.
6 in. **1912-T-9319**
Pk./20 **$1.99**
8 in. **1912-T-9318**
Pk./20 **$2.99**

Clear Party Bags
4 x 9½ in. Each pack contains 25 bags and 25 ties.
1912-T-1240
Pk./25 **$1.99**

Round
2105-T-6201

Heart
2105-T-6203

Giant Cookie Pans

Our Giant Cookie Pans help you create a jumbo pan cookie in a shape that will be a big hit for any occasion. Specially designed for one package of refrigerated dough, they are also great for brownies and pizza! Each shape is approximately ¾ in. deep and can be used with recipes that call for a standard 13 x 9 in. pan. Aluminum. **Each $6.49**

Cookie Sheets
Wilton Cookie Sheets are extra thick aluminum to heat evenly for perfect, evenly-browned bottoms.

Aluminum
Extra-thick construction.
Jumbo 14 x 20 in.
2105-T-6213 $17.99
12½ x 16½ in.
2105-T-2975 $13.99

Insulated Aluminum
Two quality aluminum layers sandwich an insulating layer of air for perfect browning without burning.
16 x 14 in.
2105-T-2644 $18.99

Cooling Grids

Chrome-Plated
Sturdy design will never rust.
13 in. Round
2305-T-130 $7.99
10 x 16 in.
2305-T-128 $5.99
14½ x 20 in.
2305-T-129 $8.99

Non-Stick
Cookies and cakes won't stick with our slick non-stick coating.
13 in. Round
2305-T-230 $9.49
10 x 16 in.
2305-T-228 $8.99
14½ x 20 in.
2305-T-229 $12.99

3-Pc. Stackable Chrome-Plated
Use singly or stack to save space while cooling three batches of cookies at the same time. Individual grids are 13½ x 9¾ x 3 in. high; stacked grids are 9¾ in. high.
2305-T-151 $12.99

See p. 148-160 for the full line of Wilton Bakeware.

Cookie Spatula
Angled stainless steel blade and smooth ergonomic handle with thumb rest—moves cookies from pan to plate with ease. Great for brownies and bar cookies, too.
409-T-6054 $6.99

Colored Sugars
Brighten up plain cookies fast with our colorful decorating sugars. Just sprinkle these extra-fine sugars on cookies before baking. Controlling the flow is easy with our flip-top shaker bottle. Certified Kosher. 4.4 oz. bottles.

Brights 4-Mix
Contains Pink, Yellow, Light Green, Lavender.
710-T-651 $4.99

Primary 4-Mix
Contains Red, Dark Green, Blue, Yellow.
710-T-650 $4.99

Candy Making

Let Wilton show you how much fun candy can be! Use our Candy Melts®*
and molds for beautiful candy in 3 easy steps—just melt, mold and serve.

Candy Melting Accessories

We've made melting chocolate and Candy Melts®* faster and easier than ever—now it's even more fun to make your own homemade candies! Our new collection is designed for melting candy for pouring or dipping and for maintaining the smooth texture to paint molds without constant reheating. It's just what the home candymaker needs!

STAY-WARM CERAMIC CANDY MELTING CUPS & BOWLS

Ceramic keeps candy melted longer for easier candy-making because microwave-safe ceramic retains heat. Great for heating and pouring dessert toppings too.

Candy Melting Cups
Cups are great for melting colors separately. Use them like an art palette for painting colors—just brush candy details into molds before filling. Holds heat up to ½ hour. Includes 6 cups (2 x 1½ in. deep) and 6 decorating brushes.
1904-T-1067 Set/12 $9.99

Candy Melting Bowls
Ideal for filling all types of Wilton molds, when making candy plaques or lollipops. Take them right to the table for easy dipping of pretzels, graham crackers or cookies. Holds heat up to 1 hour. Two, 4 x 3½ in. deep.
1904-T-1076 Set/2 $9.99

CHOCOLATE PRO® ELECTRIC MELTING POT

The fast and easy way to melt chocolate and Candy Melts®*!

- Melting base stays cool to the touch
- Removeable non-stick Melting Pot holds 2½ cups
- Easy-pour spout
- Non-skid feet keep Chocolate Pro® steady on counter

It's the fast and fun way to mold candies like a pro and to add the excitement of chocolate to your desserts. With the Chocolate Pro®, you'll be able to mold lollipops and fancy dipped-center candies. Serve elegant dipped desserts like fruit, cake, cookies and fondue. Add the great taste of chocolate to potato chips and pretzels. Create flavored chocolate sauces for ice cream or silky ganache glaze to pour over cakes. The Chocolate Pro® helps you do it all! 120 volts. CUL Listed.
2104-T-9004 $29.99

Candy Melts®*

Versatile, creamy, easy-to-melt wafers are ideal for all your candy making—molding, dipping or coating. Their delicious taste can be varied by adding our Candy Flavors.

14 oz. bag. Certified Kosher Dairy. **$2.50**

Peanut Butter 1911-T-481	**Dark Cocoa** 1911-T-358	**Light Cocoa** 1911-T-544	**Chocolate Mint** 1911-T-1920	**Lavender** 1911-T-403	**Pink** 1911-T-447
Yellow 1911-T-463	**Orange** 1911-T-1631	**Blue** 1911-T-448	**Red** 1911-T-499	**Green** 1911-T-405	**White** 1911-T-498

LOLLIPOP AND TREAT STAND

Show off your fun lollipops and other treats for the whole party to see! This lively looping metal stand neatly serves up to 18 treats for the ideal celebration centerpiece. Great for marshmallows, jelly candies and caramels too—just insert 4 in. sticks. Use the top slot to add a fun message! Assembled size 6 x 14 in. high.
1904-T-1068 $9.99

Candy Color and Flavoring Sets

Primary Candy Color Set
Concentrated oil-based colors blend easily with Candy Melts®. Includes Yellow, Orange, Red and Blue in .25 oz. jars. Certified Kosher.
1913-T-1299 Set/4 $3.99

Garden Candy Color Set
Create pretty pastel colors! Concentrated oil-based colors blend easily with Candy Melts®. Includes Pink, Green, Violet and Black in .25 oz. jars. Certified Kosher.
1913-T-1298 Set/4 $3.99

Candy Flavoring Set
Add your favorite. Includes Peppermint, Cherry, Cinnamon and Creme de Menthe in .25 oz. bottles. Certified Kosher.
1913-T-1029 Set/4 $5.49

*Brand confectionery coating.

ORDER TOLL FREE: 800-794-5866

Candy Making Tools

Squeeze Bottles

Melt candy with ease, then fill your mold without mess! Our convenient bottles are available in three sizes so you can melt just the amount of Candy Melts®* you need. Melt candy right in the bottle, then squeeze out into molds. Great way to store and reheat leftover candy.

Mini	Regular	Large
6 oz.	12 oz.	16 oz.
1904-T-1166	1904-T-1189	1904-T-1167
Pk./2 $1.99	$1.69	$1.99

Candy Melting Plate

Microwave-melt up to 11 Candy Melts®* colors at one time with less mess! Plastic with non-slip grip edge. Includes decorating brush.
1904-T-8016 $2.99

Metal Dipping Set

Professional-quality stainless steel with wooden handles. 8¾ in. long.
1904-T-925 Set/2 $9.99

Candy Dipping Set

Easy-handling spoon and fork, each 7¾ in. long.
1904-T-800 Set/2 $2.99

Decorator Brush Set

Plastic, durable bristles, easy-to-hold handle.
2104-T-9355 Set/3 $1.49

Easy-Pour Funnel

Push-button controls flow of candy. 5 x 4 in. diameter, nylon.
1904-T-552 $3.99

Candy Thermometer

Precise measurement essential for preparing hard candy, nougat, more.
1904-T-1200 $14.99

Candy Wraps and Boxes

Your homemade candy deserves a beautiful presentation. Wilton has everything you need to wrap and package your candy like a pro. Designed to keep candies fresh, protected and attractive for gift giving.

Candy Gift Boxes

For attractive gift giving and stay-fresh storage.

1 lb. White Candy Boxes 1904-T-1344 Pk./2 $1.99
½ lb. Candy Boxes Pk./3 $1.99

White	1904-T-1150	Red	1904-T-1152
Gold	1904-T-1151	Silver	1904-T-1153

NEW!

Tented Candy Gift Boxes

Stand-up design with front window will give your home made candy gift the ideal showcase. 3¼ in. wide x 5¾ in. high x 1⅝ deep. White.
1904-T-1087 Pk./3 $1.99

Candy Cups

Crisply-pleated, just like professionals use. White glassine-coated paper.

1¼ in. Diameter.
1912-T-1245 Pk./75 $1.49
1 in. Diameter.
1912-T-1243 Pk./100 $1.49

Candy Bar Boxes

Designed to hold candies made in our Candy Bar Molds (below), the window displays your special message.
Pk./10 $3.99

White
1904-T-1157
Silver
1904-T-1159

Candy Box Liners

Padded paper liners cushion candy and prevent breakage. Fits ½ lb. Candy Gift Boxes.
1904-T-1191 Pk./4 $1.49

Gold Elastic Ties

Pre-tied with a bow. Use with Candy Gift Boxes.
1904-T-1186 Pk./5 $1.49

"Home Made" Box Seals

Let everyone know the care you put into your candy gift, with these embossed seals. Add this "home made" touch whenever you give baked goods, too!
1904-T-8936 Pk./24 $0.99

NEW!

Foil Wrappers

Bright, shiny coverings for candy and lollipops! 4 x 4 in. squares.
Pk./50 $1.99

Gold
1904-T-1197
Silver
1904-T-1196
Red
1904-T-1198

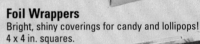

Truffle Boxes

An elegant look, with a lock-close top that forms a perfect "bow." Holds 2-3 pieces of candy.
Pk./4 $1.99

White
1904-T-1154
Silver
1904-T-1155
Gold
1904-T-1156

CANDY BAR MOLDS

Create a sweet memory for your guests . . . a candy bar featuring your special message.

Molding is easy using Candy Melts®* (p. 166). Present them beautifully in Candy Bar Boxes (above). Each candy bar measures 3¼ x 1¾ x ¼ in. deep. Mold has 1 design, 4 cavities. **$1.99**

Add-A-Message
2115-T-1356

Our Wedding
2115-T-1409

Thank You
2115-T-1410

Candy Molds

More fun shapes and greater detail make Wilton Candy Molds the world's favorite way to create candy. Look at the variety! You can do it all, from exciting kids' party treats to elegant wedding and shower favors. Molding and coloring couldn't be easier when you use Candy Melts®*. Look for terrific design ideas and molding instructions on every mold package. For specific Holiday designs, see our Seasonal Section, p. 193-213.

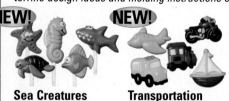

NEW!

Sea Creatures Lollipop
5 designs, 5 cavities.
2115-T-1414 $1.99

NEW! Transportation
5 designs, 5 cavities.
2115-T-1413 $1.99

NEW!

NEW!

Wedding Favor
3 designs, 6 cavities.
2115-T-4446 $1.99

Baby Treats
5 designs, 5 cavities.
2115-T-4447 $1.99

10-PACK CANDY MOLD SET

NEW! Be ready for any celebration with this great variety of theme molds! Includes 72 total shapes and 114 total cavities for fun candy messages, sports treats, flowers and more.
2115-T-1724 Pk./10 $9.99

Alphabet 26 designs, 26 cavities	Transportation 6 designs, 7 cavities	Sports Champ 7 designs, 7 cavities	Celebration 5 designs, 10 cavities
Numbers 10 designs, 10 cavities			
Hearts 1 design, 15 cavities	Peanut Butter Cups 1 design, 11 cavities	Snack Time 6 designs, 12 cavities	Fruit Lollipop 5 designs, 5 cavities	Garden Flowers 5 designs, 11 cavities

Alphabet
26 designs, 26 cavities.
2115-T-1563 $1.99

Numerals
10 designs, 10 cavities.
2115-T-1564 $1.99

Ice Cream
3 designs, 9 cavities.
2115-T-4367 $1.99

Roses in Bloom
1 design, 10 cavities.
2115-T-1738 $1.99

Stars
1 design, 12 cavities,
2115-T-1554 $1.99

Dancing Daisies Lollipop
1 design, 9 cavities.
2115-T-1430 $1.99

Rubber Ducky
1 design, 6 cavities.
2115-T-1565 $1.99

Party Time Lollipop
6 designs, 8 cavities.
2115-T-1516 $1.99

Seashells
5 designs, 11 cavities.
2115-T-1561 $1.99

Summer Fun
5 designs, 11 cavities.
2115-T-1741 $1.99

Roses and Buds Lollipop
3 designs, 9 cavities.
(4 lollipop).
2115-T-1708 $1.99

Wedding Shower Lollipop
5 designs, 10 cavities.
(4 lollipop).
2115-T-1711 $1.99

Smiley Face Lollipop
1 design, 9 cavities.
2115-T-1715 $1.99

2-PACK CANDY MOLD SETS

Girl Power
10 designs, 10 cavities.
2115-T-1604 Pk./2 $2.99

Baby
10 designs, 10 cavities.
2115-T-1605 Pk./2 $2.99

Pets
10 designs, 11 cavities.
2115-T-1606 Pk./2 $2.99

Garden Goodies Lollipop
10 designs, 10 cavities.
2115-T-1607 Pk./2 $2.99

Summer Fun Lollipop
10 designs, 10 cavities.
2115-T-1608 Pk./2 $2.99

LARGE CANDY AND LOLLIPOP MOLDS

NEW!

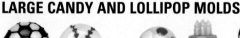

Sports Lollipop
4 designs, 4 cavities.
2115-T-4432 $1.99

Party/Birthday Lollipop
4 designs, 4 cavities.
2115-T-4434 $1.99

Double Heart Lollipop
2 designs, 4 cavities.
2115-T-4440 $1.99

Pinwheel Lollipop
2 designs, 3 cavities.
2115-T-4443 $1.99

Cross/Bible Lollipop
4 designs, 6 cavities
(2 lollipop).
2115-T-4435 $1.99

Candy Bar
1 design, three 4-block cavities.
2115-T-4431 $1.99

*Brand confectionery coating.

ORDER TOLL FREE: 800-794-5866

Pretzel Molds

Easy to mold; position pretzel rod, add your favorite melted Candy Melts®* and refrigerate to set. Ideal for lollipop sticks, too. 1 design, 6 cavities. **$1.99**

NEW!

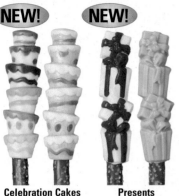

Celebration Cakes
2115-T-4429

NEW!

Presents
2115-T-4442

Smiley Face
2115-T-4437

Flowers
2115-T-4436

PRETZEL MOLDING KIT
NEW!

Everything you need—just add pretzels!

With this kit it's easy to mold tempting pretzel pops perfect for gifts, favors and celebrations. Just melt the Candy Melts®*, place a pretzel in the mold and fill with candy. You can also create dazzling designs by painting candy details in the mold before adding the pretzel. Serve them with style in the clear treat bags included—so everyone can see how great your pretzels look! Includes 2 Swirl Pretzel Molds, 5 oz. White Candy Melts®, 5 oz. Light Cocoa Candy Melts® and 20 Clear Treat Bags with twist ties. Certified Kosher.
2104-T-1650 $6.99

SILICONE CANDY & CRAFT MOLDS

Use these versatile silicone molds to make a fun-shaped treat for your next celebration. Their flexible design is perfect for molding candy plaques, large-size cookies or creative ice molds. Great with Wilton Candy Melts®*!

- High-heat silicone is oven-safe to 500°F
- Stain and odor resistant
- Reusable
- Dishwasher safe

Butterfly
Mold area is
5⅜ x 5½ x ½ in. deep.
2115-T-1038 $4.99

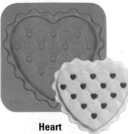

Heart
Mold area is
6¼ x 6 x ½ in. deep.
2115-T-1039 $4.99

Teddy Bear
Mold area is
4¼ x 5½ x ½ in. deep.
2115-T-1040 $4.99

CLASSIC CANDY MOLDS

Wilton has a great selection of traditional shapes for creating elegant gift assortments and party trays.

Cordial Cups
Mold a candy "glass" for dessert liqueurs, or fill with whipped cream and float in cocoa or coffee. 1 design, 6 cavities.
2115-T-1535 $1.99

Peanut Butter Cups
1 design, 10 cavities.
2115-T-1522 $1.99

Deep Heart Truffles
1 design, 7 cavities.
2117-T-100 $1.99

Truffles
1 design,
12 cavities.
**2115-T-1521
$1.99**

Roses
3 designs,
12 cavities.
**2115-T-1713
$1.99**

Gift Truffles
1 design,
13 cavities.
**2115-T-1728
$1.99**

Mint Discs
1 design,
16 cavities.
**2115-T-1739
$1.99**

Accessories

Create the perfect pop with sticks in every size, cool colors too! Clear wrappers make giving easy.

Lollipop Tags **NEW!**
Write a name or a message, draw a design, then slide the tag onto your lollipop stick. Perfect for party lollipops, cookie pops, candy gift mugs.
Pk./12 $1.99
Pennant 1904-T-1088
Star 1904-T-1089
Flower 1904-T-1071
(not shown)

Drawstring Lollipop Bags **NEW!**
Fill with your favorite candies, then pull the drawstring to close—a fun way to give. Clear bags are also great for cookies, nuts and other treats. 4½ x 5½ in.
1912-T-9469 Pk./15 $1.99

Rainbow Lollipop Sticks
Add pizzazz to your pops! Food-safe plastic sticks; 5 each red, yellow, blue and green. Not for oven or microwave use. 4 in.
1912-T-9316 Pk./20 $1.99

Lollipop Sticks
Sturdy paper sticks in 4 sizes. Not for oven use.
4 in.
1912-T-1006 Pk./50 $1.99
6 in.
1912-T-1007 Pk./35 $1.99
8 in.
1912-T-9320 Pk./25 $1.99
11¾ in.
1912-T-1212 Pk./20 $3.99

Lollipop Wrapping Kit
Cover your candy lollipops and special treats for gift-giving! Contains 18 sticks, (4 in.) 18 bags, 18 twist ties.
1904-T-1193 $1.99

Clear Treat Bags Only
3 x 4 in. **1912-T-2347 Pk./50 $2.69**

Dipped Spoons Kit
Fun to make, use or give. Use with the Dipped Spoons Mold, plus your favorite Candy Melts®* and Candy Flavors. Includes 6 plastic spoons, 6 bags, 6 twist ties and instructions.
1904-T-1192 $1.99

Dipped Spoons Mold
Use with the Dipped Spoons Kit or use your own spoons, along with Wilton Candy Melts®* and Candy Flavors, to create candy-coated spoons that stir in flavor. Contains mold (1 design, 6 cavities) and instructions.
2115-T-1722 $1.99

Famous Favorites

Wilton helps you make kids feel like stars! We have a great cast of today's favorite faces and themes on fun party products for cakes, cookies and more.

NEW!

Cake Pan
Kids will follow *Diego* everywhere—they've watched him race to the rescue on TV, and now he's ready to save the party with the perfect birthday cake! The fun detailed design really captures his adventurous attitude. 16 x 10 x 2 in. deep. Aluminum.
2105-T-4250 $12.99

Party Toppers
Diego scopes out all the party fun on these colorful toppers. They're easy ways to complete your treats! Handpainted, food-safe plastic is great on cupcakes, brownies, cakes and more. 2 in. high.
2113-T-4250 Set/6 $3.99

Candle
Handpainted, clean-burning with colorful details.
3¼ in. high.
2811-T-4250 $3.99

Icing Color Set
Includes four .5 oz. jars: Skin Tone, Brown, Blue and Black. Certified Kosher.
601-T-4250 Set/4 $4.99

Icing Decorations
Mint-flavored edible sugar shapes to decorate cupcakes, cookies, ice cream and cake. Certified Kosher.
710-T-4250 Pk./9 $2.49

Baking Cups
Standard size, microwave-safe paper. 2 in. diameter.
415-T-4250 Pk./50 $1.69

Treat Bags
Fill with candy, cookies and other goodies; great for gifts too! Includes sixteen 4 x 9½ in. bags with twist ties.
1912-T-4250 Pk./16 $1.99

Fun Pix®
Fun for cupcakes, brownies, ice cream and more. Paper, 3¼ in. high.
2113-T-4251 Pk./24 $1.29

ORDER TOLL FREE: 800-794-5866

NEW!

Cake Pan

Some of the best adventures can happen right in your own backyard—like an amazing party featuring this high-spirited *Pablo* cake! It's easy to see *Pablo's* fun-loving, adventurous spirit. He's sure to bring a smile to every kid at the celebration! 15 x 10 x 2 in. deep. Aluminum.
2105-T-7515 $12.99

Candle

Handpainted, clean-burning with fun details. 2¾ in. high.
2811-T-7516 $3.99

Icing Color Set

Includes four .5 oz. jars: Red, Blue, Gold and Black. Certified Kosher.
601-T-7515 Set/4 $4.99

Icing Decorations

Mint-flavored edible sugar shapes to decorate cupcakes, cookies, ice cream and cake. Certified Kosher.
710-T-7515 Pk./9 $2.49

Baking Cups

Standard size, microwave-safe paper. 2 in. diameter.
415-T-7515 Pk./50 $1.69

Treat Bags

Fill with candy, cookies and other goodies; great for gifts and surprises, too! Includes sixteen 4 x 9½ in. bags with twist ties.
1912-T-7515 Pk./16 $1.99

ORDER ONLINE: WWW.WILTON.COM

Cake Pan
Tink makes birthday wishes come true! She brings fun to the celebration on a cake that captures the twinkle in her eye and the magic in her smile. 10 ½ x 12 x 2 in. deep. Aluminum.
2105-T-5110 $12.99

Candle
Handpainted, clean-burning with colorful details.
3 in. high.
**2811-T-5110
$3.99**

Party Toppers
Top your treats with *Tink* and create enchantment! Handpainted, food-safe plastic is great on cupcakes, brownies, cakes and other treats. 2¼ in. high.
2113-T-5110 Set/6 $3.99

Icing Decorations
Mint-flavored edible sugar shapes to decorate cupcakes, cookies, ice cream and cake. Certified Kosher.
710-T-5110 Pk./9 $2.49

Fun Pix®
Fun for cupcakes, brownies, ice cream and more. Paper, 3½ in. high.
2113-T-5111 Pk./24 $1.29

Icing Color Set
Includes four .5 oz. jars: Blue, Yellow, Red, Skin Tone. Certified Kosher.
**601-T-5110
Set/4 $4.99**

Baking Cups
Standard size, microwave-safe paper. 2 in. diameter.
**415-T-5110
Pk./50 $1.69**

Treat Bags
Fill with candy, cookies and other goodies; great for gifts and surprises, too! Includes sixteen 4 x 9½ in. bags with twist ties.
**1912-T-5110
Pk./16 $1.99**

© Disney
Please visit Disney Fairies at DisneyFairies.com

NEW!

Cake Pan

Enter *Ariel's* world of enchantment under the sea! Her sweet new look will captivate kids and bring all the thrills of the *Little Mermaid* story to your celebration. 10 ½ x 11 ¾ x 2 in. Aluminum.
2105-T-4355 $12.99

Candle

Handpainted, clean-burning with fun details. 3 in. high.
**2811-T-4355
$3.99**

Party Toppers

When *Ariel* surfaces on party desserts, there's a new wave of birthday excitement! Handpainted, food-safe plastic is great on cupcakes, brownies, cakes and other treats. 1¾ in. high.
2113-T-4355 Set/6 $3.99

Icing Decorations

Mint-flavored edible sugar shapes to decorate cupcakes, cookies, ice cream and cake. Certified Kosher.
710-T-4355 Pk./9 $2.49

Icing Color Set

Includes four .5 oz. jars: Skin Tone, Red (2), Teal. Certified Kosher.
**601-T-4355
Set/4 $4.99**

Baking Cups

Standard size, microwave-safe paper. 2 in. diameter.
415-T-4355 Pk./50 $1.69

Treat Bags

Fill with candy, cookies and other goodies; great for gifts and surprises, too! Includes sixteen 4 x 9½ in. bags with twist ties.
1912-T-4355 Pk./16 $1.99

© Disney

Fun Pix®
Fun for cupcakes, brownies, ice cream and more. Paper, 3 in. high.
2113-T-6402 Pk./24 $1.29

Cake Pan
Any party is a joy ride when you serve a cake starring *Lightning McQueen*! All the fun details you love on the big screen are here. One-mix pan is 13¾ x 6¼ x 2¾ in. deep. Aluminum.
2105-T-6400 $12.99

Icing Decorations
Mint-flavored edible sugar shapes to decorate cupcakes, cookies, ice cream and cake. Certified Kosher.
710-T-6400 Pk./9 $2.49

Party Toppers
Rev up the fun with treats topped with your favorites from *Disney/Pixar Cars*! Handpainted, food-safe plastic is great on cupcakes, brownies, cakes and other treats. 1¼ in. high.
2113-T-6400 Set/6 $3.99

Baking Cups
Standard size, microwave-safe paper. 2 in. diameter.
415-T-6400
Pk./50 $1.69

Candle
Handpainted, clean-burning with fun details. 3½ in. high.
2811-T-6400 $3.99

Icing Color Set
Includes four .5 oz. jars: Red, Blue, Yellow, Black. Certified Kosher.
601-T-6400
Set/4 $4.99

Treat Bags
Fill with candy, cookies and other goodies; great for gifts and surprises, too! Includes sixteen 4 x 9½ in. bags with twist ties.
1912-T-6400 Pk./16 $1.99

©Disney/Pixar

ORDER TOLL FREE: 800-794-5866

Cake Pan
Everyone's favorite seafaring star will make a big splash at the party. One-mix pan is 13½ x 11¾ x 2 in. deep. Aluminum.
2105-T-5130 $12.99

Party Toppers
He's surfing your party goodies on these cool handpainted toppers. Food-safe plastic to use on cupcakes, brownies, cakes and other treats. 2 in. high.
**2113-T-5130
Set/6 $3.99**

Candle
SpongeBob is swimming in loot—giving you a cake to treasure! Handpainted, clean-burning with colorful details. 3½ in. high.
**2811-T-5130
$3.99**

Icing Color Set
Includes four .5 oz. jars: Yellow, Red, Blue and Brown. Certified Kosher.
**601-T-5130
Set/4 $4.99**

Icing Decorations
Mint-flavored edible sugar shapes to decorate cupcakes, cookies, ice cream and cake. Certified Kosher.
710-T-5130 Pk./9 $2.49

Shaped Sprinkles
4-cell container is convenient for pouring and storing. Includes *SpongeBob* (in 2 cells), Flower and Patrick shapes. 2.8 oz. Certified Kosher.
710-T-5131 $5.99

Baking Cups
Standard size, microwave-safe paper. 2 in. diameter.
415-T-5130 Pk./50 $1.69

Treat Bags
Fill with candy, cookies and other goodies; great for gifts and surprises, too! Includes sixteen 4 x 9½ in. bags with twist ties.
**1912-T-5130
Pk./16 $1.99**

Cake Pan

Wherever *Dora* goes, it's always "una fiesta"! Discover a world of party excitement with this great pan. One-mix pan is 13¾ x 10 x 2 in. deep. Aluminum.
2105-T-6300 $12.99

Party Toppers

Dora is ready to top your delightful party treats! Handpainted, food-safe plastic is great on cupcakes, brownies, cakes and other treats. 2¼ in. high.
2113-T-6300 Set/6 $3.99

Candle

Handpainted, clean-burning with colorful details. 3¼ in. high.
2811-T-6300 $3.99

Icing Color Set

Includes four .5 oz. jars: Red, Pink, Brown and Skin Tone. Certified Kosher.
601-T-6300 Set/4 $4.99

Icing Decorations

Mint-flavored edible sugar shapes to decorate cupcakes, cookies, ice cream and cake. Certified Kosher.
710-T-6300 Pk./8 $2.49

Baking Cups

Standard size, microwave-safe paper. 2 in. diameter.
415-T-6300 Pk./50 $1.69

Treat Bags

Fill with candy, cookies and other goodies; great for gifts and surprises, too! Includes sixteen 4 x 9½ in. bags with twist ties.
1912-T-6300 Pk./16 $1.99

ORDER TOLL FREE: 800-794-5866

THE AMAZING SPIDER-MAN

Cake Pan
The Wizard of Webs is back in action, on a pan that will grab every guest! Kids will love the great costume detail. One-mix pan is 9 x 12 x 2 in. deep. Aluminum.
2105-T-5052
$12.99

Party Toppers
He's ready to sling his next web on these exciting handpainted toppers. Food-safe plastic to use on cupcakes, brownies, cakes and other treats. 2¼ in. high.
2113-T-5052 Set/6 $3.99

Candle
Handpainted, clean-burning with exciting details. 3½ in. high.
2811-T-5052
$3.99

Icing Color Set
Includes four .5 oz. jars: Light Blue, Dark Blue, Red and Black. Certified Kosher.
601-T-5052
Set/4 $4.99

Icing Decorations
Mint-flavored edible sugar shapes to decorate cupcakes, cookies, ice cream and cake. Certified Kosher.
710-T-5052 Pk./9 $2.49

Baking Cups
Standard size, microwave-safe paper. 2 in. diameter.
415-T-5052 Pk./50 $1.69

Treat Bags
Fill with candy, cookies and other goodies; great for gifts and surprises, too! Includes sixteen 4 x 9½ in. bags with twist ties.
1912-T-5052 Pk./16 $1.99

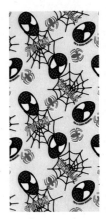

SCOOBY-DOO!

Candle
Handpainted, clean-burning with colorful details. 3¾ in. high.
2811-T-3227 $3.99

Baking Cups
Standard size, microwave-safe paper. 2 in. diameter.
415-T-3227
Pk./50 $1.69

Cake Pan
As usual, *Scooby* gets right next to the food! This fun pan shows him about to put his canines into a big burger. One-mix pan is 10½ x 12 x 2 in. deep. Aluminum.
2105-T-3227 $12.99

Shaped Sprinkles
Shake up your *Scooby-Doo!* treats. Convenient 4-cell container designed for easy pouring and storing. Includes *Mystery Machine, Scooby-Doo!*, bone and bat shapes. 2.55 oz. Certified Kosher.
710-T-3207 $5.99

Treat Bags
Fill with candy, cookies and other goodies; great for gifts and surprises, too! Includes sixteen 4 x 9½ in. bags with twist ties.
1912-T-3227
Pk./16 $1.99

Party Toppers
Scooby-Doo! is begging for attention on these fun handpainted toppers. Food-safe plastic to decorate cupcakes, brownies, cakes and other treats. 2½ in. high.
2113-T-3206 Set/6 $3.99

Icing Decorations
Mint-flavored edible sugar shapes to decorate cupcakes, cookies, ice cream and cake. Certified Kosher.
710-T-3206 Pk./9 $2.49

SUPERMAN

Candle
Handpainted, clean-burning with fun details. 2½ in. high.
2811-T-3350 $3.99

Baking Cups
Standard size, microwave-safe paper. 2 in. diameter.
415-T-3350
Pk./50 $1.69

Cake Pan
Superman™ is back to save the world and rescue your celebration! Call on this mighty World Hero for a cake that will thrill every kid—and featuring a bold new look for the *Man of Steel™*. One-mix pan is 13½ x 11½ x 2 in. deep. Aluminum.
2105-T-3350 $12.99

Party Toppers
Top your treats with these exciting action figures. Handpainted, food-safe plastic is great on cupcakes, brownies, cakes and other treats. 2¼ in. high.
2113-T-3350 Set/6 $3.99

Treat Bags
Fill with candy, cookies and other goodies; great for gifts and surprises, too! Includes sixteen 4 x 9½ in. bags with twist ties.
1912-T-3350
Pk./16 $1.99

Icing Decorations
Mint-flavored edible sugar shapes to decorate cupcakes, cookies, ice cream and cake. Certified Kosher.
710-T-3350 Pk./9 $2.49

ORDER TOLL FREE: 800-794-5866

Pooh #1 Hunny Pot
2811-T-3102

Pooh and Presents
2811-T-3100

Candles
Pooh is ready for the party. Handpainted, clean-burning with colorful details. 2-3 in. high.
$3.99

Icing Color Set
Includes four .5 oz. jars: *Pooh* (gold), Red, Green and Black. Certified Kosher.
601-T-3100
Set/4 $4.99

Baking Cups
Standard size, microwave-safe paper. 2 in. diameter.
415-T-3100
Pk./50 $1.69

Treat Bags
Fill with candy, cookies and other goodies; great for gifts and surprises, too! Includes sixteen 4 x 9½ in. bags with twist ties.
1912-T-3100
Pk./16 $1.99

Pooh Cake Pan
He's always ready for a fun party, with his birthday balloon in hand and a happy smile on his face. One-mix pan is 13¾ x 7¾ x 2 in. deep. Aluminum.
2105-T-3100 $12.99

Icing Decorations
Mint-flavored edible sugar shapes to decorate cupcakes, cookies, ice cream and cake. Certified Kosher.
710-T-3100 Pk./9 $2.49

Based on the "Winnie The Pooh" works, by A.A. Milne and E.H. Shepard.
© Disney

SESAME STREET

Elmo with Crayons Candle
Elmo brings smiles to the party. Handpainted, clean-burning with colorful details. 3½ in. high.
2811-T-3463 $3.99

Parade Cake Top Set
A fun birthday parade right on your cake. *Cookie Monster, Zoe, Elmo, Big Bird* in food-safe plastic. 1½ to 4 in. high.
2113-T-3460 Set/4 $4.99

Baking Cups
Standard size, microwave-safe paper. 2 in. diameter.
415-T-3461
Pk./50 $1.69

Elmo Face Cake Pan
He's sweet, lovable and popular with kids of all ages. One-mix pan is 13½ x 10½ x 2 in. deep. Aluminum.
2105-T-3461 $12.99

Icing Decorations
Mint-flavored edible sugar shapes to decorate cupcakes, cookies, ice cream and cakes. Certified Kosher.
710-T-3460 Pk./9 $2.49

Treat Bags
Fill with candy, cookies and other goodies; great for gifts and surprises, too! Includes sixteen 4 x 9½ in. bags with twist ties.
1912-T-3461
Pk./16 $1.99

Sesame Workshop, the nonprofit educational organization behind Sesame Street, puts the proceeds it receives from sales of its products right back into Sesame Street and its other projects for children at home and around the world.
Learn more at www.sesameworkshop.org

Sesame Workshop®, Sesame Street® and associated characters, trademarks and design elements are owned and licensed by Sesame Workshop. ©2007 Sesame Workshop. All Rights Reserved.

Icing Color Set

Includes four .5 oz. jars of Teal, Blue, Yellow and Orange. Certified Kosher.
601-T-2424
Set/4 $4.99

Candle

Hand-painted, clean-burning with adorable details. 3 in. high.
2811-T-2424 $3.99

Baking Cups

Standard size, microwave-safe paper. 2 in. diameter.
415-T-2424
Pk./50 $1.69

Treat Bags

Fill with candy, cookies and other goodies; great for gifts and surprises, too! Includes sixteen 4 x 9½ in. bags with twist ties.
1912-T-2424
Pk./16 $1.99

Icing Decorations

Mint-flavored edible sugar shapes to decorate cupcakes, cookies, ice cream and cake. Certified Kosher.
710-T-2424 Pk./9 $2.49

Cake Pan

With this pan, kids can enjoy a different *Care Bear* every time! The label includes instructions and patterns for 4 of the most popular "care"acters—it's easy to give *Wish Bear™*, *Love-a-lot Bear™*, *Share Bear™* and *Good Luck Bear™* their distinctive colors and personalities. One-mix pan is 13 x 9½ x 2 in. deep. Aluminum.
2105-T-2424 $12.99

Icing Color Set

Includes four .5 oz. jars: Red, Brown, Green and Skin Tone. Certified Kosher.
601-T-7040
Set/4 $4.99

Candle

Handpainted, clean-burning with fun details. 3¼ in. high.
2811-T-7040 $3.99

Baking Cups

Standard size, microwave-safe paper. 2 in. diameter.
415-T-7040
Pk./50 $1.69

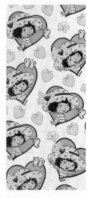

Treat Bags

Fill with candy, cookies and other goodies; great for gifts and surprises, too! Includes sixteen 4 x 9½ in. bags with twist ties.
1912-T-7040
Pk./16 $1.99

Cake Pan

Everyone loves her fun and colorful look! From her bouncy hat to her sweet smile, she adds a "berry" happy touch to the party. One-mix pan is 11¼ x 10½ x 2 in. deep. Aluminum.
2105-T-7040 $12.99

Icing Decorations

Mint-flavored edible sugar shapes to decorate cupcakes, cookies, ice cream and cake. Certified Kosher.
710-T-7041 Pk./9 $2.49

ORDER TOLL FREE: 800-794-5866

Cake Pan
Start your party with a cake your pit crew will love—decorated with the excitement of *NASCAR*. It's ready to customize with your favorite driver's number and colors! Perfect for birthdays or race days. One-mix pan is 15¾ x 8¾ x 2 in. deep. Aluminum.
2105-T-2500 $12.99

Icing Decorations
Mint-flavored edible sugar shapes to decorate cupcakes, cookies, ice cream and cake. Certified Kosher.
710-T-2500 Pk./9 $2.49

Baking Cups
Standard size, microwave-safe paper. 2 in. diameter.
415-T-2500 Pk./50 $1.69

Candle
Handpainted, clean-burning with colorful details. 3 in. high.
2811-T-2500 $3.99

Icing Color Set
Includes four .5 oz. jars: Black, Red, Yellow and Blue. Certified Kosher.
601-T-2500 Set/4 $4.99

ICING COLOR SET
NET WT 2 OZ (56 g)

Treat Bags
Fill with candy, cookies and other goodies; great for gifts and surprises, too! Includes sixteen 4 x 9½ in. bags with twist ties.
1912-T-2500 Pk./16 $1.99

NASCAR is a registered trademark of the National Association for Stock Car Auto Racing, Inc.

NEW!

Icing Decorations
Mint-flavored edible sugar shapes to decorate cupcakes, cookies, ice cream and cake. Certified Kosher.
710-T-2400 Pk./9 $2.49

Candle
Handpainted, clean-burning with fun details. 2½ in. high.
2811-T-2400 $3.99

Baking Cups
Standard size, microwave-safe paper. 2 in. diameter.
415-T-2400 Pk./50 $1.69

Treat Bags
Fill with candy, cookies and other goodies; great for gifts and surprises, too! Includes sixteen 4 x 9½ in. bags with twist ties.
1912-T-2400 Pk./16 $1.99

Entertaining

Every big event needs a main attraction—Wilton Fountains will be the most popular stop at the party! Each great-looking design will complement your celebration décor.

Celebrate!® Party Fountain

NEW!

The fountain that's filled with design possibilities!

- Easy to assemble—no tools needed!
- Quiet, no-splash design
- Precision spouts for a neat, even flow
- Contoured rim is the perfect fill line
- Illuminated base adds a dramatic glow
- Holds up to 3 gallons

The Celebrate! Party Fountain is the most versatile beverage fountain you can buy. It's made to be customized to your celebration! Add drama and sparkle with its illuminated base, or display unlit and accented with favorite flowers, holiday decorations and more. Tailor the light color to match your décor. Top off the fountain 2 ways—use the included ornamental plate to show off favorite figurines, floral bouquets and holiday accents. Or use the graceful tulip top to create a simple, elegant silhouette. No tools needed—just assemble pieces using numbers as guides, then add up to 3 gallons of your favorite beverage. Not designed to heat or cool beverages or for use with beverages containing pulp. 120V; UL listed.
2104-T-9009 $149.99

Chocolate Pro® Chocolate Fountain

- Holds 4 lbs. of melted chocolate
- Tiers come apart for easy cleaning
- Three adjustable feet, plus bubble level, allow perfect leveling from all angles

Bring the excitement of chocolate dipping to your next party! The Chocolate Pro® Chocolate Fountain makes it easy to enjoy delicious hand-dipped desserts any time! The graceful canopy style creates an elegant flow from all 3 levels; the bowl is designed to keep chocolate melted and flowing.

Wit the Chocolate Pro®, any celebration becomes more special. Let your guests dip cake and cookies for a flavorful finishing touch. Great for fruit, or try a sweet and salty combination by dipping potato chips and pretzels. 120V; UL listed.
2104-T-9008 $99.99

Chocolate Pro®
FOUNTAIN AND FONDUE CHOCOLATE

The best real melting chocolate for fountains and fondues is here! Made from premium ingredients for superior melting and a delicious chocolate taste. Ideal texture and rich flavor for making dipped desserts. No tempering needed! 2 lbs.
2104-T-2618 $14.99

Party

You've written the guest list—now start your decorating list here! From baking cups to candles, cake toppers to treat bags, Wilton has the great-looking designs you want.

Theme Party Products

Give your party personality! See how easy it is to pull your look together with the great selection of Wilton theme products. You'll discover favorite subjects including jungle animals, colorful flowers, over-the-hill tombstones and sports for every season. Find candles, party bags, baking cups, candy molds, cake pans and more—all with the Wilton touch of fun design and detail.

JUNGLE PALS

Kids will just love these adorable creatures for birthdays, school parties and special events.

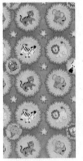

Baking Cups
Standard size.
415-T-1012
Pk./50 $1.49

Friendly Lion Pan
He'll be the pride of all your celebrations! One-mix pan is 12¾ x 10¾ x 2 in. deep. Aluminum.
2105-T-1012 $11.99

Icing Decorations
Certified Kosher.
710-T-1012 Pk./12 $2.29

Party Bags
20 plastic bags, 20 ties included. 4 x 9½ in.
1912-T-1012
Pk./20 $1.99

Fun Pix®
Approx.
3⅛ in. high.
2113-T-1012
Set/24 $1.99

Jungle Animals Topper Set
1¾ to 3 in. high.
2113-T-2095 Set/4 $3.99

Candles
Approx.
2 in. high.
2811-T-1012
Set/4 $3.49

DANCING DAISY FLOWER

Pick this daisy for Mother's Day, wedding showers and birthdays for any garden-lover.

Pan
One perfect flower makes bunches of great cakes and desserts!
One-mix pan is 12 x 12 x 2 in. deep. Aluminum.
2105-T-1016 $11.99

Icing Decorations
Certified Kosher.
710-T-353 Pk./12 $2.29

Candles
Approx. 2 in. high.
2811-T-217
Set/6 $3.49

Lollipop Mold
1 design, 9 cavities.
2115-T-1430 $1.99

Baking Cups
Standard size.
415-T-7812
Pk./50 $1.49

Party Bags
20 plastic bags, 20 ties included.
4 x 9½ in.
1912-T-7813
Pk./20 $1.99

Theme Party Products

PARTY TIME

What a great way to cap off any celebration, from birthdays to that New Year's Eve bash!

Party Hat Pan
Customize cakes with your favorite colors and fun designs—ideal for molded desserts and salads too. One-mix pan is 10 x 13½ x 2 in. deep. Aluminum.
2105-T-3317 $11.99

Party/Birthday Large Lollipop Mold
4 designs, 4 cavities.
2115-T-4434 $1.99

Party Bags
20 plastic bags, 20 ties included.
4 x 9½ in.
**1912-T-4365
Pk./20 $1.99**

Baking Cups
Standard size.
**415-T-5365
Pk./50 $1.49**

Icing Decorations
Certified Kosher.
**710-T-7205
Pk./12 $2.29**

Candles
Approx. 1½ in. high.
2811-T-860 Set/4 $3.49

ICE CREAM

A refreshing look for any celebration, from birthdays to backyard barbecues.

Ice Cream Cone Pan
Like a real ice cream cone, create endless flavor and color combinations. One-mix pan is 13¾ x 9¼ x 2 in. deep. Aluminum.
2105-T-2087 $11.99

Candy Mold
3 designs, 9 cavities.
2115-T-4367 $1.99

Party Bags
20 plastic bags, 20 ties included.
4 x 9½ in.
**1912-T-3106
Pk./20 $1.99**

Baking Cups
Standard size.
**415-T-121
Pk./50 $1.49**

Candles
Approx. 2¼ in. high.
2811-T-9349 Set/4 $3.49

OVER THE HILL

The secret of aging is keeping your sense of humor! These Wilton products help anyone face those big birthdays with a smile!

Icon Candles
Candles that feature a fun hand-carved tombstone. Instant fun, great size for cupcakes too! 2½ in. high.
2811-T-8417
Pk./10 $1.99

Candle Picks
3 in. high.
2811-T-786 Set/13 $1.99

Candle
2¼ in. high.
2811-T-553 $1.99

SMILEY FACE

Have a nice party! This friendly face has a way of making everyone happy at birthdays, housewarmings and welcome home parties.

Lollipop Mold
1 design, 6 cavities.
2115-T-1715 $1.99

Party Bags
20 plastic bags, 20 ties included.
4 x 9½ in.
1912-T-2361
Pk./20 $1.99

Baking Cups
Standard size.
415-T-261
Pk./50 $1.49

Candles
1½ in. high.
2811-T-9351
Set/6 $3.49

Pretzel Mold
Easy to mold; 1 design, 6 cavities.
2115-T-4437
$1.99

Candle Picks
2½ in. high.
2811-T-6327 Set/4 $3.49

Chunky Candles
Thicker candles to energize any cake! They feature bold textured spirals and a fun hand-carved shape on top. 3¼ in. high.
Pk./4 $3.49

Smiley Stars
2811-T-6325

Smiley Flames
2811-T-6326

RUBBER DUCKY

This bath-time favorite will make the biggest splash for birthdays, baby showers and school celebrations.

3-D Cake Pan
Five adorable designs included. Two-piece pan takes 5½ cups batter. Aluminum.
2105-T-2094 $14.99

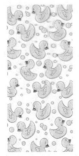

Icing Decorations
Certified Kosher.
710-T-293
Pk./12 $2.29

Baking Cups
Standard size.
415-T-378
Pk./50 $1.49

Candy Mold
1 design, 6 cavities.
2115-T-1565 $1.99

Party Bags
20 plastic bags, 20 ties included. 4 x 9½ in.
1912-T-1275 Pk./20 $1.99

Candles
Handpainted details, clean-burning design. 1½ in. high.
2811-T-9337 Set/6 $3.49

Theme Party Products
BASEBALL/SOFTBALL

From Little League to World Series celebrations, cover the bases with 3-D cakes, bobbling player toppers and hit candles.

Mini Ball Pan
Ice two mini balls and push together for a 3-D effect. One cake mix makes 10–12 mini balls. Six cavities, each 3½ x 3½ x 1½ in. deep. Aluminum.
2105-T-1760 **$11.99**

Soccer Ball Pan
One-mix pan is 8¾ x 8¾ x 3½ in. deep. Aluminum.
2105-T-2044
$11.99

Icing Decorations
Certified Kosher.
710-T-475
Pk./9 **$2.29**

Sports Ball Pan Set
Includes two 6 in. diameter half-ball pans and two metal baking stands. Each pan half takes 2½ cups batter. Aluminum.
2105-T-6506 **Set/4 $11.99**

Baking Cups
Standard size.
415-T-298
Pk./50 **$1.49**

Take Me Out To The Ballgame Candles
Approx. 2 in. high.
2811-T-9341
Set/4 **$3.49**

Bobbling Cake Toppers
Food-safe, with hand-painted detail. 4½ in. high.
Baseball   Softball
2113-T-5242 **$3.99**   2113-T-5240 **$3.99**

Sports Lollipop Mold
Makes favorite sports balls from every season. 4 designs, 4 cavities.
2115-T-4432 **$1.99**

HOCKEY

Topper Set With Decals
Includes 1 topper, 6 candleholders, 6 candles, 1 sheet of decals.
2811-T-8422 **Set/14 $4.99**

Baseball Topper Set*
Batter, catcher, three fielders and pitcher, 2⅛ to 2¾ in. high.
2113-T-2155 **Set/6 $2.99**

Topper Set with Decals
Includes 1 topper, 6 candleholders, 6 candles, 1 sheet of decals.
2811-T-8425 **Set/14 $4.99**

*CAUTION: Contains small parts. Not recommended for use by children 3 years and under.

FOOTBALL

Touching down at Super Bowl parties, homecomings, award dinners and much more.

First and Ten Football Pan
One-mix pan is 12 x 7¾ x 3 in. deep. Aluminum.
2105-T-6504 **$11.99**

Icing Decorations
Certified Kosher.
710-T-478 Pk./9 **$2.29**

Baking Cups
Standard 415-T-5152
Pk./75 **$1.99**

Mini 415-T-5154
Pk./100 **$1.99**

Party Bags
20 plastic bags, 20 ties included. 4 x 9½ in.
1912-T-1053
Pk./20 **$1.99**

Sports Lollipop Mold
Makes favorite sports balls from every season.
4 design, 4 cavities.
2115-T-4432 **$1.99**

Topper Set with Decals
Includes 1 topper, 6 candleholders, 6 candles, 1 sheet of decals.
2811-T-8424 Set/14 **$4.99**

Football Topper Set*
Eight players and two goal posts, 1½ to 4½ in. high.
2113-T-2236
Set/10
$2.99

SOCCER

A great way to reward a season or a game well played!

Soccer Ball Pan
One-mix pan is 8¾ x 8¾ x 3½ in. deep. Aluminum.
2105-T-2044 **$11.99**

Bobbling Cake Toppers
Food-safe, with hand-painted detail. 4½ in. high.

Male Soccer
2113-T-5238 **$3.99**

Female Soccer
2113-T-5239 **$3.99**

Sports Lollipop Mold
Makes favorite sports balls from every season.
4 design, 4 cavities.
2115-T-4432 **$1.99**

Icing Decorations
Certified Kosher.
710-T-477
Pk./9 **$2.29**

Baking Cups
Standard size.
415-T-296 Pk./50 **$1.49**

Topper Set with Decals
Includes 1 topper, 6 candleholders, 6 candles, 1 sheet of decals.
2811-T-8421 Set/14 **$4.99**

Soccer Topper Set*
Seven players and two nets, 1¾ to 2 in. high.
2113-T-9002
Set/9 **$2.99**

---

*CAUTION: Contains small parts. Not recommended for use by children 3 years and under.

Theme Party Products

BASKETBALL

Slam dunk winners! Create thrilling cakes and candies.

Soccer Ball Pan
One-mix pan is 8¾ x 8¾ x 3½ in. deep. Aluminum.
2105-T-2044 $11.99

Sports Lollipop Mold
Makes favorite sports balls from every season. 4 design, 4 cavities.
2115-T-4432 $1.99

Topper Set with Decals
Includes 1 topper, 6 candleholders, 6 candles, 1 sheet of decals.
2811-T-8423 Set/14 $4.99

GOLF

Great ways to top cakes with perfect form.

Topper Set with Decals
Includes 1 topper, 6 candleholders, 6 candles, 1 sheet of decals.
2811-T-8420 Set/14 $4.99

Golf Topper Set*
Includes 4½ in. high golfer plus three each: 2½ in. wide greens, 4 in. high flags, 5 in. clubs and golf balls.
1306-T-7274 Set/13 $2.99

Bobbling Cake Topper
Food-safe, with hand-painted detail. 4½ in. high.
2113-T-5237 $3.99

FISHING

Land the perfect cake for your angler, with bright candles and toppers.

Tropical Fish Pan
Everyone will be hooked by this fish—it's a keeper! One-mix pan is 11½ x 12½ x 2 in. deep. Aluminum.
2105-T-1014 $11.99

Frustrated Fisherman Topper*
4½ in. high.
2113-T-2384 $3.49

Tropical Fish Candles
Approx. 1½ in. high.
2811-T-9333 Set/4 $3.49

Bobbling Cake Topper
Food-safe, with hand-painted detail. 4½ in. high.
2113-T-5236 $3.99

*CAUTION: Contains small parts. Not recommended for use by children 3 years and under.

ORDER TOLL FREE: 800-794-5866

PARTY

Baking Cups

The easiest way to dress up a cupcake! Ideal for holding candy and nuts, too.

Made of microwave-safe paper unless otherwise noted. Jumbo cups are 2¼ in. diameter, standard cups are 2 in. diameter, mini cups are 1¼ in. diameter, bon bon cups are 1 in. diameter.

Dazzling Dots $1.49
Standard
415-T-582 Pk./50
Mini
415-T-1141 Pk./75

Snappy Stripes $1.49
Standard
415-T-581 Pk./50
Mini
415-T-1140 Pk./75

White $1.49
Jumbo 415-T-2503 Pk/50
Standard 415-T-2505 Pk./75
Mini 415-T-2507 Pk./100

Assorted Pastel $1.49
25 pink, 25 yellow, 25 blue.
Standard 415-T-394
Pk./75

Gold Foil $1.49
Wax-laminated paper on foil.
Standard 415-T-206 Pk./24
Bon Bon 415-T-306 Pk./75

Silver Foil $1.49
Standard 415-T-207
(24 pure aluminum/24 paper)
Bon Bon 415-T-307
(36 pure aluminum/36 paper)

Petite Loaf Cups*
Microwave-safe paper. White.
415-T-450 Pk./50 $1.49

*Petite Loaf Cups are 3¼ x 2 in. and fit Petite Loaf Pan p. 154.

Nut and Party Cups
Mini 1¼ oz.
415-T-500 Pk./36 $1.69
Standard 3¼ oz.
415-T-400 Pk./24 $1.69

Party Bags

Wrap up cookies, candies, favors and more with color and fun!
Contains 20, 4 x 9½ in. bags and 20 twist ties, unless otherwise noted.
Pk./20 $1.99

Clear (not shown)
1912-T-1240
Pk./25 $1.99

Dazzling Dots 1912-T-1090 **Snappy Stripes** 1912-T-1089 **Wedding Cake** 1912-T-1086 **Wedding** 1912-T-2364 **Colorful Stars** 1912-T-2362

Baby 1912-T-2365 **Blue** 1912-T-2356 **Yellow** 1912-T-2359 **Pink** 1912-T-2363 **Red** 1912-T-2357

PIZAZZ

A dazzling reflective pattern in 2 great colors.

Contains 8, 4 x 9½ in. bags and 8 twist ties.
Pk./8 $1.99

Silver Pizazz 1912-T-1020 **Gold Pizazz** 1912-T-1022

Icing Decorations

Wilton Icing Decorations are perfect for topping cupcakes, cookies and ice cream. Mint-flavored edible shapes are Certified Kosher.

HAPPY BIRTHDAY Alphabet/Numerals
710-T-494 Pk./70 $2.29

HAPPY BIRTHDAY Script Alphabet
710-T-546 Pk./62 $2.29

Happy Birthday with Balloons
710-T-547 Pk./21 $2.29

Add-A-Message Fun Pix®
Serve party cupcakes in an exciting new way—clip on messages, pictures and more with these colorful plastic picks! Great for place markers, announcing awards at banquets and favorite sayings. Four fun colors to go with your favorite baking cups. 3 in. high.
2113-T-7611 Pk./12 $1.99

ORDER ONLINE: WWW.WILTON.COM

NUMERALS

Festive way to mark age or year. Edged in green unless specified.
3 in. high. $0.79

#2 2811-T-9102
#3 2811-T-9103
#4 2811-T-9104
#5 2811-T-9105
#6 2811-T-9106
#7 2811-T-9107
#8 2811-T-9108
#9 2811-T-9109
#0 2811-T-9100
? 2811-T-9110

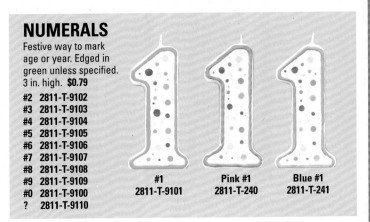

#1 2811-T-9101 **Pink #1** 2811-T-240 **Blue #1** 2811-T-241

Candles

CANDLE SETS

Wilton gives you more choices! Top your cake with candles in the perfect colors—and check out our exciting designs.

Farm
Approx.
1⅝ in. high.
2811-T-9347
Set/4 $3.49

Firefighting
Approx.
1½ in. high.
2811-T-9339
Set/4 $3.49

Baby Things
Approx. 2 in. high.
2811-T-855 Set/4 $3.49

Fiesta
Approx. 1¾ in. high.
2811-T-9345 Set/4 $3.49

**Home
Improvement Tools**
Approx. 2¼ in. high.
2811-T-9136 Set/5 $3.49

Construction Vehicles
Approx. 1¾ in. long.
2811-T-858 Set/4 $3.49

Race Cars
Approx. 1¾ in. high.
2811-T-9135 Set/4 $3.49

**Beach
Sandals**
⅜ in. high;
⅞ in. long.
2811-T-9352
Set/6 $3.49

Margaritas
1¼ in. high.
2811-T-9343
Set/6 $3.49

Champagne Bottles
2 in. high.
2811-T-163 Set/6 $3.49

Beer Cans
1¾ in. high.
2811-T-9326
Set/6 $3.49

NOVELTY

Glow-in-the-Dark

They light up the room even before you light them! These luminous candles will lend an extra touch of fun to any celebration. Assorted colors: white, yellow, green, blue. 2½ in. high.
**2811-T-165
Pk./10 $1.99**

Glow Candle Set

Turn out the lights and get ready to serve your cake in a thrilling glow of color. Set of 4 light stick candle holders with candles gives cakes an aura of excitement that lasts up to 6 hours. No batteries needed—the glow starts when you bend the light sticks. Includes 4 each light sticks, connectors and candles. 6½ in. high.
**2811-T-6215
Set/12 $4.99**

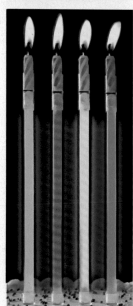

PICK SETS

Put your celebration message in lights! These bright candle picks are a unique and easy way to pick up the party theme on your cake top. Fun colors are just right for the occasion.

Happy Birthday
3 in. high.
2811-T-785
Set/15 $1.99

Congratulations
3 in. high.
2811-T-787 Set/15 $1.99

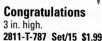

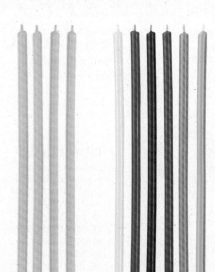

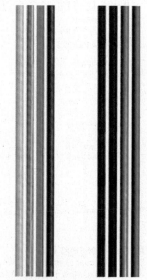

Longs
Sized right for larger cakes or for making a bold statement on any cake. 5⅞ in. high. **Pk./12 $1.99**

White	Multicolor
2811-T-773	2811-T-777

Slenders
6½ in. high.
2811-T-1188
Pk./24 $0.79

"Trick" Sparklers
Blow 'em out—they relight!
6½ in. high. **Pk./18 $0.99**

Assorted	Red and Blue
2811-T-1230	2811-T-704

RAINBOW COLORS

Curly
Twisting, turning fun. 3 in. high.
2811-T-9127
Pk./12 $1.49

Candle Holders
Protects cakes and keeps candles secure. Great colors, 1 in. high.
2811-T-552
Pk./24 $0.99

CLASSIC

Pearlized
Watch them shimmer from the moment you light them! 2½ in. high.
Pk./10 $1.99
White
2811-T-3658
Multicolor
2811-T-3665

Glitter
2½ in. high.
Pk./10 $0.99
White
2811-T-248
Pink 2811-T-244
Blue 2811-T-246
Black
2811-T-247

Celebration
2½ in. high.
Pk./24 $0.69
White 2811-T-207
Pink 2811-T-213
Red 2811-T-209
Blue 2811-T-210
Black 2811-T-224

Assorted Celebration
Classic spirals in attractive two-tones. 2½ in. high.
2811-T-215
Pk./24 $0.69

"Trick"
Blow 'em out —they relight! 2½ in. high. Assorted: White, Yellow, Pink, Blue.
2811-T-220
Pk./10 $0.99

Silver and Gold
2¼ in. high.
Pk./10
$1.49
Silver 2811-T-9123
Gold 2811-T-9122

Shimmer
2½ in. high.
2811-T-3663
Pk./8 $1.99

Lattice
2½ in. high.
2811-T-3656
Pk./8 $1.99

Tricolor
2½ in. high.
2811-T-779
Pk./10 $1.99

Crayons
3¼ in. high. $1.49
2811-T-226 Pk./8
2½ in. high. $1.49
2811-T-227 Pk./10

Triangle "Trick" Sparklers
2½ in. high.
2811-T-278
Pk./9 $0.99

Wavy "Trick" Sparklers
2½ in. high.
2811-T-272
Pk./10 $1.99

Rounds
2½ in. high.
2811-T-284
$0.69

Party Thins
8 in. high.
2811-T-239
Pk./20
$0.99

HOT COLORS

Shimmer
2½ in. high.
2811-T-3662
Pk./8 $1.99

Lattice
2½ in. high.
2811-T-3655
Pk./8 $1.99

Twist
2½ in. high.
2811-T-3659
Pk./8 $2.49

Rounds
2½ in. high.
2811-T-225
Pk./24 $0.69

SOFT COLORS

Shimmer
2½ in. high.
2811-T-3664
Pk./8 $1.99

Lattice
2½ in. high.
2811-T-3657
Pk./8 $1.99

Tricolor
2½ in. high.
2811-T-782
Pk./10 $1.99

Wavy "Trick" Sparklers
2½ in. high.
2811-T-289
Pk./10 $1.99

Tricolor
2½ in. high.
2811-T-781
Pk./10
$1.99

Crayons
3¼ in. high.
2811-T-282
Pk./8 $1.49

Triangle "Trick" Sparklers
2½ in. high.
2811-T-276
Pk./9 $0.99

Wavy "Trick" Sparklers
2½ in. high.
2811-T-270
Pk./10 $1.99

Party Thins
8 in. high.
2811-T-237
Pk./20
$0.99

Crayons
3¼ in. high.
2811-T-292
Pk./8 $1.49

Triangle "Trick" Sparklers
2½ in. high.
2811-T-288
Pk./9 $0.99

Rounds
2½ in. high.
2811-T-291
$0.69

Party Thins
8 in. high.
2811-T-255
Pk./20
$0.99

Musical Candle
Plays "Happy Birthday To You".
4¾ in. high.
2811-T-1231 $3.69

ORDER ONLINE: WWW.WILTON.COM

Cake Toppers

With Wilton toppers, a decorated cake is just minutes away! The excellent detail you expect from Wilton is evident in every design.

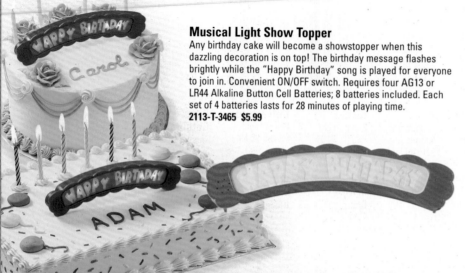

Musical Light Show Topper
Any birthday cake will become a showstopper when this dazzling decoration is on top! The birthday message flashes brightly while the "Happy Birthday" song is played for everyone to join in. Convenient ON/OFF switch. Requires four AG13 or LR44 Alkaline Button Cell Batteries; 8 batteries included. Each set of 4 batteries lasts for 28 minutes of playing time.
2113-T-3465 $5.99

Carousel Separator Set
Snaps together fast—sturdy pony pillars and separator plates provide strong support. Set includes four 9 in. high pony pillars and two 10 in. diameter separator plates.
2103-T-1139 Set/6 $12.99

DOLL PICKS

Mini Doll Pick Set
4¼ in. high with pick.
1511-T-1019 Set/4 $5.99

Teen Doll Pick
Her hair and face are prettier than ever—she'll give your Wonder Mold cakes a realism and sophistication unlike anything you've seen. 7¾ in. high with pick. $2.99
Brunette 2815-T-101
Blond 2815-T-102
Ethnic 2815-T-103

Circus Animals Set*
Handpainted performers, 2½ to 3 in. high.
2113-T-9422 Set/4 $3.99

Dinosaur Party Set*
Reptile revelry! 1¾ to 2½ in. high.
2113-T-9420 Set/4 $3.99

Tumbling Bears Set*
Adorable acrobats, 2 to 2½ in. high.
2113-T-9421 Set/4 $3.99

Small Derby Clowns Set*
2 in. high with pick.
2113-T-2759 Set/6 $1.99

Circus Balloons Set
12 in a bunch, 3 bunches per set, 6½ in. high.
2113-T-2366 Set/36 $2.99

*CAUTION: Contains small parts. Not recommended for use by children 3 years and under

RELIGIOUS

Inspiring decorations add a beautiful touch to spiritual events—Christening, Communion, Confirmation, and more!

Inspirational Cross
Polished resin with finely sculpted scroll and bead highlighting. 5½ in. high.
202-T-398 $14.99

NEW!

Faith Cross Cake Pick
Sparkling cross decoration looks beautiful in cake tops, centerpieces, floral arrangements. Accented with rhinestones, crafted of painted resin. Food safe. 4 in. high cross with 2 in. pick.
1006-T-489 $14.99

NEW!

Faith Cross Favor Accents
Detailed cross accents add an elegant look to favors, decorations, and more! 1 in. long plastic. Tie on with ribbon or attach with hot glue.
Silver 1006-T-4501 Pk./20 $1.99
White 1006-T-7149 Pk./20 $1.99

Communion Girl†
3½ in. high.
2113-T-7878 $3.49

Communion Boy†
3½ in. high.
2113-T-7886 $3.49

† Designed by Ellen Williams

ORDER TOLL FREE: 800-794-5866

Seasonal

Wilton makes every time of year worth celebrating! With so many fun ways to serve cakes, cookies and other treats, it's easy to let everyone taste the excitement of each season.

HALLOWEEN

Bakeware
SILICONE MOLDS

Discover the convenience and easy release of flexible silicone bakeware! Freezer, refrigerator, microwave and dishwasher safe—oven safe to 500°F.

NEW!

Pumpkin Shaped Mini Pumpkin Mold
One mix makes 20-24 pumpkins. 6 cavities, each 2½ x 1½ in. deep.
2105-T-4878 $9.99

NEW!

Petite Pumpkin Mold
One mix makes 40-48 pumpkins. 12 cavities, each 2 x 1 in. deep.
2105-T-4876 $9.99

NEW!

Mini Ghost Mold
One mix makes 20-24 ghosts. 6 cavities, each 2½ x 1½ in. deep.
2105-T-4877 $9.99

Mini Jack-O-Lantern Mold
One mix makes 20-24 jack-o-lanterns. 6 cavities, each 2½ x 1½ in. deep.
2105-T-4815 $9.99

Spooky Ghost Pan
A welcome vision at all your Halloween happenings—from costume parties at home to celebrations at school. Great for easy-to-decorate cakes and gelatin desserts. One-mix pan is 11½ x 11½ x 2 in. deep. Aluminum.
2105-T-2090 $8.99

Iridescents! Jack-O-Lantern Pan
This bright, colorful shape is as much fun for serving party treats as it is for baking! Designed for quick, easy cake decorating. Also ideal for crisped rice cereal treats, molded gelatin, bread dough and more. One-mix pan is 11¾ x 11⅛ x 2 in. deep. Aluminum.
2105-T-2059 $6.49

Non-Stick Mini Pumpkin and Ghost Pan
Perfect size for trick-or-treaters! Non-stick steel releases treats easily. One mix makes 24-28 treats. 6 cavities, each 2¾ x 1¼ in. deep.
2105-T-1540 $6.99

Petite Jack-O-Lantern Pan
Make personal petite smiling pumpkins. One mix makes 9-13 dozen jack-o-lanterns. 12 cavities, each 2 x 1⅛ in. deep. Aluminum.
2105-T-8462 $10.99

Mini Ghost Pan
Create gobs of goblins at one time! One mix makes 9-15 ghosts ready for decorating. 6 cavities, each 4 x 4⅞ x 1⅜ in. deep. Aluminum.
2105-T-3845 $11.99

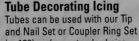

Colors & Icings

HALLOWEEN COLOR GUIDE

Orange	Black	Violet	White

Halloween Icing Colors Set
.5 oz. jars of Black and Orange. Certified Kosher.
601-T-3010 Set/2 $2.99

Color Mist™ Food Color Spray
Gives decorators the versatility and dazzling effects of an airbrush in a convenient can! Use it to transform a plain iced cake with sensational color, add splashes of holiday color to iced cookies and cupcakes. No mess, taste-free formula. 1.5 oz. Certified Kosher. $2.99

Orange	710-T-5507
Black	710-T-5506
Violet	710-T-5504

FoodWriter™ Edible Color Markers
Use like ink markers to add fun, dazzling color to countless foods. Kids love 'em! Decorate on fondant, color flow, royal icing designs and cookies. Includes Black and Orange markers. .35 oz. Certified Kosher.
609-T-101 Set/2 $3.99

Ready-to-Decorate Icing
Anyone can decorate with Wilton Ready-to-Decorate Icing! Our brilliant colors and 4 decorating tips make it a breeze to add an exciting finishing touch to treats—without mixing or mess. 6.4 oz. Certified Kosher. $3.99

Orange	710-T-4410
Black	710-T-4404
Violet	710-T-4408
White	710-T-4402

Tube Decorating Icing
Tubes can be used with our Tip and Nail Set or Coupler Ring Set (p. 136) and any standard size Wilton metal tip. Colors match Wilton Icing Colors (p. 136). 4.25 oz. Certified Kosher. $1.99

Orange	704-T-212
Black	704-T-206
Violet	704-T-242
White	704-T-200

Tube Decorating Gel
Transparent gels are great for writing messages and decorating cakes and cookies. Colors match Wilton Icing Colors (p. 136). .75 oz. Certified Kosher. $1.49

Orange	704-T-312
Black	704-T-306
Violet	704-T-342
White	704-T-302

Party

Baking Cups
Microwave-safe paper. Standard size, 2 in. diameter, Mini size, 1¼ in. diameter.

Standard Pk./75 **$1.99**
Mini Pk./100 **$1.99**

Happy Haunters
Standard 415-T-961
Mini 415-T-962

Spooky Ghosts
Standard 415-T-1601
Mini 415-T-2027

Smiling Pumpkins
Standard 415-T-324
Mini 415-T-7572

Wacky Witch Silly-Feet! Silicone Baking Cups
Give your Halloween treats feet and watch your guests step up to grab them! Bright silicone cups are perfect for creating cupcakes with character. Add fun faces with icing or candy to make witches, ghosts and more. Also great for holding candy, fruit and other treats.
Standard 415-T-9430 Pk./4 **$9.99**

Party Bags
Colorful Halloween designs for candy and cookie treats. Unless otherwise noted, 20 plastic bags, 20 ties included. 4 x 9 ½ in.
Pk./20 **$1.99**

Happy Haunters
1912-T-2389

Spooky Ghosts
1912-T-1040

Smiling Pumpkins
1912-T-1224

Silicone Baking Cups
No muffin pan needed! Bake and serve in these reusable oven-safe cups.
Standard 415-T-9408
Pk./12 **$9.99**

Shaped Smiling Pumpkin with Drawstring
Large bags are 9½ x 7 in.
1912-T-2126 Pk./15

Icing Decorations
Perfect for topping cupcakes, cookies and ice cream. Mint-flavored. Certified Kosher. **$2.29**

Petite Ghosts
710-T-3030 Pk./12

Smiling Pumpkins
710-T-7200 Pk./12

Fun Pix®
Add a spooky touch to cakes, cupcakes, ice cream and more. Approx. 3½ in. high.
$1.99

Happy Haunters
2113-T-9216
Pk./12

Smiling Pumpkins
2113-T-7505
Pk./24

Foil Pumpkins
2113-T-713
Pk./12

Candy

Candy Melts®*
Ideal for molding, dipping or coating. Artificially vanilla flavored unless otherwise indicated. 14 oz. bag. Certified Kosher Dairy. **$2.50**

Orange	1911-T-1631	Yellow	1911-T-463
Dark Green	1911-T-405	Dark Cocoa	1911-T-358
Light Cocoa	1911-T-544	Chocolate Mint	1911-T-1920
White	1911-T-498	Lavender	1911-T-403

*Brand confectionery coating.

Halloween Candy Necklace Kit
It's the perfect party activity—kit makes 8 tasty necklaces! Give each kid their own candy necklace pack and watch them have a ball stringing their own treats to wear and share. They'll love the cool colors and great flavors—and stringing the candy beads and charm is a breeze. Includes 8 necklace packs; each pack contains over 50 candy beads (artificial orange and grape flavors), 1 candy pumpkin charm (artificial orange flavor) and 17 ½ in. elastic string.
2104-T-1274 **$2.99**

Halloween Pretzel Mold
1 design, 6 cavities.
2115-T-1500 **$1.99**

Happy Haunters Lollipop Mold
4 designs, 4 cavities.
2115-T-1436 **$1.99**

Monsters Candy Mold
4 designs, 4 cavities.
2115-T-1752 **$1.99**

Smiling Pumpkins Lollipop Mold
1 design, 7 cavities.
2115-T-1750 **$1.99**

Jack-O-Lantern Lollipop Mold
1 design, 8 cavities.
2115-T-1704 **$1.99**

Halloween MEGA PACK Candy Making Kit
Everything you need to make creepy lollipops, pretzels and candies for your trick-or-treaters. It's easy and fun—with lots of fun shapes and colorful Candy Melts®! Kit includes: 3 molds: Pumpkin and Mummy Pretzel (2 designs, 6 cavities), Ghost/Pumpkin/Cat Lollipop (3 designs, 6 cavities), Spider/Ghost/Pumpkin Candy (3 designs, 7 cavities); 20 oz. Candy Melts brand confectionery coating (5 oz. each Orange, White, Light Cocoa and Green); 20 Lollipop Sticks (6 in.); 4 Disposable Decorating Bags; Decorating Brush and 20 Party Bags/Ties (10 each Purple and Orange).
2104-T-1433 **$9.99**

Spooky Ghost Candy Mold
1 design, 8 cavities.
2115-T-1407 **$1.99**

See pages 166-169 for more Wilton candy items.

Holds 1 standard cupcake.
415-T-1212 Pk./3 $2.99

NEW!

Holds 4 standard cupcakes.
415-T-3220 Pk./3 $4.99

Happy Haunters Cupcake Boxes

Brightly-patterned window boxes are the perfect way to hold and display your cupcakes! Each box includes an insert with recessed space to hold standard cupcakes safely in place. Easy to fold assembly; great for gifts and favors! Choose 1- or 4-cupcake size.

Jack-O-Lantern Cookie Treat Pan

Create cookie blossoms, rice cereal treats and candy pops. Recipe included. Six-cavity pan, each cavity measures 3¼ x ¼ in. deep. Aluminum.
2105-T-8100 $8.99

Cookie Treat Sticks
6 in. 1912-T-9319 Pk./20 $1.99
8 in. 1912-T-9318 Pk./20 $2.99

Ghost
2113-T-3464

Pumpkin
2113-T-3463

Bobbling Cupcake Toppers
Food-safe design features hand-painted details that make plain cupcakes more exciting. 2¼ in. high.
Pk./6 $2.99

Halloween Marshmallow Toppers
A fun new way to top cupcakes, cookies, ice cream and more! Soft, delicious marshmallow in happy holiday shapes.
710-T-458 Pk./6 $1.99

NEW!

Halloween Cupcake and Cookie Stencils
Just place one of the fun designs over your baked treat, then sprinkle with Wilton Cake Sparkles™ or Colored Sugars (sold at right) or spray with Color Mist™ Food Color Spray (p. 193). 8 designs.
417-T-499 $1.99

Pre-Baked Cookie Kits

No baking, just fun! Everything you need is included to make great haunted designs.

NEW!

NEW!

NEW!

Pre-Baked Halloween Cookie Kit
Decorate 8 spooky pumpkin-shaped cookies! It's easy and fun for the whole family. Includes 8 pre-baked cookies (approximately 4 in. high), creamy orange icing mix, colorful candies (spice drops, mini round candies and spearmint leaves) and decorating instructions.
2104-T-4320 $9.99

Pre-Baked and Pre-Assembled Halloween Cookie House Kit
Everyone will have a howling good time decorating this spooky house! It's the perfect centerpiece for home, school or office celebrations—so easy and fun to make. Includes pre-baked, pre-assembled cookie house (measures 7 x 4 x 8 in. high), orange and black decorating icing mixes, colorful candy (purple and orange mini round candies, orange, yellow and black jelly beans, purple round candies), 1 ghost icing decoration, 2 round decorating tips, 2 disposable decorating bags, cardboard base and complete decorating instructions.
2104-T-4319 $12.99

Pre-Baked Halloween Cookie House Kit
Easy to assemble and fun to decorate—it's the ideal family activity for Halloween. Includes 10 pre-baked gingerbread house pieces (assembled house measures 7 ¾ x 4 x 8 ½ in. high), orange and black decorating icing mixes, 1 ghost icing decoration, colorful candy (purple and orange mini round candies, jelly beans and candy corn), 2 decorating tips, 2 disposable decorating bags, cardboard base, complete assembly and decorating instructions.
2104-T-4318 $12.99

Sprinkles

INDIVIDUAL BOTTLES

Shake up your Halloween treats with fun colors and designs. Try our new Jumbo Sprinkles—big bold toppers perfect for brownies, cookies and more. Plastic bottles for convenient pouring and storing. Certified Kosher.
Jumbo Sprinkles $3.99   Sprinkles $2.29

NEW!

NEW!

Jumbo Pumpkin
3.5 oz. bottle
710-T-566

Jumbo Ghost
3 oz. bottle
710-T-567

Hallow Pumpkin Mix
2.5 oz. bottle
710-T-182

Halloween Confetti
2.5 oz. bottle
710-T-184

Halloween Nonpareils
3 oz. bottle
710-T-584

Ghost Mix
2.5 oz. bottle
710-T-767

Orange Sugar
3.25 oz. bottle
710-T-759

Black Sugar
3.25 oz. bottle
710-T-762

Lavender Sugar
3.25 oz. bottle
710-T-758

Sparkling Sugars
Coarse texture; brilliant sparkle. 8 oz. Certified Kosher. $4.49

Orange/White
710-T-572

Cake Sparkles™
Edible glitter, .25 oz. bottle. Certified Kosher. $2.89

Orange
703-T-1308

Black
703-T-1302

Purple
703-T-1266

ASSORTMENTS

4-Mix Halloween
Includes Halloween Mix, Halloween Nonpareils, Black and Orange Sugars. 4.4 oz. Certified Kosher.
710-T-728 $4.99

6-Mix Halloween Pumpkin
Includes Black and Orange Nonpareils, Halloween Confetti, Halloween Pumpkin Mix, Black, Orange and Purple Sugars. 7.1 oz. Certified Kosher.
710-T-185 $5.99

Cookie Cutters

Halloween Push 'N Print™ Cutter Set

NEW!

Serve cookies that make a great impression—use Push 'N Print Cutters to emboss a fun design before baking! It's so easy! Load one of the 3 imprint disks in the cutter, cut the cookie, then press the plunger with disk still in place to imprint the design. Bake, cool and serve a treat that's perfect for celebrations and cookie gift baskets. Great for embossed fondant decorations too! Disks are 2⅞ in. diameter. Recipe included.
2308-T-4002 Set/4 $6.99

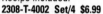

COMFORT GRIP™ CUTTERS

These easy-grip cutters with extra-deep sides are perfect for cutting so many favorite foods into spectacular shapes. The cushion grip gives you comfortable control even when cutting thick desserts. Recipe included. Stainless steel sides, 4½ x 4½ x 1½ in. deep.
$2.99

**Pumpkin
2310-T-600**

**Monster Head
2310-T-643**

**Witch's Hat
2310-T-630**

**Ghost
2310-T-607**

GRIPPY™ CUTTERS

4 Pc. Grippy™ Set

Safe, easy cutting, with a comfortable grip and deep plastic sides. Four shapes include ghost, cat, pumpkin and bat, approx. 3 ½ in.
2311-T-257 Set/4 $3.99

COOKIE SCOOP

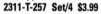

Festive color and convenient design make holiday baking more fun! Scoops and releases approx. 1 Tablespoon of dough with ease. Dishwasher safe plastic.
**417-T-324
$2.49**

METAL CUTTERS

Put variety in your cookie-making with fun Halloween multi-shape sets. There are styles to please everyone. Recipe included.

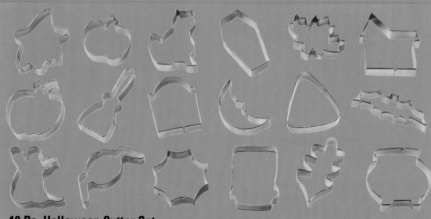

18 Pc. Halloween Cutter Set

Set of 18 includes witch, pumpkin, cat, coffin, maple leaf, house, apple, witch's broom, tombstone, moon, candy corn, bat, ghost, spider, spider web, Frankenstein, oak leaf and cauldron, each approx. 3 in.
2308-T-1131 Set/18 $9.99

3 Pc. Halloween Cutter Set

NEW!

Set of 3 includes pumpkin, ghost and cat. Each approx. 3 in. Colored aluminum.
2308-T-1265 Set/3 $3.49

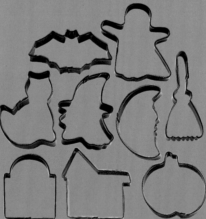

9 Pc. Halloween Cutter Set

Set includes bat, ghost, cat, witch, moon, witch's broom, tombstone, house and pumpkin, each approx. 3 to 3¾ in. Colored aluminum.
2308-T-2501 Set/9 $9.99

4 Pc. Spooky Shapes Cutter Set

Set includes moon, pumpkin, witch and ghost, each approx. 3 in. Coated metal.
2308-T-1200 Set/4 $4.49

12 Pc. Halloween Mini Cutter Set

Set includes pumpkin, skull, witch's hat, tombstone, bat, acorn, cat, house, maple leaf, moon, oak leaf and ghost, each approx. 1½ in.
2308-T-1246 Set/12 $4.99

Nesting Cutter Sets

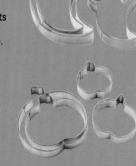

Create boo-tiful Halloween treats in 4 sizes. Each cuts neatly and is easy to handle. Sizes from 2¼ to 4 ½ in.
Set/4 $4.49

**Ghosts
2308-T-1238**

**Pumpkins
2308-T-1210**

6 Pc. Halloween Mini Cutter Set

Set includes cat, bat, pumpkin, ghost, moon and skull, each approx. 1½ in.
**2308-T-1211
Set/6 $2.99**

ORDER TOLL FREE: 800-794-5866

CHRISTMAS
Bakeware
SILICONE MOLDS

Discover the convenience and easy release of flexible silicone bakeware! Freezer, refrigerator, microwave and dishwasher safe—oven safe to 500°F.

Petite Tree Mold
One mix makes 40-48 trees. 12 cavities, each 2 x 1 in. deep.
2105-T-4898 $9.99

Mini Tree Mold
One mix makes 20-24 trees. 6 cavities, each 2½ x 1 in. deep.
2105-T-4830 $9.99

Mini Snowflake Mold
One mix makes 20-24 snowflakes. 6 cavities, each 2½ x 1½ in. deep.
2105-T-4831 $9.99

Non-Stick Mini Snowman and Mitten Pan
Perfect size for holiday gift basket treats! Non-stick steel releases treats easily. One mix makes 24-28 snowmen and mittens. 6 cavities, each 2¾ x 1¼ in. deep.
2105-T-3513 $6.99

NEW!
Non-Stick Mini Holiday Pan
So versatile! Includes 12 classic shapes for your single-serving holiday cookies and molded desserts. Easy-release non-stick steel delivers great detail. 12 cavities, each approximately 2¾ x 2¼ x ½ in. deep.
2105-T-8122 $9.99

DIMENSIONS® DECORATIVE BAKEWARE

With Dimensions non-stick cast aluminum bakeware, anyone can create Christmas desserts with elegant shapes and spectacular detail. Heavyweight cast aluminum conducts heat extremely evenly. Premium non-stick surface for easy release and cleanup. Aluminum.

Gift
11⅛ x 9⅝ x 1½ in. deep. 11 cup capacity.
2105-T-5027 $27.99

Snowflake
12 in. x 2¾ in.; 11 cup capacity.*
2105-T-5030 $27.99

4-Cavity Mini Snowflakes
Each cavity is 5 x 2¼ in. deep and holds 1½ cups.
2105-T-5028 $27.99

Step-By-Step Snowman Pan
Just bake, ice and decorate. He's also perfect for molding gelatin and ice cream, salads, baking bread and more. One-mix pan is 12 x 9¼ x 2 in. deep. Aluminum.
2105-T-2083 $6.49

Iridescents! Tree Pan
This bright, colorful shape is as much fun for serving party treats as it is for baking! Designed for quick, easy decorating. Also ideal for crisped rice cereal treats, molded gelatin, bread dough and more. One-mix pan is 14 x 10 x 2 in. deep. Aluminum.
2105-T-2081 $6.49

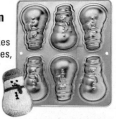

Mini Snowman Pan
Bake a blizzard of snowmen! One mix makes 12-18 snowmen. 6 cavities, each 2⅞ x 4⅝ x 1⅞ in. deep. Aluminum.
2105-T-472 $11.99

Bite-Size Gingerbread Boy Pan
Bake plenty of fun little guys for everyone. One mix makes 24-36 boys. 9 cavities, each 2¾ x 3⅜ x ¾ in. deep. Aluminum.
2105-T-926 $11.99

Colors & Icings
CHRISTMAS COLOR GUIDE

| Red | Kelly Green | Leaf Green | White |

Holiday Icing Colors Set
.5 oz. jars, Red-Red and Kelly Green. Certified Kosher.
601-T-3011 Pk./2 $2.99

Color Mist™ Food Color Spray
The dazzling effects of an airbrush in a convenient can! Use it to transform a plain iced cake with sensational color, add splashes of holiday color to iced cookies and cupcakes. No mess, taste-free formula. 1.5 oz. Certified Kosher. $2.99
Green 710-T-5503
Red 710-T-5500

FoodWriter™ Edible Color Markers
Use like ink markers to add fun, dazzling color to countless foods. Kids love 'em! Decorate on fondant, color flow, royal icing designs and cookies. Includes .35 oz. Green and Red markers. Certified Kosher.
609-T-102 Set/2 $3.99

Ready-to-Decorate Icing
Anyone can decorate with Wilton Ready-to-Decorate Icing! Our brilliant colors and four decorating tips make it a breeze to add an exciting finishing touch to treats—without mixing or mess. 6.4 oz. Certified Kosher. $3.99
Green 710-T-4401
Red 710-T-4400
White 710-T-4402

Tube Decorating Icing
Can be used with our Tip and Nail Set or Coupler Ring Set (p. 135) and any standard size Wilton metal tip. Colors match Wilton Icing Colors (p. 135). 4.25 oz. Certified Kosher. $1.99
Kelly Green 704-T-227
Red 704-T-218
White 704-T-200

Tube Decorating Gel
Transparent gels are great for writing messages and decorating cakes and cookies. Colors match Wilton Icing Colors (p. 135). .75 oz. Certified Kosher. $1.49
Leaf Green 704-T-324
Red 704-T-318
White 704-T-302

Party

Baking Cups
Microwave-safe paper. Standard size, 2 in. diameter; Mini size, 1¼ in. diameter.
Standard Pk./75 **$1.99**
Mini Pk./100 **$1.99**

Shaped Party Bags with Drawstring
Large bags are 9½ x 7 in.
$1.99

Shaped Shiver Me Snowman
1912-T-9142 Pk./15

Shaped Santa
1912-T-1328 Pk./15

NEW!

Shiver Me Snowman
Standard 415-T-5766
Mini 415-T-5765

Santa
Standard 415-T-5295
Mini 415-T-5405

Party Bags
NEW!
Colorful Christmas designs for candy and cookie treats. 20 plastic bags, 20 ties included. 4 x 9½ in.
Pk./20 $1.99

Shiver Me Snowman
1912-T-9140

Santa
1912-T-1325

Santa Icing Decorations
Perfect for topping cupcakes, cookies and ice cream. Mint-flavored. Certified Kosher.
710-T-697 $2.29 Pk./12

NEW!

Santa Silly-Feet! Silicone Baking Cups
Give your holiday treats feet and watch your guests step up to grab them! Bright silicone cups are perfect for creating cupcakes with character. Add fun faces with icing or candy to make Santa, elves and more. Also great for holding candy, fruit and other treats.
Standard 415-T-9439 Pk./4 $9.99

Silicone Baking Cups
NEW!
No muffin pan needed! Bake and serve in these reusable oven-safe cups.
Standard
415-T-9405 Pk./12 $9.99
Mini
415-T-9412 Pk./12 $7.99

Fun Pix®
NEW!
Add a fun holiday touch to cakes, cupcakes, ice cream and more. 3½ in. high.
Pk./24 $1.99

Shiver Me Snowman
2113-T-720

Santa
2113-T-7610

Candy

Santa Pretzel Mold
Easy to mold, fun to eat. Position pretzel rod, spoon in your favorite melted Candy Melts®* and refrigerate to set. Use with lollipop sticks, too. 1 design, 6 cavities.
2115-T-1501 $1.99

Twinkling Trees Lollipop Mold
1 design, 10 cavities.
2115-T-1406 $1.99

Snowflake Lollipop Mold
1 design, 6 cavities.
2115-T-1705 $1.99

Christmas Character Lollipop Mold
3 designs, 6 cavities.
2115-T-1567 $1.99

NEW!

Christmas MEGA Candy Making Kit
Everything you need to make jolly holiday candies for parties and stocking stuffers! It's easy and fun—with lots of fun shapes and colorful Candy Melts®! Kit includes: 3 fun-shaped molds: Candy Cane & North Pole Pretzel (2 designs, 5 cavities), Holiday Tree Lollipop (1 design, 10 cavities), Jolly Santa Candy (2 designs, 4 cavities); 20 oz. Wilton Candy Melts® Brand confectionery coating (5 oz. each Red, Green, White, Light Cocoa), 20 (6 in.) Lollipop Sticks; 4 Disposable Decorating Bags; 1 Decorating Brush, 20 Party Bags with Ties (10 each Red and Green.
2104-T-4680 $9.99

Candy Melts®*
Ideal for molding, dipping or coating. Artificially vanilla flavored unless otherwise indicated. 14 oz. bag. Certified Kosher Dairy. **$2.50**

Red	1911-T-499	**Dark Cocoa**	1911-T-358
White	1911-T-498	**Chocolate Mint**	1911-T-1920
Dark Green	1911-T-405	**Yellow**	1911-T-463
Light Cocoa	1911-T-544		

*Brand confectionery coating.

See pages 166-169 for more Wilton candy items.

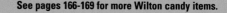

Bon Bon Cups
Perfect for candy!
1 in. diam.
Red Foil
415-T-314
Pk./75 $1.49
Silver Foil
415-T-307
Pk./72 $1.49
(36 pure aluminum
36 paper)
Gold Foil
415-T-306 Pk./75 $1.49

Red/Green Mini Cups
Mixed, glassine
paper. 1 in.
1912-T-1247
Pk./72 $1.49

Christmas Cupcake and Cookie Stencils
Turn plain treats into holiday visions.
Just place one of the fun designs
over your baked treat, then sprinkle
with Wilton Cake Sparkles™ or
Colored Sugars (shown at right)
or use FoodWriter™ Edible Color
Markers or Color Mist™ Food Color
Spray (p. 197). 8 designs.
417-T-510 $1.99

Santa Bobbling Cupcake Toppers
Top off that special treat with
this fun bobbling topper.
Food-safe design features handpainted detail that makes even
plain cupcakes more exciting.
2 in. high.
2113-T-2005 Pk./6 $2.99

Petite Loaf Baking Cups
For gift breads. Fits Petite Loaf
Pan (p.154). Microwave-safe
paper. White.
415-T-450 Pk./50 $1.49

Christmas Cookie Tree Cutter Kit
Create a beautiful Yule tree as a perfect holiday centerpiece
—it's easy and fun! Just bake, stack and decorate. Kit includes
10 plastic star cookie cutters in graduated sizes from small
to large, 3 disposable decorating bags, round decorating tip,
cookie and icing recipes, baking and decorating instructions
for 4 great designs. Tree measures approx. 8 x 11 in. high.
2104-T-1555 $7.99

Christmas Tree
2105-T-8101

Snowman
2105-T-8107

Cookie Treat Pans
Treats on a stick are so easy; just press dough
or rice cereal treat mixture into the pan, insert a
cookie stick, then bake, cool and decorate. Each
pan makes six individual treats, approx. 4 x ½ in.
deep. Recipe included. Aluminum. $8.99

Cookie Treat Sticks
6 in. 1912-T-9319 Pk./20 $1.99
8 in. 1912-T-9318 Pk./20 $2.99

Star
2105-T-8102

Plastic Cutters
Great shapes for
end-of-year
celebrations!
3 x 4 in.
high.
$0.69

Christmas Tree
2303-T-132

5-Pt. Star
2303-T-135

Holiday Red Cookie Scoop
Festive color and convenient design make
holiday baking more fun! Scoops and
releases approx. 1 tablespoon of dough
with ease. Dishwasher safe plastic.
417-T-320 $2.49

Sprinkles

JUMBO SPRINKLES
Try our new Jumbo Sprinkles—big bold toppers perfect for cookies,
brownies and more. Plastic bottles for convenient pouring and
storing. Certified Kosher. $3.99

NEW!

NEW!

NEW!

Trees
2.8 oz. bottle
710-T-568

Snowflakes
2.6 oz. bottle
710-T-569

Gingerbread Boys
2.5 oz. bottle
710-T-586

INDIVIDUAL BOTTLES
Shake up your holiday treats with fun colors and designs. Plastic
bottles for convenient pouring and storing. Certified Kosher.

NEW!

Peppermint Crunch
7 oz. bottle
710-T-1108 $4.49

Twinkling Trees Mix
2.5 oz. bottle
710-T-696 $2.29

Christmas Confetti
2.5 oz. bottle
710-T-172 $2.29

Christmas Nonpareils
3 oz. bottle
710-T-585 $2.29

Cinnamon Drops
3 oz. bottle
710-T-769 $2.29

Snowflake Mix
2.5 oz. bottle
710-T-797 $2.29

Chocolate Jimmies
2.5 oz. bottle
710-T-774 $2.29

Red Sugar
3.25 oz. bottle
710-T-766 $2.29

Dark Green Sugar
3.25 oz. bottle
710-T-764 $2.29

Sparkling Sugars
Easy-pour sugars have a coarse texture and brilliant sparkle.
8 oz. bottle. Certified Kosher. $4.49

Holiday Mix
710-T-308

Red/ White
710-T-998

Green/ White
710-T-997

Cake Sparkles™
Edible glitter in .25 oz. bottle. Certified Kosher. $2.89

Red
703-T-1284

Green
703-T-1278

White
703-T-1290

ASSORTMENTS

4-Mix
Includes
Christmas
Trees Mix,
Christmas
Nonpareils,
Dark Green and Red Sugars.
3.95 oz. Certified Kosher.
710-T-729 $4.99

6-Mix
Includes
Christmas
Nonpareils,
Confetti,
Twinkling Trees
Mix, Green, Red and White
Sugars. 7.1 oz. Certified Kosher.
710-T-755 $5.99

Cookie Cutters

NEW!

Christmas Push 'N Print™ Cutter Set

Serve cookies that make a great impression—use Push 'N Print Cutters to emboss a fun design before baking! It's so easy! Load one of the 3 imprint disks in the cutter, cut the cookie, then press the plunger with disk still in place to imprint the design. Bake, cool and serve a treat that's perfect for celebrations and cookie gift baskets. Great for embossed fondant decorations too! Disks are 2⅞ in. diameter. Recipe included.
2308-T-4003 Set/4 $6.99

COMFORT GRIP™ CUTTERS

These easy-grip cutters with extra-deep sides are perfect for cutting so many favorite foods into spectacular shapes. The cushion grip gives you comfortable control even when cutting thick desserts. Recipe included. Stainless steel sides, 4½ x 4½ x 1½ in. deep.
$2.99

Candy Cane
2310-T-644

Santa Hat
2310-T-640

Christmas Tree
2310-T-604

Gingerbread Boy
2310-T-602

Mitten
2310-T-639

Snowman
2310-T-634

Star
2310-T-631

GRIPPY™ CUTTER SET

Safe, easy cutting, with a comfortable grip and deep plastic sides. Four shapes include stocking, tree, star and gingerbread boy, each approx. 3½ in.
2311-T-260 Set/4 $3.99

White Cookie Icing

Use this quick-setting microwavable icing to cover your cookies with a shiny finish —perfect for decorating with colorful Wilton Icing Writer™ accents! Easy to use—just heat and squeeze onto cookies using the convenient cap. Sets smooth in just 45 minutes. 10 oz. bottle covers 12 (3 in.) cookies. Certified Kosher.
704-T-481 $4.49

METAL CUTTERS

Put variety in your cookie-making with fun Christmas multi-shape sets. There are styles to please everyone. Recipe included.

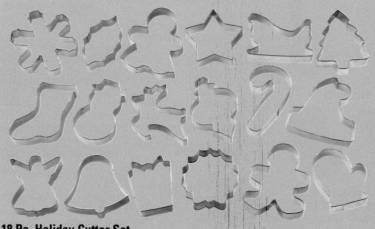

18 Pc. Holiday Cutter Set
Snowflake, holly leaf, gingerbread girl, star, sleigh, tree, stocking, snowman, reindeer, ornament, candy cane, Santa hat, angel, bell, gift, wreath, gingerbread boy and mitten. Each approx. 3 in.
2308-T-1132 Set/18 $9.99

NEW!

3 Pc. Christmas Cutter Set
Set of 3 includes snowflake, gingerbread boy and tree, each approx. 3 to 3¾ in. Colored aluminum.
2308-T-1266 Set/3 $3.49

9 Pc. Holiday Cutter Set
Candy cane, gingerbread girl, stocking, angel, star, bell, snowman, tree and gingerbread boy, each approx. 3 to 3¾ in. Colored aluminum.
2308-T-2500 Set/9 $9.99

4 Pc. Jolly Shapes Cutter Set
Stocking, star, tree and candy cane, each approx. 3 in. Coated metal.
2308-T-1201 Set/4 $4.49

12 Pc. Holiday Mini Cutter Set
Star, angel, gingerbread girl, stocking, candy cane, teddy bear, bell, holly leaf, tree, gingerbread boy, ornament, and sleigh. Each approx. 1½ in.
2308-T-1250 Set/12 $4.99

6 Pc. Holiday Mini Cutter Set
Bell, gingerbread boy, holly leaf, tree, candy cane and angel, each approx. 1½ in.
2308-T-1214 Set/6 $2.99

4 Pc. Nesting Cutter Sets
Bake your favorite holiday shapes in four fun sizes! Quality metal cuts neatly and is easy to handle. Sizes from 5 to 2½ in.
Set/4 $4.49

Snowflakes
2308-T-1244

Gingerbread Boys
2308-T-1239

Cookie Presses

Cookie Pro ULTRA II

Making traditional spritz cookies has never been so easy! Cookie Pro Ultra II is designed to be the easiest to fill, most comfortable press you've ever used. And, with 12 terrific shapes, plus 4 fun mini cookie designs, your holiday cookie baskets will be more festive than ever! Includes complete instructions and delicious recipes.
2104-T-4018 Set/17 $24.99

Twelve Disks in Festive Shapes

Plus 4 BONUS Disks For Mini Cookies!

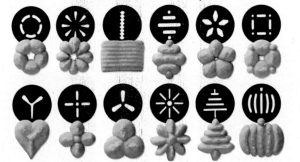

COOKIE MASTER™ *Plus*
Cordless Cookie Press

Our cordless cookie press is so powerful and easy to operate, you'll use it all year to create cookies, appetizers, desserts and more. Exclusive patented reverse action means there's no need to take press apart for refilling. Ergonomic design is shaped to fit in your hand for excellent comfort.

Includes 12 aluminum disks in classic and seasonal shapes, 4 accent tips for decorating and filling and 2 bonus recipe booklets—sweet and savory. Uses 4 AA batteries, not included.
2104-T-4008 Set/19 $39.99

12 Disk Designs

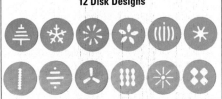

4 Accent Tips

COMFORT GRIP™
Cookie Press

Experience a classic press that is truly comfortable. Its ergonomic handle feels great in your hand and the easy-squeeze action releases perfectly shaped dough. Clear barrel takes the guesswork out of refilling. Fluted bottom raises press off the cookie sheet for better-defined shapes. Includes 12 cookie disks in a variety of shapes and our classic spritz recipe.
2104-T-4011 Set/13 $12.99

12 Disk Designs

Bakeware
RECIPE RIGHT® NON-STICK

Built with all the right qualities for better baking results. Pan dimensions are embossed on handles for easy reference. Heavy-gauge construction means pans spread heat evenly and won't warp. Non-stick coating provides exceptionally quick release and easy cleanup.
5 year warranty. Aluminum.

15 x 10 in. Cookie Sheet
2105-T-967 $4.49

12 Cup Muffin Pan
2105-T-954 $5.49

24 Cup Mini Muffin Pan
2105-T-914 $8.99

Bake Easy!™ Non-Stick Spray

This convenient non-stick spray helps your baked goods release perfectly. Just a light, even coating does the job. Use Bake Easy! for all mixes and recipes —cookies, muffins, cupcakes, brownies, breads and more. Versatile for all types of baking and cooking. 6 oz.
702-T-6018 $2.99

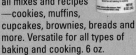

Gingerbread Kits

NEW!

Pre-Baked Ultimate Gingerbread House Kit
This house is so huge, with tons of icing and colorful candy, that everyone can have fun! Includes pre-baked house pieces and trees, 3 pks. icing mix, decorating bags, 2 tips, icing decorations, candy and complete instructions. House measures 10¾ x 9 x 11¾ in. high.
2104-T-1353 $39.99

Pre-Baked Gingerbread Boy Cookie Decorating Kit
Decorate 8 fun cookies! Great for gifts or special treats. Includes cookies, icing mix, colorful candies, decorating bag, tip and complete instructions.
2104-T-1090 $9.99

Pre-Baked Gingerbread House Kit
Includes pre-baked house pieces, icing mix, assorted candies, decorating bag and tip, cardboard base and complete instructions and decorating ideas. House measures 5¼ x 5½ x 4¾ in. high.
2104-T-1537 $9.99

Pre-Baked/Pre-Assembled Gingerbread House Kit
Includes assembled house with cardboard base, icing mix, candies, decorating bag and tip and complete instructions and decorating ideas. House measures 5½ x 5½ x 4½ in. high.
2104-T-1516 $12.99

Pre-Baked Gingerbread House Kit
Includes pre-baked gingerbread pieces, icing mix, assorted candies, decorating bag and tip, cardboard base and complete instructions and decorating ideas. House measures 8 x 7 x 6½ in. high.
2104-T-1509 $12.99

Pre-Baked Gingerbread Tree Kit
Just stack pre-baked star cookies, decorate with icing and candy and add the star icing decoration tree top! Includes cookies, white and green icing mix, icing decorations, candies, 2 decorating tips, 2 decorating bags and complete instructions. Tree measures 5½ x 8¼ in. high.
2104-T-2621 $9.99

HANUKKAH

Hanukkah Cookie Cutter Set
Includes Torah, menorah, 6-point star and dreidel, each approx. 3 in. Colored metal.
2308-T-1262
Set/4 $4.49

6-Point Star Cookie Cutter
3 x 4 in. high, plastic.
2303-T-122 $0.69

Colored Sugar
Plastic bottles for pouring and storing. 3.25 oz. Certified Kosher. **$2.29**

Blue	Yellow
710-T-750	710-T-754

Cake Sparkles™
Edible glitter, .25 oz. bottle. Certified Kosher. **$2.89**

Blue	Yellow	White
703-T-1314	703-T-1272	703-T-1290

Hanukkah Lollipop Mold
5 designs, 10 cavities.
2115-T-1405
$1.99

Candy Melts®*
Ideal for all your candy making—molding, dipping or coating. Artificially vanilla flavored unless otherwise indicated. 14 oz. bag. Certified Kosher Dairy. **$2.50**

Blue	1911-T-448	Light Cocoa	1911-T-544
Yellow	1911-T-463	Dark Cocoa	1911-T-358
White	1911-T-498	Chocolate Mint	1911-T-1920

*Brand confectionery coating.

See pages 166-169 for more Wilton candy items.

Colors & Icings

HANUKKAH COLOR GUIDE

Blue	Yellow	White

Color Mist™ Food Color Spray
The dazzling effects of an airbrush in a convenient can! Use it to transform a plain iced cake with sensational color, add splashes of holiday color to iced cookies and cupcakes. No mess, taste-free formula. 1.5 oz. Certified Kosher.
$2.99

Blue	710-T-5501
Yellow	710-T-5502

Ready-to-Decorate Icing
Anyone can decorate with Wilton Ready-to-Decorate Icing! Our brilliant colors and 4 decorating tips make it a breeze to add an exciting finishing touch to treats without mixing or mess. 6.4 oz. Certified Kosher. **$3.99**

Blue	710-T-4407
Yellow	710-T-4409
White	710-T-4402

Tube Decorating Icing
Tubes can be used with our Tip and Nail Set or Coupler Ring Set (p. 136) and any standard size Wilton metal tip. Colors match Wilton Icing Colors (p. 136). 4.25 oz. Certified Kosher. **$1.99**

Blue	704-T-248
Yellow	704-T-236
White	704-T-200

Tube Decorating Gel
Transparent gels are great for writing messages and decorating cakes and cookies. Colors match Wilton Icing Colors (p. 136). .75 oz. Certified Kosher. **$1.49**

Blue	704-T-348
Yellow	704-T-336
White	704-T-302

VALENTINE
Bakeware
DIMENSIONS®
DECORATIVE BAKEWARE

With Dimensions non-stick cast aluminum bakeware, anyone can create Valentine desserts with elegant shapes and spectacular detail. Heavyweight cast aluminum conducts heat extremely evenly. Premium non-stick surface for easy release and cleanup. Aluminum.

Mini Heart (above)
Each heart is 4 x 2 in. deep. Six 1 cup cavities.
2105-T-5012 $27.99

Also available, pans shown on p. 150:

Queen Of Hearts
9 x 3¼ in. deep. 10 cup capacity.
2105-T-5001 $27.99

Crown Of Hearts
11 x 2½ in. deep. 10 cup capacity.
2105-T-5011 $27.99

9 in. Non-Stick Heart Pan
Your classic heart cake will release perfectly. Cleanup is easy too. 9 x 2¼ in. deep. Non-stick steel.
2105-T-410 $10.99

Heart Tart Pan
Create luscious desserts and entrees with classic fluted edges. Removable bottom. 10 x 1 in. deep. Non-stick steel.
2105-T-452 $9.99

Silicone Heart Molds

Discover the convenience and easy release of flexible silicone bakeware! Freezer, refrigerator, microwave and dishwasher safe—oven safe to 500°F. One mix makes 40-48 petite hearts; 20-24 mini hearts. 12 petite cavities, each 1½ x1½ x 1 in. deep; 6 mini cavities, each 2⅝ x 2½ x 1½ in. deep.

12-Cavity Petite Heart Mold
2105-T-4860 $9.99

6-Cavity Mini Heart Mold
2105-T-4012 $9.99

Heart Springform Pans
Create elegant Valentine cheesecakes with these easy-releasing non-stick pans. Springlock sides, removable bottom for easy serving. Non-stick steel.

9 x 2¾ in. Standard
2105-T-419
$16.99

4 x 1¾ in. Mini
2105-T-457
$7.99

Heart Pans
For graceful expressions of love on Valentine's Day or anytime, in just the size you need. 2 in. deep. Aluminum.

6 in.
2105-T-600 $6.49

9 in.
2105-T-5176 $7.99

12 in.
2105-T-607 $11.99

Non-Stick Mini Heart Pan

Perfect size for party petit fours, molded salads and more. Non-stick steel releases treats easily. One mix makes 20-24 hearts; 6 cavities, each 2¼ x 2⅜ x 1 ¼ in. deep.
2105-T-1539 $6.99

SweetHeart Pan

Its gently curving shape gives the classic heart a more romantic flair. This cake will charm guests for birthdays, Mother's Day, Valentine's Day, showers and more. One-mix pan is 10¼ x 2 in. deep. Aluminum.
2105-T-1197 $11.99

Mini Heart Pan

Great size for petit fours, individual brownies and more. One mix makes 12-18 hearts. 6 cavities, each 3½ x 1 in. deep. Aluminum.
2105-T-11044 $11.99

Petite Heart Pan

Bite-size muffins, brownies and cookies will win hearts. One mix makes 10-15 dozen hearts. 12 cavities, each 1¾ x 1⅝ x ½ in. deep. Aluminum.
2105-T-2432 $10.99

Colors & Icings
VALENTINE COLOR GUIDE

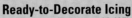

Red	Pink	Violet	White

Color Mist™ Food Color Spray
Gives decorators the versatility and dazzling effects of an airbrush in a convenient can! Use it to transform a plain iced cake with sensational color, add splashes of holiday color to iced cookies and cupcakes. No mess, taste-free formula. 1.5 oz. Certified Kosher. $2.99

Red	710-T-5500
Pink	710-T-5505
Violet	710-T-5504

Valentine Icing Colors Set
Red-Red and Pink in .5 oz. jars. Certified Kosher.
601-T-5570 Set/2 $2.99

Ready-to-Decorate Icing

Anyone can decorate with Wilton Ready-to-Decorate Icing! Our brilliant colors and 4 decorator tips make it a breeze to add an exciting finishing touch to treats without mixing or mess. 6.4 oz. Certified Kosher. $3.99

Red	710-T-4400
Pink	710-T-4406
Violet	710-T-4408
White	710-T-4402

Tube Decorating Icing
Tubes can be used with our Tip and Nail Set or Coupler Ring Set (p. 136) and any standard size Wilton metal tip. Colors match Wilton Icing Colors (p. 136). 4.25 oz. Certified Kosher. $1.99

| Red | 704-T-218 | Violet | 704-T-242 |
| Pink | 704-T-230 | White | 704-T-200 |

Tube Decorating Gel
Transparent gels are great for writing messages and decorating cakes and cookies. Colors match Wilton Icing Colors (p. 136). .75 oz. Certified Kosher. $1.49

| Red | 704-T-318 | Violet | 704-T-342 |
| Pink | 704-T-330 | White | 704-T-302 |

Party

Baking Cups
Microwave-safe paper. Standard size, 2 in. diameter, Mini size, 1¼ in. diameter.
Standard Pk/75 $1.99
Mini Pk/100 $1.99

NEW!

Hearts Remembered
Standard 415-T-518
Mini 415-T-519

Love Heart
Standard 415-T-462
Mini 415-T-461

Party Bags
Colorful solid red and Valentine designs for candy and cookie treats. 20 plastic bags, 20 ties included. 4 x 9½ in.
Pk./20 $1.99

Red Party Bags
1912-T-2357

Hearts Remembered
1912-T-1292

NEW!

Love Heart
1912-T-2398

Icing Decorations
Perfect for topping cupcakes, cookies and ice cream. Mint-flavored. Certified Kosher. **$2.29**

Hearts Remembered
710-T-824 Pk./18

Bon Bon Cups
Wax-laminated paper on red foil. 1 in. diameter
415-T-314 Pk./75 $1.49

Candy

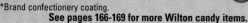

NEW!

Heart Pretzel Mold
1 design, 6 cavities.
2115-T-3025 $1.99

Double Heart Large Lollipop Mold
2 designs, 4 cavities.
2115-T-4440 $1.99

Hearts Candy Mold
1 design, 15 cavities.
2115-T-1712 $1.99

Roses and Buds Lollipop Mold
3 designs, 9 cavities.
2115-T-1708 $1.99

Heart Lollipop Mold
2 designs, 8 cavities.
2115-T-1709 $1.99

Candy Melts®*
Ideal for molding, dipping or coating. Artificially vanilla flavored unless otherwise indicated. 14 oz. bag. Certified Kosher Dairy. **$2.50**

Red	1911-T-499	Light Cocoa	1911-T-544
Pink	1911-T-447	Dark Cocoa	1911-T-358
White	1911-T-498		

*Brand confectionery coating.
See pages 166-169 for more Wilton candy items.

Sprinkles

INDIVIDUAL BOTTLES

NEW!

Shake up your Valentine treats with fun colors and designs. Certified Kosher. **$2.29**

Chocolate Hearts
2.5 oz. bottle
710-T-622

Hearts Confetti
2.5 oz. bottle
710-T-968

Valentine Nonpareils
3 oz. bottle
710-T-625

Hearts Mix
2.5 oz. bottle
710-T-854

Kisses Mix
2.5 oz. bottle
710-T-855

Sugars
3.25 oz. bottle. Certified Kosher. **$2.29**

Red
710-T-766

Pink
710-T-756

Lavender
710-T-758

Sparkling Sugars
Easy-pour sugars have a coarse texture and brilliant sparkle. 8 oz. bottle. Certified Kosher. **$4.49**

Red/White
710-T-367

Pink/White
710-T-366

Cake Sparkles™
Edible glitter, .25 oz. bottle. Certified Kosher. **$2.89**

Red
703-T-1284

Pink
703-T-1260

Purple
703-T-1266

ASSORTMENTS

3-Mix
Includes Red/White, Pink/White and White Sparkling Sugars. Certified Kosher.
710-T-372 $5.99

4-Mix
Includes Heart Mix, Sweetheart Nonpareils, Pink and Red Sugars. Certified Kosher.
710-T-730 $4.99

6-Mix
Includes Kisses Mix, Heart Mix, Sweetheart Nonpareils, Pink, Red and Lavender Sugars. Certified Kosher.
710-T-738 $5.99

HEART DOILIES
Serve Valentine treats on heart doilies with pretty lace-look edges.

10 in. Red
2104-T-90710 Pk./9 $1.99

10 in. White
2104-T-90610 Pk./9 $1.99

6 in. Red
2104-T-90706
Pk./12 $1.99

6 in. White
2104-T-90606
Pk./12 $1.99

3½ in. Red
2104-T-90703
Pk./12 $1.99

3½ in. White
2104-T-90603
Pk./12 $1.99

PLASTIC COOKIE CUTTERS

Nesting Hearts Cutter Set
Great for cookies, imprinting patterns in icing, cutting bread shapes and more. Plastic in sizes from 1¼ to 4⅛ in.
2304-T-115 Set/6 $2.99

Heart Cutter
Plastic, 3 x 4 in.
2303-T-100
$0.69

ORDER TOLL FREE: 800-794-5866

Cookie

Sweetheart Cupcake and Cookie Stencils
Turn plain treats into visions of love. Just place one of the fun designs over your baked treat, then sprinkle with Wilton Cake Sparkles™ or Colored Sugars (p. 204) or spray with Color Mist™ Food Color Spray (p. 203). 8 designs.
417-T-494 $1.99

Comfort Grip™ Cutters
Cushion-grip cutters with extra-deep stainless steel sides are perfect for cutting many favorite foods into Valentine shapes. The cushion grip gives you comfortable control even when cutting into thick desserts. Recipe included. 4½ x 4½ x 1½ in. deep. **$2.99**

NEW! Double Heart 2310-T-647

NEW! Lips 2310-T-646

Heart 2310-T-616

METAL CUTTERS
Put variety in your cookie-making with fun Valentine multi-shape sets. Recipe included.

Valentine Cutter Collection
Vivid Valentine colors bring a touch of romance to cookie-baking. Great variety of hearts, hugs and kisses designs. Sizes range from 1 to 5 in. Colored aluminum.
2308-T-2502 Set/9 $9.99

Valentine Mini Cutter Set
Double heart, crinkle heart, O, heart with arrow, heart and X, each approx. 1½ in.
2308-T-1255 Set/6 $2.99

From The Heart Nesting Cutter Set
Nesting metal cutters give you a choice of sizes, with two crinkled shapes. Largest cutter is approximately 5 in.
2308-T-1203 Set/4 $4.49

Hearts Cutter Set
Love comes in all shapes and sizes. Includes 7 different heart cutter designs from stylized to traditional. Sizes range from 1½ to 3 in.
2308-T-1237 Set/7 $4.99

Heart Cutter
Quality metal cuts neatly and is easy to handle. 3 in. wide.
2308-T-1003 $0.69

Heart Giant Cookie Pan
Create a giant-sized pan cookie or brownie in a heart shape that will be a big hit. Ideal for refrigerated dough and brownie mix. Recipe included. Pan is 11½ x 10½ x ½ in. deep. Aluminum.
2105-T-6203 $6.49

Heart Cookie Treat Pan
Just press cookie dough into pan, insert a cookie stick, then bake, cool and decorate. Also great for adding fun shapes to other goodies like rice cereal treats and candy pops. Each pan makes 6 individual treats, 3½ in. x ¼ in. deep. Aluminum.
2105-T-8104 $8.99

Cookie Treat Sticks
6 in. 1912-T-9319 Pk./20 $1.99
8 in. 1912-T-9318 Pk./20 $2.99

ST. PATRICK'S DAY

Shamrock Pan
Celebrate St. Patrick's Day with this fun symbol of joy and celebration. Also great for school parties, birthdays, sports celebrations and much more. One-mix pan is 11¾ x 2 in. deep. Aluminum.
2105-T-185 $8.99

Shamrock Foil Fun Pix®
Add a shimmering, lucky touch to cakes, cupcakes, ice cream and more. Approximately 3½ in. high.
2113-T-1347 Pk./12 $1.99

Shamrock Icing Decorations
Sugar-flavored. Certified Kosher.
710-T-286 Pk./9 $2.29

Shamrock Sprinkle Mix
Shake up your St. Patrick's Day treats! Plastic 2.5 oz. bottle for convenient pouring and storing. Certified Kosher.
710-T-7485 $2.29

Shamrock Lollipop Mold
1 design, 5 cavities.
2115-T-1545 $1.99

Shamrock Comfort Grip™ Cookie Cutter
Cushion-grip with extra-deep stainless steel sides gives you comfortable control even when cutting into thick desserts. Recipe included. 4½ x 1½ in. deep.
2310-T-648 $2.99

Shamrock Baking Cups
Microwave-safe paper. Standard size, 2 in. diameter, Mini size, 1¼ in. diameter. $1.99
Standard 415-T-1410 Pk./75
Mini 415-T-1411 Pk./100

Shamrock Party Bags
20 plastic bags, 20 twist ties included. 4 x 9½ in.
1912-T-2233 Pk./20 $1.99

NEW!

Shamrock Green Metal Cookie Cutter
Quality metal cuts neatly. Approx. 3 in.
2308-T-1320 $0.79

Shamrock Metal Cookie Cutter
Quality metal cuts neatly and is easy to handle. Approx. 3 in.
2308-T-1011 $0.69

4-Leaf Clover Cookie Cutter
Cut cookies, sandwiches and use in crafts. Plastic; 3 in. wide.
2303-T-134 $0.69

Bakeware

Step-By-Step Bunny Pan

Just what you need to get springtime celebrations hopping—just bake, ice and decorate! He's also perfect for molding gelatin, ice cream, salads and more. One-mix pan is 9¾ x 14 x 2 in. deep. Aluminum.
2105-T-2074 $6.49

3-D Bunny Pan

Sure to get everyone's attention at your holiday brunch and beyond. Instructions for 5 different decorating ideas included. Two-piece pan is 7¼ x 4¾ x 7 in. high. Pan takes 4½ cups of pound cake batter. No heating core needed. Aluminum.
2105-T-2042 Set/2 $12.99

Stand-Up Lamb Pan

A gentle symbol of springtime. This 3-D lamb will charm everyone at your Easter table. Instructions included. Two-piece pan makes lamb 10 x 4½ x 7 in. high; takes 6 cups of pound cake batter. Aluminum.
2105-T-2010 Set/2 $12.99

Silicone Mini Flower Mold

Discover the convenience and easy release of flexible silicone bakeware! Freezer, refrigerator, microwave and dishwasher safe; oven safe to 500°F. One mix makes 20-24 flowers. 6 cavities, each 2¾ x 1½ in. deep.
2105-T-4034 $9.99

Decorated Egg Pan

Great for molded desserts as well as cakes. Decorating instructions for 5 different designs included. One-mix pan is 9 x 11 x 3½ in. deep. Aluminum.
2105-T-174 $8.99

3-D Egg Pan

Hatch a great Easter centerpiece! Two-piece pan takes just one cake mix. Includes 2 ring bases for level baking of each half. Each half is 9 x 6 x 2¾ in. Aluminum.
2105-T-4793 Set/4 $12.99

Cross Pan

Truly inspiring for holidays, Christenings and other religious occasions. Bevel design is excellent with rolled fondant. One-mix pan is 14½ x 11⅛ x 2 in. deep. Instructions included. Aluminum.
2105-T-2509 $8.99

6-Cavity Non-Stick Mini Cake Pans

NEW!

Mini cakes are fun to serve at Easter brunch or wrap them up and add to baskets. Easy-release, easy-clean non-stick steel bakes cakes with great detail. Also excellent for brownies, ice cream molds, muffins and more.

Decorated Egg

NEW!

Six cavities, each 4⅛ x 2¹⁵⁄₁₆ x 1½ in. deep. One mix makes about 14 cakes.
2105-T-1550 $9.99

Bunny
Six cavities, each 4 x 2⅝ x 1⁹⁄₁₆ in. deep. One mix makes about 18 cakes.
2105-T-1551 $9.99

Mini Egg Pan

Make colorful place markers for the holiday table. One mix makes about 24-36 eggs. 8 cavities, each 3¼ x 2½ x 1 in. deep. Aluminum.
2105-T-2118 $11.99

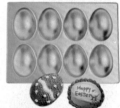

Bunny Cookie Treat Pan

Just press cookie dough into pan, insert a cookie stick, then bake, cool and decorate. Each pan makes 6 individual treats, 3½ x 2¾ x ¼ in. deep. Aluminum.
2105-T-8106 $8.99

Cookie Treat Sticks
6 in. 1912-T-9319 Pk./20 $1.99
8 in. 1912-T-9318 Pk./20 $2.99

Colors & Icings

EASTER COLOR GUIDE

Pink	Violet	Yellow	Green/ Leaf Green	White

Easter Icing Colors Set

Lemon Yellow and Violet in .5 oz. jars. Certified Kosher.
601-T-5571 Set/2 $2.99

Color Mist™ Food Color Spray

Gives decorators the versatility and dazzling effects of an airbrush in a convenient can! Use it to transform a plain iced cake with sensational color, add splashes of holiday color to iced cookies and cupcakes. No mess, taste-free formula. 1.5 oz. Certified Kosher. **$2.99**
Pink 710-T-5505 Yellow 710-T-5502
Violet 710-T-5504 Green 710-T-5503

FoodWriter™ Edible Color Markers

Use like ink markers to add fun and dazzling color to countless foods. Kids love 'em! Decorate on fondant, color flow, royal icing designs and cookies. Includes Pink and Purple markers. .35 oz. Certified Kosher.
609-T-104 Set/2 $3.99

Ready-to-Decorate Icing

Anyone can decorate with Wilton Ready-to-Decorate Icing! Our brilliant colors and 4 decorating tips make it a breeze to add an exciting finishing touch to treats without mixing or mess.
6.4 oz. Certified Kosher. **$3.99**
Pink 710-T-4406   Green 710-T-4401
Violet 710-T-4408   White 710-T-4402
Yellow 710-T-4409

Tube Decorating Icing

Tubes can be used with our Tip and Nail Set or Coupler Ring Set (p. 136) and any standard size Wilton metal tip. Colors match Wilton Icing Colors (p. 136). 4.25 oz. Certified Kosher. **$1.99**
Pink 704-T-230   Leaf Green 704-T-224
Violet 704-T-242   White 704-T-200
Yellow 704-T-236

Tube Decorating Gel

Great for writing messages and decorating cakes and cookies. Colors match Wilton Icing Colors (p. 136). .75 oz. Certified Kosher. **$1.49**
Pink 704-T-330   Green 704-T-324
Violet 704-T-342   White 704-T-302
Yellow 704-T-336

Party

Baking Cups
Microwave-safe paper. Standard size, 2 in. diameter, Mini size, 1¼ in. diameter,
Standard Pk./75 $1.99
Mini Pk./100 $1.99

NEW!

Spring Party
Standard 415-T-4761
Mini 415-T-4762

Bunnies & Chicks
Standard 415-T-416
Mini 415-T-547

Assorted Pastel
25 pink, 25 yellow, 25 blue.
Standard 415-T-9396 Pk./75 $1.49
Mini 415-T-9397 Pk./100 $1.49

Party Bags
Colorful Easter designs for candy and cookie treats. 20 plastic bags, 20 ties included. 4 x 9½ in.
Pk./20 $1.99

NEW!

Pastel Silicone Baking Cups
No muffin pan needed! Bake and serve in these reusable oven-safe cups in pretty pastels.
Standard size, 2 in. diameter.
415-T-9413 Set/12 $9.99

Bunny Shaped Party Bags
Colorful Easter designs for candy and cookie treats. 6⅞ x 9½ in. high.
1912-T-5150
Pk./20 $1.99

Spring Party
1912-T-1204

Bunnies & Chicks
1912-T-3104

Icing Decorations
Perfect for topping cupcakes, cookies and ice cream. Mint-flavored. Certified Kosher.
$2.29

Petite Eggs
710-T-528 Pk./12

Bunnies & Chicks
710-T-368 Pk./12

Bunnies and Chicks Fun Pix®
Add a fun touch to cakes, cupcakes, ice cream and more. Approx. 3½ in. high.
2113-T-3303 Pk./24 $1.99

DOILIES

Serve springtime treats on sweet pastel doilies in 4 in., 8 in. and 10 in. sizes. Pretty lace-look edges. Includes 4 doilies in each size. **$2.99**

Pink 2104-T-5560 Pk./12

Yellow 2104-T-5559 Pk./12

Cookie

Pre-Baked and Pre-Assembled Bunny Hutch Cookie House Kit
It's the perfect springtime project and a cute centerpiece for your Easter table. So hop to it—everything is included: a pre-baked, pre-built hutch, yellow and pink decorating icing mixes, candies, icing decorations, 2 cookie bunny ears, 2 decorating bags and tips, cardboard base and complete instructions with great decorating ideas. Hutch measures 5½ x 5¼ x 6 in. high.
2104-T-1594 $12.99

Candy

Candy Melts®*
Ideal for molding, dipping or coating. Artificially vanilla flavored unless otherwise indicated. 14 oz. bag. Certified Kosher Dairy. **$2.50**

Pink	1911-T-447
Lavender	1911-T-403
Yellow	1911-T-463
Blue	1911-T-448
White	1911-T-498
Chocolate Mint	1911-T-1920
Light Cocoa	1911-T-544
Dark Cocoa	1911-T-358

*Brand confectionery coating.

Lil' Bunnies Mini Candy Mold
4 designs, 12 cavities.
2115-T-1544 $1.99

Hoppy Easter Lollipop Mold
8 designs, 9 cavities.
2115-T-1718 $1.99

See pages 166-169 for more Wilton candy items.

Easter Cupcake & Cookie Stencils
Turn plain treats into spring sensations with a stenciled Easter design. Place one of the designs over your baked treat, then sprinkle with Wilton Cake Sparkles™ or Colored Sugars (p. 208) or spray with Color Mist™ Food Color Spray (p. 206). 8 designs.
417-T-496 Set/8 $1.99

Sprinkles

INDIVIDUAL BOTTLES

Shake up your Easter treats! Plastic bottles for convenient pouring and storing. Certified Kosher. **$2.29**

Colorful Egg Mix 2.5 oz. bottle 710-T-7486

Spring Confetti 2.5 oz. bottle 710-T-1278

Bunny/Ducks Mix 2.5 oz. bottle 710-T-870

Soft Pink Sugar 3.25 oz. bottle 710-T-896

Soft Lavender Sugar 3.25 oz. bottle 710-T-897

Soft Yellow Sugar 3.25 oz. bottle 710-T-895

Soft Green Sugar 3.25 oz. bottle 710-T-898

Sparkling Sugars

Easy-pour sugars have a coarse texture and brilliant sparkle. 8 oz. Certified Kosher. **$4.49**

Pink/White 710-T-369

Lavender/White 710-T-371

Yellow/ White 710-T-370

ASSORTMENTS

3-Mix
Includes Pastel Green, Yellow and Pink Sparkling Sugars. 8.4 oz. Certified Kosher.
710-T-373 **$5.99**

4-Mix
Includes Yellow Sugar, Lt. Green Sugar, Springtime Nonpareils and Bunnies/Ducks Mix. 3.75 oz. Certified Kosher.
710-T-736 **$4.99**

6-Mix
Includes Bunny/Ducks Sprinkle Mix, Colorful Egg Mix, Spring Confetti, Lavender, Pink and Green Sugars. 6.9 oz. Certified Kosher.
710-T-740 **$5.99**

Cookie Cutters

METAL CUTTERS

Put variety in your cookie-making with fun Easter multi-shape sets. There are styles to please everyone. Recipe included.

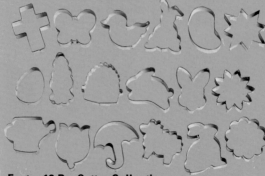

Easter 18 Pc. Cutter Collection
Cross, butterfly, chick, bunny, jelly bean, sun, egg, carrot, basket, leaping bunny, bunny face, daisy, sprinkling can, tulip, umbrella, lamb, rabbit and flower cutters are approx. 3 in.
2308-T-1134 Set/18 **$9.99**

Easter 12 Pc. Mini Cutter Collection
Bunny face, egg, cross, sun, carrot, chick, flower, tulip, sprinkling can, umbrella, bunny and butterfly cutters are approx. 1½ in.
2308-T-1254 Set/12 **$4.99**

Easter Mini Cutter Set
Butterfly, daisy, tulip, bunny face, chick and bunny, each approx. 1½ in. Metal.
2308-T-1209 Set/6 **$2.99**

Colorful Cutter Sets
Our metal cutters look great with their bright colors and fun shapes. Perfect for hanging until your next cookie-baking bash.

NEW!

Easter Colored Metal Cutter Set
Set of 3 includes bunny, tulip and butterfly, each approx. 3 to 3½ in. Colored aluminum.
2308-T-1216 Set/3 **$3.49**

Hoppy Easter Cutter Set
Springtime favorites in pastels of the season. Tulip, egg, butterfly and bunny. Coated metal. Each approx. 3½ in.
2308-T-1207 Set/4 **$4.49**

Easter 9 Pc. Cutter Collection
Lamb, chick, tulip, flower, bunny, egg, butterfly, bunny face, and carrot cutters are approx. 3 in. Colored aluminum.
2308-T-2503 Set/9 **$9.99**

COMFORT GRIP™ CUTTERS

Cushion-grip cutters with extra-deep stainless steel sides are perfect for cutting so many foods into seasonal shapes. Provides comfortable control even when cutting thick desserts. Recipe included. Approx. 4½ x 1½ in. deep. **$2.99**

Bunny 2310-T-626

Chick 2310-T-625

GRIPPY™ CUTTER SET

Safe, easy cutting, with a comfortable grip and deep plastic sides. Includes egg, butterfly, flower and bunny, approx. 3½ in.
2311-T-258 Set/4 **$3.99**

PLASTIC CUTTERS

Child-safe design means kids can have a great time helping. And remember all the fun ways to use our cutters—for bread shapes, stencils, sun catchers and so much more.

Easter Egg Canister Cutter Set
A fun and convenient egg canister holds a collection of Easter cutters for holiday cookies. Ten cutters, each approx. 3½ in.
2304-T-95 Set/10 **$5.99**

Easter Bite-Size Cutter Set
Bunny, tulip, chick, egg and bunny face shapes. Each approx. 1½ in.
2303-T-9319 Set/5 **$2.49**

Nesting Bunnies Cutter Set
Sizes from 1¼ to 4⅛ in.
2303-T-9270 Set/4 **$2.99**

Cross 2303-T-141

Duck 2303-T-148

Egg 2303-T-119

Individual Cutters
Each approx. 3 x 4 in. **$0.69**

ORDER TOLL FREE: 800-794-5866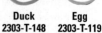

COMMUNION

Cross Pan

Beveled design is excellent with rolled fondant. One-mix pan is 14½ x 11⅛ x 2 in. deep. Instructions included. Aluminum.
2105-T-2509
$8.99

FAITH CROSS ACCESSORIES **NEW!**

Stationery
Beautifully designed in white 80 lb. card stock with white pearlized trim. Professionally print at home at **www.wiltonprint.com.**

Invitations
Border and cross accent. Invitation: 5½ x 8½ in.; envelope: 5¾ x 8¾ in.
1008-T-775 Pk./12 $4.99

Thank You Cards
Folded cards with script and cross on front. Card: 5½ x 4¼ in.; envelope: 5¾ x approx. 4½ in.
1008-T-776 Pk./12 $4.99

Seals
Self adhesive, silver tone, 1 in. diameter.
1008-T-779 Pk./24 $1.99

Faith Cross Cake Pick
Perfect for religious celebrations. Painted resin. Food-safe. 5 in. high.
1006-T-4475 $14.99

TOPPERS

Inspirational Cross
Beautifully designed in sculpted resin. 5½ in. high.
202-T-398 $14.99

Communion Girl*
3½ in. high.
2113-T-7878 $3.49

Communion Boy*
3½ in. high.
2113-T-7886 $3.49

*Designed by Ellen Williams.

Centerpiece
Stunning silver and white design, crafted in heavy card stock with honeycomb paper base. Assembled measures 7¾ x 9¾ in. high.
1006-T-7148 $2.99

6 Ft. Garland
Silver printed crosses on white paper garland make a beautiful, inspirational decoration for your celebration. 6 ft. long, accordion folded. Unfold and use tape or ribbon to hang.
1006-T-498 $5.99

Favor Boxes
Distinctive favor boxes are perfect for your celebration. Fill with Wilton Jordan Almonds or favor candy (candy not included). Crafted of paper, easy to assemble. 2½ wide x 1¾ in deep.
1006-T-7150 $5.99

Favor Accents
Detailed crosses add elegance to favors, decorations, and more! 1 in. long plastic. Tie on with your ribbon or attach with hot glue.
Pk./20 $1.99
Silver 1006-T-4501
White 1006-T-7149

PATRIOTIC

Bakeware

Stars and Stripes Pan
Decorate a grand old flag cake perfect for that July 4th cookout. Accent Old Glory with Piping Gel and fresh summer fruit. One-mix pan is 13 x 9 x 2 in. Aluminum.
2105-T-183 $8.99

Ribbon Pan
If there's a cause dear to your heart, bring it some attention with a color-cued ribbon cake or molded dessert. Decorate in the colors that represent your special cause for charity events, school activities or school fundraisers. One-mix pan is 15¼ x 9 x 2 in. deep. Aluminum.
2105-T-1017 $11.99

Star Pan
Your colorful star cake will set off sparks on the 4th and brighten parties all year long. One-mix pan is 12¾ x 1⅞ in. deep. Aluminum.
2105-T-2512 $11.99

Silicone Mini Star Mold
Microwave freezer, refrigerator, and dishwasher safe oven safe to 500°F. One mix makes 20-24 stars. 6 cavities, each 2⅝ x 2½ x 1½ in. deep.
2105-T-4819 $9.99

Mini Star Pan
One mix makes 12-16 stars. 6 cavities, 4¾ x 1 in. deep. Aluminum.
2105-T-1235 $12.99

Star Cookie Treat Pan
Just press cookie dough into pan, insert a cookie stick, then bake, cool and decorate. Makes 6 individual treats, 3½ x ¼ in. deep. Aluminum.
2105-T-8102 $8.99

Cookie Treat Sticks
6 in. **1912-T-9319 Pk./20 $1.99**
8 in. **1912-T-9318 Pk./20 $2.99**

Colors & Icings

PATRIOTIC COLOR GUIDE

| Red | White | Blue |

Color Mist™ Food Color Spray
Dazzling effects of an airbrush in a convenient can! Transform a plain iced cake with sensational color, add splashes of color to iced cookies and cupcakes. No mess, taste-free formula. 1.5 oz. Certified Kosher. **$2.99**

Red	710-T-5500
Blue	710-T-5501

Ready-to-Decorate Icing
Anyone can decorate with Wilton Ready-to-Decorate Icing! Our brilliant colors and 4 decorating tips make it a breeze to add an exciting finishing touch to treats without mixing or mess. 6.4 oz. Certified Kosher. **$3.99**

Red	710-T-4400
White	710-T-4402
Blue	710-T-4407

Tube Decorating Gel
Transparent gels are great for writing messages and decorating cakes and cookies. Colors match Wilton Icing Colors (p. 136). .75 oz. Certified Kosher. **$1.49**

Red	704-T-318
White	704-T-302
Royal Blue	704-T-348

Tube Decorating Icing
Tubes can be used with our Tip and Nail Set or Coupler Ring Set (p. 136) and any standard size Wilton metal tip. Colors match Wilton Icing Colors (p. 136). 4.25 oz. Certified Kosher. **$1.99**

Red	704-T-218
White	704-T-200
Royal Blue	704-T-248

Party

Baking Cups
Microwave-safe paper. Standard size, 2 in. diameter.
Pk./75 $1.99

Old Glory
415-T-2236

Patriotic Stars
415-T-2235

Party Bags
Colorful Patriotic designs for candy and cookie treats. 20 plastic bags, 20 twist ties included.
4 x 9½ in.
Pk./20 $1.99

Old Glory
1912-T-3056

Patriotic Stars
1912-T-1254

Icing Decorations
Perfect for topping cupcakes, cookies and ice cream. Mint-flavored. Certified Kosher. $2.29

Patriotic Flags
710-T-726 Pk./9

Patriotic Stars
710-T-942 Pk./21

CANDLES

Patriotic
Feature bold textured spirals and a fun hand-carved star on top.
3¼ in. high.
2811-T-1122
Pk./4 $3.49

Beer Cans
1¾ in. high.
2811-T-9326
Set/6 $3.49

Red and Blue Sparklers
6½ in. high.
2811-T-704
Pk./18 $0.99

PARTY PICKS

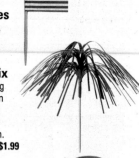

Stars and Stripes
3 in. high mini flags.
2113-T-704
Pk./40 $1.29

Patriotic Foil Pix
Looks like a dazzling fireworks display on your holiday treats! Great for cakes, cupcakes. 4 in. high.
2113-T-712 Pk./12 $1.99

Uncle Sam Bobbling Cupcake Toppers
Top off that special treat with these fun bobbling toppers. Food-safe design features hand-painted details that make even plain cupcakes more exciting. 2 in. high.
2113-T-1273 Pk./6 $2.99

Patriotic Cupcake & Cookie Stencils
Turn plain treats into American classics. Just place one of the fun designs over your baked treat, then sprinkle with Wilton Cake Sparkles™ or Colored Sugars (p. 211) or spray with Color Mist™ Food Color Spray (p. 209). 8 designs.
417-T-498 $1.99

Candy **NEW!**

Stars Candy Mold
1 design, 12 cavities,
2115-T-1554 $1.99

See pages 166-169 for more Wilton candy items.

Patriotic Pretzel Mold
3 designs, 6 cavities.
2115-T-4439 $1.99

Candy Melts®*
Ideal for molding, dipping or coating. Artificially vanilla flavored unless otherwise indicated. 14 oz. bag. Certified Kosher Dairy. $2.50

Red	1911-T-499	Chocolate Mint	1911-T-1920
White	1911-T-498	Light Cocoa	1911-T-544
Blue	1911-T-448	Dark Cocoa	1911-T-358

*Brand confectionery coating.

COOKIE CUTTERS

Stars Nesting Metal Cutter Set
A parade of small to large stars to create fun cookies for the 4th or all year long. Sizes from 5 to 2½ in.
2308-T-1215
Set/4 $4.49

Comfort Grip™ Cutters
Cushion-grip cutters with extra-deep stainless steel sides are perfect for cutting so many favorite foods into patriotic shapes. The cushion grip gives you comfortable control even when cutting into thick desserts. Recipe included.
4½ x 1½ in. deep. $2.99

Patriotic Colored Metal Cutter Set
Bold colors add to the fun! Set of 4 favorite shapes includes star, USA, flag and shooting star. Sizes from 3 to 3½ in.
2308-T-1257 Set/4 $4.49

Star Metal Cookie Cutter
Quality metal is clean-cutting and easy to handle. 3 in.
2308-T-1008 $0.69

Nesting Stars Cutter Set
Plastic.
1⅝ to 4⅝ in.
2304-T-704
Set/6 $2.99

NEW!

Flag
2310-T-651

Star
2310-T-605

ORDER TOLL FREE: 800-794-5866

CUPCAKES 'N MORE® DESSERT STANDS

Individually decorated cupcakes are the perfect way to add a personal touch to celebrations. Now, with Cupcakes 'N More, you have the perfect way to serve them, featuring bold silver-finished wire spirals to securely hold each cupcake.

38 Count Standard
15 x 18 in. wide. Holds 38 cupcakes (shown above).
307-T-651 **$39.99**

23 Count Standard 12 x 13 in. wide. Holds 23 standard cupcakes.
307-T-826 **$29.99**

13 Count Standard 9¼ x 9 in. wide. Holds 13 standard cupcakes.
307-T-831 **$12.99**

24 Count Mini 10½ x 9 in. wide. Holds 24 mini cupcakes.
307-T-250 **$14.99**

Sprinkles

INDIVIDUAL BOTTLES

Plastic bottles for easy pouring and storing. Certified Kosher. **$2.29**

Patriotic Mix
2.5 oz. bottle
710-T-786

Patriotic Nonpareils
3 oz. bottle
710-T-1123

Red Sugar
3.25 oz. bottle
710-T-766

Blue Sugar
3.25 oz. bottle
710-T-750

Cake Sparkles™

Edible glitter, .25 oz. bottle. Certified Kosher. **$2.89**

Red
703-T-1284

Blue
703-T-1314

6-Mix Assortment

Includes Red and Blue Jimmies and Patriotic Mix, Red and Blue Sugar and Patriotic Sprinkle Sparks. Certified Kosher.
710-T-656 **$5.99**

GRADUATION

Smiley Grad Pan

Our grinning grad is a smart choice to honor any student who's made the grade—boy or girl, kindergartner to collegian. One-mix pan is 10¼ x 12 x 2 in. deep. Aluminum.
2105-T-2073 **$8.99**

Topping Off Success Pan

Decorate in your grad's school colors. One-mix pan is 14¾ x 11¾ x 2 in. deep. Aluminum.
2105-T-2038 **$8.99**

Book Pans

Books detail any of life's important chapters, including graduation. Aluminum.

One-Mix
13 x 9½ x 2 in. deep.
2105-T-972 **$11.99**

Two-Mix
11½ x 15 x 2¾ in. deep. Serves up to 30.
2105-T-2521 **$15.99**

Candy

NEW!

NEW!

Graduation Pretzel Mold

3 designs, 6 cavities.
2115-T-1445 **$1.99**

Graduation Lollipop Mold

6 designs, 8 cavities,
2115-T-1729 **$1.99**

Candy Melts®*

Ideal for all your candy molding, dipping or coating. Artificially vanilla flavored unless otherwise indicated. 14 oz. bag. Certified Kosher Dairy. **$2.50**

Yellow	1911-T-463
White	1911-T-498
Blue	1911-T-448
Chocolate Mint	1911-T-1920
Light Cocoa	1911-T-544
Dark Cocoa	1911-T-358

*Brand confectionery coating.

See pages 166-169 for more Wilton candy items.

Autograph Mat

A party memento to be filled with greetings from every guest for the grad to treasure forever. Includes black pen. Fits into your 11 x 14 in. frame, holds 5 x 7 in. photo.
1009-T-241 **$5.99**

ORDER ONLINE: WWW.WILTON.COM

Party

Baking Cups
Microwave-safe paper. Standard size, 2 in. diameter.
Pk./75 $1.99

Graduation
415-T-4594

Smiley Grad
415-T-4592

Party Bags
Colorful grad designs for candy and cookie treats. 20 plastic bags, 20 ties included. 4 x 9 ½ in.
Pk./20 $1.99

Graduation
1912-T-9241

Smiley Grad
1912-T-1130

Icing Decorations
Perfect on cupcakes, cookies and ice cream. Mint-flavored. Certified Kosher. $2.29

Graduation
710-T-1125 Pk./12

Petite Smiley Grad
710-T-503 Pk./12

Grad Fun Pix®
Add a fun touch to cakes, cupcakes, ice cream and more. Approx. 3 ½ in. high.
2113-T-717 Pk./24 $1.99

Toppers

BOBBLING TOPPERS
Top off that special cake with these fun bobbling toppers and watch heads turn. The food-safe design features hand-painted detail.

Bobbling Cake Toppers
Wax, approx. 4 ¼ in. high. $3.99

Female Grad
2113-T-462

Male Grad
2113-T-461

Bobbling Cupcake Toppers
Makes even plain cupcakes more exciting. Plastic, approx. 2 in. high.
Pk./6 $2.99

Female Grad
2113-T-1275

Male Grad
2113-T-1274

Graduation Caps Set
Great party favors or cake toppers. Plastic 2 in. high.
Set/2 $1.99
White 2113-T-1800
Black 2113-T-1801

Graduation Toppers
Capture the day's excitement with our beautifully-detailed plastic toppers on your special cake. Approx. 4 ¼ in. high.

Female Graduate
2113-T-1821 $1.99

Male Graduate
2113-T-1823 $1.99

Glowing Graduate
Girl.
2113-T-1833 $1.99

Successful Graduate
Boy.
2113-T-4549 $1.99

Candle Set
3 caps, 3 diplomas, ½ to 2 in. high.
2811-T-1800
Set/6 $3.49

Champagne Bottle Candles
2 in. high.
2811-T-163
Set/6 $3.49

Graduation Cap Colored Metal Cutter
NEW!
Quality metal cuts neatly and is easy to handle. Colored aluminum. Approx. 3 ½ in.
509-T-319 $0.79

AUTUMN

Silicone Mini Leaf and Pumpkin Mold
NEW!
Discover the convenience and easy release of flexible silicone bakeware! Freezer, refrigerator, microwave and dishwasher safe; oven safe to 500°F. One mix makes 20-24 cakes. 6 cavities, each 2⅝ x 2½ x 1½ in. deep.
2105-T-4874 $9.99

Pumpkin Pie Pan
Holds one 15 oz. can of pumpkin pie filling. Use for apple, peach and cherry pies, too! Ideal for ready-to-bake pie crusts. 9 x 1½ in. deep. Aluminum.
2105-T-3970 $7.49

Candy

Mini Leaves Candy Mold
2 designs, 12 cavities.
2115-T-1540 $1.99

Harvest Lollipop Mold
4 designs, 8 cavities.
2115-T-3056 $1.99

Pumpkins Candy Mold
1 design, 11 cavities.
2115-T-1558 $1.99

See pages 166-169 for more Wilton candy items.

Candy Melts®*
Ideal for all your candy making—molding, dipping or coating. Artificially vanilla flavored unless otherwise indicated. 14 oz. bag. Certified Kosher Dairy. $2.50

Red	1911-T-499	Dark Cocoa	1911-T-358
Light Cocoa	1911-T-544	Chocolate Mint	1911-T-1920
Orange	1911-T-1631	White	1911-T-498
Yellow	1911-T-463	Peanut Butter	1911-T-481
Dark Green	1911-T-405		

*Brand confectionery coating.

ORDER TOLL FREE: 800-794-5866

Sprinkles

NEW!

INDIVIDUAL BOTTLES

Plastic bottles for convenient pouring and storing. Certified Kosher.
$2.29

Jumbo Leaves Mix
3.25 oz. bottle
710-T-565 **$3.99**

Leaves Mix
2.5 oz. bottle
710-T-787

Red Sugar
3.25 oz. bottle
710-T-766

Dark Green Sugar
3.25 oz.bottle
710-T-764

Cake Sparkles™

Edible glitter in .25 oz. bottle. Certified Kosher.
$2.89

Red
703-T-1284

Dark Green
703-T-1278

Orange
703-T-1308

Yellow
703-T-1272

ASSORTMENT

6-Mix

Includes Yellow, Red, Orange and Light Green Sugar, Leaves Mix and Chocolate Jimmies. Certified Kosher.
710-T-751 **$5.99**

Autumn Icing Colors Set

Golden Yellow and Orange in .5 oz. jars. Certified Kosher.
601-T-5583
Set/2 $2.99

Icing Decorations

Wilton Icing Decorations are perfect for topping cupcakes, cookies and ice cream. Mint-flavored. Certified Kosher. **$2.29**

Petite Leaves
710-T-230 Pk./12

Leaves
710-T-3003 Pk./12

Party

Baking Cups

Microwave-safe paper. Standard size, 2 in. diameter; mini size, 1¼ in diameter.
Standard Pk./75
Mini Pk./100
$1.99

Autumn Leaves Standard
415-T-431
Mini
415-T-433

Harvest Standard
415-T-2160
Mini
415-T-417

Party Bags

Colorful Autumn designs for candy and cookie treats. 20 plastic bags, 20 ties included. 4 x 9 ½ in.
Pk./20
$1.99

Autumn Leaves
1912-T-1430

Harvest
1912-T-1288

NEW!

Scarecrow Fun Pix®

Add an autumn touch to cakes, cupcakes, ice cream and more. Approx. 3½ in. high.
2113-T-9217
Pk./12 $1.99

Cookie

Autumn Cupcake & Cookie Stencils

Turn plain treats into visions of the season with a stenciled Autumn design. Just place one of the fun designs over your baked treat, then sprinkle with Wilton Cake Sparkles™ or Colored Sugars (shown at left) or spray with Color Mist™ Food Color Spray (p. 136). 8 designs.
417-T-495 $1.99

COMFORT GRIP™ CUTTERS

Cushion grip cutters have extra-deep stainless steel sides. Great for cutting, cushion grip gives comfortable control. Recipe included. Approx. 4½ x 1½ in. deep.
$2.99

Oak Leaf
2310-T-633

Maple Leaf
2310-T-632

Pumpkin
2310-T-600

METAL CUTTERS

Sure-to-please shapes. Recipe included.

Leaves and Acorns Nesting Cutter Set
Set of 9: Graduated acorns, oak and maple leaves, (3 each). 1¾ to 3¾ in.
2308-T-2000 Set/9 $5.99

Harvest Mini Metal Cutter Set
Set of 6: oak leaf, maple leaf, apple, pumpkin, elm leaf and acorn, approx. 1½ in.
2308-T-1217 Set/6 $2.99

Harvest Cutter Set

NEW!

Set of 3 includes pumpkin, turkey and leaf, each approx. 3 to 3½ in.
2308-T-1264 Set/3 $3.49

NEW!

Turkey Cutter
Quality metal cuts neatly and is easy to handle. 3 in. Colored aluminum.
2308-T-1319 $0.79

Wedding Style

Wilton has a beautiful selection of products for today's bride. From toasting glasses to garters to favors, we'll help you design the wedding day of your dreams!

Wedding Ensembles

Fulfill your wedding day dreams with the finest coordinated wedding accessories. Nicely presented, a complete collection makes a beautiful gift. Or enjoy the flexibility of choosing individual accessories that personalize the wedding day!

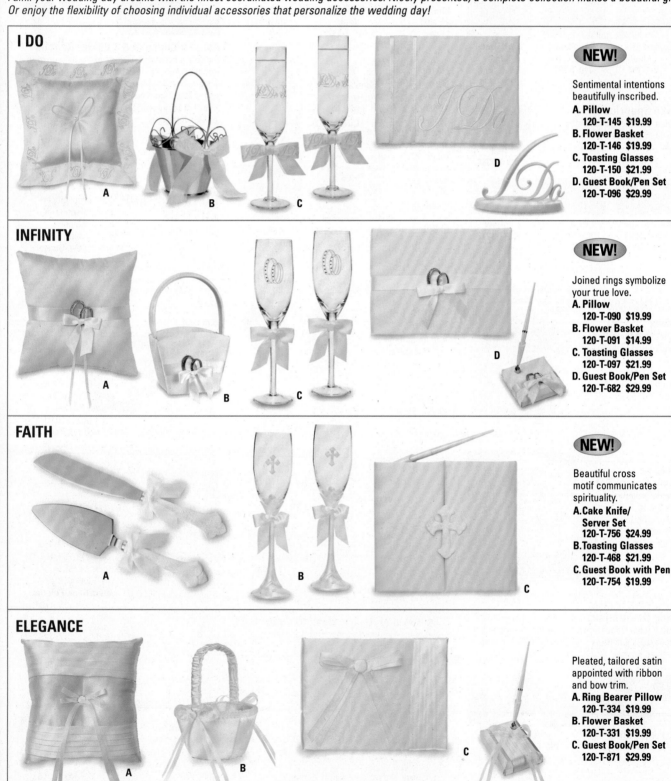

I DO

NEW!

Sentimental intentions beautifully inscribed.
- **A. Pillow**
  120-T-145 $19.99
- **B. Flower Basket**
  120-T-146 $19.99
- **C. Toasting Glasses**
  120-T-150 $21.99
- **D. Guest Book/Pen Set**
  120-T-096 $29.99

INFINITY

NEW!

Joined rings symbolize your true love.
- **A. Pillow**
  120-T-090 $19.99
- **B. Flower Basket**
  120-T-091 $14.99
- **C. Toasting Glasses**
  120-T-097 $21.99
- **D. Guest Book/Pen Set**
  120-T-682 $29.99

FAITH

NEW!

Beautiful cross motif communicates spirituality.
- **A. Cake Knife/ Server Set**
  120-T-756 $24.99
- **B. Toasting Glasses**
  120-T-468 $21.99
- **C. Guest Book with Pen**
  120-T-754 $19.99

ELEGANCE

Pleated, tailored satin appointed with ribbon and bow trim.
- **A. Ring Bearer Pillow**
  120-T-334 $19.99
- **B. Flower Basket**
  120-T-331 $19.99
- **C. Guest Book/Pen Set**
  120-T-871 $29.99

ORDER TOLL FREE: 800-794-5866

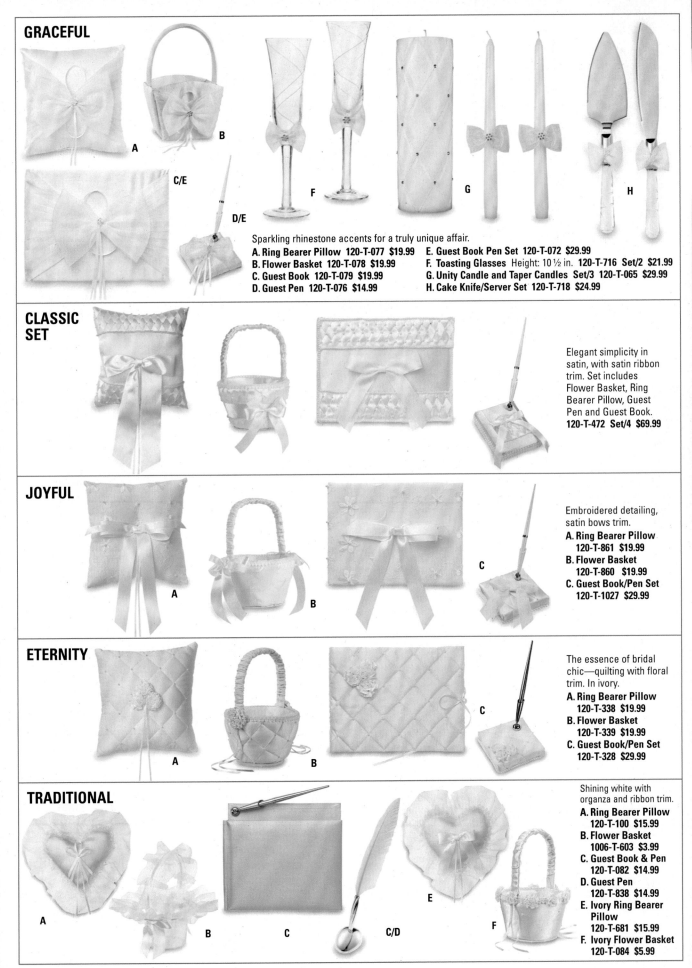

GRACEFUL

Sparkling rhinestone accents for a truly unique affair.

A. **Ring Bearer Pillow** 120-T-077 $19.99
B. **Flower Basket** 120-T-078 $19.99
C. **Guest Book** 120-T-079 $19.99
D. **Guest Pen** 120-T-076 $14.99
E. **Guest Book Pen Set** 120-T-072 $29.99
F. **Toasting Glasses** Height: 10 ½ in. 120-T-716 Set/2 $21.99
G. **Unity Candle and Taper Candles** Set/3 120-T-065 $29.99
H. **Cake Knife/Server Set** 120-T-718 $24.99

CLASSIC SET

Elegant simplicity in satin, with satin ribbon trim. Set includes Flower Basket, Ring Bearer Pillow, Guest Pen and Guest Book.
120-T-472 Set/4 $69.99

JOYFUL

Embroidered detailing, satin bows trim.

A. **Ring Bearer Pillow** 120-T-861 $19.99
B. **Flower Basket** 120-T-860 $19.99
C. **Guest Book/Pen Set** 120-T-1027 $29.99

ETERNITY

The essence of bridal chic—quilting with floral trim. In ivory.

A. **Ring Bearer Pillow** 120-T-338 $19.99
B. **Flower Basket** 120-T-339 $19.99
C. **Guest Book/Pen Set** 120-T-328 $29.99

TRADITIONAL

Shining white with organza and ribbon trim.

A. **Ring Bearer Pillow** 120-T-100 $15.99
B. **Flower Basket** 1006-T-603 $3.99
C. **Guest Book & Pen** 120-T-082 $14.99
D. **Guest Pen** 120-T-838 $14.99
E. **Ivory Ring Bearer Pillow** 120-T-681 $15.99
F. **Ivory Flower Basket** 120-T-084 $5.99

TIMELESS

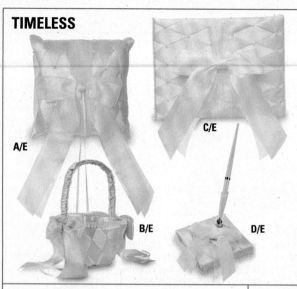

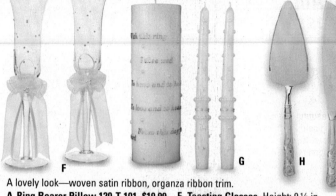

A lovely look—woven satin ribbon, organza ribbon trim.

A. Ring Bearer Pillow 120-T-101 $19.99
B. Flower Basket 120-T-604 $19.99
C. Guest Book 120-T-829 $19.99
D. Guest Pen 120-T-831 $14.99
E. Complete Set of 4 120-T-460 $69.99

F. Toasting Glasses Height: 9 ½ in.
   120-T-783 Set/2 $21.99
G. Unity Candle and Taper Candles
   Set/3 120-T-064 $29.99
H. Cake Knife/Server Set 120-T-4004 $29.99

SILVER SWIRL

NEW!

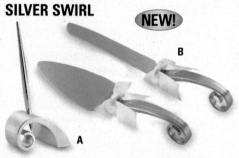

A twist on a contemporary look—brilliant silver swirls customize your day.
A. Guest Pen 120-T-751 $14.99
B. Cake Knife/Server Set 120-T-094 $24.99

CANDLE SETS

Swirl
Ornate sculpted design. Unity Candle is 9 in. high x 3 in. diameter; Taper Candles are 10 in. high.
Unity Candle
120-T-140 $19.99
Taper Candles
120-T-447
Set/2 $4.99

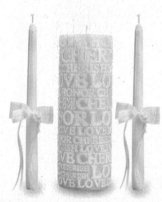

Love, Honor, Cherish
Contemporary lettering. Unity Candle is 9 in. high x 3 in. diameter; Taper Candles are 10 in. high.
120-T-066
Set/3 $29.99

CRYSTAL-LOOK

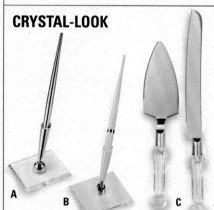

Glamorous crystal-look accents complete your wedding day.
A. Silver Guest Pen
   120-T-152 $5.99
B. White Guest Pen
   120-T-814 $5.99
C. Cake Knife/
   Server Set
   120-T-839 $24.99

Glass Candleholder Set
Bring the beauty and shimmer of crystal-look glass to your candle lighting ceremony. Ribbon trim. Unity candleholder is 5¾ in. high; holds a pillar candle up to 3¾ in. diameter. Each taper candleholder is 4¼ in. high; holds a standard size taper. Candles not included.
120-T-088 Set/3 $34.99

HEART SILVER

Heart Silver Toasting Glasses and Servers Ensemble
Bring the ultimate look of romance to your celebration.
120-T-232
Set/4 $49.99

TOASTING GLASSES

Fluted
Height: 10 in.
120-T-784
Set/2 $21.99

Bride and Groom
Height: 8 ⅜ in.
120-T-708
Set/2 $21.99

ORDER TOLL FREE: 800-794-5866

Wedding Day Accessories

FLORAL ACCESSORIES

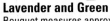

NEW! **NEW!** **NEW!**

Wedding Bouquets
Perfect, beautiful blooms to keep or to use during the bouquet toss. Hand-crafted, fine faux flowers.

White Rose Boutonniere

Perfect for weddings, prom, special occasions
1006-T-694 $4.99

Something Blue
Bouquet measures approx. 9½ in. diameter x 7½ in.
120-T-427 $24.99

Lavender and Green
Bouquet measures approx. 9½ in. diameter x 7½ in.
120-T-646 $24.99

Pastel Rose
Bouquet measures approx. 9½ in. diameter x 7 in.
120-T-103 $24.99

French
Bouquet measures approx. 9½ in. diameter x 7½ in.
120-T-1013 $24.99

Fresh Look Bouquet Holder

Make bouquets for the wedding party! It's easy to do, using your favorite silk or fabric flowers.
1006-T-611 $7.99

Scented Soap Petals **NEW!**

Fragrant, colorful accents perfect for sachets, favor bags, welcome baskets for guests, decorative accents. Approx. 300 petals.
120-T-571 $9.99

Silver Bouquet Holder

Arrange the bride's favorite flowers in this keepsake holder. Silver-plated. 7½ in. long.
120-T-651 $12.99

Bouquet Collar
Slip over stems to dress up any bouquet. White Organza; 10½ in. diameter.
1006-T-992 $1.99

Flower Petals
Fill the flower girl's basket, scatter on the cake table, decorate favors. Lifelike 2½ in. diameter flower petals. Approx. 300 petals.
$9.99

Lavender Hydrangea
1006-T-879

White Rose
1006-T-698

Blush Rose
1006-T-697

Red Rose
1006-T-695

WEDDING REMEMBRANCES
Beautiful things keep your wonderful wedding memories alive.

NEW!

NEW!

Bridal Handkerchief
Carry it as the "something blue" on your wedding day. Washable cotton, 10 in. square.
1006-T-398 $4.99

Tossing Garter
Ribbon, pearl and lace trim.
Blue 120-T-402 $5.99
White 120-T-401 $5.99

Bridal Autograph Pillow
Fun alternative to the guest book and great bride's keepsake! Guests write their "advice" to the bride. Includes pen. Pillow measures 10 x 10 in.
120-T-230 $14.99

Autograph Mat
Let guests create wonderful wedding memories. Each size holds 5 x 7 in. photo, includes black pen.
11 x 14 in. fits 11 x 14 in. frame.
1009-T-508 $5.99

8 x 10 in. fits 8 x 10 in. frame.
1009-T-1103 $3.99

NEW!

NEW!

Rhinestone Heart Hair Picks

Delicate, sparkling hair accessories make a chic addition to every hairstyle. Designed to be worn with or without a veil. Silver-plated metal, appointed with rhinestones.
1006-T-4464 Set/2 $9.99

NEW!

NEW!

Pearl and Rhinestone Hair Picks

Delicate, sparkling hair accessories make a chic addition to every hairstyle. Designed to be worn with or without a veil. Silver-plated metal, appointed with rhinestones and faux pearls.
1006-T-4466 Set/2 $9.99

addition rstyle. to be worn without a Silver-plated tal, appointed with hinestones.
1006-T-4463 Set/2 $9.99

NEW!

Rhinestone Hair Picks

Delicate, sparkling hair accessories make a chic addition to every hairstyle. Designed to be worn with or without a veil. Silver-plated metal, appointed with rhinestones and faux pearls.
1006-T-4469 Set/2 $9.99

Cathedral Length Veil

Look and feel like a princess! Formal cathedral length, sheer netting. Use with any headpiece, tiara; with hair picks or alone. Comb included. Veil measures 102 in. long x 72 in. wide.
120-T-163 $19.99

Wedding Day Décor
CENTERPIECES

Lighted Lantern

Straight from the pages of decorating magazines, these lighted lanterns create a party setting styled to your celebration—indoors or out! Hang or use as a centerpiece. Uses two AAA batteries, not included. 9½ in. high x 8 in. wide
1006-T-278 $4.99

Celebration Tree

Use it as a party decoration, displayed on the gift table, and as a centerpiece on reception tables. Easy to assemble. Metal construction. Assembled tree measures approx. 14 in. high x 11 in. wide. (Favors and decorations shown not included.)
1006-T-571 $9.99

See matching place card holders on p. 223!

See matching favor containers on p. 221!

Heart Basket

Makes a stunning table centerpiece—fill it with flowers, candy, favors, more. Includes a clear liner to securely hold smaller contents. Silver-tone metal basket measures 3¾ in. high x 5⁷⁄₁₆ in. diameter at rim. (Decorations and candy shown not included.)
1006-T-998 $4.99

Always festive, paper decorations are trendy, fun, and economical too! Easy to assemble. Reusable, fold to store flat.

Blossoming Bride
7 in. wide x 9¼ in. high.
120-T-841 $2.99

Wedding Dress
7 in. wide x 10 in. high.
120-T-547 $2.99

Wedding Day Décor

NEW!

NEW!

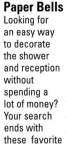

Flameless Votives
Add the romantic glow of candlelight with safe, no flame candles. Includes: 8 flameless votives (with 8 replaceable CR2032 batteries included), 8 holders. Average battery life: 24 hours.
1006-T-7137 Set/8 $15.99

Heart Wreaths
Beautiful, full floral accents bring romance to your celebration—perfect for bridal showers, wedding and anniversary receptions. Use the attached ribbon loop to hang, or cut ribbon loop and tie on to attach.
7 in. **1006-T-7127 $7.99**
12 in. **1006-T-7126 $9.99**

Satin Chair Cover
Distinguish wedding party and special guest seating at your celebration —fits most standard folding and party chairs. Fabric dye changes both cover into perfect-colored accents for your wedding day!
1006-T-131 $9.99

Tulle Spool
Create beautiful bows, swags and puffs, even use as ribbon for gift wrap! Simply cut to desired length. 6 in. wide x 50 yards long.
1005-T-442 $7.99

Paper Bells
Looking for an easy way to decorate the shower and reception without spending a lot of money? Your search ends with these favorite shapes—bells, the all-time favorite icon of the wedding day! Crafted in paper, easy to assemble. Ribbon not included.
Medium 6⅝ x 8 in.
1006-T-270 Pk./3 $4.99
Small 3¼ x 4 in.
1006-T-276 Pk./7 $4.99

Sparkling Ice*
Container size: 1½ in. high x 4½ in. diameter.
1006-T-342 $9.99

*WARNING: CHOKING HAZARD– Small parts. Not intended for children. Not a toy–for decorative use only.

BRIDAL GARLANDS
Romantic garland adds a soft glow to your wedding ambiance! You'll find so many uses for the ceremony and reception. Drape on pews and line the aisles, place along table edges and around the cake, wrap around pillars. Lighted garlands are battery operated (uses 2 D Batteries, not included).

Lighted Organza Rose
6 Ft. Length **1006-T-584 $23.99**

Lighted White Rose
6 Ft. Length **1006-T-350 $23.99**

Rose Garland
Non-lighting; roses strung together by organza ribbon. 6 foot length.
1006-T-917 $9.99

Car Decorating Kit
Eye-catching decorations trim the bride and groom's getaway vehicle with style! Includes: Magnetic "Just Married" sign, window clings, pre-fluffed pom-poms, streamers, balloons. Crafted of weather-resistant materials, reusable (except balloons).
1006-T-483 $14.99

RECEPTION GIFT CARD HOLDERS
Attractively keep the wedding gift cards together at the reception. Tulle, ribbon and flowers not included. Use the Tulle Spool (sold above) for creating puffs that decorate the Gift Card Holders.

Gift Shape
Whimsical gift box design of sturdy metal construction with faux gem trim, extra long slot for envelopes, box opens from the top, heart-shaped lock and key. 10¾ in. high x 8 in. long x 8 in. deep.
120-T-220 $24.99

Horizontal
White painted wire. After the reception, use as a display for flowers or photos. 12 in. high x 10 in. long x 7 in. deep.
120-T-875 $24.99

Vertical
White painted wire. After the reception, use as a display for flowers or photos. 16½ in. high x 7 in. long x 7 in. deep.
120-T-330 $24.99

Mailbox
Personalize the flag with a photo or saying at www. wiltonprint.com. Includes easy to assemble mailbox, 2 printable labels, 1 test sheet. White printed corrugated cardboard. 12 in. high x 15¼ in. wide x 10¼ in. deep.
1006-T-396 $14.99

Wishing Well
A charming display for any shower, wedding, or anniversary celebration. White printed corrugated cardboard, easy to assemble. 30½ in. high x 16 in. wide x 14 in. deep.
1006-T-395 $14.99

Favor-Making Kits

Fun and festive kits personalize your favors with ease!

Silver Scoop Favor Kit

Scoop up a treat for your guests, wrap in tulle circle and add a personalized tag. Print the tags at **www.wiltonprint. com**. Silver-plated scoops measure 4 ¼ in. long. Food safe. Kit includes 24 scoops, 24 (9 in.) tulle circles, 24 (12 in.) satin ribbons, 24 printable tags, 2 test sheets. Candy not included.
1006-T-177 Pk./24 $24.99

Clear Vase Favor Kit

Fill these crystal clear vases with candy or flowers and arrange one at each guests' place setting. Print the tags at **www.wiltonprint.com**. Vases measure 3 in. high. Food safe. Kit includes 16 vases, 16 (12 in.) satin ribbons, 16 printable tags, 2 test sheets. Candy not included.
1006-T-252 Pk./16 $24.99

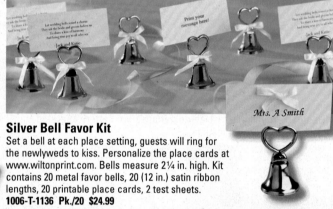

Square Pail Favor Kit

Make elegant favors with personalized tags perfect for all occasions. Print the tags at **www.wiltonprint. com**. Food safe pails measure 2 in. high. Kit contains 18 favor pails, 18 (12 in.) satin ribbon lengths, 18 printable tags, 2 test sheets. Candy not included.
1006-T-1137 Pk./18 $24.99

Silver Bell Favor Kit

Set a bell at each place setting, guests will ring for the newlyweds to kiss. Personalize the place cards at www.wiltonprint.com. Bells measure 2¼ in. high. Kit contains 20 metal favor bells, 20 (12 in.) satin ribbon lengths, 20 printable place cards, 2 test sheets.
1006-T-1136 Pk./20 $24.99

Favor Tins Mega Kits

Create personalized favor tins for your celebration using your computer, or hand design. Includes 25 tins, 25 adhesive labels and strips, complete instructions. Just download template from **www.wiltonprint.com**. Candy not included.
1006-T-8038 Pk./25 $19.99

Love Potion Favor Kit

Fill to match your celebration theme and surprise your guests. Personalize the stickers at www.wiltonprint.com. Bottles measure 2¾ in. high. Kit includes 24 glass bottles with slotted corks. 24 (12 in.) satin ribbon lengths, funnel for easy filling, 24 printable stickers, 2 test sheets. Candy not included.
1006-T-1009 Pk./24 $24.99

CD Favor Tins

Create personalized CD labels for your celebration using your computer, or hand design. Includes 12 tins, 12 adhesive labels and complete instructions. Just download template from **www.wiltonprint.com**.
1006-T-4474 Pk./12 $24.99

Candle Favors

Add a romantic touch to showers, receptions, every celebration. Includes 12 lightly-scented 4 in. mini candles, and 3 in. candle holders already decorated with white organza bows.
1006-T-643 Pk./12 $14.99

Heart Favor Mega Kits

Make 24 favors with heart containers, tulle circles, ribbon and favor tags. Candy not included.
1006-T-924 Pk./24 $24.99

Goblet Favor Mega Kits

Make 24 favors with goblet containers, tulle circles, ribbon and favor tags. Candy not included.
1006-T-923 Pk./24 $24.99

Drawstring Wrappers

Create 12 cute favors in no time at all! Kit includes pre-assembled drawstring wrapper and favor tags. Just fill and tie.
White   1006-T-921 Pk./12 $12.99
Lavender 1006-T-922 Pk./12 $12.99

Favor Containers

These beautiful containers hold favors for shower, wedding and anniversary celebrations. Perfect for mints, almonds, potpourri and small gifts.

NEW!

Faith Favor Box
1 ¾ in. high x 2 ½ in. wide. Paper.
1006-T-7150
Pk./10 $5.99

Flirty Fleur Favor Box
2¼ in. high x 2¼ in. wide. Paper.
1006-T-936 Pk./10 $4.99

Sweet Heart Favor Bag
6 in. high x 3¼ wide x 1¾ in. deep. Includes sheer white ribbon. Paper.
1006-T-940 Pk./10 $4.99

Flirty Fleur Favor Bag
6 in. high x 3¼ wide x 1¾ in. deep. Includes sheer white ribbon. Paper.
1006-T-941 Pk./10 $4.99

Simple Yet Elegant Favor Bag
6 in. high x 3¼ wide x 1¾ in. deep.Includes sheer white ribbon. Paper.
1006-T-939 Pk./10 $4.99

Silver Heart Box
2 in. high x 2 in. wide. Metal.
1006-T-169 $1.29

See matching centerpiece on p. 218!

Silver Heart Patterned Basket
3½ in. high x 3 in. wide. Metal.
1006-T-338 $1.29

Tuxedo
4 in. high. Paper.
1006-T-514
Pk./10 $9.99

Ivory Chest
2½ in. high x 2¼ in. long x 1½ in. wide. Paper.
1006-T-515 Pk./20 $9.99

Heart Tab
2¼ in. high x 2¼ in. long x 2¼ in. wide. Paper.
1006-T-517 Pk./20 $9.99

Silver Heart Pillow
1 in. high x 3 in. long x 2¼ in. wide. Paper.
1006-T-557 Pk./20 $9.99

Champagne Glass
Clear. 2 in. high. Plastic.
1006-T-614 Pk./12 $2.49

CAKE SLICE BOXES

Favor Cake Box
Shaped and decorated like a slice of wedding cake. 20 boxes fit together to form a round cake tier. 4¼ in. long x 2¾ in. high.
1006-T-629 Pk./20 $6.99

Cake Slice Boxes
Bakery style boxes measure 5 in. square x 3½ in. high.
415-T-955
Pk./5 $3.49

Tulle Sachets; Organza and Tulle Circles

Perfect for favors, rose petals, rice, treats, gifts.

Drawstring Sachet Bags
Sheer organza fabric pouch closes with a pull of the ribbons. 3¾ x 4 in. Pk./12 $5.99

White
1006-T-173

Ivory
1006-T-176

Lavender
1006-T-189

Red
1006-T-188

Black
1006-T-1126

Also available:
4½ x 6¾ in. size. White.
1006-T-184 Pk./12 $7.99

Organza Circles with Ribbon Trim
Organza trimmed with ribbon makes the prettiest favors, decorations, and crafts. 9 in. diameter.
Pk./25 $5.99
White 1005-T-426 Pink 1005-T-107
Ivory 1005-T-106

White Tulle Circles
Makes beautiful favors and decorations! Sheer mesh fabric measures 9 in. diameter.
1005-T-7882
Pk./75 $5.99

Candy

Trendy and traditional candies make great fillers for favors and candy dishes at showers, weddings, celebrations!

NEW!   **NEW!**

Wedding Rings
35 pieces per package. Sweet/ tart fruit flavored. Each measures 1⅛ in. high x 1 wide.
1006-T-6170 $3.99

Mini Pastels
10 oz. bag. Fruit flavored.
1006-T-904 $3.99

Wedding Bells
12 oz. bag. Sweet/ tart fruit flavored.
1006-T-1140 $5.99

Mint Drops
16 oz. bag. Assorted. Certified Kosher.
1006-T-788 $5.99

Wedding Message Hearts
10 oz. bag; approx. 90 pieces. Mint flavored.
1006-T-371 $3.99

Pillow Mints
10 oz. bag. approx. 205 pieces. Assorted. Certified Kosher.
1006-T-858 $3.99

Jordan Almonds
16 oz.; approx. 100 pc. Certified Kosher.
Assorted
1006-T-779 $7.99
White
1006-T-778 $7.99

Favors
WEDDING BUBBLES

Celebrate the wedding by showering the newly married couple with shimmering bubbles. It's a fun trend and a great way to wish the bride and groom good luck!

Contains 24 .6 oz. bottles of bubbles with wands. Decorate with Favor Band (shown below) and Tulle or Organza Circles (shown on p. 221).
1007-T-8000 Pk./24 $4.99

Pop Out Streamers
Great for weddings, graduations, birthdays, New Year's celebrations, surprise parties. Just aim and press lever. Each contains ten silver foil streamers that stay attached to tube for easy disposal. Streamers are over 10 feet long. Spring loaded, the streamers do not contain gunpowder or other explosives.
1006-T-932 Pkg./14 $24.99

NEW!

Large Bling Ring
Makes a big impression as a package tie-on, party favor, napkin ring. Measures 3 x 4 in.
1006-T-282 $1.49

NEW!

Notepad Favors
Perfect as favors and thank you gifts! Matchbook style pads measure 2¾ in. and have 40 sheets.
1006-T-1135 Pk./10 $4.99

Love Knot Wands
Use after the ceremony or at the reception. 36 wands are packed in a convenient tray for reception table use. Ribbon not included. Each wand contains .16 fl. oz. bubble solution.
1007-T-8017 Pk./36 $9.99

Celebration Bells
Ring for a special kiss after the ceremony and at the reception. Hand to guests exiting the church, and place one at each setting at the reception. Contains 24 bells, poem tags and ties. Bell measures 1¼ in. tall.
Silver
1007-T-8012 Pk./24 $6.49
White
1007-T-8013 Pk./24 $6.49

Silver-tone Pens
Perfect as shower, reception, and anniversary favors. Convenient to have on hand for games at showers and parties. Black ink. Ribbon not included.
1006-T-1008 Pk./6 $9.99

Place Cards and Holders

An elegant way to indicate seating arrangements; and a stunning display for photos, special notes and thanks for your guests.

NEW!

Silver Double Bell Place Cards
Perfect for wedding and anniversary!
1006-T-627 Pk./70 $4.99

Silver Double Heart Place Cards
Use for every life celebration!
1006-T-752 Pk./40 $2.29

Sweet Heart Glass Place Card Holders
Clip on back to attach to rim of glass or napkin ring. Approx. 4¾ in. high x 2½ in. wide. (Ribbon and card inserts not included.) Paper.
1006-T-933 Pk./20 $4.99

Wedding Dress Place Card Holders
Charming place card holder can also display photos, menu, thank you notes. (Place cards not included.)
120-T-842 Pk./6 $5.99

See matching centerpiece on p. 218!

Favor Frames

Insert a favorite photo or use as a place card holder by adding your guest's name.

"Glass" Slippers
Heel is slotted to hold place card. 1¾ in. high x 1 in. wide x 2 in. deep. Plastic.
1006-T-370 Pk./12 $5.99

Fleur-De-Lis
2½ in. high x 3½ in. wide. Silver-tone plastic.
1006-T-376 Pk./5 $5.99

Single Heart
1 in. high x 1 in. wide. Metal.
1009-T-239 $0.99

Favor Accents and Leaves

Romantic accents add sparkling beauty and elegance to favors, table decorations!

NEW!

Thank You Tags
Send a message of gratitude —tie to favor boxes or bags. Stamped tin. Measures 1¾ in. diameter.
1006-T-987 Pk./12 $1.99

NEW!

Sweetheart Charms
Shows the sweet, sentimental sign of love. Stamped tin. Measures 1¼ x ¾ in.
1006-T-411 Pk./12 $1.99

NEW!

Double Bell Charms
Ring the good news of the bride and groom! Stamped tin. Measures 1⅜ x 1 in.
1006-T-1132 Pk./12 $1.99

NEW!

Clear Heart Charms
Crystal-look hearts add shimmer and elegance. Plastic. Measures ¾ in. diameter.
1006-T-1558 Pk./12 $1.99

NEW!

Love Charms
Spell it out for all to see. Stamped tin. Measures 1½ in. long.
1006-T-573 Pk./12 $1.99

NEW!

Faith Cross Favor Accents
Detailed cross accents add an elegant look to favors, decorations, and more! 1 in. long plastic. Tie on with ribbon or attach with hot glue. Pk./20 $1.99
Silver 1006-T-4501
White 1006-T-7149

Engagement Rings
Sparkling favor accents to add beauty to favors, table decorations, centerpieces. Faux diamond measures ¼ in. diameter.
1006-T-115 Pk./12 $1.99

Wedding Bands
¾ in. diameter.
Pk./48 $1.99
Silver 1006-T-101
Gold 1006-T-100
Pk./288 $6.99
Silver 1006-T-422
Gold 1006-T-421

Bling Rings
Use these sparkling favor accents to add beauty to favors, table decorations. Faux diamond measures 1 in. diameter.
1006-T-919 Pk./12 $4.99

Thank You Tags
Clear oval tags, imprinted in silver are threaded on 11¾ in. organza ribbon lengths. Tie onto favors, wine glass stems, napkins and more.
1006-T-927 Pk./20 $4.99

Lily Spray
9 in. long.
1006-T-503
Pk./12 $1.99

White Pearl Spray
8 in. long.
1006-T-506
Pk./12 $2.49

Glittered Doves
Coated with non-edible glitter. Do not place directly on cake.
2 x 1½ in.
1006-T-166
Pk./12 $1.99

White Pearl Beading
Molded on one continuous 5-yard strand. Remove pearls before cutting and serving cake.
Small (4 mm) 211-T-1989 $2.99
Large (6 mm) 211-T-1990 $3.99

Satin Stripe Favor Bands
Functional and decorative, a pretty way to accent favors. Use on Drawstring Sachets, Wedding Bubbles bottles and more for an instant decoration. 2 in. wide.
1007-T-8014 Pk./12 $2.99

Gold
1⅞ in. long.
1005-T-6518
Pk./144 $3.99
1¼ in. long.
1005-T-6712
Pk./144 $3.49

Silver
1⅞ in. long.
1005-T-6526
Pk./144 $3.99
1¼ in. long.
1005-T-6720
Pk./144 $3.49

Green
2½ in. long leaf, 2½ in. stem.
1005-T-401
Pk./12 $1.49

Candy Bar Molds

Create a sweet memory for your guests, a candy bar featuring a special message.

Molding is easy using Wilton Candy Melts® (p. 166). Present them beautifully in Candy Bar Boxes. Each bar measures 3¼ in. wide x 1¾ in. tall x ¼ in. deep. 1 design, 4 cavities. $1.99

Candy Bar Boxes
The window displays your special message.
Pk./10 $3.99
White 1904-T-1157
Silver 1904-T-1159

Our Wedding
2115-T-1409

Thank You
2115-T-1410

Add-A-Message
2115-T-1356

Bridal Shower Accessories

Personalized extras add more to your celebration.

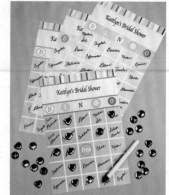

Favor Box with Tissue Puff
Fill with scented soap petals, small gifts, candy. Boxes measure 2 ½ in. wide x 1 ¾ in. high.
120-T-570 Pk./20 $9.99

Autograph Plate
Create a distinctive keepsake for the bride right at the celebration—a fun alternative to a guest book. Crafted in melamine, 12 in. diameter. Includes marker.
120-T-575 $9.99

Bling Placecard Kit
Every trendy party starts with bling—for girlfriends, fun-to-wear shower favors, place cards. Print the cards at www. wiltonprint.com, tie on with ribbon. Kit includes 20 rings in assorted colors (blue, lavender, yellow, pink), 20 cards, 20 ribbon lengths (each 14 in. long), 2 test sheets.
120-T-577 Pk./20 $9.99

Bridal Party Bingo
Personalize the bingo cards for your event at www.wiltonprint,. com. Guests write the names of gifts they think the bride will receive in the spaces on the cards. Then, play like traditional bingo. Includes bingo for 12: 12 cards, 12 packets gem markers, 12 pencils.
120-T-576 Pk./12 $9.99

Bachelorette Party Accessories

Gather the bridesmaids and girlfriends for the best party ever!

Garter
Brightly colored and flirty—fun for the bachelorette party! Crafted of satin, ribbon and lace.
1004-T-1509 $1.99

Autograph Mat
Frame your favorite girlfriend photo and have everyone sign the mat—makes a great keepsake for the bride! Holds 5 x 7 in. photo, fits 8 x 10 in. frame. Includes pen.
1006-T-896 $3.99

Bride-To-Be Tiara with Veil
Flirty and stylish accessory. Silver-tone tiara with faux gemstones.
1006-T-631 $3.99

Glow Bracelets
Light up the party with brightly colored, glow in the dark bracelets for everyone to wear. Perfect for every bachelorette event. 24 assorted colors.
1004-T-1501 Pk./24 $3.99

Name Tags
Identify your party-goers at a glance. Pressure sensitive tags have space for name. Each tag measures 2½ in. high x 3½ in. long.
1006-T-418 Pk./12 $2.99

Buttons
Wear these fun, colorful buttons as badges of honor—they tell just who you are in the wedding party. 2½ in. diameter.
1006-T-417 Pk./6 $4.99

Bride-To-Be Sash
Satin ribbon proudly tells the world you are about to be married. One size fits most. 38 in. long, 4 in. wide.
1006-T-981 $3.99

Wedding Cakes

From the keepsake figurine on top to the impressive stand below, Wilton has something special just for your wedding cake!

Wedding Figurines

More brides choose Wilton figurines to top their wedding cakes. The rich, sculpted crafting, realistic detailing and romantic designs make these figurines perfect wedding day keepsakes.

Always and Forever Petite Embrace
Height: 3¾ in.
Base: 2½ in. diameter. Resin.
202-T-311 **$21.99**

Bianca
Height: 5½ in.
Base: 3¾ x 3½ in. Resin.
202-T-207 **$24.99**

Clear Bianca
Height: 5½ in.
Base: 3¾ x 3½ in. Acrylic.
Perfect on Lighted Revolving Base (sold on p. 227).
202-T-424 **$24.99**

Always and Forever
Height: 6½ in. Base: 7 x 5 in.
Resin, plastic, fabric.
118-T-200 **$37.99**

Always and Forever Musical Ornament
Plays "The Wedding March". Height: 7¼ in.
Base: 4¼ in. diameter. Resin.
215-T-310 **$49.99**

HUMOROUS WEDDING FIGURINES

Add a lighthearted touch to the celebration. Sure to bring a smile to the face of anyone who has ever planned a wedding!

IT LIGHTS!

Castle
Lights from within using 2 D batteries (not included).
Height: 7½ in.
Base: 4½ in. Resin.
111-T-2804 **$59.99**

With This Ring
Height: 4½ in.
Base: 3½ diameter.
Resin.
202-T-313 **$24.99**

Ball and Chain
Height: 4¼ in.
Base: 3½ in. Resin.
115-T-7143 **$19.99**

Runaway Bride
Height: 4 in.
Base: 3¼ in. Resin.
115-T-7142 **$19.99**

The Tiff
Height: 4 in. Base:
2¼ x 2 in. Resin.
115-T-103 **$14.99**

NEW! **NEW!**

Threshold of Happiness
Height: 5 in.
Base: 3¼ x 2 in.
Resin.
202-T-202 **$24.99**

From This Day Forward
Height: 5 in.
Base: 3¼ x 2 in.
Resin.
202-T-319 **$24.99**

Oh No You Don't
Height: 4¼ in. Base: 6 x 3 in. Resin.
115-T-102 **$19.99** Ethnic 115-T-104 **$19.99**

Now I Have You
Height: 4¼ in. Base: 4¼ x 3¾ in. Resin.
115-T-101 **$19.99**

Just Married
Height: 5 in.
Base: 5 x 3¼ in. Resin.
110-T-864 $44.99

Elegance
Height: 5½ in.
Base: 5 x 3 in. Resin.
110-T-863 $34.99

Forever In Your Eyes
Height: 6 in.
Base: 5 in. diameter. Resin.
110-T-903 $39.99

NEW!

Sweet Couple
Clever topper sits on the edge of the cake—perfect when you want a distinctive cake decoration.
Height: 4¼ in.
Base: 1¾ in. Resin.
1006-T-7145 $14.99

Expression of Love
Height: 7¾ in.
Base: 4½ in. diameter.
Poly resin, plastic, fabric.
101-T-931 $35.99

Sweetness
Height: 7¾ in.
Base: 4½ in. diameter.
Poly resin, plastic, fabric.
101-T-153 $29.99

Ethnic Expression of Love
Height: 7¾ in. Base: 4½ in. diameter.
Poly resin, plastic, fabric.
101-T-933 $35.99
Couple Only
Height: 4½ in. Base: 2¼ x 1¾ in. Poly resin.
202-T-306 $6.99

Love's Duet
Height: 6 in.
Base: 2½ x 2¼ in.
Poly resin.
202-T-402
$14.99
Ethnic
202-T-412
$14.99

Our Day
Height: 4¾ in.
Base: 2 x 1¾ in. Poly resin.
Blonde/ White Gown
202-T-409
$6.99

Brunette/ Ivory Gown
(not shown)
202-T-415 $6.99

Classic Couple
Add a touch of nostalgia. Plastic.
Height: 4½ in. Base: 2 x 3 in.
Brunette 202-T-1422 $6.99
Blonde (not shown) 202-T-1423 $6.99
Ethnic 202-T-1421 $6.99

Lasting Love
Height: 4½ in.
Base: 2¼ x 1¾ in.
Poly resin.
202-T-302 $6.99

Spring Song
Height: 9½ in. Base: 4⅝ in. diameter.
Plastic, fabric flowers.
111-T-2802 $19.99
Kissing Lovebirds 5½ in. high. Plastic.
1002-T-206 $4.99

Petite Spring Song
Height: 7 in.
Base: 3¼ in. diameter.
Plastic, fabric flowers.
106-T-159 $12.99

Simple Joys
Height: 8 in.
Base: 4½ in. diameter.
Plastic, fabric flowers, fabric.
103-T-150 $24.99

Devotion
Height: 7 in.
Base: 4 x 2½ in. Ceramic.
111-T-2803 $34.99

ORDER TOLL FREE: 800-794-5866

NEW!

Two Rings
Height: 5½ in.
Base: 3¾ in. diameter.
Plastic, resin.
1006-T-1121 $34.99

Enduring Love
Height: 5 in.
Base: 7 x 5 in. oval.
Plastic, tulle.
103-T-235 $35.99

Inspirational Cross
Height: 5½ in.
Base: 2 x 1½ in.
Resin.
202-T-398 $14.99

Reflections
Porcelain couple.
Height: 8 in.
Base: 4¾ in. diameter.
Plastic, fabric flowers, tulle.
117-T-268 $25.99

CAKE PICKS

NEW!

The new look—stunning picks draw attention to your celebration—perfect for cake tops, floral arrangements, bouquets and centerpieces. Beautifully appointed with rhinestones, crafted of painted resin. Food-safe. Approximately 5-5¼ in. high overall.

Decorative
NEW!
Perfect for wedding and anniversary celebrations.

Faith Cross
1006-T-4475 $14.99

Infinity Rings
1008-T-805 $14.99

Double Hearts
1006-T-985 $14.99

Anniversary
Silver 25th
1008-T-758 $14.99
Gold 50th
1008-T-762 $14.99

Specialty Toppers

Follow today's trends of decorating the cake with new shapes, fantasy themes, and designs that mirror other elements of your special day!

Song Of Love Cake Jewelry
Handcrafted of metal with sparkling rhinestones, painted hues, butterflies and flowers.
Height: 4½ in.
Base: 4 in. diameter.
120-T-492 $39.99

LA QUINCEAÑERA
Honor her on her 15th birthday celebration. Use as cake top decoration or as a favor.
Height: 4½ in.
Base: 2¾ in. diameter.
Plastic.
203-T-305 $3.99

ANNIVERSARY ORNAMENTS

Petite 50th
Height: 5¾ in.
Base: 3¼ in. diameter.
Plastic.
105-T-4273 $9.99

Petite 25th
Silver tone.
105-T-4265 $9.99

50 Years of Happiness
Height: 10 in.
Base: 4⅝ in. diameter. Plastic, fabric flowers.
102-T-223 $19.99

Ornament Settings and Bases

A beautiful beginning to a cake top ornament you create. Simply add the figurine of your choice, and trim with flowers, fabric tulle and accents.

IT LIGHTS!

Romantic Heart
2 pieces, 4⅝ in. diameter.
Plastic.
201-T-7332 $2.99

Lighted Revolving Base
Select just light, just rotate or both at the same time. Uses 3 AA batteries (not included).
Height: 2 in. Diameter: 5 in.
201-T-453 $24.99

Chapel Windows
Use with base or alone.
6½ x 5 x 1 in. deep. Plastic
205-T-3060 $4.99

Gazebo Set
Easy to assemble plastic. 5 x 9 in. high.
205-T-3061 $4.99

Floral Arch
Height: 10 in.
Base: 4⅝ in. diameter.
Plastic, fabric flowers.
210-T-1987 $9.99

Cake Assembly Sets

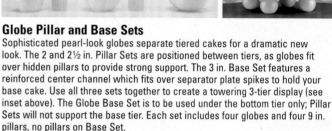

Fluted Bowl Separator Set

The translucent bowl separator makes it easy to add designer color treatments that complement your tiered cake. Simply fill it with fresh or silk flowers, tulle or patterned fabric, or use it on its own. The curving, fluted design adds a fresh new element that works for a variety of wedding and shower cakes. Setup couldn't be simpler: the included separator plates are spiked to fit inside the top and bottom openings of the bowl for a secure presentation. Set includes 4 in. high fluted bowl and 2 smooth-edge separator plates (6 and 10 in. diameter). Holds cakes up to 9 in. diameter.
303-T-823 Set/3 $19.99

Globe Pillar and Base Sets

Sophisticated pearl-look globes separate tiered cakes for a dramatic new look. The 2 and 2½ in. Pillar Sets are positioned between tiers, as globes fit over hidden pillars to provide strong support. The 3 in. Base Set features a reinforced center channel which fits over separator plate spikes to hold your base cake. Use all three sets together to create a towering 3-tier display (see inset above). The Globe Base Set is to be used under the bottom tier only; Pillar Sets will not support the base tier. Each set includes four globes and four 9 in. pillars, no pillars on Base Set.

2 in. 303-T-822 Set/8 $7.99   **2½ in. 303-T-824 Set/8 $9.99**
3 in. Globe Base Set 303-T-825 Set/4 $9.99
9 in. Replacement Pillars Set 303-T-4005 Set/4 $3.99

Spiral Separator Sets

Add an elegant touch to your special occasion cakes with these beautifully scrolled separators. The curling, openwork design in white coated metal gives cakes a light, garden style design. Setup couldn't be simpler—the smooth-edge plates are spiked to fit inside the top and bottom rings for a secure presentation. Use sets together for a high-rising construction of 3 separated tiers or use on their own to hold 2 or 3 stacked tiers.

10 in. Set
Includes 7 x 4¼ in. high wire separator ring, 2 smooth-edge separator plates, 8 and 10 in. diameter. Holds 6, 8 or 9 in. round cakes.
303-T-8176 Set/3 $19.99

14 in. Set
Includes 10½ x 4¼ in. high wire separator ring, 2 smooth-edge separator plates, 10 and 14 in. diameter. Holds round cakes 12 in. or smaller.
303-T-8175 Set/3 $29.99

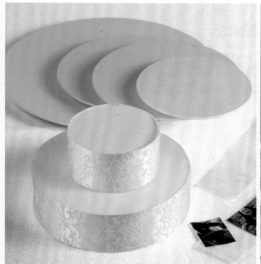

Tailored Tiers Cake Display Set

Satin-look separators add beautiful texture to any tiered cake design. The elegant patterned fabric which covers the foam separators will complement most wedding, shower and anniversary designs and looks wonderful with floral arrangements. As an added bonus, use the included acetate photo wraps to customize the separators with treasured family photos, wrapping paper or an alternate fabric. It's a great way to personalize your cake for those special occasions. Set includes 2 satin brocade wrapped craft foam separators (4¼ and 7¼ in. diameter x 2 in. high), 4 smooth-edge separator plates (one 6 in., two 8 in., one 12 in. diameter) and 2 acetate photo wraps. The 4¼ in. separator holds cakes up to 6 in. diameter when used with 8 in. top plate; the 7¼ in. separator holds cakes up to 10 in. diameter when used with 12 in. top plate.
304-T-8174 Set/8 $29.99

Crystal-Clear Cake Divider Set

- Sparkling clear twist legs beautifully accent your cake
- Designed for towering cakes from 6 to 14 in. diameter
- An elegant combination with Wilton Crystal-Look accessories

Clear plastic twist legs penetrate cake, rest on plate (dowel rods not needed). Includes 6, 8, 10, 12, 14 and 16 in. plastic separator plates plus 24 legs.
301-T-9450 Set/30 $49.99

Additional Plates
6 in. **302-T-9730** $2.99
8 in. **302-T-9749** $3.99
10 in. **302-T-9757** $4.99
12 in. **302-T-9765** $6.99
14 in. **302-T-9773** $8.99
16 in. **302-T-9780** $10.99

7½ in. Twist Legs
303-T-9794 Pk./4 $3.99

9 in. Twist Legs
Add more height to your tiers.
303-T-977 Pk./4 $4.99

Grecian Pillar and Plate Set
A deluxe money-saving collection for the serious cake decorator. Decorator Preferred® scalloped-edge separator plates and 5 in. pillars. Includes 54 pieces: two each 6 in., 8 in., 10 in., 12 in. and 14 in. plates; 20 Grecian pillars and 24 pegs.
SAVE 27% on set
301-T-8380 Set/54 $49.99

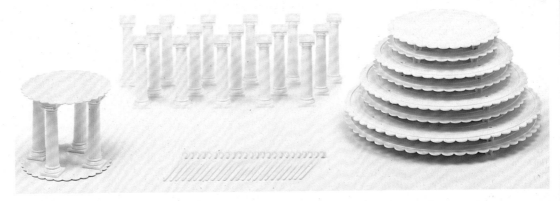

Roman Column Tier Set
Stately Roman pillars and scalloped-edge plates create beautiful settings for all tiered cakes. Includes 8 pieces: six 13¾ in. Roman columns and two super strong 18 in. round Decorator Preferred® separator plates. Lovely with the Kolor-Flo Fountain (sold on pg. 232).
301-T-1981 Set/8 $39.99

Arched Tier Set
Dramatic when used with Kolor-Flo Fountain (sold on pg. 232). Includes 14 pieces: Six 13 in. arched columns, two super strong 18 in. round Decorator Preferred® separator plates and six angelic cherubs to attach to columns with royal icing or glue.
301-T-1982 Set/14 $45.99

Curved Pillars
Modern, pearlized pillars bring a contemporary look to any classic tiered cake design.
2½ in. 303-T-658 Pk./4 $4.99
5 in. 303-T-659 Pk./4 $6.99

"Hidden" Pillars
Separate cake tiers slightly and create a floating illusion. Pushed into tiers as dowel rods, they fit onto all white separator plates except Tall Tier. Trimmable, hollow plastic. 6 in. high.
303-T-8 Pk./4 $2.99

Grecian Pillars
Elegantly scrolled and ribbed.
3 in. 303-T-3606 Pk./4 $2.99
5 in. 303-T-3703 Pk./4 $3.99
7 in. 303-T-3705 Pk./4 $4.99

Crystal-Look Pillars
Use with Crystal-Look Plates (sold on pg. 231) and Crystal Bridge and Graceful Stairway Set (sold on pg. 232).
3 in. 303-T-2171 Pk./4 $3.49
5 in. 303-T-2196 Pk./4 $4.99
7 in. 303-T-2197 Pk./4 $4.99
*13¾ in. 303-T-2242 $3.99
*Sold singly. Use only with 17 in. Crystal-Look plate (sold on pg. 231).

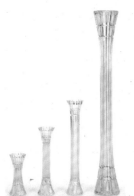

Arched Pillars
Grecian-inspired with arched support.
4½ in. 303-T-452 Pk./4 $3.99
6½ in. 303-T-657 Pk./4 $4.99
13 in. 303-T-9720 Pk./2 $7.99

Roman Columns
Handsome pillars may be used with 16 and 18 in. plates and the Kolor-Flo Fountain (sold on pg. 232).
10¼ in. 303-T-8136 Pk./2 $5.99
13¾ in. 303-T-2130 Pk./2 $6.99

Baker's Best® Disposable Pillars with Rings
Single plate pillars.
7 in. 303-T-4000 Pk./4 $2.99
9 in. 303-T-4001 Pk./4 $3.49

Crystal-Look Spiked Pillars
Single plate pillars. Double cake circles for extra support.
7 in. 303-T-2322 Pk./4 $4.49
9 in. 303-T-2324 Pk./4 $5.49

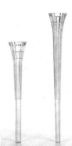

Grecian Spiked Pillars
Single plate pillars. Wide base for increased stability.
5 in. 303-T-3708 Pk./4 $2.49
7 in. 303-T-3710 Pk./4 $3.49
9 in. 303-T-3712 Pk./4 $4.49

Cake Displays

Stunning Wilton Cake Displays are the perfect way to show off your special wedding cake. Take a look—there's one perfectly suited to your wedding cake size and design.

NEW!

FEATURED ON OUR COVER AND SPECIAL SECTION!

NEW!

Graceful Tiers Cake Stand

The three-tiered, scrollwork stand features crystal-clear plates which nest securely in each section. Ideal for garden-themed wedding cakes, but also perfect to display cupcakes, muffins, candies, fruit and more. Set includes cream-colored powder-coated metal stand, 14½ wide x 29½ high; 3 clear plastic separator plates, 8, 10 and 12 in. diameter, to hold 6, 8 and 10 in. round cakes; 1 wrench for tightening bolts on bottom tier, all hardware; easy assembly instructions.
307-T-841 $49.99

Romantic Castle Cake Set

Create a fairy tale for your wedding. Everything you need to transform your tiered cake into a fantasy castle is included: three sizes of detailed turret towers with removable peak pieces, lattice windows, a paneled door and roof pieces. Easy to assemble. Complete assembly and decorating ideas included for princess, medieval and candy castle designs. See 7 exciting castle ideas in our Special Section (p. 88) and many more designs on-line at www.wilton.com!
301-T-910 Set/32 $19.99

Cakes 'N More™ 3-Tier Party Stand

Contemporary stairstep stand with crystal-clear plates puts the focus where it belongs—on your stunning cake and desserts! Constructed in metal with chrome-plated finish, stand holds 3 different size cake plates—8, 10 and 12 in. (included). Easy to set up and take apart.
307-T-859 $29.99
Replacement Plates Set
302-T-7925 $9.99

Tall Tier Cake Stand

Display your multi-tiered cakes up to 6 tiers high with this majestic stand. Lace-look plates enhance every cake design and hold tiers from 6 to 16 in. diameter. Easier to assemble than pillar construction, the twist-together center columns and strong, interchangeable plates provide stability.

Basic Set
Includes: 5 twist-apart columns, 6½ in. high; top nut and bottom bolt; 18 in. footed base plate; 8, 10, 12, 14 and 16 in. separator plates (interchangeable, except footed base plate). Plastic.
304-T-7915 Set/13 $45.99

Replacement Parts
Top Column Cap Nut **304-T-7923 $0.79**
Bottom Column Bolt **304-T-7941 $0.99**

Additional Plates
8 in.	**302-T-7894**	**$3.99**	14 in.	**302-T-7940** **$8.99**
10 in.	**302-T-7908**	**$4.99**	16 in.	**302-T-7967** **$11.99**
12 in.	**302-T-7924**	**$5.99**	18 in.	**302-T-7983** **$14.99**

Additional Columns
6½ in. **303-T-7910 $1.99**
7¾ in. **304-T-5009 $2.99**
13½ in. **303-T-703 $4.99**

Glue-On Plate Legs
Convert 14 or 16 in. separator plate into a footed base plate. Order 6 legs for each plate.
304-T-7930 $0.59

Lady Windemere-Look 4-Arm Base (For Use With Tall-Tier Stand)
Easily adds 4 base cakes to your tall tier cake. The 4-arm base can be used with any plate from the basic set, except the 18 in. footed base plate. Up to 3 graduated tiers can be added to the center columns. Includes 20 in. diameter 4-arm base with 4 stability pegs and base bolt. Use with 13½ in. column, bottom column bolt and four 12 in. plates, sold above.
304-T-8245 $11.99
Additional Base Bolt 304-T-8253 $0.59

Candlelight Cake Stand

Elegant scrollwork and soft candlelight show off your cake. Convenient flameless votives are safe, and perfect for receptions where real candles are not permitted. Stand supports 40 lbs., use with 14 in. smooth or scallop edge separator plate, not included. Includes 21½ in. diameter x 5 in. high stand, 4 flameless votives (with 4 replaceable CR2032 batteries included), 4 holders. Average battery life: 24 hours.
307-T-351 $39.99

NEW!

Garden Cake Stand

Our beautiful Garden Cake Stand echoes the wrought-iron look found in many formal gardens. Simply place cakes on plates and set on the stand. Painted metal stand is 23 in. high x 22 in. wide and uses 10 in., 14 in. and 18 in. scalloped separator plates (p. 223). Satellite garden stands sold individually below.
307-T-860 $169.99

Satellite Garden Cake Stand
Painted metal; holds 12 in. separator plate.
307-T-861 $44.99

Cake Corer Tube (not shown)
Essential tool easily and neatly removes center from cake tiers when tall tier stand columns are used. Ice cake before using. Serrated edge removes cake center with one push. Cleans easily.
304-T-8172 $1.99

CUPCAKES 'N MORE® DESSERT STANDS

Easy to assemble!
Just stack each layer of cupcakes onto the locking center rod.

Keeps looking great!
Non-toxic, silver-finished metal has a durable non-chip finish.

Collapsible design
Stores easily and safely.

Angled holders
Give the best view of cupcake tops!

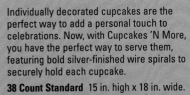

Individually decorated cupcakes are the perfect way to add a personal touch to celebrations. Now, with Cupcakes 'N More, you have the perfect way to serve them, featuring bold silver-finished wire spirals to securely hold each cupcake.

NEW!

38 Count Standard 15 in. high x 18 in. wide. Holds 38 cupcakes (shown above).
307-T-651 $39.99

23 Count Standard 12 in. high x 13 in. wide. Holds 23 cupcakes.
307-T-826 $29.99

24 Count Mini 10½ in. high x 9 in. wide. Holds 24 mini cupcakes. **NEW!**
307-T-250 $14.99

13 Count Standard
9¼ in. high x 9 in. wide.
Holds 13 standard cupcakes.
307-T-831 $12.99

FLOATING TIERS CAKE STANDS

Round

NEW! **DISASSEMBLES FOR EASY STORAGE!**

The beautiful illusion of floating tiers, made more convenient because it disassembles for easy storage. Includes base tier, center tier and top tier rings, left and right footed ring support bars, top tier connector bar, 1 long and 5 short fastening screws, 8, 12 and 16 in. separator plates which hold 6, 10 and 14 in. cakes. Assembly required, instructions included.
307-T-710 $69.99

Round

Original design—set includes 17 in. high enamel coated white metal stand, 8, 12, and 16 in. smooth separator plates; instructions.
307-T-825 $69.99

Replacement Plates
(Same plates as Crystal-Clear Cake Divider Set.)
8 in. **302-T-9749 $3.99**
12 in. **302-T-9765 $6.99**
16 in. **302-T-9780 $10.99**

Heart

Perfectly sized to heart shaped tiers. Set includes 17 in. high enamel coated white metal stand, 8, 12 and 16 in. Decorator Preferred® Heart separator plates; instructions.
307-T-872 $69.99

Replacement Plates
8 in. **302-T-60 $2.99**
12 in. **302-T-62 $4.99**
16 in. **302-T-64 $8.99**

Separator Plates

Decorator Preferred® Smooth Edge Plates

A fresh, clean shape puts the focus on your cake. Built for unmatched stability, with our patented Circles of Strength™ design. Plate feet fit securely on Wilton pillars, available in many styles (p. 229).

6 in.	302-T-4101 $2.29	14 in.	302-T-4105 $5.99
8 in.	302-T-4102 $2.99	16 in.	302-T-4106 $8.99
10 in.	302-T-4103 $3.99	18 in.	302-T-4107 $11.99
12 in.	302-T-4104 $4.99		

Decorator Preferred® Scalloped Plates

Our best, strongest separator plates with superior stability and beauty.

6 in.	302-T-6 $2.29	12 in.	302-T-12 $4.99
7 in.	302-T-7 $2.49	13 in.	302-T-13 $5.49
8 in.	302-T-8 $2.99	14 in.	302-T-14 $5.99
9 in.	302-T-9 $3.49	15 in.	302-T-15 $6.99
10 in.	302-T-10 $3.99	16 in.	302-T-16 $8.99
11 in.	302-T-11 $4.49	18 in.	302-T-18 $11.99

Decorator Preferred® Heart Plates

Perfectly sized to fit Wilton heart pans, for a stunning tiered heart creation.

8 in.	302-T-60 $2.99	14 in.	302-T-63 $5.99
10 in.	302-T-61 $3.99	16 in.	302-T-64 $8.99
12 in.	302-T-62 $4.99	18 in.	302-T-65 $11.99

Decorator Preferred® Square Plates

NEW!

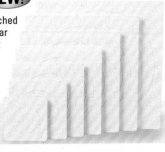

Clean lines, smooth edges, unmatched strength. Crafted for today's popular cake designs. Perfectly sized to fit Wilton Square pans.

6 in. **302-T-1801 $2.99**
8 in. **302-T-1802 $3.99**
10 in. **302-T-1803 $4.99**
12 in. **302-T-1804 $5.99**
14 in. **302-T-1805 $6.99**
16 in. **302-T-1806 $9.99**
18 in. **302-T-1807 $12.99**

Crystal-Look Plates

Wilton Crystal-Look plates have an elegance like no other, with ridged sides that look like cut crystal. Built with the strength and support Wilton is famous for. Use with Crystal-Look pillars (sold on p. 229).

7 in. **302-T-2013 $3.99**   13 in. **302-T-2078 $7.99**
9 in. **302-T-2035 $4.99**   * 17 in. **302-T-1810 $14.99**
11 in. **302-T-2051 $5.99**

*Use only with 13¾ in. Crystal-Look pillars (sold on p. 229).

17 in. Crystal-Look Plate and Pillar Set

Ideal style and height for use with fountains (sold on p. 232). Contains four 13¾ in. pillars and two 17 in. plates. (not shown)
301-T-1387 $45.99

Cake Fountains and Accessories

Kolor-Flo Fountain
Professional quality fountain looks spectacular with every tiered cake design. Water cascades dramatically from three levels; simply remove top levels for smaller fountain arrangements. Intricate light system with two bulbs for added brilliance. Use with 16 or 18 in. scalloped edge plates; 18 in. smooth edge plate (p. 223). Coordinates with our 17 in. Crystal-Look Plate and Pillar Set (p. 223). Plastic fountain bowl is 9¾ in. diameter. 110-124 V, AC motor with 65 in. cord. Pumps water electrically. Directions, replacement part information included.
306-T-2599 $109.99

Replacement Parts for Kolor-Flo Fountain

Light Bulb
306-T-1053 $5.99

Cascade /Pump Connector
306-T-1088 $3.49

Light Socket
306-T-1045 $5.49

Bottom Base
306-T-1170 $13.99

Floater Switch
306-T-1096 $14.49

Pump/Bulb Bracket
306-T-1037 $3.39

Piston
306-T-1029 $3.99

Pump
306-T-1002 $48.99

Cascade Set for Kolor-Flo Fountain
Dome shapes redirect water over surface in non-stop streams. Set includes 4 pieces: 2½ in., 4½ in., 8 in., and 11½ in. diameter.
306-T-1172 Set/4 $14.99

Upper Cascade **306-T-1118 $6.99**
Middle Cascade **306-T-1126 $8.69**
Lower Cascade **306-T-1134 $10.49**
Bowl **306-T-1142 $17.99**

Fanci Fountain
Economical fountain in crystal-clear design enhances any tiered cake. Adjustable, smooth water flow. Use with 16 or 18 in. scalloped edge plates; 18 in. smooth edge plate (p. 223). Set-up instructions included.
Height: 12 in. Diameter: 10 in.
306-T-2000 $69.99

Replacement Parts for Fanci Fountain
Bulb
306-T-1790 $1.79

Cascade Set
306-T-1791 $9.99

Fresh Flower Accessories

Crystal-Look Bowl
4½ in. diameter. 1½ in. deep.
205-T-1404 $2.99

Flower Spikes
Fill with water, push into cake, add flowers. Makes cakes safe for insertion of stems or wires. 3 in. high.
1008-T-408 Pk./12 $2.49

Fresh Flower Holders
Insert easily under cake tiers to hold blooms, greenery, pearl sprays, tulle puffs and more. Use with floral oasis to keep flowers fresh.
205-T-8500 Pk./2 $2.99

Flower Holder Ring
Put at base of Kolor-Flo Fountain as shown at right. 12½ in. diameter x 2 in. high. 1¾ in. wide opening; inside ring diameter is 8½ in. Plastic.
305-T-435 $4.99

Stairways and Bridges
Bridge the gap between lavish tiers.

Crystal Bridge and Graceful Stairway Set
Includes two stairways (16¾ in. long) and one platform (4¾ x 5 in.). Plastic.
205-T-2311 Set/3 $14.99

Filigree Bridge and Stairway Set
Includes two stairways (16¼ in. long) and one platform (4¾ x 5 in.). Plastic.
205-T-2109 Set/3 $11.99

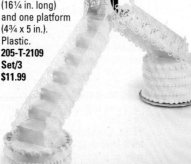

Dowel Rods and Pegs

Plastic Dowel Rods
Heavy-duty hollow plastic provides strong, sanitary support for all tiered cakes. Cut with serrated knife to desired length. Length: 12¾ in. Diam.: ¾ in.
399-T-801 Pk./4 $2.49

Wooden Dowel Rods
Cut and sharpen with strong shears and knife. Length: 12 in. Diam.: ¼ in.
399-T-1009 Pk./12 $2.99

Plastic Pegs
Insure that cake layers and separator plates atop cakes stay in place. Pegs do not add support; dowel rod cake properly before using. Length: 4 in.
399-T-762 Pk./12 $1.44

Cake Boards and Accents

Your cake will look its best when presented with quality Wilton boards, doilies and ruffled trims.

Cake Boards
Shaped cakes look best on boards cut to fit! Strong corrugated cardboard, generously-sized in rectangular shapes. Perfect for sheet and square cakes. For shaped cakes, use the pan as a pattern and cut out board to fit cake.
10 x 14 in. **2104-T-554 Pk./6 $4.79**
13 x 19 in. **2104-T-552 Pk./6 $5.29**

Cake Circles
Corrugated cardboard for strength and stability.
6 in. diameter	**2104-T-64**	Pk./10	**$3.19**
8 in. diameter	**2104-T-80**	Pk./12	**$4.19**
10 in. diameter	**2104-T-102**	Pk./12	**$5.29**
12 in. diameter	**2104-T-129**	Pk./8	**$5.29**
14 in. diameter	**2104-T-145**	Pk./6	**$5.69**
16 in. diameter	**2104-T-160**	Pk./6	**$6.29**

Silver Cake Bases
Convenient ½ in. thick silver-covered bases are grease-resistant, food-safe and reusable. Strong to hold heavy decorated cakes without an additional serving plate. Perfect for all types of cakes and craft creations.
10 in. Round	**2104-T-1187**	Pk./2	**$6.99**
12 in. Round	**2104-T-1188**	Pk./2	**$7.99**
14 in. Round	**2104-T-1189**	Pk./2	**$9.99**
16 in. Round	**2104-T-1190**	Pk./2	**$11.99**

Show 'N Serve™ Cake Boards
Scalloped edge has the look of intricate lace. Food-safe, grease-resistant coating.
10 in. diameter	**2104-T-1168**	Pk./10	**$4.49**
12 in. diameter	**2104-T-1176**	Pk./8	**$4.99**
14 in. diameter	**2104-T-1184**	Pk./6	**$5.49**
14 x 20 in. Rectangle	**2104-T-1230**	Pk./6	**$5.99**

Ruffle Boards®
Ready-to-use cake board and ruffle in one. Bleached white board and all-white ruffling complement any cake.
8 in. (for 6 in. round cake)	**415-T-950**	**$2.49**
10 in. (for 8 in. round cake)	**415-T-960**	**$2.99**
12 in. (for 10 in. round cake)	**415-T-970**	**$3.99**
14 in. (for 12 in. round cake)	**415-T-980**	**$4.49**
16 in. (for 14 in. round cake)	**415-T-990**	**$5.49**
18 in. (for 16 in. round cake)	**415-T-1000**	**$7.49**

Tuk-'N-Ruffle®
A pretty touch that attaches to edge of your serving tray or board with royal icing or tape.
60 ft. bolt per box.
White **802-T-1008 $14.99**
6 ft. pkg. White
802-T-1991 $2.99

Fanci-Foil
Serving side has a non-toxic grease-resistant surface. FDA-approved for use with food.
Continuous roll:
20 in. x 15 ft.
White **804-T-191 $7.99**
Gold **804-T-183 $7.99**
Silver **804-T-167 $7.99**

Cake Doilies
Add instant elegance to cake plates, dessert trays, entrée and sandwich servings. Use under table centerpieces and plants, for decorations and crafts, too.

Silver Foil
4 in. Round
2104-T-90404 Pk./12 $2.49
6 in. Round
2104-T-90116 Pk./18 $2.49
8 in. Round
2104-T-90006 Pk./12 $2.49
10 in. Round
2104-T-90007 Pk./6 $2.49
12 in. Round
2104-T-90412 Pk./4 $2.49

Gold Foil
4 in. Round
2104-T-90304 Pk./12 $2.49
6 in. Round
2104-T-90306 Pk./18 $2.49
8 in. Round
2104-T-90308 Pk./12 $2.49
10 in. Round
2104-T-90310 Pk./6 $2.49
12 in. Round
2104-T-90312 Pk./4 $2.49

Grease-Proof White
4 in. Round	**2104-T-90204**	Pk./30	**$1.99**
6 in. Round	**2104-T-90206**	Pk./20	**$1.99**
8 in. Round	**2104-T-90208**	Pk./16	**$1.99**
10 in. Round	**2104-T-90210**	Pk./10	**$1.99**
12 in. Round	**2104-T-90212**	Pk./6	**$1.99**
14 in. Round	**2104-T-90214**	Pk./4	**$1.99**
10 x 14 in. Rectangle	**2104-T-90224**	Pk./6	**$1.99**

Cake Accents
Romantic accents add a sparkling beauty and elegance to cakes.

White Pearl Beading
Molded on one continuous 5-yard strand. Remove before cutting and serving cake.
Small (4 mm) **211-T-1989 $2.99**
Large (6 mm) **211-T-1990 $3.99**

Scrolls
2¾ in. x 1¼ in.
Plastic.
1004-T-2801
Pk./24 $2.29

Baby

Start planning the party! From pink to blue, and themes in between, this dazzling array of Wilton products will inspire you to make the cutest things for your baby celebration.

Baby Favor Kits

All you add is candy—adorable favor containers are packaged in larger quantities to complete your favor making in no time at all!

Baby Blocks
Featuring print-your-own tags to personalize favors—it's easy to do at www.wiltonprint.com. 1¾ in. squares. Multicolor pastel assortment. Includes 20 blocks, 20 tags with printing instructions, 20 ribbons, 2 printing test sheets. (Candy and tulle not included.)
1006-T-284 Pk./20 $24.99

Drawstring Wrappers
They're pre-assembled! Just fill, tie ribbons, and add favor tag. (Candy not included.)
Pk./12 $12.99

Pink
1006-T-218
Blue
1006-T-219
White
1006-T-340

Multicolor
3 each pink, blue, yellow, mint green.
1006-T-245

Pails
Featuring print-your-own tags to personalize favors—it's easy to do at www.wiltonprint.com. Crafted of food-safe painted metal, pails measure 2 x 2⅜ in. diameter at rim. Includes 18 pails, 18 tags with printing instructions, 2 printing test sheets. (Candy, tulle, favor tie and safety pin accent not included.)
1006-T-916 Pk./18 $24.99
Pail Only 1006-T-915 $1.29 each

Rattles **NEW!**
Favorite baby icon easily makes party favors and decorations. Just add Wilton Favor Candy—each clear side hinges open for easy filling. Personalize tags at www.wiltonprint.com. Multicolor pastel assortment rattles measure 4 in. long. Includes 20 rattles, 20 ribbons, 20 printable tags, 2 test sheets. (Candy not included.)
1006-T-572 Pk./20 $24.99

Baby Bottles
Featuring print-your-own tags to personalize favors —it's easy to do at www.wiltonprint.com. Bottles measure 4 in. high, ½ in. diameter opening. Multicolor pastel assortment. Includes 24 bottles, 24 tags with printing instructions, 24 ribbons, 2 printing test sheets. (Candy and safety pin accents not included.)
1006-T-577 Pk./24 $24.99
Bottles Only 1006-T-696 Pk./6 $5.99

Cradles **NEW!**
Cute baby cradles look adorable at each place setting. Fill with your favorite candy, and print a personalized place card or message on the tag at www.wiltonprint.com. White cradles measure 2½ x 2½ x 1½ in. wide. Includes 18 cradle favor containers, 18 ribbons, 18 printable tags and 2 test sheets. (Candy not included.)
1006-T-1330 Pk./18 $24.99

Favor Containers

Perfect as favors, filled with candy and treats, and as gift and cake accents.

Drawstring Sachets
Ready to fill with Jordan Almonds, Rose Petals, Pillow Mints, small gifts. 3¾ x 4 in. high.
Pk./12 $5.99

Pink 1006-T-179
Blue 1006-T-180
Multicolor
3 each pink, blue, yellow, mint green.
1006-T-244

Tulle Circles
Sheer tulle circles come in an assortment of pretty pastel shades, perfect for all baby celebrations. Make cute favors, use in centerpieces, decorations and floral arrangements. Contains 5 each pink, lavender, blue, yellow, mint green. 9 in. diameter.
1006-T-288
Pk./25 $2.99

Pearlized Baby Cradles **NEW!**
Adorable as favors, cake toppers and table decorations. 2½ in. high, crafted in plastic.
Pink Cradle
1006-T-262 $1.99

Blue Cradle
1006-T-264 $1.99

Baby Blocks Containers*
Removable lids for easy filling. Each 1¼ in. high.
2113-T-419 Set/4 $2.99

Baby Favor Bags
Delightful container for candies, small gifts and other favor treats. 3 x 5½ in. high.
1006-T-362 Pk./12 $7.99

Baby Party Bags
Colorful designs for candy and cookie treats. 20 plastic bags, 20 ties included. 4 x 9½ in.
1912-T-2365 Pk./20 $1.99

White Flower Basket
2¼ x 3⅜ in. high. Metal. Contents shown not included.
1006-T-990 $1.29

Favor Accents

Add special touches to your baby favors, gift tie-ons and table decorations.

Baby Bracelets*
Pink, blue, yellow, mint green.
1¼ in. high.
1103-T-56
Pk./6 $2.29

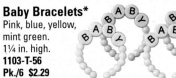

Mini Clothes Pins*
Pink, lavender, blue, yellow, mint green.
1⅜ in. high.
1103-T-27
Pk./20 $1.99

Small Safety Pins*
1½ in. long.
Pk./20 $1.99
Pink 1103-T-21
Blue 1103-T-26
Multicolor
Pink, blue, yellow, mint green.
1103-T-42

Mini Baby Bottles*
Pink, lavender, blue, yellow, mint green. 1¼ in. high.
1103-T-16 Pk./20 $1.99

Ethnic Newborn Baby Figurines*
1 in. high.
1103-T-30 Pk./6 $1.99

Newborn Baby Figurines*
1 in. high.
1103-T-62 Pk./6 $1.99

Baby Bears*
1 in. high.
Pk./6 $2.99
Blue 1103-T-7
Pink 1103-T-8
Multicolor
Pink, blue, yellow, mint green. 1103-T-46

Rocking Horses*
Three blue, three pink.
2½ in. high.
1103-T-28
Pk./6 $3.99

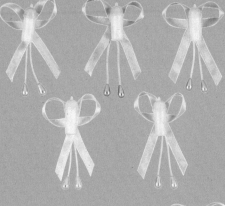

Shower Rattles*
Pink, lavender, blue, yellow, mint green.
3¾ in. high.
1103-T-29
Pk./6
$2.99

Mini Rocking Horses*
Pink, lavender, blue, yellow, mint green.
1¼ in. high.
1103-T-52 Pk./6 $1.99

Sleeping Angels Set
A precious pose, one pink and one blue. 2 in. high x 3 in. long.
2113-T-2325
Set/2 $1.99

FAVOR TIES

Instant decoration for favors, bubbles, gifts. Slip one on to close filled bags and tulle favor puffs, or use to decorate any baby favor.

Baby Bottle
Accented with a cute baby bottle.
Pk./6 $2.49
Pink
1006-T-509
Blue
1006-T-508
Multicolor
Pink, lavender, blue, yellow, mint green.
1006-T-575

Baby Pacifier
Accented with a mini pacifier.
Pk./6 $2.49
Pink
1006-T-566
Blue
1006-T-567
Multicolor
Pink, lavender, blue, yellow, mint green.
1006-T-361

Candy

Fun shapes, beautiful colors, great flavors! Wilton candy makes the perfect filler for favors, treat bags, candy dishes.

NEW!

Mini Pastels
Assorted fruit flavors.
10 oz. bag.
1006-T-904 $3.99

Baby Talk
Assorted fruit flavors.
10 oz. bag.
1006-T-1115 $3.99

Mini Pacifiers
Assorted sweet/tart fruit flavors. 12 oz. bag. Certified Kosher.
1006-T-540 $5.99

Mint Drops
Assorted colors. 16 oz. bag. Certified Kosher.
1006-T-788 $5.99

Jordan Almonds
16 oz. bag; approx. 100 pieces. Certified Kosher. $7.99
Assorted 1006-T-779
White 1006-T-778

Pillow Mints
Assorted colors. 10 oz. bag; approx. 205 pieces. Certified Kosher.
1006-T-858 $3.99

*WARNING: CHOKING HAZARD—Small parts. Not intended for children. Not a toy—for decorative use only.

BABY

Party Decorations

Adorable accents crafted in paper add a special touch to your celebration.

Baby Bottle Garland
The perfect accent for baby showers and celebrations. 8 ft. long. Paper.
1006-T-426
$3.99

Centerpiece
Cute centerpiece is easy to assemble. Paper with ribbon pull. Assembled centerpiece measures 8 x 5 x 14½ in. high.
1006-T-427 $3.99

Lighted Lantern
Hang for a spectacular effect, or use as table decorations. Uses two AAA batteries, not included. Easy to assemble; Paper, plastic, metal. 8 x 9 in. wide.
1006-T-423 $4.99

Pop Up Favor Boxes
One piece construction for easy-to-assemble quick favors. Paper. Assembled size; 2¼ in. square.
1006-T-425 Pk./10 $4.99

Baby Memories

Piggy Bank
Whimsical, yet practical, it's a great gift idea and fun accent for baby's room. Cute just as it is, or you can personalize with name and birthdate, pink or blue, or any design you choose. Crafted in ceramic. Has coin slot on top, removable plug on the bottom. 5¾ in. high. x 8 in. long.
1009-T-1113 $9.99

Best Wishes Bear
Create a precious keepsake for the new baby. Makes a great shower gift. Includes blue and pink sheer ribbons and pen. 9¼ in. high, holds 4 x 3 in. photo. Fabric covered. (Clothespin accents not included.)
1009-T-1140 $16.99

Autograph Mat
Holds a 5 x 7 in. photo, with room for autographs and good wishes from friends and family. Few gifts touch so many like this one! For use in an 11 x 14 in. frame. Pen included.
1009-T-1106 $5.99

Mini Favor Frames
Perfect shower favors, crafts, keepsakes. Hand out instead of cigars! 4 different designs per box, each 2⅞ x 2⅞ in. Holds 1½ x 1½ photo. Resin.
1009-T-1326
Pk./4 $7.99

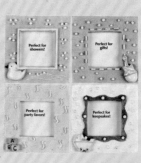

Rubber Ducky Theme

3-D Cake Pan
This bathtime favorite will make a big splash at baby showers. Five adorable designs included. Two-piece pan takes 5½ cups batter. 9 x 5 x 7 in. high. Aluminum.
2105-T-2094 $14.99

Baking Cups
Microwave-safe paper. Standard size, 2 in. diameter.
415-T-378 Pk./50 $1.49

Candles
Handpainted details, clean-burning design. 1½ in. high.
2811-T-9337
Set/6 $3.49

Candy Mold
Making candy is easy to do, complete directions are included. Reusable. Use Wilton Candy Melts®† sold on p. 162. 1 design, 6 cavities.
2115-T-1565 $1.99

†Brand confectionery coating.

Icing Decorations
Mint-flavored edible sugar shapes to decorate cupcakes, cookies, ice cream and cake. Certified Kosher.
710-T-293 Pk./12 $2.29

Party Bags
Fill with candy, cookies and other goodies; great for gifts and surprises, too! 20 plastic bags, 20 ties included. 4 x 9½ in.
1912-T-1275
Pk./20 $1.99

Cake Toppers

Baby Face
Oh-so-cute baby tops the baby shower or first birthday cake. 4 in. high; crafted in resin.
1006-T-257 $7.99

Super Mom-To-Be
Cute cake topper tells it like it is—mom does it all! 4¾ in. high; crafted in resin.
1006-T-259 $7.99

Oops!
Designed to top the baby shower cake or decorate the table, this whimsical topper also makes a great keepsake for the mother-to-be! 4¾ in. high; crafted in resin.
1006-T-1331 $7.99

Cradle
Perfect for shower or christening! Stylized cradle makes a great decoration for cake or table. 5 in. high, crafted in pearlized resin with ribbon trim.
1006-T-258 $7.99

Cake Server
What better way to cut and serve baby's cake than with a utensil designed just for the celebration? Whimsical stacked blocks spell out B-A-B-Y on the handle. Crafted in plastic with serrated edge. 10 in. long
1006-T-1312 $5.99

BABY

FAITH CROSS ACCESSORIES
Inspiring designs add a beautiful touch to spiritual events.

Stationery
Beautifully designed in white 80 lb. card stock with white pearlized trim. Professionally print at home at **www.wiltonprint.com**.
Invitations
Border and cross accent. Invitation: 5½ x 8½ in.; envelope: 5¾ x 8¾ in.
1008-T-775 Pk./12 $4.99
Thank You Cards
Folded cards with script and cross on front. Card: 5½ x 4¼ in.; envelope: 5¾ x approx. 4½ in.
1008-T-776 Pk./12 $4.99

Seals
Self adhesive, silver tone, 1 in. diameter.
1008-T-779 Pk./24 $1.99

Candy Molds
Fun-shaped, reusable molds celebrate baby over and over again. Making candy is easy to do, complete directions are included! Use with Wilton Candy Melts® brand confectionery coating, (p. 166).

Baby Treats
5 designs, 5 cavities.
2115-T-4447 $1.99

Baby Bottles Lollipop
1 design, 6 cavities.
2115-T-1560 $1.99

Baby Shower
4 designs, 11 cavities.
2115-T-1710 $1.99

Mini Baby Icons
5 designs, 20 cavities.
2115-T-1537 $1.99

Centerpiece
Stunning silver and white design, crafted in heavy card stock with honeycomb paper base. Assembled measures 7¾ x 9¾ in. high.
1006-T-7148 $2.99

6 Ft. Garland
Silver printed crosses on white paper garland make a beautiful, inspirational decoration. 6 ft. long, accordion folded. Unfold and use tape or ribbon to hang.
1006-T-498 $5.99

Favor Boxes
Distinctive boxes are perfect for your celebration. Fill with Wilton candy (not included). Paper, easy to assemble. Boxes measure 2½ x 1¾ in. high.
1006-T-7150 Pk./10 $5.99

Favor Accents
Detailed crosses add an elegant look to favors. 1 in. long plastic. Tie on with ribbon or attach with hot glue. **Pk./20 $1.99**
Silver 1006-T-4501
White 1006-T-7149

BAKEWARE

Stork Express Pan
Brings a bundle of joy to showers and baby welcome celebrations as a colorful cake, mousse or glittering gelatin mold. One-mix pan is 13 x 9½ x 2 in. deep. Aluminum.
2105-T-1191 $11.99

#1 Pan
Add the #1 cake to all the important first celebrations. One-mix pan is 12¾ x 8½ x 2 in. deep. Aluminum.
2105-T-1194 $11.99

Baby Buggy Pan
It's a precious carriage design for shower and christening, for cakes or elegant salads and gelatins. One-mix pan is 11¼ x 11¼ x 2 in. Aluminum.
2105-T-3319 $11.99

Print Your Own Stationery

*Get professional results right at home. Personalizing and printing invitations is easy to do—simply go to **www.wiltonprint.com** and see how!*

Complete Kits

Wilton Print-Your-Own Stationery is the perfect way to announce any special celebration! Complete kits are ready to personalize, print and mail! All invitation kits are crafted in 80 lb. card stock and feature distinctive accents. Invitations measure 5½ x 8½ in. Reply cards measure 5½ x 4¼ in.

See the complete line of Wilton stationery at **www.wiltonprint.com**.

The Two Of Us
Set of 25 Includes:
- 25 Invitations and Mailing Envelopes
- 25 Reply Cards and Envelopes
- 25 Pre-tied Bows with Adhesives
- 3 Test Sheets

Holds 4 x 6 image.
1008-T-709
Set/25 $24.99

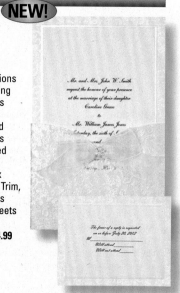

Happy Day
Set of 25 Includes:
- 25 Invitations and Mailing Envelopes
- 25 Reply Cards and Envelopes
- 25 Pre-tied Bows with Faux Diamond Trim, Adhesives
- 3 Test Sheets

1008-T-711
Set/25 $24.99

Simple Yet Elegant
Set of 25 Includes:
- 25 Invitations and Mailing Envelopes
- 25 Reply Cards and Envelopes
- 25 Pre-tied Bows with Adhesives, Circle Tags and Ball Chains
- 3 Test Sheets

1008-T-530
Set/25 $24.99
Also available in Ivory.
1008-T-531
Set/25 $24.99

Soiree
Set of 25 Includes:
- 25 Invitations and Mailing Envelopes
- 25 Reply Cards and Envelopes
- 25 Rhinestone Buckles with Ribbons
- 3 Test Sheets

1008-T-710
Set/25 $24.99

Portrait of Love
Set of 25 Includes:
- 25 Invitations and Mailing Envelopes
- 25 Reply Cards and Envelopes
- 25 Mini Frames with Adhesive Backing and Mini Frame Inserts
- 3 Test Sheets

1008-T-529
Set/25 $24.99

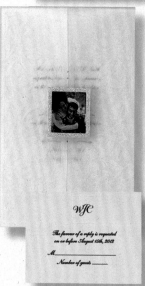

Two Hearts
Set of 50 Includes:
- 50 Invitations and Mailing Envelopes
- 50 Reply Cards and Envelopes
- 3 Test Sheets

1008-T-524
Set/50 $24.99

Joined Together
Set of 50 Includes:
- 50 Invitations and Mailing Envelopes
- 50 Reply Cards and Envelopes
- 3 Test Sheets

1008-T-522
Set/50 $24.99

Also available in Ivory with Gold.
1008-T-523
Set/50 $24.99

Flirty Fleur
Set of 50 Includes:
- 50 Invitations and Mailing Envelopes
- 50 Reply Cards and Envelopes
- 3 Test Sheets

1008-T-525
Set/50 $24.99

ORDER TOLL FREE: 800-794-5866

Learn from the Leaders in Cake Decorating!

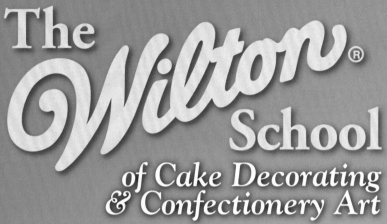

The Wilton School
of Cake Decorating & Confectionery Art
in Darien, Illinois

For 80 years The Wilton School has been home to the leading authorities in cake decorating. Today we offer more courses on more specialties than ever—all providing students with one-on-one guidance from world-class instructors. For professionals or hobbyists, there is no better place to explore cake decorating than The Wilton School.

THE MASTER COURSE
Join students from around the world at the most comprehensive cake decorating course! In 2 exciting weeks, students learn the skills to become a pro—20 borders, 15 flowers including The Wilton Rose. Learn color flow, piping gel and figure piping. All of these lead to the design, assembly and decoration of a 3-tiered wedding cake. Virtually all materials included.

SUPPLEMENTARY CLASSES *(available during the Master Course)*
Expand your skills with individual specialty courses in rolled fondant, candy making, sugar art and Isomalt design! Each session will make you a more versatile decorator.

EXPLORE OTHER GREAT CLASSES!
Real Tiered Cakes, Lambeth, Advanced Sugar Artistry, Chocolate Inspirations, Advanced Gum Paste & Fondant or Fondant Art.

1-DAY WORKSHOPS
Art of Sweet Tables, Holiday Icing Flowers, Holiday Candy Making, Wedding Cake Assembly, Cupcakes Galore and more!

CHECK OUT OUR WEEKEND AND BILINGUAL CLASSES!

For class schedules, details and enrollment, visit
www.school.wilton.com
Or call 630-810-2888 or
800-772-7111, ext. 2888.

Certificate of Approval to operate issued by the Illinois State Board of Education, 100 N. First Street, Springfield, IL 62777.